Treating the Changing Family
Handling Normative and Unusual Events

Edited by
Michele Harway

JOHN WILEY & SONS, INC.

New York • Chichester • Brisbane • Toronto • Singapore

To my family:
My husband Bruce Antman and
my two wonderful children Sasha and Alissa,
my source of support during times of stress

Library of Congress Cataloging-in-Publication Data:

Treating the changing family : handling normative and unusual events /
    edited by Michele Harway.
        p.   cm. — (Wiley series in couples and family dynamics and
    treatment)
    Includes index.
    ISBN 0-471-07905-7 (cloth : alk. paper)
    1. Family psychotherapy. 2. Family. 3. Life change events.
I. Harway, Michele. II. Series.
RC488.5.T7193   1996
616.89´156—dc20   95-11794

Printed in the United States of America

10 9 8 7 6 5 4 3 2 1

Series Preface

Our ability to form strong interpersonal bonds with romantic partners, children, parents, siblings, and other relations is a key characteristic defining our humanity. These coevolving relationships shape who we are and what we become—they can be a source of great gratification or tremendous pain. Yet, only in the mid-twentieth century did behavioral and social scientists really begin focusing on couples and family dynamics; and only in the past several decades have the theory and findings that emerged from those studies been used to develop effective therapeutic interventions for troubled couples and families.

We have made great progress in understanding the dynamics, structure, function, and interactional patterns of couples and families—and have made tremendous strides in treatment. As we stand poised on the beginning of a new millennium, however, both intimate partnerships and family relationships are in a period of tremendous flux. Economic and sociopolitical factors are changing work patterns, parenting responsibilities, and relational dynamics. Modern medicine has helped lengthen the life span, giving rise to the need for transgenerational caretaking. Cohabitation, divorce, and remarriage are quite commonplace, and these social changes make it necessary for us to rethink and broaden our definition of what constitutes a family.

Thus, it is no longer enough simply to embrace the concept of the family as a system. To understand, and effectively treat the evolving family, we must incorporate into our theoretical formulations, and therapeutic armamentarium, information derived from research and clinical practice on important emerging issues such as ethnicity, culture, religion, gender, sexual preference, family life cycle, socioeconomic status, education, physical and mental health, values, and belief systems.

The purpose of the *Wiley Series in Couples and Family Dynamics and Treatment* is to provide a forum for cutting-edge relational and family theory, practice, and research. Its scope is intended to be broad, diverse, and international. All books published in this series share a common mission—to reflect on the past, offer state-of-the-art information on the present, and speculate on, as well as attempt to shape, the future of the field.

FLORENCE W. KASLOW

Florida Couples and Family Institute
Duke University

Preface

The focus of this volume is on so-called nontraditional families. Expectations for families are placed against the backdrop of theories that describe the normative experiences of individual and family life cycles. However, it is important that clinicians be knowledgeable both about the expectations clients bring with them and the realities of functioning in the changing family.

This book is divided into five parts. Part One, provides the context for consideration of many types of families. Chapter 1 considers recent changes in family demographics and proposes that we honor family diversity rather than encourage homogenization. Theories of individual development and the family life cycle are also reviewed. Chapter 2 looks at the pervasive influence of culture not just on individual behavior but also on family functioning because what is acceptable may vary for different cultural groups. Cuéllar and Glazer consider the impact of culture on families and examine events within the context of different cultures, subcultures, and multicultural environments. Several models are presented to help clinicians better assess and understand cultural influences on family processes, and interventions are considered that take cultural influences into consideration.

Part Two considers nontraditional family constellations. In this section, we look at families that differ from the traditional nuclear family of a mother, father and children. In Chapter 3, Seibt examines nontraditional family constellations including stepfamilies and blended families, single-parent families, and binuclear families. Carlson in Chapter 4 considers families comprising gay and lesbian couples and their children.

Part Three examines challenges to the family life cycle. This includes looking at the impact of aging on families (Chapter 5, by Peake, Rosenzweig, and Williamson), and the special challenges of adoption (Chapter 6, by Schwartz).

In Part Four, we examine the impact of unusual events on the family. In Chapter 7, Marsh, Lefley, and Husted consider the catastrophic impact of serious mental illness on families and the opportunities afforded to clinicians working with such families. Williams, in Chapter 8, looks at the impact of trauma on family members of trauma survivors, and considers the role of mental health practitioners in intervening with these families. Chapter 9 considers the impact of domestic violence on families. The first section of that chapter looks at spousal abuse (by Harway and Hansen), the second examines child abuse (Rossman and Geffner), and the final section considers the growing problem of elder abuse (Deitch).

Sanchez-Hucles looks at the unique opportunities and challenges of urban living on families (Chapter 10). Chapters 11 and 12 consider the impact of illness and disability on families. Edmister, in Chapter 11, looks at approaches to helping families with disabled children; in Chapter 12, Strozier considers the special needs of families who deal with chronic illness. In Chapter 13, the impact of a special form of chronic illness, AIDS, is considered by Rosenthal, Boyd-Franklin, Steiner, and Tunnell. Part Four concludes with a consideration of families faced with addictions (Wynne, McCrady, Kahler, Liddle, Palmer, Horberg, and Schlesinger).

Part Five considers enlarging the role of the clinician by the use of psychoeducational methods, interactive technologies, and other new approaches (Chapter 15, L'Abate and Odell) and concludes with an overview and recommendations for the work of family clinicians (Chapter 16, Harway). Throughout the book, clinical case material is presented. In order to protect client confidentiality, identifying details have been changed in the case material. In addition, some cases represent composites drawn from multiple cases.

MICHELE HARWAY

Acknowledgments

A book such as this is not completed without the involvement of many individuals.

First thanks to Josephine Beebe, former President of the Division of Family Psychology of the American Psychological Association, for appointing me to chair the Committee on Critical Issues Facing the Family and allowing me the freedom to structure the Committee's work. The work of that committee forms the core of this volume, and its existence was the impetus for this book. Thanks are also in order to successive presidents of the Division of Family Psychology for continuing to support the work of the Committee: Carol Philpot, Robert Wellman, and Ronald Levant. The subcommittee chairs, most of whom have authored chapters in this volume, also deserve thanks for multiple revisions of their contribution.

Florence Kaslow, as editor of the *Wiley Series in Couples and Family Dynamics and Treatment,* deserves special appreciation for encouraging me to publish this book as part of her series.

At the Phillips Graduate Institute, several individuals have been centrally involved in the completion of the manuscript. I would like to especially acknowledge Max Frankl, who provided ongoing assistance with correspondence to chapter authors and with Kelly Franklin at John Wiley & Sons, and who helped with final preparation of the manuscript. Sally Peace was also involved in preparation of parts of the book. Thanks too to Edwin S. Cox, President of Phillips Graduate Institute, for his unfaltering support of my need to write and fill my desk with stacks of manuscripts.

It may seem inappropriate to acknowledge one's family in the preparation of an academic book, but both my family of origin and my nuclear family have provided important testing grounds for my ideas about what is expected in families. My bicultural background taught me early on that there is more than one way to be in this world. I have been able to generalize that lesson to the varieties of families in our society.

M. H.

Contents

PART ONE
Introduction

CHAPTER 1

Setting the Stage for Understanding and Treating the Changing Family

MICHELE HARWAY and KATHY WEXLER

Traditional developmental models used to understand the functioning of families (Carter & McGoldrick, 1989) and of individuals within the family (e.g., Erikson, Levinson, Gould, and others) are helpful in understanding normative experiences of families. However, these traditional models cannot by themselves teach us all we need to know about what happens to families when they must cope with extraordinary circumstances. What is the family like when a family member is mentally ill, recovering from trauma, or dealing with AIDS? What happens when the family has a child with a developmental disability? Most theories about family and individual functioning have also assumed that the traditional family is one with a working father, a stay-at-home mother, and two school-age children. Population demographics suggest that this traditional family has become a statistical minority. Yet, does family functioning change with changes in family composition?

In this book, we will look at nontraditional family constellations, consider the impact of a variety of events on families, and describe what psychotherapists can do when affected families present for therapy. Many of the constellations and events described in this volume, once rare, have become increasingly prevalent: As the AIDS epidemic spreads, more families are affected; as the "baby-boom" generation grays and life expectancies expand, more families find themselves caring for elders while raising children or launching adolescents; as the divorce rate increases, more families are headed by single parents.

One of the premises of this volume is that our traditional notion of the family no longer applies. We are suggesting a paradigmatic shift in our way of looking at the family. Our tolerance for diversity in families has been extremely constrained and families have been encouraged to blend in and take on the characteristics of the majority. This effort leads to a loss of the uniqueness that makes each individual and each family special and a rich contribution to our society. A family, we are told, fits a fairly narrow description, almost a caricature. The current model of the traditional family comes to us from the 1950s when the ideal was a family with a mother who stayed home and got rid of ring around the collar, a father who left for work every morning and returned in the evening ready for supper and slippers, Junior who was a football star, and Sis, the girl next door. This *middle-class white* family lived in its own house in suburbia with a white picket fence, drove a station wagon, and had an English sheepdog named Benjie. Even in the 1950s, however, this family was a statistical artifact, a product of the melting pot of family differences.

Today, this family is even more rare and unusual. In fact, the National Survey of Families and Households reported that in 1988, 28% of all households were headed by a single female, 16% by a single male and 5% represented cohabiting couples. The remaining 51% represented a variety of family types: "traditional" families and blended families as well as married couples with no children in the home. As we head to the end of the century, the nontraditional families will represent an even larger majority. But old ideas disappear slowly and many professionals continue to view the traditional family as the norm and any other family constellation as abnormal. As the numbers of traditional families dwindle and the numbers of nontraditional families increase, it is time to identify and celebrate the diversity in family types.

Ten years ago, much of our interest in families was focused on the special *problems* of nontraditional families. We were interested in the impacts of divorce on children, how children fared in stepfamilies, and the other problems of adjustment of the families themselves. This book proposes a shift in our way of considering these families: not as problems in the making but as viable families. This change in our way of looking at these families translates into a change in the way they see themselves. This in turn will have a profound effect on their ability to function. We need to look for the strengths and resources of these families rather than to find their pathology. Take, for example, Elise, a single mother and her two daughters. What are the strengths that have allowed the mother to cope alone with her children? What special areas of resilience have the daughters developed and how has their competence been enhanced by their family structure? By exploring the positive coping mechanisms of this family rather than focusing on how its changed family structure has resulted in problems, we reinforce family members' positive view of themselves instead of pathologizing them for being different. We thereby enable and empower them. We focus on the diversity of experience each nontraditional family brings, which enriches the culture.

The families we may encounter in our work as mental health practitioners are extremely diverse. First, though, let us define a family. Olson and DeFrain (1994) describe a family as "two or more persons who are committed to each other and who share intimacy, resources, decisions and values" (p. 9). According to this definition, a family may be the traditional family of mother and father and their children. Or, it may be one where a single parent is raising children. There are many other ways of describing today's family. Figure 1.1 presents a taxonomy of families, comprising four dimensions—biological tie, marital status, sexual orientation and gender role or employment status. The following list describes each dimension in greater detail:

- *Biological Tie.* Today's families include those in which both parents are biologically related to their children (as in the traditional family); where only one parent is biologically related (because the family has availed itself of artificial insemination or a surrogate parent, because a lesbian has had a child that she is coparenting with her partner, or because the family is in fact a blended family where a biological parent raises a child with a new parent who becomes stepparent to the child); or where the parents have no biological ties to their child (as in the case of adoption).

- *Marital Status.* Families also vary by marital status. A family may be a single-parent family (as a result of a divorce, or because an individual has chosen to have a child on her own, which has been conceived either through sexual intercourse or artificial insemination). Or the family may consist of two partners who are married to each other (either the original nuclear family or a stepfamily), or the partners may be cohabitating (in a heterosexual, gay, or lesbian relationship).

- *Sexual Orientation.* Families vary by sexual orientation, with some families being headed by a gay or lesbian couple, most by a heterosexual couple.

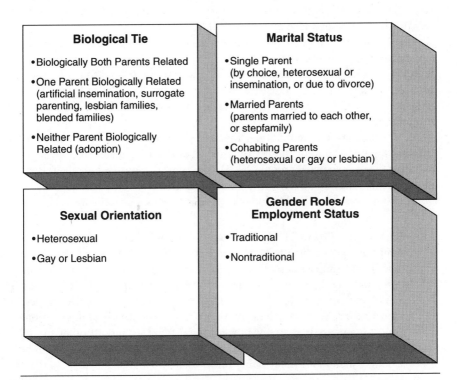

Figure 1.1   A Taxonomy of Normative Families

- *Gender Roles.* Finally, families vary according to gender roles and employment status with some being traditional in this arena (Dad works, Mom tends the home; Mom cooks and cleans, Dad mows the lawn and does household repairs) or nontraditional (where both work, or Mom works and Dad is the homemaker or where there has otherwise been a gender reversal or sharing of roles).

The complexity of family types is apparent even within the constraint of family constellation. There are other ways in which families may differ and be considered nontraditional. Many families face special challenges because one or several members have experienced something out of the ordinary. Some of those special families may include families who struggle with a chronically mentally ill member. Families with a disabled child or a family member who suffers from chronic illness or a handicap, develop special structures and patterns to cope with these difficulties. Devastating illnesses such as AIDS not only bring multiple problems to the family, but bring special social stigma that the family must overcome. When a family member has experienced trauma, the family is likely to be affected as well. Families affected by domestic violence, child abuse, partner abuse, or elder abuse have developed and capitalized on special coping abilities, as have families living in urban environments, in particular those affected by urban violence. These families used to be rare; they too are becoming more common.

Family members may be poorly motivated for family therapy (unless of a supportive type) because systemic views in particular suggest that the family's pathology is somehow to blame for the illness or trauma. Consequently, these families' special strengths must be the focus of the work. In addition, clinicians have a special responsibility to provide information, skills, and support to family members.

Let us next consider the functions that families serve. There are a number of different ways of organizing family function (these have been described by many including the sociologist Murdock, 1965). Most descriptions include the following functions—the daily living tasks, family leadership functions, cohesiveness-building functions, and the development of family values (see Figure 1.2).

1. *Daily Living Tasks.* These tasks include obtaining goods for family consumption and all the attendant preparation before they can be used. This function encompasses such activities as buying and cooking food; cleaning, repairing, or improving the family's possessions; installing equipment; sewing; child care and socialization of dependent children; and care for the sick and the elderly. How these tasks are distributed among family members may differ in traditional families and all other family types, perhaps no longer divided along gender lines. All continue to be accomplished in all functioning families.

2. *Family Leadership Functions.* The power and control functions in a family may be held by the same person all the time, or may change

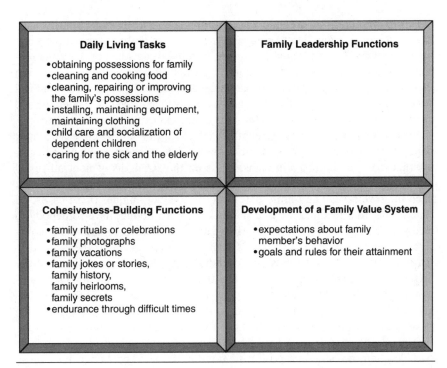

Daily Living Tasks

- obtaining possessions for family
- cleaning and cooking food
- cleaning, repairing or improving the family's possessions
- installing, maintaining equipment, maintaining clothing
- child care and socialization of dependent children
- caring for the sick and the elderly

Family Leadership Functions

Cohesiveness-Building Functions

- family rituals or celebrations
- family photographs
- family vacations
- family jokes or stories, family history, family heirlooms, family secrets
- endurance through difficult times

Development of a Family Value System

- expectations about family member's behavior
- goals and rules for their attainment

Figure 1.2   Four Dimensions of Family Functioning—Revisited

depending on the type of problem. The more flexible the family, whatever the family constellation, the more family leadership may be shared.

3. *Cohesiveness-Building Functions.* Building family cohesiveness occurs through family rituals or celebrations (some of these may need to be modified in the case of some family constellations), family photographs, family vacations, favorite jokes or stories, family secrets, family history, endurance together through difficult times, and family heirlooms. Affectional and sexual relationships further cement family bonds. Finally, family rules about participation in family events and forces to prevent group disintegration during crises and other occurrences that threaten to disrupt the family are also an important family function.

4. *Development of a Family Value System.* Expectations about how members should behave, and other expectations of the family constitute a system of values for organizing and giving direction to various family activities. A hierarchy of goals and rules for their attainment is also usually included.

A consideration of the expected functions of families underlines the fact that so-called nontraditional families are in fact quite traditional when it comes to carrying out these functions. Today's families continue to fulfill each of the functions in the preceding list. How they successfully complete those tasks attests to their areas of strength. Thus, the single mother described earlier may have to do a lot of juggling to complete the chores of daily living. At the same time, involving the children at an early age in fulfilling some of these maintenance function has led to her daughters' greater autonomy and confidence in their abilities. Family celebrations have also developed a special timing and flavor of their own, and the extended family is involved in much of the planning and carrying out of the traditions, to the greater enrichment of the entire family.

The development of these strengths has helped this family cope with their nontraditional structure. That is not to say we should ignore problems but simply that if we, as family clinicians, focus on the strengths of nontraditional families, we will be more effective in enhancing their functioning in areas that need improvement. The family described here is not unique. In all cases, *all* functioning families take care of the tasks of daily living, have somebody in charge of certain aspects of family life, find common rituals that bring cohesiveness, and develop joint values. It is important to remember then, in working with families of all types not to pathologize them when their structure differs from expectations. More critical than family constellation is how well a family functions. Thus, identifying the strengths and assets of these families and their positive coping mechanisms is the first step in therapy. Reinforcing those areas that need reinforcement can then follow more easily.

The paradigm shift described here requires mental health professionals to consider their own stereotypes of what families "should" be. Superimposing an appreciation of the strengths of the families we are treating onto traditional theories of individual development, those encompassing the family life cycle and theories of relational development, will allow us to honor the diversity of families with which we work. Carter and McGoldrick (1989) caution that the "rigid application of psychological ideas to the 'normal' life cycle can have a detrimental effect if it promotes anxious self-scrutiny that raises fears that deviating from the norms is pathological" (pp. 3–4). By shifting away from a pathology paradigm and toward one of competence, we enhance the mental health of the families we work with. By emphasizing their strengths and resources, we become enabling agents who look for competencies and empower our clients to function even more effectively.

To accomplish the paradigmatic shift suggested here, mental health professionals need a basic knowledge of what has been considered normative developmental events and stages. Thus, we will briefly review theories of development in this chapter.

THEORETICAL PERSPECTIVES ON INDIVIDUAL AND FAMILY FUNCTIONING

What do we mean by "normative development"? Normative means objective, demonstrable reality—what we would generally or normally expect to see in the real world. Yet, normative also connotes "right" or "appropriate" or "healthy" and thus connects to personal standards and expectations—what individuals, tutored by their culture, see as acceptable or normal. These images of what is right or appropriate have a great deal of power: People measure themselves and others against these norms, even when they have little empirical validity. When an event or pattern of events is considered normal, this frame makes the objective circumstances easier to accept: We smile indulgently as we recount our teenager's oppositional behavior, because it is "right on schedule," or we excuse a hysterical friend who is going through a midlife crisis.

Some models of development, particularly those describing the physical development of children, are easily validated with objective measurement. For example, we can discover with a simple survey that most human beings are walking by age 13 months, have bowel and bladder control day and night by age 4, and achieve certain norms of height and weight by certain ages (Gesell & Amatruda, 1941). Other models, particularly those describing social and emotional development, overlap little with observable reality. For example, it is impossible to demonstrate that an infant is struggling with Erikson's stage of "Trust versus Mistrust" or that an elderly adult has or has not achieved "Ego Integrity" (Erikson, 1963). In this section of Chapter 1, we will review this second type of model because the concepts behind these models have become firmly entrenched in popular consciousness and are therefore significant normative images for both the general public and the academician.

Until recently, theories of development (psychodynamic, cognitive, moral) focused on the individual as he or she progressed through time, tracking the landmarks of physical, social-emotional, and/or cognitive growth. Family therapists, sociologists, and others have lately noted the limitations of individual models, given that people require interactional systems in which to grow. It is also clear that development occurs on many interactive levels: biological changes in one person, patterns in dyads, all the way up to the complexity of social evolution and change (Breunlin, Schwartz, & Mac Kune-Karrer, 1992).

Sometimes, development is viewed as continuous, with little to demarcate stages and steps. However, the general public has more understanding of stage theories, and so this chapter will review only models that include this notion of definite stages. In stage theories, there is usually a developmental task, or key process, to be accomplished at each stage, and each stage forms a prerequisite for the next one. Sequence is important—tasks must be accomplished in order, and stages may not be skipped or hurried. At any time, the entity being studied is either early, late, or on schedule (Breunlin et al., 1992).

It is not our intent in this chapter to provide an inclusive review of all theories of development. In particular, a variety of theories of childhood and adolescent development have been well documented elsewhere. The interested reader is referred to those primary sources (e.g., early object-relations: Mahler, 1968; Klein, 1948; Winnicott, 1965; cognitive development: Piaget & Inhelder, 1959; observational learning: Bandura, 1962; moral development: Kohlberg, 1963; language acquisition: McNeill, 1970; and the psycholinguists).

Individual Theories of Development

Although we will not review in any detail the concepts of Freud, some reference must nonetheless be made to his early theories (Freud, 1953). No one really believes anymore that libido flows in some biologically programmed channel from one body orifice to another, determining adult character development in virtually irrevocable ways. Most psychologists and the general public, however, still find these notions influencing their expectations of babies and young children, and labels like "anal retentive" and "orally fixated" have entered the cultural vocabulary and are applied to adults.

In his early work, Freud (1953) argued that libidinal energy attached first to the mouth, then to the anal area, then to the genitals, was sublimated during latency, and then reattached to the genitals at puberty. Too much frustration or too much indulgence of the libidinal needs at any stage would result in fixation, with some libido still attached to an earlier body area as the person continued to mature. In adult life, dysfunctional personality traits and neurotic symptoms were seen as a result of these fixations.

Another significant psychodynamic model of individual development is that of Erik Erikson, a psychoanalyst who expanded Freud's model to include the entire life span and the social interactive element, as well as the flow of libido. In *Childhood and Society,* (Erikson, 1963), he outlined his "Eight Stages of Man," a psychosocial model in which each stage is characterized by a struggle between two elements or processes. At the oral stage, the struggle is between trust and mistrust, as the infant discovers via the primary caregiver whether the world makes any kind of sense: Is the infant fed when hungry, comforted when cranky, and so on? Is there a fit between internally experienced need and action from outside? If on balance, the correspondence is there, the infant is better prepared for the next stage—as in Freud's view, each stage builds on the one before, and fixation has a cumulative effect (Erikson, 1963).

In Erikson's model, at the anal stage, the struggle is between autonomy and shame or self doubt, as the toddler discovers the separateness between self and others, and accepts limits in addition to nurturance.

From age 3 to age 5, the child is learning "to make do" (with peers instead of the opposite-sex parent), "to make like" (in other words, to imitate and pretend and model self after the same-sex parent), and "to do with" (to play and socialize with peers). If all goes well, there is a balance of "Initiative versus Guilt."

As the child enters the fourth stage, latency, the psychosocial crisis is "Industry versus Inferiority." This is the age of industriousness—putting together science projects and participating in Girl Scout cookie sales, building clubhouses and practicing for sports, and so on. The child either feels successful and competent most of the time, or emerges from this stage with a crippling sense of inferiority.

At puberty, the fifth stage, the psychosocial crisis is "Identity versus Role Confusion" as the adolescent struggles with questions such as "Who am I?

What do I believe in?" Interestingly, this stage parallels the second stage of the model: The toddler is discovering that he or she has a self, separate from caretakers ("Autonomy") whereas the teenager is working with the *content* of that self ("Identity"). To the extent that identity is established during adolescence, the next crisis is easier to manage: "Intimacy versus Isolation." Here the task is "to lose and find oneself in another" as represented by the formation of an intimate partnership. If identity is not formed, then the choice of a love object is made as an identity issue rather than as an adult decision. For example, an immature young woman may marry a successful doctor so that she "knows who she is—a doctor's wife," rather than because she has truly formed an intimate connection with him.

The seventh stage, adulthood, involves the struggle between "Generativity and Self-absorption." Adults need "to make be" and "to take care of" something other than themselves. The most obvious way to do this is to have children, but Erikson allows for other forms of creativity and nurturance as well. At the eighth stage (the end of the life cycle), maturity, the struggle is between "Integrity and Despair," as the individual looks back at the events of his or her life and either feels the connections, the meaningfulness of choices, or is swamped with despair because it is too late to make a difference. Erikson sees the positive outcome of this stage as "Wisdom" or an integrated knowing rather than simple measurable intelligence. With this sense of integrity, death (one's own and that of others) is easier to face.

Looking over Erikson's eight stages, there is an alternation between processes of connection ("Trust versus Mistrust," "Intimacy versus Isolation") and separation ("Autonomy," "Initiative," "Identity") with an emphasis on separation and self-development. Also, with this theory, chronological age is not always an indicator of psychological maturity; not everyone makes it through the eight stages, regardless of the length of his or her life. On the other hand, some individuals make rapid progress though the stages under unusual circumstances, such as terminal illness. Most people are dealing with *all* the psychosocial crises at various times through their lives. For most, for example, it is not the case that they emerge from infancy and never have to deal with issues regarding trust again.

Whereas Freud and Erikson's theories began with the infant, and in the case of Erikson continued through the life span, a few more recent theories have described stages of development occurring during the adult years. Although the rapid physiological changes of childhood and adolescence do not continue at the same pace during the adult years, change and development occur throughout the life cycle. With the increasing realization that psychological development (and to a lesser extent physiological change) continues, theories about stages of development during the adult years have been proposed. Noteworthy among those theories is that of Havighurst (1972), who describes the stages as a series of "developmental tasks" with each time of life calling for the completion of a distinct set of tasks leading to life satisfaction with that period of life. He divides part of the life span into early adulthood and middle age. In early adulthood, the tasks to be completed are to select a mate, to learn to live with a marriage partner, to start a family, to rear children, to manage a home, to get started in an occupation, to take on civic responsibility, and to find a congenial social group. In middle age, the tasks involve achieving adult civic and social responsibility, establishing and maintaining an economic standard of living, assisting teenage children to become responsible and happy adults, developing adult leisure-time activities, relating to one's spouse as a person, accepting and adjusting to the physiological changes of middle age, and adjusting to aging parents.

Levinson et al. (1978) describe four eras of life each with distinctive characteristics, proceeding "in a systematic sequential *alternation* of stable and transitional periods (Colarusso & Nemiroff, 1981, p. 37). During the 6- or 7-year stable period, the individual is building structure and enriching life, whereas during the "intervening transitional periods of 4 to 5 years, existing life structures are modified or fundamentally changed in preparation for the next period" (p. 38). During the early adult transition, occurring at the beginning of the early adult era (roughly ages 17 through 22), the developmental task consists of resolving the feelings of dependence of adolescence and beginning to establish the self-reliance of early adulthood. At the midlife transition (between 40 and 45) the developmental task is to question the life structure laid down in the 30s and to examine whether early dreams have been realized or whether changes are necessary. Between these two transitions, which Levinson considers true developmental crises, other transitional periods occur. At each transitional period, individuals form a stronger sense of who they are and what they want to accomplish in life. Other theories describing the adult years include Gould's (1978), Vaillant's (1977), and Kovacs (1990).

It must be pointed out that the suitability of the progression of stages and life tasks described in each of these theories has been questioned for groups other than white middle-class traditional families (McGrath, 1990). At the same time, there is increasing awareness that many sociodemographic changes due to an expanded life expectancy and to reproductive technology make for many variations in the sequencing of these life tasks. Nonetheless, expectations of life tasks or stages described by Havighurst and Levinson have passed into the cultural expectation of what is normative and inform the template against which many individuals and families judge the appropriateness of their life trajectory.

Models of Family Development

Freud, Erikson, Havighurst, Levinson, and others attempted to describe the social-emotional development of individuals. In the past 20 years, family therapists, among others, have noted the limits of individual models, given that people require interactional systems in which to live and grow (Berman & Lief, 1975; Carter & McGoldrick, 1989; Falicov, 1988). A richer image of development emerges if we attend to relational systems as they progress through time, adding and losing membership, adjusting or failing to change their structure and organizing principles.

Family life cycle models (Carter & McGoldrick, 1989; Duvall, 1977) describe a series of predictable transitions or developmental tasks for the system, occurring at times of changing membership: birth, death, marriage, divorce. When the structure of the system changes, all members must adjust and adapt on a variety of levels, and symptoms are seen as a product of failed transitions. The biological and emotional development of individuals influences the ability of the system to reorganize and make transitions, but family life cycle models focus on the systemic level.

Duvall (1977), Rodgers (1976), Falicov (1988), and others have presented a variety of stage models, with anywhere from 6 to 24 stages, but the best known model is Carter and McGoldrick's (1989) 6-stage model. They acknowledge that their model describes primarily traditional middle-class families in Western industrialized societies, but the general principles behind the model can be adapted to families of any cultural or economic background. The model encompasses three generations, and includes a multigenerational component as well.

Stage 1 is labeled "Between Families: The Unattached Young Adult," and the task here is for both generations to separate and permit the exit of the young adult to form his or her own nuclear family. There must be financial independence and some intimate peer connections for the young person, and the older generation must give emotional permission to leave the family of origin. Carter and McGoldrick note that the requirement for separation, for a period of independence, is not a cultural universal: Hispanic or Asian families, for example, are quite healthy without it. Also, this stage has, until recently, been seen as unnecessary for women, who have traditionally gone from college straight into marriage.

If the separation of the generations has gone well, the next stage is easier. Called "The Joining of Families through Marriage," Stage 2 involves realignment of relationships of friends and extended family, negotiating rules and rituals from each partner's family of origin, and in general making a commitment to the new system. Although each spouse must do this on a personal level, the families are clearly involved as well.

Stage 3, "Families with Young Children" is stressful because babies make practical demands of time and energy. The entrances into the system also trigger adjustment problems for the older generation, who are now grandparents, and value conflicts that the couple felt were solved at an earlier stage now reappear. The focus becomes "Whose values and culture are to be passed on to the children?"

Stage 4 is called "The Family with Adolescents"; here the process is not really coping with entrances and exits into the system, but rather with a fundamental restructuring necessary to allow for more independence. The boundary around the family must shift from the protective white picket fence to more of a revolving door as teens exit the system to experiment and then return for nurturance.

Stage 5, "Launching Children and Moving On," involves more entrances and exits than any other stage, and some researchers (Haley, 1973) report that this stage of the life cycle is overrepresented in their clinical samples. Children are leaving home (exits) and bringing in potential spouses (entrances); the older generation is looking at retirement and the so-called midlife crisis (exits) and the aging of their own parents, with the need for more caretaking.

Stage 6, "The Family in Later Life," requires supporting the older generation without overfunctioning for them, facing death and disability, and life review and integration for the eldest generation.

The key concept in this model is that coping with entrances into and exits from the system is stressful. Hence the model can be adapted to families who divorce, remarry, and have more children, or families where the marriage comes late in life and never includes children, or cultures in which the norm is to stay with extended family and not launch. The clinician can simply consider what reorganizational task(s) the system is dealing with and use that as a guide to treatment.

Another dimension of this model is the notion of a vertical axis for stress. Whereas developmental transitions occur periodically on the horizontal axis, as the system progresses through time, the vertical axis can be used to represent ever-present elements of family lifestyle, rules, mythology, and so on, that persist through several generations. Bowen (1978) might refer to this vertical stress as undifferentiation, and might include themes such as rigid communication styles, persisting cognitive distortions (e.g., "Our family are just losers," "We are so special we are *entitled* to get into Harvard"), or dysfunctional organizational patterns (underfunctioning men married to overfunctioning women, or parentified children in every generation).

In addition to the family life cycle, there are other systemic models for the developmental stages that dyads experience. Wynne (1988) describes sequential mastery of four processes as the task of families. These include attachment/caregiving, communicating, joint problem solving, and mutuality. These are most clearly applicable to the development of parent-child relationships, but might apply to romantic relationships as well. Breunlin et al. (1992) describe a complex, recursive process of relational development, in which couples deal with six processes sequentially: attraction, liking, nurturing, coordinating meaning, setting rules, and making metarules.

All these models of development for systems have in common the notion that many other levels affect the system being studied; for example, biological development of an individual, if either behind or ahead of schedule, will naturally affect the development of the whole system.

TREATING THE CHANGING FAMILY

Some of the previously described complex interactions will be the focus of the remaining chapters of this volume. To treat the family in its many presentations, clinicians must understand both the family's expectations and the special needs and strengths of a variety of family constellations challenged by life cycle stresses and confronted by unusual events. The following chapters will provide information about various family types that can lead to effective treatment.

REFERENCES

Bandura, A. (1962). Social learning through imitation. In M. R. Jones (Ed.), *Nebraska symposium on motivation.* Lincoln: University of Nebraska Press.

Berman, E. M., & Lief, H. I. (1975). Marital therapy from a psychiatric perspective: An overview. *American Journal of Psychiatry, 132,* 6.

Bowen, M. (1978). *Family therapy in clinical practice.* New York: Aronson.

Breunlin, D., Schwartz, R., & Mac Kune-Karrer, B. (1992). *Metaframeworks: Transcending the models of family therapy.* San Francisco: Jossey-Bass.

Carter, B., & McGoldrick, M. (1989). *The changing family life cycle* (2nd ed.). Boston: Allyn & Bacon.

Colarusso, C. A., & Nemiroff, R. A. (1981). *Adult development: A new dimension in psychodynamic theory and practice.* New York: Plenum Press.

Duvall, E. M. (1977). *Marriage and family development* (5th ed.). Philadelphia: Lippincott.

Erikson, E. H. (1963). *Childhood and society* (2nd ed.). New York: W. W. Norton.

Falicov, C. J. (1988). *Family transitions: Continuity and change over the life cycle.* New York: Guilford.

Freud, S. (1953–64). *The standard edition of the complete psychological works of Sigmund Freud.* J. Strachey et al. (Eds.). London: The Hogarth Press.

Gesell, A., & Amatruda, C. S. (1941). *Developmental diagnosis: Normal and abnormal child development.* New York: Hoeber.

Gould, R. L. (1978). *Transformations: Growth and change in adult life.* New York: Simon & Schuster.

Haley, J. (1973). *Uncommon therapy.* New York: Norton.

Havighurst, R. J. (1972). *Developmental tasks and education* (3rd ed.). New York: McKay.

Klein, M. (1948). *Contributions to psycho-analysis.* London: The Hogarth Press.

Kohlberg, L. (1963). Moral development and identification. In H. W. Stevenson (Ed.), *Child psychology,* Part 1. (62nd yearbook). Chicago: University of Chicago Press.

Kovacs, A. L. (1990). *Helping men at midlife: Can the blind ever see.* Paper presented at the 1990 APA Convention. Boston, MA.

Levinson, D. J., Darrow, C. N., Klein, E. B., Levinson, M. H., & McKee, B. (1978). *The seasons of a man's life.* New York: Alfred A. Knopf.

McGrath, E. (1990). *New strategies for women in the middle.* Paper presented at the 1990 APA National Convention. Boston, MA.

McNeill, D. (1970). *The acquisition of language: The study of developmental psycholinguistics.* New York: Harper & Row.

Mahler, M. (1968). *On human symbiosis and the vicissitudes of individuation.* New York: International Universities Press.

Murdock, G. (1965). *Culture and Society.* Pittsburgh: University of Pittsburgh Press.

National Survey of Families and Households. (1988). Madison, WI: Center for Demography and Ecology. University of Wisconsin.

Olson, D. H., & DeFrain, J. (1994). *Marriage and the family: Diversity and strengths.* Mountain View, CA: Mayfield.

Piaget, J., & Inhelder, B. (1959). *La genese des structures logiques elementaires: Classifications et seriations.* Neuchatel: Delachaux et Niestle.

Rodgers, R. H. (1973). *Family interaction and transaction: The developmental approach.* Englewood Cliffs, NJ: Prentice Hall.

Vaillant, G. E. (1977). *Adaptation to life.* Boston: Little, Brown.

Winnicott, D. W. (1965). *The maturational processes and the facilitating environment.* New York: International Universities Press.

Wynne, L. C. (1988). An epigenetic model of family processes. In C. J. Falicov (Ed.), *Family transitions: Continuity and change over the life cycle.* New York: Guilford Press.

CHAPTER 2

The Impact of Culture on the Family

ISRAEL CUÉLLAR and MARK GLAZER

Culture is one of those entities that can have such an obvious and pervasive influence on behavior and, yet, be so commonly overlooked in explaining behavior. Because we are so immersed in it, we fail to see the "big picture" and lose ourselves in the details of everyday life. There are several myths about culture (Mumford, 1981) that need to be dispelled from the outset. The most prominent of these is that culture influences only trivial aspects of everyday behavior such as the design of our dress and the spice in our foods. The length of women's skirts, whether people wear an earring in the right, or left earlobe, or through the nose are examples of such details—superficial and interesting perhaps—but certainly not elements that make individuals profoundly different from one another. For some, this is the sum total of the influence of culture, representing the first myth. As others have pointed out, culture gives meaning to life itself and forms the foundation for a system of beliefs and values that we hold most dear to our heart and soul. History has shown that we will fight and die for these ideals, certainly not trivial in their influence over our behavior.

Another myth is that we can discard cultural influences as easily as we can replace a coat or dress with another that suits our needs. Again, history has shown that many of the garments of culture remain with us throughout our life span; they endure like our genetics from generation to generation, and thus may become more endearing with time. Efforts to remove them by others in particular may result in greater clinging to them and more resistance by those who wear them.

Still another myth is that only others are affected by culture (Mumford, 1981), that somehow we are not as subject to culture as others. We are all equally affected by culture, although in differing ways. It is therefore important to examine cultural impacts of the dominant as well as the minority cultures and their mutual interactions.

There is much diversity within any given ethnocultural group or subgroup. Therefore, most generalizations are not true for all members of any given group. There are some common cultural characteristics mutually influencing any given cultural or subcultural group (cultural norms). Additionally, there are cultural elements whose influence cuts across ethnocultural groups (cultural commonalities) (Chung, 1992). In environments where there are many multicultural or mixed cultural elements and where the processes of acculturation are accelerated, we would expect an even greater number of cultural commonalities.

Anthropologists, sociologists, and social psychologists have helped us understand the pervasive and enduring influence of culture on our behavior. This chapter will examine cultural influences on normative and nonnormative events in families. It begins with an understanding of how culture plays a role in defining what is normal and what is not with regard to events and behavior as well as to the definition of "family." The chapter will examine nonnormative events within the context of different cultures, subcultures, and multicultural environments. The influence of culture on families from a developmental lifespan perspective will be employed through various models that emphasize the rich, dynamic, interactional systems that influence family functioning. Models are presented to help clinicians, in particular, better assess and understand cultural influences on family processes. Finally, intervention approaches are discussed that take into consideration the cultural influences on family functioning.

Culture impacts families in a number of ways. This chapter will examine the following premises:

1. Culture determines the definition of a family.
2. Cultural contexts determine the conflict and tensions present in a family, and determine the adaptations required.
3. Culture determines the norms for a given family.
4. Culture determines the perception of normative and nonnormative events and the acceptance or reaction, including manifestations, of those events.
5. Culture determines which interventions are most effective.

THE DEFINITION OF CULTURE

Linton (1945), a cultural anthropologist, defined culture as "shared, learned behavior, transmitted from one generation to the other." An important aspect of Linton's definition is that culture is behavior. Marsella and Kameoka (1989) add significantly to Linton's definition "for purposes of adjustment, adaptation and growth." Marsella and Kameoka further add that there are both external and internal referents to culture. To some, these are respectively synonymous with macro and micro aspects of culture. The external or macro aspects of culture include such factors as architecture, artifacts, roles, and institutions. The internal referents, or micro level components of culture include cognitions, ideas, values, and beliefs. Marsella and Kameoka also include "epistemologies or consciousness" as internal referents of culture.

Among the various component parts of culture are language, music, foods, customs, ideas, and values. These component parts have a differential effect or impact on behavior. During the developmental processes, individuals are exposed to these aspects of one or more cultures to varying degrees. Some of these effects are superficial and others are rather deep and integral to the personality of the individual undergoing the process of acculturation. In the United States, there are many ethnocultural minority groups such as African American, Cuban American, Mexican American, Japanese American, and Native American. Ethnocultural groups are not limited to minority populations. It is our supposition that the white mainstream American cultural group, which we generally refer to when we say "majority population," is a cultural group also, even though it is composed of mixed ethnicities. There are many white (European American) ethnocultural subgroups in the United States (e.g., German, Irish, Greek, Italian; R. E. Roberts, personal communication, August, 2, 1994). There is also a mainstream American cultural group of mixed ethnicity that includes people of color. These various cultural groups and ethnocultural groups are in constant interaction with one another. There is no way to escape culture and its influence. Some exchange or interaction is always going on between and among cultures. These cultures are dynamic and are constantly changing, just as are the individuals who compose the membership of each cultural group.

TYPES OF CULTURES

Triandis (1994a) describes cultures by their social behavior patterns: (a) sharing, (b) authority ranking, (c) equality matching, and (d) market pricing. Cultures that emphasize sharing and authority-ranking patterns tend to be traditional, simple, and homogeneous, whereas those that emphasize equality matching and market pricing tend to be complex and heterogeneous. These two types are respectively referred to by Triandis as Collectivistic and Individualistic.

Triandis (1994b) describes *Collectivistic Cultures* as those that emphasize (a) the views, needs, and goals of some collective; (b) shared beliefs with the collective; (c) emotional attachment to the collective; (d) cooperative and self-sacrificing behavior toward the collective. *Individualistic Cultures* emphasize that (a) the views, needs, and goals of the individual (self) are paramount, (b) that beliefs distinguish individuals from the group creating an autonomous person, (c) that social behavior is independent from the collective.

Markus and Kitayama (1994) provide strong evidence to indicate that the formation of the self is influenced by whether we grow up in a collectivistic culture or an individualistic culture. Markus and Kitayama note that in an individualistic culture, the self is independent (e.g., white mainstream American culture), but in a collectivistic culture the self is interdependent, part of a whole (e.g., the Japanese and other Asian cultures). This difference may be the source of much cross-cultural discomfort.

THE PROCESS OF ACCULTURATION

The mutual interactions of individuals from different cultures define the *acculturation process*. Redfield, Linton, and Herkovitz (1936) define acculturation as a process that includes all the changes that result from the firsthand contact and interaction of groups of individuals having distinct cultures. Acculturation phenomena, like culture, have both external and internal referents.

Both macro and micro level acculturation changes are constantly taking place within American society. During the process of acculturation, some of these subcultural components are undergoing change at differential rates. For example, people acquire language rather quickly from another culture but are slower to acquire cultural values and deeply held beliefs. At the profoundest level, culture influences the meaning individuals give to life and the interpretation of life itself. People are in various stages of the acculturation process with regard to any number of cultures. For example, some people are essentially monocultural, whereas others are, in varying degrees or proportions, bicultural or multicultural and have incorporated major aspects of two, three, or more cultures.

MODES OF ACCULTURATION

There are four basic modes of acculturation according to Berry (Berry, 1980; Berry & Kim, 1988): Separation, Assimilation, Integration, and Marginalization. Because acculturation processes involve both macro and micro level changes, they include social and structural aspects of society, in this case, subgroups and components of society such as families. Thus, investigators can easily identify modes of acculturation with regard to family adaptations or *Family Acculturative Styles*. Adapting Berry's modes of acculturation to families, the following five family acculturative types can be hypothesized. Some families (Traditional Oriented Non-resistive Style) are composed of first-generation parents and first-generation children who are traditionally oriented with regard to that culture and have minimal exposure to the majority culture. These families are open to acculturation but have had little opportunity. They probably have not lived long in the United States or for some reason have had little exposure to the host culture. For example, Martá and José have immigrated to the United States in the past 2 years from El Salvador with their 6- and 8-year-old sons. They live in a primarily Salvadorean neighborhood in Los Angeles and spend much of their time with distant relatives and friends.

The second style of cultural family adaptation is the *Integrated Bicultural Family,* which adheres fairly equally to two cultures: Tom, a first-generation American of German descent is married to Chin, a Chinese American. They live in a middle-class suburb of Dallas. They fully integrate elements of their native cultures including language (German and Chinese, respectively) with elements of mainstream American culture. Integration involves some adoption and adaptation resulting in a kind of balance with regard to orientation and acceptance of two or more cultures.

The third type, *Assimilated Family Style,* has virtually no residual traditional orientation or character; essentially, it is fully assimilated within the larger, majority, mainstream American culture. John Bielanski, a second-generation Polish American, is married to a third-generation Mexican American. Their children speak neither Polish nor Spanish and are fully "melted" or assimilated into the American mainstream culture.

In the fourth variety, the *Separatist Family Style,* the family as a whole tends to resist acculturation forces and pressures. There is active opposition to the forces of acculturation. This family does not feel comfortable adapting to mainstream American ways of life. Jerome Dakota is a Native American who feels his family doesn't have to buy into mainstream American ways of life and prefers to hold onto tribal beliefs about life and nature.

The fifth family acculturative type is the *Marginalized Family Style,* in which some or all of the family members seem to have lost their identity with both the traditional and the majority culture. Thus, cultural conflicts have generated a family in which some of the members have identity conflict with regard to cultural orientation resulting in adaptation problems or difficulties. This family as a whole doesn't identify with mainstream culture or its culture of ethnic origin.

Acculturation processes are highly correlated with socioeconomic status (Negy & Woods, 1992). Socioeconomic status has a major influence in many cases. Families in the United States undergoing the process of acculturation would most likely experience very different acculturative processes and stressors depending on their socioeconomic status.

Acculturation, enculturation, and socialization are closely associated but different from one another. Enculturation is the process of learning one's own culture; socialization is the process by which we learn those behaviors that are appropriate within a given culture. The primary agents of socialization are believed to be the family (home), school, and peers (Lefrançois, 1993).

A phenomenon of interest with regard to acculturative processes in families is "*Acculturation Gap*" (Szapocznik & Kurtines, 1980), which exists generally but not exclusively between first-generation parents and their second-generation children who have adopted different views, morals, and values from those of their parents. Luisa is a 15-year-old teenage girl from a traditionally oriented Hispanic family who wants to date, go out with her friends, spend the night with friends, or stay out until early hours of the morning, be alone with her boyfriend, own and drive her own car, and so on. Her parents believe it is wrong for her to do these things. The teenager has acculturated more rapidly than her parents; she is rejecting their traditional ways and her parents are rejecting her acculturated ways. Acculturation gap does not always lead to conflicts. In some immigrant families, the children may be in better touch with social norms than their parents and serve them as translators, mediators, or guides.

Cultural conflicts exist not only within a family but between groups. Conflicts arise because of the differences between ethnocultural groups. Differences also make for strengths, interactions, harmony, interrelationships, and accelerated change. Some differences are not easily reconciled as they involve fundamental discrepancies in world views, perceptions, and meaning.

Acculturation phenomena can produce unique sources of stress on the individual and the immediate family. Stonequest (1937) writes about the conflict of cultures and their impact on psychological development. He reports that where cultural dissimilarities with regard to certain basic beliefs, ideas, and values are at odds with one another, a special type of psychological tension is generated. The individual may not be aware of these tensions, at least initially, and the family, as a unit, may not recognize the acculturative aspects or the tensions that exist within it. However, at certain stages of marginalization, the conflict of cultures becomes overt and prominent. Stonequest's stages of marginalization include a crisis stage, that is generally a precipitant to the development of marginalization—a state of identity confusion in which an individual no longer identifies with the majority culture or with the culture of ethnic origin (Stonequest, 1937).

CULTURE AND THE FAMILY

Cultural influences can change the basic structure of a family and can alter or interrupt family development. The definition of a family unit may be culture specific: What constitutes a family unit in one culture is not so in another. The types of families within a single ethnocultural group can be so varied that, in some cases, it may be difficult to assess the cultural norm for a given subcultural group.

Family and Norms

An important way culture affects families is through the establishment of normative and nonnormative behavior. For example, in a study of 544 of the world's societies, Murdock (1957) found that polygamy was sanctioned in 76% of the societies and monogamy in only 24% of societies.

Norms or standards are developed by a culture and simultaneously are imposed on that culture. Roles are defined (Burgess & Locke, 1953) as "organization of behavior in response to group expectations." Parental expectations are imposed on the children, and early behavior habits are established that form normative behavior when imposed simultaneously by many parents and families on their children. The individuals developing and living within a given culture learn to follow the standards of that culture. Standards are norms or typical kinds of behaviors expected or demanded of us. Some of our roles are less fixed than others depending on the culture. The roles prescribed by a given culture have a functional basis and are dynamic; they respond to the changing demands of society—the thoughts or ideas for a particular population group. For example, family views about parenting, childbearing, discipline, and gender roles are prescribed by a culture and are established as norms or standards that individuals try to meet, replicate, or model through their behavior.

Family Attitudes

A particular culture will prescribe standards, or "normal attitudes," toward a variety of behavioral dimensions such as childbearing. Firm rules and regulations, the appropriate steps for achieving greater privileges, and discipline approaches are behaviors that are driven by sets of values and attitudes. Certain traditional cultural orientations dictate much structure and discipline, and stipulate prerequisites to gaining privileges, rewards, and freedoms. Some cultures also prescribe or dictate individual responsibility for behavior, whereas others adhere more to collective responsibility (see Triandis, 1994a). Self-discipline appears to be an important cultural characteristic of Japanese Americans and some European cultures. Forms of discipline also are culture specific. The enormous reaction in the United States to the flogging with a cane of a young adult American male in Singapore in 1994 exemplifies how deeply ingrained and different cultural attitudes and values can be.

What occurs as a sanctioned practice in Singapore may be defined as "child/adult abuse" in another culture. Some traditional cultures stress highly differentiated gender roles for males and females, whereas other cultures may have vague, flexible, or dynamic gender role standards.

Culture is known to determine the very definition of what is normal and abnormal behavior. Mental illness, according to many is culture specific. Certainly, many core concepts integral to the definition of "family" are culture specific. In the United States, a family is generally defined as consisting of a man and woman, who are bonded both legally and emotionally; who may have children or other extended family members living with them; who also have shared sets of behaviors toward childbearing, gender role differentiation, and other standards; and who also have shared values. Obviously, there are many variations to this definition of an American family (as described in Chapters 1 and 3). Nevertheless, the family is the unit of society that forms, perhaps in most cultures, the building blocks of society and culture.

Divorce, once statistically rare, has now become the norm with 50% of marriages ending in separation or divorce (Lefrançois, 1993). Simply because an event is statistically normal does not make the event normal. Relationship difficulties are normal but when marital discord is serious, neither the events (e.g., divorce) nor the feelings associated with these events are normative. Relationship difficulties can lead to great distress, depression, and suicide and are involved in many family homicides (Lefrançois, 1993). Tolerance for divorce, abuse, infidelity, and drunkenness in the spouse can be culturally determined. Where divorce is against the mores of one or both marriage partners, tolerance for abusive behavior may be greater in that marriage. Thus, nonnormative events, such as infidelity or drunkenness, can become the norm in a family where other more powerful standards of behavior override and allow for their tolerance. This hierarchical aspect to our values causes some to override the influence of others.

Burgess and Locke (1953) proposed three phases in the development of our culturally acquired behavior (most of these phases occur within the context of family). The first phase takes place when we are children as our parents and family shape and form our internal referents. The second phase occurs during adolescence when we substitute our peers' expectations for those of our parents, and the third phase occurs when as young adults, we formulate our own scheme of expectations and values to guide our behavior. These are not mutually exclusive processes, but certainly, the influence of culture in imposing mores, norms, roles, expectations, and standards on the behavior of its members has great significance.

Cultural transmission can be rule-governed or contingency-governed behavior (Skinner, 1972). That is, we are not always aware of the rules of the culture (rule-governed) but learn to make the "culturally appropriate" responses (contingency-governed) when the situation presents itself. Mainstream American culture appears to be largely rule-governed, but in many less developed countries, culture is to a larger extent contingency-governed.

Parenting

Cultural values often clash in the area of parenting issues. Some cultures attach great weight to differential gender roles whereas others do not. Individuals undergoing the process of acculturation, commonly within a family context, have to resolve these important gender role differences where they exist. An individual may choose to remain traditional in gender role and parenting behaviors. These central areas requiring resolution in acculturating families are sensitive to family instability. Many of the problems that cause families to seek therapists or marriage counselors involve parenting difficulties. The division of labor in the household, primarily between husband and wife, generally represents some sort of cooperative arrangement and agreement about gender roles. This sets the cultural base for each family. When families are raising children, husband and wife further determine the specific gender roles that they will reinforce and thus impart to their children. These gender roles play a part in disciplining, educating, orienting, and guiding children. It is possible that the shared subcultural gender role agreement bonding husband and wife also begins the process of family development, societal structural development, and eventually cultural-species development. The sum in each case (family unit) is greater than the individual parts, because each family unit provides an additional cultural vehicle. The family unit is, or at least historically has been, the major functional cultural transmission component/unit of culture.

Many of the challenges that families face and that are addressed more fully in other chapters in this book (e.g., single parenting, gay and lesbian families, aging family members, adoption, chronic mental illness, family violence, spousal abuse) can be exacerbated by "culture conflicts" within the family unit or between the family unit and its greater cultural context. Clinicians need to be sensitive to cultural clashes that may have a potential impact on assessment, diagnosis, manifestations, and/or treatment and resolution of family problems.

CULTURE, EMOTIONS, AND DYSFUNCTION

The literature indicates that emotions can be shaped and used by cultural contingencies as social behavior regulatory mechanisms (Kitayama & Markus, 1994). Emotions are believed to be an important part of culture and serve the function of transmitting socially shared meaning (Frijda & Mesquita, 1994). These authors note that associations accompanied by emotions are assumed to be learned more rapidly. They believe that emotions are among the prime means for the transmission of socially shared meaning. Appraisal and perception of events, both normative and nonnormative, are filtered through culturally based emotional and cognitive processes. Frijda and Mesquita believe that a culture develops sensitivities to certain transgressions; these, in turn, are used as regulatory processes through the emotions of guilt, shame, anger, and grief. They believe that emotions exist to fulfill regulatory social functions. For example, an individual who does not conform to a culturally prescribed gender role may be ostracized by the in-group and made to feel shame, or mortification.

An important area in which culture has impact is in shaping, if not creating, dysfunctional or psychopathological behavior. One way in which culture impacts psychopathology is through symptom manifestations. A number of *culture-bound syndromes* (Lambo, 1965; Simons & Hughes, 1993; Weidman & Sussex, 1971) are believed to be "culturally shaped" and result in unique symptom clusters. Examples of such syndromes in Hispanics are *Susto* (Rubel, 1964; Simons & Hughes, 1993) and *Ataque de Nervios* (Garrison, 1977; Simons & Hughes, 1993). *Susto* refers to a psychological state resulting most likely from trauma in which the spirit is dislodged from the body. *Ataque de Nervios* is a culturally recognized and accepted anxiety reaction that may include loss of consciousness, dyspnea, shouting, swearing, falling to the ground, and convulsions, and which serves as a cry for help. Culture influences the content as well as underlying dynamics of symptoms. In Mexican American families, religious hallucinations or hallucinations of deceased relatives may be more common than in other cultural groups. Paranoid symptoms in Mexican Americans frequently include references to being *embrujado* (hexed), whereas technical cultural references such as having electrodes implanted in the brain are, based on the personal experience of the first author, found more commonly in other non-Hispanic white ethnocultural groups. The American Psychiatric Association *Diagnostic and Statistical Manual of Mental Disorders 4th edition (DSM-IV)* (1995) acknowledges that culture-bound syndromes are not limited to diverse immigrant groups but may be found in industrialized cultures as well. Bulimia, anorexia nervosa, and an assortment of other clinical phenomena including "mass murderers" may be examples of syndromes shaped by mainstream American Culture.

CROSS-CULTURAL FAMILY ASSESSMENT

Many limitations are evident in the multicultural application of instrumentation in the field of clinical family assessment and therapy. Many of the assessment instruments available in the field of family assessment have been developed and used largely with white, middle-class American groups (Fischer & Corcoran, 1994). Some of these instruments are appropriate for use with subcultural, ethnic, or other populations such as minority clients and extremely poor clients, whereas other instruments are not. Specifically, instruments that base their results on reference group norms are appropriate only for individuals who are represented in that population. Table 2.1 shows examples of the kind of scales that are undoubtedly influenced by cultural practices but do not have different norms for different cultural groups. The essential question is, To what extent are these scales applicable with clients other than white, middle-class Americans?

The context of the use of questionnaires and scales may have a different meaning in different ethnic or other population groups. Four cultural considerations must be recognized in cross-cultural assessment and family assessment (Marsella & Kameoka, 1989). These considerations center on the concept of equivalence: linguistic, conceptual, scale, and norm. Although they are all important, space limitations permit us to discuss only norm equivalence. It is essential to ascertain whether each client who is substantially different from the norm group knows how to use the questionnaire and understands the meaning of every item. This administrative procedure can be cumbersome and awkward, but cross-cultural reliability and validity of an instrument, in particular the rapid assessment instruments noted in Table 2.1, cannot be assumed. Investigators need to establish such claims for each subcultural group or population not included in the normative sample on which the instrument was originally developed. Essentially, there are concerns regarding the reliability and validity of an instrument in a cross-cultural context that has not been empirically investigated. Content bias, construct bias, response set bias, and differential predictivity are always possible if norm equivalence is lacking (Moran, 1990).

MODELS AND INTERVENTION STRATEGIES

Kleinman, Eisenberg, and Good (1978) proposed a model of intervention for cross-cultural work that has applicability to the delivery of family services or any human service. This model emphasizes "compatibility." Kleinman et al. propose that some compatibility is necessary to achieve effective therapeutic services. With increased compatibility between the providers and the consumers of services, consumers are most likely to be compliant, and reap the greatest benefits from those services. Kleinman's thesis is that without compatibility, consumers withdraw, are more resistive, and fail to obtain maximum benefits. Compatibility assessment is required to assess differences between the providers and the consumers that might create barriers to the delivery of services.

TABLE 2.1   Examples of Family Assessment Instruments That May Yield Different Norms/Results for Culturally Diverse Groups

Family Crisis Oriented Personal Evaluation Scales (F-Copes). Identifies problem-solving and behavioral strategies utilized by families in difficult or problematic situations (McCubbin & Thompson, 1991).

Family Coping Inventory (FCI). Measures how spouses perceive their own responses to a family separation that is permanent (e.g., divorce); for extended period (e.g., military assignment); or that recurs repeatedly (e.g., business travel) (McCubbin & Thompson, 1991).

Co-Dependency Inventory (CODI). Studies co-dependency in family and friends of substance abusers (Stonebrink, 1988).

Adolescent-Family Inventory of Life Events and Changes (A-File). Measures an adolescent's perceptions of life events and changes experienced by his or her family (McCubbin & Thompson, 1991).

Marital Conventionalization Scale (MCS). Measures the extent to which a person distorts the appraisal of his or her marriage in the direction of social desirability (Edmonds, 1967).

Marital Alternatives Scale (MAS). Measures the perception of how much better or worse off a person would be without his or her present spouse, and how easily that spouse would be replaced with one of comparable quality (Udry, 1981).

Family Functioning Scale (FFS). Measures general dimensions of family functioning, positive family affect, family communication, family conflicts, family worries, and family rituals/supports (Tavitian, Lubiner, Green, Grebstein, & Velicer, 1987).

Parent Affect Test (PAT). A 40-item instrument designed to measure two aspects of parental response to child behavior: anger and pleasure (Linehan, Paul, & Egan, 1983).

Parental Authority Questionnaire (PAQ). A 30-item instrument that measures parental authority, or discipline practices, from the point of the view of the child of any age (Buri, 1991).

Kansas Parental Satisfaction Scale (KPS). A 3-item scale designed to measure satisfaction with oneself as a parent, the behavior of one's children, and one's relationship with one's children (James, Schumm, & Hall, 1985).

Index of Family Relations (IFR). A 25-item scale designed to measure the extent, severity, or magnitude of problems that family members have in their relationships with one another (Hudson, 1992).

In providing family services cross-culturally, it is important to evaluate the family for ideas, religious beliefs, customs, practices, and values that might differ from those of the therapist or of those delivering family services. McGoldrick (1982) stresses that clinicians have to struggle consciously with their own subjectivity and to recognize the limitations of any belief systems in their own work. Mac Kune-Karrer (Breunlin, Schwartz, & Mac Kune-Karrer, 1992) suggests that to understand cultural influences and even to consider what might be normative in a client's culture, the clinician has to have done some exploration of his or her culture of origin. A clinician who holds on to the notion of the great American melting pot, may never understand how to connect with a client's cultural background.

Examining the fit between the client and the therapist's cultural background involves looking at cultural dimensions such as immigration and acculturative status, economics, education, ethnicity, religion, gender, age, race, minority or majority status, and regional background. For example, Dr. S., a family therapist, is a Cuban immigrant from a wealthy, educated family. In the early 1950s, when he was a child, his family came to Washington, DC, as political refugees. He is largely of European ancestry; one parent was a Jewish refugee from the Nazis. Even though his mother tongue is Spanish, his background is a poor fit with that of Jorge, an 18-year-old recent immigrant from Mexico with a grade school education and a largely Indian ethnic background. Dr. S. will have to work to recognize the differences between himself and the client as well as identify their areas of similarity. Respect for the disparities that exist is important in this model because intentional or unintentional negative references to customary practices may result in consumers dropping out of the service system altogether. Where differences exist, they may involve very dissimilar normative behavior. The greater the divergence between consumers and providers of care, the greater the likelihood of misdiagnosis, noncompliance, and reduced therapeutic effectiveness. A practical guideline in conducting cross-cultural assessments is to find out how the client or family views the problem, its causes, and its resolutions. This provides the practitioner with valuable information for assessing potential cultural variables and barriers to treatment in a given family.

The model proposed by Cuéllar and Arnold (1988) to help understand the role of culture on illness behavior and its treatment is referred to as the *Concentric Circles Model*. This model is depicted by three embedded circles with the innermost circle representing physical/biological influences; the second circle, which surrounds the first, representing physical/environmental influences; and the third outermost circle representing sociocultural influences on behavior. This is the model most people seem to have of culture—a superficial influence at best—consistent with a common myth about culture. Although culture may appear to be just another exogenous variable with regard to potential influences, in truth, its role extends much further. It is important nonetheless to examine this simplistic view of culture before discussing its more meaningful role.

In the Concentric Circles Model, the innermost ring of influence involves nonnormative events having physical, organic, or biological impacts such as an organic illness or disease. These are viewed as primary and have priority status. Physical injuries in this model would tend to have the greatest impact on an individual and the family. These can be life threatening and are the primary and central focus of concern to the patient and to his or her family, as well as that of the physician or other health-care provider. The next level of the model focuses on environmental impacts as nonnormative events. Examples of this layer of influence are (a) an accident not involving physical injuries, (b) one's home burning, or (c) a natural catastrophe such as an earthquake, or war. The outermost layer of the model is reserved for sociocultural influences and events that impact individuals and families. A death in the family, a divorce, separation, or remarriage are examples of events in this category.

These nonnormative events can directly affect family functioning and adjustment. However, because culture can play a role in the very definition of a nonnormative event as well the reaction to the event, the relative influence of cultural variables extends far beyond its significance as reflected by the Concentric Circles Model. This added significance of the impact of culture on nonnormative events is described more fully by the PARA (Perception, Acceptance, Reaction, Adjustment) Linear Model (Cuéllar & Arnold, 1988).

This second model for viewing the relative impact of cultural processes on nonnormative events is consistent with Angel's view of culture being not merely another variable but rather the one that comprises the context for the operation of all other variables (Angel, 1994). The impact of culture on nonnormative events in a family is determined by both the character and the context of the nonnormative event, with culture forming an important component of that context.

In the PARA Linear Model, culture affects the individuals Perception (P) of the event. As mentioned already, to some, an event may be seen as normal, whereas for others it may not be normal at all (e.g., teenage marriage).

At the next level, culture affects our response. Our perception of the event determines whether we will respond with Acceptance (A) or Reaction (R). This is not too much unlike the way anthropologists see the clash between cultures resulting in acceptance, adoption, or reaction (Redfield, Linton, & Herskovitz, 1936).

The last sequence of events in which culture enters into the equation of influence based on the PARA Linear Model relates to Adjustment (A). Many nonnormative events, by their nature, have a long-lasting impact on individuals and their families. Long-term adjustment is affected by idiosyncratic and culture-bound perspectives. Certain contexts facilitate the adjustment process, including rehabilitation efforts, whereas others hinder it.

This clash between culturally prescribed roles and what is expected of the individual in adjusting to injuries or disability is sometimes quite stressful and represents a significant aspect of overall adjustment outcome. For example, Luis, a married, Mexican American with school-age children, was very traditional in his cultural orientation particularly with regard to his Mexican male role. He was used to assuming financial responsibility for his family and enjoyed the control it provided him in family matters. He became disabled as a result of a back injury, arthritis of his hands, and depression. Severe marital and family conflicts arose when he could not adjust to allowing his wife to become the breadwinner and to assume control of many family matters. He became increasingly depressed because conflicts at home worsened over several years during which he became inflexible in reversing certain learned gender roles.

Marital counseling was required to teach him the value and importance of his new role as husband and father without losing dignity and self-respect.

The way a person perceives an event has a profound influence on the interpretation and meaning given to that event. Asian families perceive mental illness within the family as shameful, which results in delays in seeking help or treatment (Gaw, 1993). Mexican American families may, in addition to perceiving mental illness as shameful, perceive mental illness as "supernatural" and may seek help through *curanderos* as opposed to mainstream practitioners. Curanderos are folk psychiatrists who utilize religious symbols and folk practices to mobilize supernatural healing power. Both Chinese and Mexican Americans believe in "wind illness." Mexican Americans refer to wind illness as *mal aire* and Chinese refer to it as *p'a-leng.* The typical patient develops a culturally specific fear of being cold, wears several layers of clothing, avoids chills or drafts, takes tonics, closes windows even in warm weather, and fears becoming ill from exposure to air (Simons & Hughes, 1993). Thus assessing the family's view of the source or cause of the problem is important to determine significant perceptual differences, and these may suggest likely areas for therapeutic work.

Interventions have to be tailored to the relative needs of individuals and their families. Interventions appropriate for one cultural group may be contraindicated for another. For example, Paniagua (1994) suggests that inviting the client to bring a church member to the session to help discuss the problem may be quite appropriate in some African American families. Asian American families, however, emphasize shame and confidentiality, and Paniagua points out that inviting nonfamily participants may not be appropriate in such cases.

Individuals' perceptions of what they expect from family therapy vary cross-culturally in addition to the variance in perception of illness and other non-normative events. Some clients (e.g., members of some Native American and some Hispanic groups) might expect the therapist to integrate their traditional healing practices with mainstream, Western, or modern healing practices. Native Americans and Hispanics may expect the therapist to be directive. Asian American clients expect problem-solving approaches and negotiation as opposed to direct confrontation (Berg & Jaya, 1993). Paniagua (1994) provides many practical guidelines for assessing and treating culturally diverse individuals and their families.

In summary, the PARA Linear Model places cultural influences in a primary role tying it to the perception, definition, and meaning of life events. Thus, cultural influence is not peripheral but central and is embedded in defining the problem itself. Its influence carries over to all other aspects of the problem including the client's reactions and adjustment.

CULTURAL PSYCHODYNAMICS

The following two cases serve as examples of cultural influences on family functioning and the need to incorporate psycho-social-cultural dynamic perspectives in family therapy.

Case 1:

Josefa ("Josey") is a 15-year-old Mexican American girl with a dark complexion and strong Indian-Asian physical features (many Latinos have mixtures of Caucasian, Indian, African, and/or Asian physical features). Both her parents also have strong Indian-Asian features, and she grew-up in a region of the United States where there were very few other Latinos. She was verbally abused by an older brother throughout her childhood and had very poor self-esteem. She began to withdraw, would lock herself in her room, had virtually no friends, and would spend an inordinate amount of time (between 2 and 3 hours) applying makeup to her face every morning before school. Most of her time applying makeup was aimed at trying to change her eyes, which she particularly disliked. She developed oppositional tendencies toward her parents and seemed to be ashamed of them. She was critical of her parents' heavy Spanish accent and angrily corrected them at every opportunity in an arrogant manner. She did not want to eat with her parents and preferred to take food to her room, where she ate alone. Like many teenagers, she attached a high value to popular brand-name items in food, clothes, and the like. She would not have anything to do with generic brands.

Her relationship with her parents had deteriorated over the past several years going back to an incident in which her parents had disapproved of her makeup. The more her father tried to help her, the more defiant and oppositional she became. Her father concluded that he could not tolerate her constant rejection of him and decided he would "no longer have anything to do with her."

Case 2:

Amparo, a 30-year-old, married, Mexican American woman was committed to the local mental health inpatient unit with auditory hallucinations. She was also exhibiting paranoid and grandiose delusional ideation. She believed herself to be a *bruja* (female witch) and engaged in private, daily rituals involving the burning of candles in her home. She would not talk to anybody about her witchcraft activities, and her husband was most concerned about a possible fire in the home. He also expressed concern over once finding a doll with needles and pins embedded in it among her paraphernalia. She refused to take any psychological tests whatsoever in the hospital and was extremely distrustful, secretive, and suspicious. She expressed the belief that the Virgin Mary, mother of Jesus Christ, was jealous of her supernatural powers. Following her admission, it was also learned that her husband was excessively jealous and did not allow her to leave the home without him. She suspected he was having an affair.

In both cases, culture plays an important role with regard to psychodynamics, symptomatology, and choice of treatment interventions. For both patients, family therapy is necessary as more than one family member is affected by the nonnormative events, and it is fairly clear how cultural context is directly related to symptom manifestation and family functioning. Underlying psychological difficulties affect the family member, the identified client, that are intricately tied to and compounded by cultural factors and cultural context. In neither case would psychotropic medication or individual therapy alone resolve the problems, as contextual factors involving family dynamics and culture are embedded in the problem.

In Case 1, Josey felt a need to belong and be accepted by her peers, which in and of itself is not unusual for teenagers; however, she saw her physical features and ethnicity as barriers to her acceptance. Therefore, she did not accept herself, much less like herself. She felt "different" in a setting in which she perceived that difference to be associated with peer rejection, nonacceptance, and stigmatization. Because her self-esteem was too weak to tolerate these nonnormative, adolescent psychosocial pressures, she began to withdraw as a means of coping. She blamed her parents and learned to resent and despise them. An important dynamic consideration was that her parents did little to convey their pride in their cultural heritage. Involving the entire family in changing interactions was necessary. Self-esteem building for Josey necessitated changes in parental behavior concurrent with individual counseling. Instilling ethnocultural pride in the entire family was crucial but not until Josey was accepted by her peers were significant psychological improvements noted. Her identity development and eventual identity closure were intertwined with her ethnic identity and with cultural/contextual/environmental factors.

In Case 2, Amparo's involvement in *brujeria* (witchcraft) was motivated by a need to balance power within her marriage. Family therapy was crucial to resolving the dynamics directly related to her symptoms. The belief that she had supernatural powers fortified her in her battle to regain dignity and self-esteem within her marriage and family. Even though her ritualistic behavior resulted in part in her hospitalization, it also frightened her husband enough that he eventually changed his behavior toward her, allowed his wife more freedom and control, and stopped his infidelity. Interestingly, Hispanic staff at the hospital where Amparo was being treated, tried to distance themselves from notions of supernatural spirits and downplayed this behavior. There was disagreement within the Hispanic provider group as to the extent to which some of her "delusions" were actually culturally shaped and "normal" behavior as opposed to representing delusional thinking. Medication was helpful in reducing some of Amparo's symptoms, but it alone was not sufficient in resolving family dysfunctional behavior. Shared negotiation tactics (Kleinman, Eisenberg, & Good, 1978) were employed in resolving marital dysfunctional behavior.

CONCLUSION

An example of the impact of culture on a nonnormative family event is presented of a family member who is suffering from a chronic, severe mental illness. A mental disorder would have great potential impact not only on the ill individual but also on his or her immediate family (Chapter 7 details the impact in more detail). How both the individual and the family react and adjust to this nonnormative event varies on a case-by-case basis. Some families, for example, nurture dependence, some nurture interdependence, and still others nurture independence. Some families deny, others are totally overwhelmed, whereas others become strong advocates for research and services. For some, life goes on unaltered; others are devastated and permanently scarred. There are obviously many possible reactions to discovering that a family member has a mental illness. The impact of culture determines what form this reaction will take. In different cultures, the same behaviors have a very different meaning and interpretation. For example, an individual experiencing hallucinations may have power within one culture and be given special status whereas in another culture, the same hallucinations may lead to being isolated, discriminated against, and stigmatized. What this chapter has attempted to show is that culture influences our behavior, thoughts, beliefs, and emotions in profound ways. Our culture determines the extent to which we stigmatize mental illness, perceive it as a curse, as a medical illness, as normal or abnormal behavior, and so on. Even the extent to which we react emotionally (e.g., feelings of guilt) is culturally determined. The family may react by increasing any preexisting dysfunctional tendencies and complicate the recovery of the illness. Our behaviors, attitudes, and beliefs are formed in large part from membership, participation, and from learning that transpired within our family and that characterizes the ethnocultural group(s) with which we identify. Psychotherapeutic processes aimed at family intervention frequently require individual cognitive changes, behavior changes, and changes in attitudes, that are in direct contradiction to existing ideas, beliefs, and behaviors. Thus, in the process of helping families, we operate in a culturally determined environment. Family therapists should obtain some level of cultural competence in their professional training (Dana, 1993) if they are to navigate skillfully within that environment.

Family therapists and clinicians have the task of helping families cope with many nonnormative events. An understanding of cultural influences on families is a good beginning point toward reaching the ideal or proficiency level of cultural competence. However, simply reading about Iran, for example, when a Persian family presents itself for therapy is not sufficient. Asking specific questions such as "What do you think are the problems, their causes, and their solutions?" is another step. Learning about our own ethnocentric biases or resistances is also important. Looking for areas of cultural fit between client and therapist is critical. Dana (1994) points out that the task of becoming culturally competent to provide assessment and therapeutic services for even one group that is culturally different from mainstream white-Americans is enormous. McGoldrick (1982) is correct in stating that no therapist can become an expert in all ethnic groups but that an attitude of openness to cultural variability and to understanding the relativity of our own values is what is most essential for clinicians to learn.

REFERENCES

American Psychiatric Association. (1995). *Diagnostic and Statistical Manual of Mental Disorders* (4th ed.). Washington, DC: Author.

Angel, R. (1994). The impact of culture and social class on health status and medical care use. In S. K. Hoppe & W. H. Holtzman (Eds.), *Search for a common language in psychiatric assessment.* The University of Texas, Texas-World Health Organization Collaborating Center. Hogg Foundation for Mental Health.

Berg, I. K., & Jaya, A. (1993). Different and same: Family therapy with Asian-American families. *Journal of Marital and Family Therapy, 19,* 31–38.

Berry, J. W. (1980). Acculturation as varieties of adaptation. In A. M. Padilla (Ed.), *Acculturation: Theory, models and some new findings.* Boulder, CO: Westview.

Berry, J. W., & Kim, U. (1988). Acculturation and mental health. In P. Dasen, J. W. Berry, & N. Sartorious (Eds.), *Health and cross-cultural psychology: Towards application* (pp. 207–236). London: Sage.

Breunlin, D., Schwartz, R., & Mac Kune-Karrer, B. (1992). *Metaframeworks: Transcending the models of family therapy.* San Francisco: Jossey-Bass.

Burgess, E. W., & Locke, H. J. (1953). *The family* (2nd ed.). New York: American Book Company.

Buri, J. R. (1991). Parental authority questionnaire. *Journal of Personality and Social Assessment, 57,* 110–119.

Chung, D. K. (1992). Asian cultural commonalities: A comparison with mainstream American culture. In D. K. Chung, K. Murase, & F. Ross-Sheriff (Eds.), *Social work practice with Asian Americans* (pp. 27–44). Newbury Park, CA: Sage.

Cuéllar, I., & Arnold, B. (1988, July/August). Cultural considerations and rehabilitation of disabled Mexican Americans. *Journal of Rehabilitation, 54* (3), 35–41.

Dana, R. (1993). *Multicultural assessment perspectives for professional psychology.* Boston: Allyn and Bacon.

Dana, R. H. (1994, midwinter). How can we invest assessment procedures with knowledge of Mexican Americans as cultural beings? In R. H. Dana (Chair), *Assessment of clients as cultural entities.* Symposium conducted at the 1994 midwinter meeting of the Society for Personality Assessment, Chicago, IL.

Edmonds, V. H. (1967, November). Marital conventionalization: Definition and measurement. *Journal of Marriage and the Family, 29,* 681–688.

Fischer, J., & Corcoran, K. (1994). *Measures for clinical practice: A sourcebook Vol. 1: Couples, families and children* (2nd ed.). New York: The Free Press.

Frijda, N. H., & Mesquita, B. (1994). The social roles and functions of emotions. In S. Kitayama & H. R. Markus (Eds.), *Emotion and culture: Empirical studies of mutual influence* (pp. 51–87). Washington, DC: American Psychological Association.

Garrison, V. (1977). The Puerto Rican syndrome in psychiatry. In V. Crapanzano & V. Garrison (Eds.), *Case studies in spirit possession.* New York: Wiley.

Gaw, A. C. (1993). *Culture ethnicity and mental illness.* Washington, DC: American Psychiatric Press.

Hudson, W. W. (1992). *The WALMYR Assessment Scales Scoring Manual.* Tempe, AZ: WALMYR.

James, D. E., Schumm, W. R., & Hall, J. (1985). Characteristics of the Kansas Parental Satisfaction Scale among two samples of married parents. *Psychological Reports, 57,* 163–169.

Kitayama, S., & Markus, H. R. (1994). Introduction to cultural psychology and emotions. In S. Kitayama & H. R. Markus (Eds.), *Emotions and culture: Empirical studies of mutual influence.* Washington, DC: American Psychological Association.

Kleinman, A. M., Eisenberg, L., & Good, B. (1978). Culture illness and cure: Clinical lessons from anthropological and cross-cultural research. *Annals of Internal Medicine, 88* (2), 251–258.

Lambo, T. A. (1965). Schizophrenia and borderline states: Cross-cultural variations in psychiatric symptomatology. In A. V. S. de Reuck & R. Porter (Eds.), *Transcultural psychiatry.* Boston: Little, Brown.

Lefrançois, G. R. (1993). *The lifespan* (4th ed.). Belmont, CA: Wadsworth.

Linehan, M. M., Paul, E., & Egan, K. J. (1983). The parent affect test: Development, validity and reliability. *Journal of Clinical Child Psychology, 12,* 161–166.

Linton, R. (1945). *The cultural background of personality.* New York: Appleton-Century-Crofts.

McCubbin, H. I., & Thompson, A. I. (Eds.). (1991). *Family assessment inventories for research and practice.* Madison: University of Wisconsin.

McGoldrick, M. (1982). *Ethnicity and family therapy: An overview.* In M. McGoldrick, J. K. Pearce, & J. Giordano (Eds.), *Ethnicity and family therapy.* New York: Guilford.

Markus, H. R., & Kitayama, S. (1994). The cultural construction of self and emotion: Implications for social behavior. In S. Kitayama & H. R. Markus (Eds.), *Emotion and culture: Empirical studies of mutual influence* (pp. 89–130). Washington DC: American Psychological Association.

Marsella, A. J., & Kameoka, V. A. (1989). Ethnocultural issues in the assessment of psychopathology. In S. Wetzler (Ed.), *Measuring mental illness: Psychometric assessment for clinicians.* Washington, DC: American Psychiatric Press.

Moran, M. P. (1990). The problem of cultural bias in personality assessment. In C. R. Reynolds & R. W. Kamphaus (Eds.), *The handbook of psychological and educational assessment of children.* New York: Guilford.

Mumford, E. (1981). Culture: Life perspectives and the social meaning of illness. In R. C. Simon & H. Pardes (Eds.), *Understanding human behavior in health and illness.* Baltimore, MD: Williams and Wilkins.

Murdock, G. P. (1957). World ethnographic sample. *American Anthropologist, 59,* 676–688.

Negy, C., & Woods, D. J. (1992, May). A note on the relationship between acculturation and socio-economic status. *Hispanic Journal of Behavioral Sciences, 14*(2), 248–251.

Paniagua, F. (1994). *Assessing and treating culturally diverse clients: A practical guide.* Thousand Oaks, CA: Sage.

Redfield, R., Linton, R., & Herkovitz, M. J. (1936). Memorandum on acculturation. *American Anthropologist, 38,* 149–152.

Rubel, A. J. (1964). The epidemiology of folk illness: Susto in Hispanic Americans. *Ethnology, 3,* 268–283.

Simons, R. C., & Hughes, C. C. (1993). Culture-bound syndromes. In A. C. Gaw (Ed.), *Culture, ethnicity and mental illness.* Washington, DC: American Psychiatric Press.

Skinner, B. F. (1972). *Beyond freedom and dignity.* New York: Alfred A. Knopf.

Stonebrink, S. (1988). *A measure of co-dependency and the impact of socio-cultural characteristics.* Unpublished master's thesis, University of Hawaii, School of Social Work.

Stonequest, E. V. (1937). *The marginal man: A study in personality and culture conflict.* New York: Russell & Russell.

Szapocznik, J., & Kurtines, W. (1980). Acculturation, biculturalism and adjustment among Cuban Americans. In A. M. Padilla (Ed.), *Acculturation: Theory, models and some new findings,* pp. 139–159. Boulder, CO: Westview.

Tavitian, M. L., Lubiner, J. L., Green, L., Grebstein, L. C., & Velicer, W. F. (1987). Dimensions of family functioning. *Journal of Social Behavior and Personality, 2,* 191–204.

Triandis, H. C. (1994a). Culture and social behavior. In W. J. Lonner & R. Malpass (Eds.), *Psychology and culture* (pp. 169–173). Boston: Allyn and Bacon.

Triandis, H. C. (1994b). Major cultural syndromes and emotions. In S. Kitayama & H. R. Markus (Ed.), *Emotion and culture: Empirical studies of mutual influence* (pp. 285–306). Washington, DC: American Psychological Association.

Udry, J. R. (1981). Marital alternatives and marital disruption. *Journal of Marriage and the Family, 43,* 889–897.

Weidman, H. H., & Sussex, J. N. (1971). Cultural values and ego functioning in relation to the atypical culture-bound reactive syndromes. *International Journal of Social Psychiatry, 17,* 83–100.

PART TWO

Nontraditional Family Constellations

CHAPTER 3

Nontraditional Families

Families? What are they like today? How have they changed and how are they different from those of previous generations? The fantasy images people have carried around in their heads about the structure, composition, size, and function of families have changed dramatically in the past 25 or more years (Glick, 1988). The *Father Knows Best* TV series that ran decades ago, encapsulates many of the fantasies that people still have today about how family life should be. The mythical family of a working father, a stay-at-home mother, and two or three school-age children is more the exception than the rule in today's world.

Perhaps the most notable shift that has happened in modern family life has been the shift in emphasis toward meeting the personal, emotional, companionship needs of its members (Edwards, 1987). Today, people marry or live together for love, companionship, and the satisfaction of their emotional needs (Gergen & Gergen, 1988). Perhaps one of the consequences of this shift has been the disappointment many individuals experience when they feel their personal needs and expectations are not met. There is no way of knowing how much the failure of romantic fantasies and unrealistic expectations has contributed to the high divorce rate.

There are countless definitions of "family," but they often fail to cover non-traditional affiliations. The following definition by Lamanna and Riedmann (1985) accounts for many of these variations in families:

> A *family* is any group of persons united by the ties of marriage, blood, or adoption, or any sexually expressive relationship, in which (1) the people are committed to one another in an intimate, interpersonal relationship, (2) the members see their identity as importantly attached to the group, and (3) the group has an identity of its own. (p. 19)

With this definition in mind, it might be useful to categorize some of the many possible variations that do not fit the *Father Knows Best* model. Their differences are often found in their structure and the relationships that exist among the members themselves. We can no longer assume that the word family is synonymous with the *traditional nuclear family*.

The *single-parent* family consists of a parent, who may or may not have been married, and one or more children (McLanahan, Wedemeyer, & Adelberg, 1981). Whether or not there has been a marriage, the children are emotionally being parented and the household maintained by only one parent.

The *binuclear family,* a term used by Ahrons and Rodgers, views the divorced nuclear family as split into two new nuclear families—one headed by the mother; the other headed by the father. These families include whatever children were in the original family and may be headed by a single parent or two parents if former spouses have remarried (Ahrons & Rodgers, 1987). Children often feel divided loyalties trying to juggle their lives between the two. Ahrons uses the term binuclear to make what she considers to be a most important statement: The nuclear family is no longer living as one unit but rather now is functioning as two separate units. This really reflects the idea that *divorce does not end the family but only restructures it.* For the children, mom lives in one house and dad lives in another but *this is still their nuclear family.*

Stepfamily is a term often applied to describe the configuration that forms when either or both the husband and wife have children when they remarry (or marry). Some authors speak of this type of family as *blended* or *reconstituted* (Dowling, 1983). Many people seem to imply that such families only come about through the legal process of marrying. Based on my experience, however, the definition of what constitutes a stepfamily has to be broadened to include not only those couples who legally marry but also those who come together with children in committed relationships without formal legal marriage (heterosexual or same sex). Some would label these as *cohabiting families,* not *stepfamilies.*

ONE-PARENT FAMILIES

One of the most significant changes that has occurred since the 1970s has been the marked increase in the number of households with one or more children that are headed by a single parent (Sporakowski, 1988). Not only has there continued to be a high rate of separation and divorce, there has also been an increased number of out-of-wedlock births resulting in a proportionately large increase in this type of family (Norton & Glick, 1986). Also during these years, adoption by singles has increased (Feigelman & Silverman, 1983). The number of one-parent families more than doubled (from 3.8 million to 9.7 million) between 1970 and 1990. Mothers headed 88% of these and fathers only 12% (U.S. Bureau of Census, 1991b).

This growing nontraditional family type is described well in the book, *Single Parents by Choice: A Growing Trend in Family Life* (Miller, 1992). It focuses on four groups: (a) single, biological mothers (planned or unplanned pregnancies); (b) singles (men and women) who have adopted children (both infants and older); (c) divorced parents in sole and joint custody arrangements; and (d) gay and lesbian parents. Because the issues around adoption and gay and lesbian families are addressed in more detail in Chapters 4 and 6 of this book, the focus here will be primarily on general issues common to single-parent families.

Special Needs and Concerns

Education and Support

Single-parent families have special needs as they cope with the tasks of raising their children. They especially need *support and education* (Johnson, 1986; Porter & Chatelain, 1981). Our society puts so much emphasis on couples as the norm for parenting children that the single parent often feels out of place or not quite normal. These families need to receive credit for doing an excellent job of raising children and often providing for the needs of the children through the concerned involvement of the parent.

Miller (1992) states it well when she observes:

> The presence of both a strong support system and an emotionally and physically stable environment are of especial importance to single-parent families. Whether the support comes from the community, the extended family, or friends, it has a particular significance for a parent carrying the entire burden of raising a child alone. (p. 203)

Public education is important. Single parents in particular and society as a whole need to know that this type of nontraditional family is an integral part of daily living. The children raised by single parents can be just as healthy and normal as those raised in the traditional two-parent family. In fact despite the obstacles, children in most single-parent families, are provided with the love and nurturing that all children need and deserve. Single parents need to be reassured that what they are doing is normal and that they are not "messing up" their children. Education and support go hand in hand.

Finances

Because the overwhelming majority of these households are maintained by women, one of the most basic concerns is *the financial status of these households.* One-third of these families live below the poverty level (U.S. Bureau of the Census, 1991b). In a society where the cost of food, housing, and transportation seems to be ever increasing, it is common knowledge that one income is seldom enough to care for a family. When the financial responsibility is on a woman's shoulders, her more limited earning potential ($.70 for every dollar earned by a man with equal education; Taeuber, 1991) is an even greater liability. Yet most often, these mothers do a remarkable job providing for their children.

Inadequate Child Care

Faced with having to support the family alone, the need for adequate child care ranks as a major concern for many of these households (Turner & Smith, 1983).

Care for children under 5 is most often provided in the child's or another's home. This expanding family group needs more day-care and group-care programs for the children of working mothers (Hofferth & Phillips, 1987).

Being a "Supermom"

Single mothers, faced with both breadwinning and homemaking tasks, often *have difficulty performing all family functions well* (Burden, 1986; Sanik & Mauldin, 1986). Because survival is a first priority, household chores and tasks (e.g., cleaning, dishes, food preparation) are often neglected—there just is not enough time in the day. In spite of this reality, culture and society have imposed such expectations on women to be heart and soul of family life that it is very difficult for single mothers not to feel these dual responsibilities. The only solution is trying to be "Supermom." In the stress of survival—just trying to make it through the week—it is likely there is not enough time and energy left for both doing the household tasks and providing physical and emotional care to the children. Priorities have to be set; either one or the other has to be neglected (Quinn & Allen, 1989). Otherwise, Supermom could end up burning out and not being there for her children.

Being a "Superdad"

Although single fathers who are heading up the household do not experience as severe financial pressures as single mothers (Norton & Glick, 1986), nonetheless this is still the most common complaint. However, *not being able to spend enough time with their children* is also a major concern (Risman, 1986). Commitments to jobs and careers have often been a higher priority for men than women. Thus the responsibility involved in being primarily responsible for the care of children can place much intrapsychic stress on the man (Greif, 1988).

Single fathers with such a personal child-care role frequently feel compelled to prove their competency as suitable parents. They are well schooled in the stereotypical gender role of breadwinners. What may be new, however, is learning how to have one-to-one, nurturing personal relationships with their children. Many single fathers feel they must meet this challenge by becoming "Superdad" and "Father of the Year." A major stress factor often comes from having to change their circle of friends and rebuild their social life (Greif, 1988). Most single fathers prove to be competent and satisfied in their new role (Risman, 1986).

Isolation and Loneliness

In American society, much of adult mainstream social activity is organized for couples. This often leaves the single parent feeling isolated and cut off *in meeting his or her normal emotional needs for affection and companionship* (Smith, 1980). Unfortunately, many adults end up relating to their children more like peers or confidantes or friends. This deprives the child of a parent. More single parents are turning to groups and networks that have been developed to meet their social and emotional needs. These networks are important to their psychological well-being (McLanahan, Wedemeyer, & Adelberg, 1981). One such group, "Parents without Partners," was organized both to help with parenting the children and to meet such adult social and emotional needs.

Therapeutic and Educational Interventions

So much attention has been placed on what is wrong with single-parent families. More attention needs to be directed toward what is right and how to help these families find solutions that will encourage and build success. From the vantage point of over 25 years of clinical, supervisory, and teaching experience, I believe the following goals described in the article "Successful Single Parents" (Olsen & Haynes, 1993, p. 262) can serve as useful guidelines for helping professionals:

1. Acceptance of the responsibilities and challenges in single-parent families.
2. Prioritization of the parental role.
3. Employment of consistent, nonpunitive discipline.
4. Emphasis on open communication.
5. Ability to foster individuality within a supportive family unit.
6. Recognition of need for self-nurturance.
7. Rituals and traditions.

The following sections describe several ways helping professionals can work with single parents to achieve these goals.

Acceptance

Therapists and educators need to take the lead in reeducating our society and single-parent families. Without glossing over the struggles and challenges single parents face on a day-to-day basis, the emphasis needs to be on the positives: a commitment to the family, appreciation and affection for the family members, open, honest, straightforward communication; adequate time together, spiritual well-being and the ability to cope with the stresses and crises of daily living in a creative fashion (Stinnett & DeFrain, 1985).

Prioritization of Parenting

This shift to focusing on being the best possible parent is a necessary one. It is probably a bigger leap for fathers who have traditionally focused on work/career as a higher priority. Now the single parent must put the needs of his or her children first. This shift could have an impact on decisions about moving, changing jobs, being more involved in youth activities, and so on. Therapists can assist by helping single parents sort out the ambivalance they may feel. They can also help them find ways to make both roles possible and satisfying.

Discipline

It is hard enough for two parents to be consistent and nonpunitive with discipline. It is even harder for the single parent, who does not want to be "the bad guy," to provide the balance between being structured and consistent while being empowering and democratic. Therapists and educators can assist single parents on an individual basis to better understand what is normal child and adolescent development, what are appropriate and effective ways of disciplining, and how one copes with more difficult acting-out behavior. Family therapy is a recommended approach because it allows the therapist to model what is being taught. Books, audio, tapes, and videotapes can be used effectively as part of this psychoeducation. Parenting classes and support groups can be most useful. It is a different ball game when the single parent takes on disciplining the children without the support of a partner. It helps to know others who are struggling with similar issues.

Open Communication

Frequently, family upheavals (e.g., divorce or death), disrupt the trust levels in a family. Where there is custody and visitation, children are often caught in the conflicts between their parents. When a parent has died or disappeared, denial often is used as the coping mechanism: "If we don't discuss it, maybe the pain will go away." It is imperative that therapists help all family members to communicate their feelings openingly and honestly. Such communication can build bridges and promote trusting relationships. In divorcing families where the parents have been wrapped up in spousal conflicts, the helping professionals need to be sensitive to the feelings of the children. This is especially true if parents have triangled the child(ren) into the marriage and have encouraged them to take sides in support of one parent or the other. The children may have denied their feelings to protect the parent(s) from any further pain and hurt.

Foster Individuality

If the helping professionals have been able to assist members of the single-parent family to practice the skills addressed in the first four areas, it is likely that both adults and children will begin to experience their own individuality within the context of a family that has become more supportive. Individual efforts will merit personal attention even as the evolving single-parent family achieves its own special identity. Divorced parents frequently find themselves having closer relationships with their children postdivorce than they ever did while they were married. This can be a goal in therapy or education.

Self-Nurturance

Although it is important for the single parent to devote every effort to provide for the well-being of the children, it is equally vital for the health of single-parent families that the parents also nurture themselves. Helping professionals can be instrumental in teaching the art of self-care and nurturance. It is often easier for the single parent to focus on the children's needs than to deal with his or her own needs. Single parents need to be taught that if they do not care for their own emotional, physical, spiritual, or social needs, they could easily feel overwhelmed by the needs they are expected to provide for their children. Self-care is not selfishness.

Rituals and Traditions

There is real comfort and reassurance in maintaining the old and developing the new in families. Therapists and educators can help single-parent families identify the traditions that remain beneficial in the present circumstances. They can also assist these families to create new rituals that can help the family cope and thrive in the face of change and uncertainty.

THE DIVORCED FAMILY

In the past, couples often stayed together "for the sake of the children" even though the marriage itself might have been unsatisfying. That appears to be changing. According to the U.S. Census Bureau, during the 1980s, approximately 61% of all households with dependent children included both biological parents, 24% were headed by single parents, 12% were remarried or stepfamilies, and the remaining 3% consisted of other configurations. (U.S. Bureau of Census, 1989)

Prior to the 1960s, couples seeking a divorce needed to base this decision on issues of immorality or fault (Miller, 1992):

> Divorce was difficult to undergo even in the most favorable of circumstances, and bad feelings were often made worse because one spouse had to come up with grounds based on immorality (often fabricated) against the other. This happened all too often even when both parties had agreed to divorce. (p. 108)

In California, in 1970, the legislature passed the first "no-fault" divorce law. This required only that one spouse assert (Miller, 1992):

> Irreconcilable differences have caused the irremediable breakdown of the marriage. . . . Divorce was no longer based on issues of moral judgment; rather it was looked on as a private decision in which each partner was to be treated equally. It was the hope that such changes would reduce much of the acrimony surrounding divorce proceedings and, consequently, would be less destructive to the children. (p. 108)

In any divorce where children are involved, one of the most important struggles the adults face is separating their *spousal issues from their parenting responsibilities*. Even though the marital partners end up legally dissolving their marital relationship, the one thing that is not dissolved is the parenting relationship with one another and the parenting relationship they continue to have with their children. *Divorce ends the marriage but not the family. Divorce restructures the family.*

Ahrons expresses this idea when she says:

> The key idea . . . is that of the "binuclear family." . . . This term reflects our basic point of view that, while *marriages* may be discontinued, *families*—especially those in which there are children—continue after marital disruption. They do so with the focus on the two ex-spouse parents now located in separate households—two nuclei to which children and parents alike, as well as others, must relate. (1980, p. ix)

The Emotional Trauma for Adults

For whatever reasons, many people who marry seem to look unconsciously to marriage as something akin to the universal healer of childhood wounds and disappointments. Many couples marry with the dream that life is going to get better or happier. When these expectations are unfulfilled, divorce often seems to be the only solution. For many, the broken promises and shattered dreams result in deep feelings of disappointment, hopelessness, despair, revenge, and retaliation. For others, the decision to divorce may be a real relief: "I've done everything and this is the right decision for me." The emotional impact is more traumatic when one spouse wants the divorce and the other does not. The former may be euphoric; the latter, despondent—maybe even suicidal.

The trauma has often been compared with the loss of a loved one who dies, but at least in death, *there is a finality.* With divorce, the ex-spouses continue to be part of the lives of the family members. The *restructured* family goes on. The adults need to put aside their *spousal issues* and continue to be involved in *coparenting* their children. And the children still have a *living* parent to deal with either actively or sporadically or in absentia.

The Attitudes of Society

When a family has suffered a loss through death, family and friends rally around the survivors and offer comfort, support, sympathy. In the case of the divorcing family, the experience is often quite the opposite; many still view divorce as a *failure.* Friends frequently shy away: "They drop you like a hot potato"; or they feel they must take sides. Family members also often either take sides or stay out of it stating, "That's their business." Thus it is very difficult for family members to deal with the impact of divorce publicly. These negative stereotypes are lessening as some people today reflect on their parents' marriage and say: "They didn't divorce *but they should have!*" Others grew up in a divorced family and are more accepting of divorce as part of life.

The Battle with Loneliness

The pain that is at the very core of loneliness is often more intense than has previously been experienced. Many divorcing adults withdraw to protect themselves from further hurt. They isolate themselves from friends and family hoping that others do not see how much they are hurting. The unaccustomed quiet, isolation, loneliness, especially for the noncustodial parent, can be stifling, a constant reminder of shattered dreams. To compensate for these experiences, the divorcing adult often swings from one extreme to another. Fisher (1992) describes them this way:

> ... "busyholics," with an activity for each night of the week and two on Saturdays and Sundays. . . . This busy-loneliness varies in length and intensity from person to person. . . . Eventually all get tired and begin to realize there must be more to life than running from the ghost of loneliness. Then they begin to slow down into the aloneness stage. (pp. 75–76)

The Financial Strains

Especially for mothers with custody of the children following divorce, the reduction in income is often dramatic—40% to 50% less than before. This factor alone can have a significant impact on many aspects of postdivorce family life. The custodial parent must become totally responsible for housing and child care. Even if the mother has not been working full time previously, now there is pressure to take on that full financial responsibility. Often it is necessary to sell the family residence, uproot from the neighborhood and schools, and relocate based on a lower standard of living. All these stresses are particularly evident in the first 2 years following the actual separation.

Therapeutic and Educational Interventions

In my years of experience working with divorcing families, a number of important beliefs and interventions have emerged. In working with the adults who are emotionally impacted by the divorce, it is most beneficial for helping professionals:

1. To lend a empathetic ear allowing the person to tell his or her "story" about the marriage and the divorce; there is a desperate need to be heard, and after awhile friends often get tired of hearing the story over and over again.
2. To normalize the often intense emotional reactions the person is going through; Trafford (1984) describes this experience as "Crazy Time"; because the emotions are often so intense, therapists tend to see these people at their worst.
3. To give permission for grieving the losses that are involved in giving up a spouse and the dream of "one happy family;" the process is comparable to death and dying and could take one, two, or more years.
4. To educate and inform about the stages and duration of the divorcing process; it is not uncommon for the legal divorce to happen long before the emotional healing; bibliotherapy can often be most useful especially the

works of Fisher (1992), Trafford (1984), Berman (1991), and numerous other authors.

5. To encourage participation in groups for divorcing persons; this not only gives the opportunity to be heard, it also helps in the healing and socialization processes.

The Emotional Trauma for the Children

Divorce is an adult decision that can have a very significant (positive or negative) impact on a child's life and development. If the family life has been filled with violence or abuse (see Chapter 9) or neglect, or drugs and alcohol (see Chapter 14), the decision to divorce probably will come as a great relief. For other children, the divorce may send shock waves through the family. Their family—the very source of their emotional and psychological stability—can be jolted from its foundations like a home in an earthquake.

These reactions vary greatly from child to child. Much will depend on the developmental level of each child including chronological and emotional age, gender, temperament, and ability to cope with stressful experiences. With all the emotionality involved, divorce can rate as highly on the stress scale as death in a family. Several authors (Blau, 1994; Francke, 1983; Kalter, 1990) have addressed these issues of children's needs and their reactions, during the divorcing process. What is important to remember is that divorce is not simply a one-time event but rather is an ongoing process that continues over time to impact the restructured family as both the adults and the children make multiple transitions and the growing children face new challenges. The adjustments are rarely smooth and peaceful:

> Most children show some problems in the first 2 years following their parents' divorce. After this initial crisis period, some children exhibit remarkable resiliency and emerge as well-functioning, competent, or even enhanced individuals. . . . although 20% of children are showing extreme levels of behavior problems even beyond the crisis period of the divorce transition, 80% are functioning within the normal range. (Hetherington, Law, & O'Conner, 1993, pp. 222–223)

Common Thoughts and Feelings of Children

In many years of clinical and supervisory practice with divorcing families, I have found that children exhibit a wide variety of thoughts and feelings that seem to overwhelm them. Some of the most common ones are:

Reunification. Many children hope and dream of their parents getting back together, both at the time of the breakup and many years later. To add to the child's confusion, frequently at least one of the parents may harbor similar wishes.

Responsibility. Often, divorcing parents end up battling over parenting issues rather than their spousal differences. When they split up fighting about parenting, this leaves the children feeling, "If I had done my homework or gotten good grades or cleaned my room, my parents would still be together; it's my fault they're divorcing."

Loyalties. Children want to love both parents, and they want both to love them; often they feel trapped in the middle. It becomes a giant emotional tug-of-war.

Power and Helplessness. What a double bind! Children often feel they can or should make things better and get the parents back together. At the same time, they frequently feel no control in their lives. The adults have made the decisions without attending to the feelings and needs of the children.

Abandonment. There is a loss of love and security. Who is going to leave next? What does the future hold for them? "Am I going to be kicked out next like daddy if I'm not good?" "Why doesn't daddy come and see me? Why did he leave me?"

Hurt and Sadness. Children across the board may experience these feelings but those more likely to feel intense sadness and hurt are school-age children. "Particularly boys are hard hit at this stage. They are old enough to understand what the divorce means and to pine over memories of the family together but young enough to feel completely defenseless" (Blau, 1994, p. 114). This often shows up in denial, not wanting to talk, withdrawal, with the child believing: "If I don't talk about it, everything will be just fine."

Confusion and Frustration. Caught in the middle between warring parents can lead to great confusion and frustration for the children. Parents often lean on their children for comfort and support. Sometimes they pressure them to take sides. The children may respond to the parents in a self-protective fashion. They may tell the parents what they want to hear or they may play one parent against another in a manipulative way. Regressive behaviors by the children can be another way of coping with these emotions.

Anger. For preteen children (9 to 12), the news of divorce may trigger an explosive response. "They may express anger, verbal and sometimes physical; they can be contrary or blatantly rebellious. . . . They may take out their anger on their peers; their schoolwork is likely to suffer; they may even get into more serious trouble—like lying and stealing" (Blau, 1994, p. 116). Siblings, teachers, children at school, destruction of property, and harm to animals can often be targets of the anger they may feel toward their parents and the divorce.

Embarrassment. Children are often embarrassed that their parent have somehow failed. This perhaps reflects the societal myth that the "together" family is the successful one and the "broken" family represents failure. Also if mother remarries and changes her name, the child may feel awkward in social situations where introductions are necessary (e.g., at school).

Joy and relief. Not every divorce is experienced with such negative feelings. For some children, the separation and divorce may bring joy and relief—"Finally, it's over!" This is especially true when the conflicts, fighting, violence, abuse, drugs and alcohol have been so much part of daily living that children lived in fear and trepidation. For some children, these feelings may only come over time with acceptance of the reality that their family really is better off divorced and at peace rather than together in constant tension and conflict.

Therapeutic and Educational Interventions

The adults in a divorcing family demand a lot of attention as they struggle with their emotional issues. As a result, the needs of the children often are put into the background. They frequently "take care of" their parents by holding in their feelings and appearing to be "doing just fine." In my clinical experience, it is imperative that therapists and educators assist the children in the following ways:

1. Acknowledge that their family is going through a stressful transition.
2. Create for them a safe and supportive environment whether it be in school or therapy, at home, or on visitations to the non custodial parent.
3. Give them permission to freely express all their feelings without fear of reprisal.
4. Teach them coping skills for dealing with their parents, siblings, and peers.
5. Help them understand divorce, how it is an adult struggle and how the family is not ended but rather restructured.
6. Help increase their self-esteem and relieve their guilt teaching them that they are not responsible for the divorce.
7. Work to make it possible for the children to have freedom of access to each parent without being put in the middle.
8. Provide support/information groups both at school and in therapy centers where children can meet with others from divorcing families and better understand that "they are not alone."

Children usually will find it easier to cope when their parents learn to separate spousal issues from parenting issues. They need to become "coparents" rather than warring ones. If this shift can happen, then the children have a better chance of adjusting.

Stability and Success in the Divorcing Family

Although spouses *legally* dissolve their spousal relationships through divorce, usually, they continue to be parents to their children. There are many ties that bind, especially emotional ones, that go into making a success of such a monumental task. Undoubtably, the crucial part for the parents is learning to continue to coparent their children while setting aside their very emotional ex-spousal issues.

> Being "caught in the middle," rather than divorce per se, or loss of contact with a noncustodial parent, has the most adverse effect on children's behavior and psychological well-being. . . . Children, especially older children, are able to function well over time in independent, noninterfering households. As long as they are not involved in parental conflict, children are able to cope well even if these households have different rules and expectation. (Hetherington, 1993, p. 214)

Largely to the degree that the adults learn to coexist and cooperatively function as parents, their children will reap the benefits. Blau (1994, pp. 32–33) outlines what she believes are essential ingredients in helping divorced spouses work cooperatively in coparenting their children:

Key 1 Heal yourself—so you can get on with your own life, without leaning on your kids.

Key 2 Act maturely—whether or not you really *feel* it; you and your co-parent are the adults.

Key 3 Listen to your children; understand their needs.

Key 4 Respect each other's competence as parents and love for the children.

Key 5 Divide parenting time—somehow, in some way, so that the children feel they still have two parents.

Key 6 Accept each other's differences—even though . . . one is laid back and the other a disciplinarian, one's fanatically neat, the other is a slob.

Key 7 Communicate about (and with) the children—directly, not *through* them.

Key 8 Step out of gender roles. Mom learns how to fix a bike . . . and Dad can take his daughter shopping.

Key 9 Recognize and accept that change is inevitable and therefore can be anticipated.

Key 10 Know that coparenting is forever; be prepared to handle . . . milestones in your children's lives with a minimum of stress and encourage your respective families to do the same.

Although most parents and their children experience the divorcing process as initially painful and stressful, over time both are able to adjust to two-home (binuclear), single-parent living provided there is not continuing or escalating parental conflict. Divorce in families is not the end of the world. These restructured families can be filled with opportunities for personal growth, more peaceful family living, and meaningful one-to-one personal relationships with each parent.

REMARRIAGES AND STEPFAMILIES

Stepfamilies are families emerging out of hope. Being a remarried parent or a stepparent is different from being a parent in a first-marriage family . . . Successful stepfamilies accept and understand these differences and allow themselves the necessary time to accomplish the tasks that lead to successful integration. (Visher & Visher, 1993, p. 251)

The number of households that include stepparents and stepchildren has increased dramatically. According to the 1987 National Survey of Families and Households (NSFH), 33% of the U.S. population was in some type of "step" situation/household (Glick, 1991). It is Glick's prediction that by the year 2000 there will be more stepfamilies than any other type of American family (Glick & Lin, 1986).

In spite of these realities, Emily Visher and John Visher (1993), the most prominent and respected spokespersons for stepfamilies, predict an uphill struggle for these families:

Our impression is that it will take many more years for society to overcome the influence of the old fairy tales, the negative bias toward divorce and remarriage, and the idealization of the nuclear family, so that marriages other than first marriages will be accepted as positive, albeit challenging, life cycle stages. (p. 236)

Broadening the Definition of "Family"

Most people associate "family" with "being married." When working with step-families clinicians must broaden the definition of family. There are many adults, with children, who choose to be together in emotionally and psychologically committed relationships who are not legally remarried. These groupings nonetheless view themselves as stepfamilies. Who is viewed as having "membership" in these newly formed families is also subjective and depends on each adult and child involved. Just because two adults (one or both with children) fall in love and join in a committed relationship does not mean the children will automatically be just as enthusiastic about this new configuration. There are good reasons for such reluctance or resistance.

Of Spaceships and Aliens

Many a stepparent has exclaimed in frustration: "I feel like I'm an *alien* in this family! His kids treat me like I'm an *invader from Mars!*" These reactions may not be so far-fetched when we consider how stepfamilies come into being. We can learn a valuable lesson from science fiction that helps us better understand families and stepfamilies (Seibt, 1990).

Drawing from the *Star Trek* television series, we know that when a star-cruiser encounters an unknown or enemy spaceship, the starcruiser's first response is to self-protect by activating its invisible, protective "force field"; this shield keeps it safe. Families are much like spaceships—they protect themselves from outsiders and alien invaders (the enemy) by putting up "invisible, emotional force fields, shields" (Seibt, 1993). Family members may fight among themselves but let there be a threat from the outside and they will band together to protect the family from such dangers.

Because stepfamilies are most frequently *born of loss*—divorce or death—the protection factor is an important consideration. After a death or divorce, the reorganized, single-parent family often bonds itself into a very close unit emotionally. This closeness is vital to its survival. To ward off any real or perceived invaders, the family members may automatically put up the family's invisible protective emotional shield. It becomes a case of "us against the world, circle the wagons" as the single-parent family seeks to stabilize itself.

Children, naturally, become highly protective of their relationships with the individual parents. If they feel they lost out when their parents divorced, then it makes a lot of sense that if and when either parent decides to *lift the protective shield* around the family spaceship and bring aboard (begin dating) another adult, the children could feel their "space has been invaded" This adult (potential stepparent?) probably has no emotional, psychological ties with the children; this is truly a "stranger, an alien invader from Mars."

Often in the formation of stepfamily relationships, the adults look at this new family as a positive opportunity for growth and happiness. For the children, on the other hand, this outsider represents a threat to the security of the parent-child relationship. Whereas the adults often come out feeling like winners, the children just as frequently feel like losers.

A Word of Caution to Therapists and Educators

It is very important that helping professionals have a clear understanding of the issues and dynamics of stepfamily living. These families are unique and potentially very complex. In their functioning, we can readily see family systems operating in the most complicated fashion. With a thorough knowledge of family systems and stepfamily dynamics, professionals are better prepared to cope with the turmoil that these families encounter (Seibt, 1991).

Martin and Martin (1992) in their book on therapy with stepfamilies express this very clearly:

> For a therapist untrained in working with stepfamilies, therapeutic contact with them can feel like being ringmaster for a disorganized circus. In correlation with its degree of dysfunction, a stepfamily can take every conceivable twist and turn. The methods that work with traditional families may not work with stepfamilies at all. (p. 2)

It has been my experience that in the early stages of working with stepfamilies, one of the first interventions of benefit is *education about what is normal and can be expected in stepfamily development.* The metaphor or comparison with aliens, spaceships, and invisible force fields is readily understood by most. Normalizing their many and varied feelings frequently relieves a great deal of anxiety and allows them to step back and look at the situation with a little more objectivity.

Unfortunately, the only models of family that most stepfamilies compare themselves with are the intact, traditional family or *The Brady Bunch.* It is most helpful to reassure stepfamilies that their family structure is unique, different, and very special and there is no "right way" to become the ideal stepfamily. At the same time, clinicians can offer guidelines for working on the blending process and can reiterate that *becoming a stepfamily is a process that takes time* (3 to 5 years on average—not simply a few weeks or a few months).

As part of the education process with stepfamilies, they need to understand:

- The myths and unrealistic expectations that are prevalent in our culture.
- The unique stepfamily characteristics.
- The primacy of the couple relationship.
- The developmental stages that stepfamilies normally traverse.

Understanding Stepfamily Dynamics

Myths and Unrealistic Expectations

"I feel like *the wicked stepmother*" is a common reaction of many stepparents in their frustration of trying to meet the needs of their stepchildren. This myth is so much part of our culture that stepfamilies cannot seem to get around it. As one stepfather said, "When we told the children we were getting married (after living together for six months), the youngest daughter reacted by asking, 'Does that mean *now you're going to be mean?*'"

At the other extreme is the *Instant Love* myth and expectation. Stepfamilies and society tend to believe that in these "instant families" there should be "instant love." It just does not happen this way. Because adults fall in love does not mean they instantly love the children who are part of the "package deal." Nor do the children have instant feelings of love for the newly arrived stepparent. Love takes time, patience, respect, and trust. It can be especially hard for the children to accept this stranger aboard ship as a member of "my" family.

The Vishers (1993) state it clearly: "In successful remarriage families, this myth of instant love is understood and rejected; the stepfamily members relax their expectations about their feelings, and often relationships slowly blossom into caring and loving bonds that last a lifetime" (p. 245).

Stepfamilies are not the same as first-marriage, nuclear families. Yet society has in the past measured stepfamily success by comparing them with nuclear families. You can reconstitute orange juice from concentrate but you don't "reconstitute" nuclear families when stepfamilies are formed. Each stepfamily is *unique* and needs to be valued as a family unto itself.

Stepfamily Characteristics and Tasks

The Vishers (1988, p. 10), call our attention to seven characteristics that distinguish stepfamilies from nuclear, intact families. With each characteristic the Vishers also outline the corresponding task facing the stepfamily:

Stepfamily Characteristics	Stepfamily Tasks
1. Begins after many losses and changes.	1. Dealing with losses and changes.
2. Incongruent individual, marital, family life cycles.	2. Negotiating different developmental needs.
3. Children and adults all come with expectations from previous families.	3. Establishing new traditions.
4. Parent-child relationships predate the new couple.	4. Developing a solid couple bond and forming new relationships.
5. Biological parent elsewhere in actuality or in memory.	5. Creating a "Parenting Coalition."
6. Children often members of two households.	6. Accepting continual shifts in household composition.
7. Legal relationship between stepparent and children is ambiguous or nonexistent.	7. Risking involvement despite little societal support.

That *the parent-child relationship precedes the new couple relationship* is one of the most significant factors that must be considered. Children need closeness and stability to feel secure, and usually their parents will provide such security. Naturally, divorce and death strike at the very heart of these attachments. Thus a new couple relationship could well feel like a major threat to the already existing parent-child bond. In so many ways, the incoming stepparent is at a distinct disadvantage, in a "one-down" position. It is a most uncomfortable position for an adult to feel like an outsider looking in through the invisible family shield, unable to be part of the ongoing parent-child relationship. However, until the child feels trusting enough to welcome this stranger aboard ship, the adults (parent and stepparent) need to refrain from trying to force such bonds to happen. Children need to set this pace.

What roles do stepparents have in newly forming stepfamilies? This is an extremely important question facing the adults. It is especially relevant when discipline issues arise. If the stepparent has only a tentative, fragile bond with the stepchildren, how can either feel secure with the stepparent being involved in limit-setting or discipline? There is much confusion for both adults and children. The old line, "You can't tell me what to do, you're not my dad [mom]," is accurate. A stepparent does not automatically become an authority figure just because he or she is married to or living with the child's bioparent.

The "parenting" role is not a given; it has to be earned, achieved over time and based on respect and an emerging psychological relationship. In the beginning, the most appropriate role for a new stepparent would probably be as a "caring adult friend" who is involved in the child's life and supportive of the bioparent (Seibt, 1994). Otherwise this thorny issue can generate intense conflict and bitter hostility. This is especially true when the children are preteens or adolescents. They already have two biological parents to differentiate from; they do not need to break away from another "parent figure."

The Couple Relationship

This needs to be a first priority in any newly forming stepfamily. It is crucial that children feel secure, and the most visible source of such security would be a stable, loving couple who can provide for their needs. Realistically, what generally takes center stage is the acting-out behavior of the children, especially when they feel threatened or stressed by the alien stepparent. Their shields are up and the couple feels compelled to focus on the children's needs.

So often, couples who take the plunge into stepfamily living have no time or energy for one another. If the couple does not make adequate time and space for meaningful "couple bonding," how are they going to be supportive of one another when the unexpected crises of normal stepfamily living suddenly erupt? Unless their relationship is stable and caring, under stress each bioparent (where each adult has children) is likely to stand up for his or her children. This can result in two warring camps where "children come first." In the first two years of stepfamily living, the key to eventual stability for the children and stepfamily unity has to be emergence of a solid, stable, loving couple relationship. And even then, there is no guarantee that all children in the stepfamily will accept what is happening.

The Vishers (1993) indicate:

> Not only does their new couple relationship bring happiness to the adults, it reduces the children's anxiety about another parental breakup, creates an atmosphere in which the maintaining of the parent/child relationship can be respected by the stepparent, and encourages warm steprelationships. It provides the children with a model of a couple who are happy together and can work as a team to meet family challenges. (p. 247)

The Developmental Stages in Stepfamilies

When a parent has a pretty clear idea about what is normal behavior for a 2- or 3-year-old or what is within normal range for acting-out adolescents, this can be reassuring. Understanding developmental models serves to guide parents, educators and clinicians. If there is one cry that has haunted stepfamilies, it has been: "We don't *know* what is *normal! Help!*"

Thanks to the research of Papernow, we now have identified the various stages of individual and family development as they apply to stepfamilies. Papernow (1993) has classified these as: "the three *Early Stages:* Fantasy, Immersion, and Awareness; The two *Middle Stages:* Mobilization and Action; and the two *Later Stages:* Contact and Resolution" (p. 13).

I have expanded Papernow's model by drawing on some group therapy concepts of how the group process works: Groups begin by "Forming" (getting started); then they often experience "Storming" (restructuring) as leadership is challenged; once they become more cohesive, "Norming" (pulling together-unifying) occurs; then this results in "Performing" (working together as a "family") (Seibt, 1994). The "Forming" corresponds to the *Early Stages,* the "Storming" and "Norming" come during the *Middle Stages* and the "Performing" is certainly reflective of the *Later Stages.*

Early Stages

Initially, stepfamilies are filled with high hopes and expectations about healing past hurts and making this new version of family better than the past one (Forming). When this does not happen as anticipated, there are feelings of confusion, resentment, depression, and failure. The stepparent often says: "It's dad and his kids; and I'm the outsider!" There are still *two separate emotional units.* Thus the new member faces "a crucial developmental task: getting to know the strangers she or he has joined" (Papernow, 1993, p. 14).

Middle Stages

This awareness pushes the stepfamily toward confronting the issues (Storming) of stepfamily and biological family needs. The stepparent may really need to "rock the boat without jumping off." As the family members begin to renegotiate new agreements, the family can gradually restructure itself. The bioparent-child bonds need to be "unfrozen" and clearer emphasis placed on the couple, the stepparent-stepchild, stepsiblings, and the stepfamily itself. Norming begins to happen. To this point in stepfamily development, it has often been an uphill struggle requiring lots of hard work, patience, and gradually emerging respect and trust. It may take four or more years to achieve this level of development.

Later Stages

At long last, the stepfamily is in a performing mode. Their history and experiences together have solidified their unification. The emphasis in its development is no longer on "step" but rather on "family." The stepparent's role is finally clear: "'intimate outsider' . . . intimate enough to be a confidante, outside enough to provide support and mentoring" (Papernow, 1993, p. 16).

This is a description of an *ideal* progression. It rarely happens in a neat and orderly fashion as most stepfamilies can testify. Each family is unique, and under stress there are often regressions to an earlier stage. Some members, especially children, may take longer or may never adjust. "Preliminary data about the amount of time this process takes indicates that faster families complete the entire Stepfamily Cycle in about 4 years. Average-paced families take about 7 years to reach Resolution, and slower families remain in the Early Stages longer than 4 years, a few for as many as 12 years" (Papernow, 1993, p. 18).

Therapeutic and Educational Interventions/Goals

During the many years of working with stepfamilies in clinical practice and personally being a stepfather, I have found a number of interventions to be useful:

1. Educate about stepfamily functioning; normalize their experiences; engender hope for success thus reducing their anxiety and building their self-esteem.
2. Give permission for all members to vent their feelings (positive and negative).
3. Devote time to mourning all the losses and changes that are being experienced.
4. Educate about unrealistic expectations and myths common in stepfamilies; give permission to let go of these.
5. Help the family restructure itself with a strong, open, caring, trusting, respectful couple alliance that can provide safety and stability for the children.
6. Establish clear boundaries within the family and with outside systems; help clarify the roles for each family member; teach stepparents how to become "friends" rather than assuming a "parenting" roles.
7. Help family members learn to listen to and respect one another's differences; encourage appreciation for previous histories, traditions, customs, rules, and rituals.
8. Encourage one-to-one relationships between stepparents and stepchildren; validate the continuing importance of parent-child relationships.
9. Give all permission to take lots of time (3 to 5 years) because this is a developing process; encourage patience and a good sense of humor, flexibility, and compromise.
10. Finally, encourage these families to be involved in support groups, classes, and organizations that understand their struggles and issues.

The future outlook for remarriages and stepfamilies is optimistic. Even though these families face an overwhelming number of obstacles, a recent article in *Psychology Today* (Rutter, 1994), reporting on the research of Mavis Hetherington, stated: "80 percent of children of divorce and remarriage do *not* have behavior problems, despite the expectations and challenges, compared to 90 percent of children of first marriage families. Kids whose parents divorce and remarry are not doomed" (p. 33).

As a matter of fact, children in stepfamilies acquire multiple role models— they get a chance to see their parents happier with other people than they were with each other. They learn the value of flexibility and compromise. Stepfamilies are neither better nor worse than intact, traditional families, but they certainly are unique and special. They often do try harder.

CONCLUSION

As our society is evolving and changing and new patterns are emerging, many nontraditional families (single-parent, divorced, remarried) need education and support in their journeys through these new and uncharted waters. Being in a nontraditional family is different from being in a traditional, intact first-marriage family. To succeed in the face of these differences, it is necessary for these families to know that their experiences are normal. It is also critical not to label these families as dysfunctional. Family members need to understand that although the tasks they face in their unique situation are challenging, they are not impossible. Helping professionals need to be knowledgeable about and open to these nontraditional families. The guidelines set forth in this chapter can help clinicians work with single-parent, divorced, or remarried families. Perhaps these families can be seen as living laboratories for studying what it takes to succeed in all family situations.

REFERENCES

Ahrons, C. R., & Rodgers, R. (1987). *Divorced families: A multidisciplinary view.* New York: Norton.

Berman, C. (1991). *Adult children of divorce speak out: About growing up and moving beyond parental divorce.* New York: Simon and Schuster.

Blau, M. (1994). *Families apart: Ten keys to successful co-parenting.* New York: G.P. Putnam's Sons.

Burden, D. S. (1986). Single parents and the work setting: The impact of multiple job and homelife responsibilities. *Family Relations, 35,* 37–43.

Dowling, C. (1983). The relative explosion. *Psychology Today, 17,* 54–59.

Edwards, J. N. (1987). Changing family structure and youthful well-being. *Journal of Family Issues, 8,* 355–372.

Feigelman, W., & Silverman, A. (1983). Single parent adoptions. *Chosen children: New patterns of adoptive relations.* New York: Praeger.

Fisher, B. (1992). *Rebuilding when your relationship ends.* San Luis Obispo, CA: Impact.

Francke, L. B. (1983). *Growing up divorced.* New York: Simon and Schuster.

Gergen, K., & Gergen, M. (1988). It's a love story. *Psychology Today, 22,* 48–49.

Glick, P. C. (1988). Fifteen years of family demography: A record of social change. *Journal of Marriage and the Family, 50,* 861–873.

Glick, P. C. (1991, October). *Address to the Annual Conference,* Stepfamily Association of America, Lincoln, NE

Glick, P. C., & Lin, S. (1986). Recent changes in divorce and remarriage. *Journal of Marriage and Family, 48,* 737–747.

Greif, G. L. (1988). Single fathers: Helping them cope with day-to-day problems. *Medical Aspects of Human Sexuality, 22,* 18–25.

Hetherington, E. M., Law, T., & O'Connor, T. (1993). Divorce: Challenges, changes, and new chances. In F. Walsh (Ed.), *Normal family processes* (2nd ed., pp. 208–233). New York: Guilford.

Hofferth, S. L., & Phillips, D. A. (1987). Child care in the United States, 1970 to 1975. *Journal of Marriage and the Family, 49,* 559–571.

Johnson, B. H. (1986). Single mothers following separation and divorce: Making it on your own. *Family Relations, 35,* 189–197.

Kalter, N. (1990). *Growing up with divorce: Helping your child avoid immediate and later emotional problems.* New York: Free Press.

Lamanna, M. A., & Reidmann, A. (1985). *Marriages and families: Making choices throughout the life cycle* (2nd ed.). Belmont, CA: Wadsworth.

McLanahan, S., Wedemeyer N. V., & Adelberg, T. (1981). Network structure, social support, and psychological well-being in a single-parent family. *Journal of Marriage and the Family, 43,* 601–612.

Martin, D., & Martin, M. (1992). *Stepfamilies in therapy: Understanding systems, assessment, and intervention.* San Francisco: Jossey-Bass.

Miller, N. (1992). *Single parents by choice.* New York: Insight Books.

Norton, A. J., & Glick, P. G. (1986). One-parent families: A social and economic profile. *Family Relations, 35,* 9–13.

Olsen, M., & Haynes, J. (1993, May). Successful single parents. *The Journal of Contemporary Human Services,* pp. 259–267.

Papernow, P. (1993). *Becoming a stepfamily: Patterns of development in remarried families.* San Francisco: Jossey-Bass.

Porter, B. R., & Chatelain, R. S. (1981). Family life education for single parent families. *Family Relations, 30,* 517–525.

Quinn, P., & Allen, K. R. (1989). Facing challenges and making compromises: How single mothers endure. *Family Relations, 38,* 390–395.

Risman, B. J. (1986). Can men "mother"? Life as a single father. *Family Relations, 35,* 95–102.

Rutter, V. (1994, May/June). Lessons from stepfamilies. *Psychology Today,* pp. 30–33, 60–67.

Sanik, M. M., & Mauldin, T. (1986). Single verses two-parent families: A comparison of mother's time. *Family Relations, 35,* 53–56.

Seibt, T. (1990). *Strengthening stepfamilies with teens: Mission impossible?* Presentation at the 48th Annual American Association of Marriage and Family Therapists. Washington, DC

Seibt, T. (1991). *The changing family: Stepfamilies with teenagers.* Presentation at the 49th Annual American Association of Marriage and Family Therapists. Dallas, TX.

Seibt, T. (1993). *Stepfamilies with teenagers: A challenge to family therapists.* Presentation at the 51st Annual American Association of Marriage Family Therapists Conference. Anaheim, CA.

Seibt, T. (1994, October). Teenager's in stepfamilies: What's the difference? *Employee Assistance: Solutions to Problems, 7*(3) 15–23.

Smith, M. J. (1980). The social consequences of single parenthood: A longitudinal perspective. *Family Relations, 29,* 75–81.

Sporakowski, M. J. (1988). A therapist's views on the consequences of change for the contemporary family. *Family Relations, 37,* 373–378.

Stinnett, N., & DeFrain, J. (1985). *Secrets of strong families.* Boston: Little, Brown.

Taeuber, C. (Ed.). (1991). *Statistical handbook on women in America.* Phoenix, Arizona: Oryx.

Trafford, A. (1984). *Crazy time: Surviving divorce.* New York: Bantam.

Turner, P. H., & Smith, R. M. (1983). Single parents and day care. *Family Relations, 32,* 215–226.

U.S. Bureau of the Census. (1989). *Statistical abstract of the United States: 1989* (190th ed.). Washington, DC: U.S. Government Printing Office.

U.S. Bureau of the Census. (1991a). Households, families, marital status, and living arrangements: March 1991. *Current Population Reports,* ser. p-20. Washington, DC: U.S. Government Printing Office.

U.S. Bureau of the Census. (1991b). *Statistical abstract of the United States: 1991* (111th ed.). Washington, DC: U.S. Government Printing Office.

Visher, E., & Visher, J. (1988). *Old loyalties, new ties: Therapeutic strategies with stepfamilies.* New York: Brunner/Mazel.

Visher, E., & Visher, J. (1993). Remarriage families and stepparenting. In F. Walsh (Ed.), *Normal family processes* (2nd ed.). New York: Guilford.

CHAPTER 4

Gay and Lesbian Families

KAREN CARLSON

This chapter is an attempt to look at the special treatment needs of the grow-ing numbers of gay and lesbian families. These families are nonnormative in that many of the traditional theories of human and family development are not as accurate in describing them as they may be in describing heterosexual indi-viduals and families (Cass, 1984). Moreover, not much has been written about gay and lesbian families. Homosexuality is not necessarily a nonnormative event but rather an ongoing way of being that a family must organize and reor-ganize around. In the interest of expanding the definition of family, one must acknowledge that gay and lesbian couples are indeed families and that the fam-ily therapy modality certainly applies to these family units. However, in the in-terest of space and specificity, this chapter defines lesbian and gay families as those family units who are involved in some aspect of child rearing.

Clinicians who work with this population must appreciate the organizational process of gay and lesbian families as well as the general ideology from which a gay or lesbian person operates (Margolis, Becker, & Jackson-Brewer, 1987). Although some of the struggles represented in this chapter are unique to gay and lesbian families, in no way is this chapter meant to imply that treatment is indicated simply because a family is gay or lesbian. Also, there is no single gay or lesbian family identity.

TRIANGULAR MODEL OF ASSESSING GAY AND LESBIAN FAMILIES

Lesbian and gay families are as varied and diverse as heterosexual families. They present with a full range of clinical issues, generic and idiosyncratic (Bozett, 1987; Gonsiorek, 1984). In considering the constellation of clinical

The author would like to thank the following people for their help in the writing of this chapter: Gloria Ashby, Elena DeVos, Dave Fischer, Michele Harway, Barbara Jones, James Neal, and Kathy Wexler.

She would like to send a message of appreciation to all gay and lesbian families in-cluding her own.

issues that may be present, it is important to determine three key pieces of information. First, one must understand the genesis of the family. Because children are not a natural extension of gay and lesbian sex, the clinician needs to know how this family originated. For example, the family that originated from artificial insemination will have different issues than the family that originated from heterosexual divorce (Rowland, 1985; Wallerstein, 1985). Second, one must consider where in the family life cycle the family is now (Goldenberg & Goldenberg, 1985). The homosexual family life cycle has all the same stresses and transitions as the heterosexual one plus several features that are particular to the homosexual family alone. Third, the clinician must be aware of the ongoing process of the parent's homosexual identity formation (De Cecco, 1984) tracking the ever-shifting question of where in the "coming out" process this parent is.

Family Genesis

The notion of determining family genesis is much more complex in lesbian and gay families than in heterosexual families. In fact, one would probably never consider asking a heterosexual family how they came to be a family because it is implicit in the culture. "We just turned off the ball game early one Sunday and nine months later . . ." Because children are not a natural extension of homosexual sex, it bears ascertaining. Were these children a conscious mutual choice? Were they the result of a heterosexual marriage? Multiple categories exist for the classification of the genesis of lesbian and gay families, as shown in Figure 4.1.

Lesbian and gay families that formed after heterosexual divorce have typical blended family issues, as discussed in Chapter 3. The loss of the heterosexual marriage must be grieved. Sometimes this is sensitive work, particularly when the newly "out" homosexual is joyfully welcoming his or her long-lost sexuality. The children may attempt to explicate the loss for the parent in a number of ways, such as with acting-out behaviors.

Prolonged custody disputes are not uncommon. The emotionally unsupported heterosexual former spouse may have nowhere else to take his or her conscious and unconscious pain and grievances but to the legal system. Once the battle enters the legal arena, the gay or lesbian family is at risk. There is a lack of objective legal standards that could make the outcome of these cases sensible and predictable (Hitchens, 1979–1980). Gay and lesbian parents in ongoing custody disputes may well be traumatized by a court system that at best is homophobic and demeaning; in such cases, much more often than in heterosexual custody battles, the court finds reason to deny custody. The residue of laws that made and in some geographical locales continue to make homosexuality criminal is present and real.

Children in general, are greatly affected by custody disputes (Wallerstein, 1985). Children of gay and lesbian families are likewise affected (Patterson, 1994). The clinician working with children of gay and lesbian parents needs to

	Lesbian Families	Gay Families
Adoption	Non-biological mother with formal or informal custody Adoptive single mother Adoptive couple	Non-biological father with formal or informal custody Adoptive single father Adoptive couple
Divorce	Divorced biological mother Divorced biological mother with partner Two divorced biological mothers	Divorced biological father Divorced biological father with partner Two divorced biological fathers
Donor/Surrogate	Single biological mother, donor father Couple, donor father Single biological mother, known father Couple, known father	Single biological father, surrogate mother Couple, surrogate mother Single biological father co-parenting with biological mother Couple co-parenting with biological mother
Other	Child product of consenual sex Child product of rape Co-parenting with a gay man Heterosexually married lesbian mother	Co-parenting with a lesbian Heterosexually married gay father

Figure 4.1   Multiple Categories of Gay and Lesbian Families

ascertain the child's internal experience of the family battle that forces them to stretch themselves across a huge schism. Edward, an 8-year-old boy, whose gay father and heterosexual mother were engaged in the 2nd year of a 3-year custody battle for Edward and his younger brother described the world-weariness that this can provoke. One of Edward's favorite activities in therapy was to use wood scraps and a hot melt glue gun to erect complex and sometimes beautiful houses that he would wind up smashing. In treating this child, I was responsible for writing a report to the court regarding what I thought was the best custody arraignment. I was trying to ascertain which parent Edward would most like to live with. I told him a story about a porcupine and a mole who had built a home together under the earth. They lived together in peace for awhile until one day the porcupine turned around in his home and poked the mole with his sharp quills. He hadn't meant to hurt the mole but his very presence in the narrow home caused the mole great pain. The mole with her fine digging skills could easily make a new home; the problem was they had two children. Edward who had been enjoying the story up to this point pulled back and interrupted. He said with the profound wisdom of a child, "Hey Karen, let's just let the judge decide." Children should never be made to choose one parent over another.

On the other hand, artificial insemination in lesbian families has a different configuration of issues. Whereas children here are a conscious choice and involvement in the legal system is minimal (sometimes the nonbiological mother adopts), this particular origin presents logistical and emotional considerations. A healthy sperm donor must first be found. Then, the emerging lesbian family must come in contact with a medical system that may be unaccustomed to such nontraditional needs (Potter, 1985).

The nonbiological mother is particularly at risk. She has no legal protection. She must learn to negotiate within a culture that may be inclined to exclude her. Invisibility in general (Guth, 1978) and within traditional health-care systems is a particularly potent problem (Potter, 1985). Although Potter's research documents the problem of lesbian invisibility in terms of lesbians using health-care systems due to illness, her findings certainly would apply to lesbians using health-care systems for obstetric services as well. Since lesbians struggle with invisibility in the larger culture, it is possible that old wounds may reopen during a partner's pregnancy. At the same time, the nonbiological partner is witness to her pregnant mate's visibility as she literally and metaphorically grows in substance and credibility.

When children are old enough to understand their place in the dominant culture, the artificially inseminated child may ask, "Who (or where) is my father?" (Rowland, 1985). Resolving this loss issue for the child may rekindle both parents' own loss issues. The lesbian parent may grieve that she is not able to provide a family closer to the stereotypical cultural ideal. Family members may need to explicate their phenomenological notion of the ideal family: minivan, Daddy, golden retriever; whatever the images are, they need to be fully explored for grief to resolve. One client, 4½-year-old William, described his ideal family picture: "The family is going to see *The Lion King*. The kids don't ever get scared when the daddy lion dies. The mother is a lesbian, she can take care of the children when the dad is out of town." William, a child of artificial insemination and a forthright lesbian mother, is putting together a notion of the American family that includes Disney and his lesbian mother.

The category of "other" genesis is a metaphorical salad bar of possibilities (see Figure 4.1). The child could be a product of lesbian rape during a hate crime. The child of two gay men could have been conceived from consensual sex with a friend who agrees to give up the child as a favor. There are situations too numerous and diverse to cover here. But it is stressed that without knowing the genesis of the gay or lesbian family, the clinician lacks a certain foundation to fully understand the presenting issues.

The Family Life Cycle

Another point of the assessment triangle is the homosexual family life cycle. Gay and lesbian families have all the same stresses and transitions as heterosexual families in their journeys through the life cycle (Erikson, 1959; Rowland, 1982). Parenting may be distilled into certain recurring themes that recycle again and again with various levels of intensity. Attachment and separation are certainly two of those themes. The parent must hold steady while the child, whether age 2 or 22, struggles with the push-pull of "Back off, I can do it myself" and "Come here, I need you." At each developmental stage, or as the old themes are repeated anew, the gay and lesbian family may have further, special issues as well.

One example: Adjusting to new parenthood is particularly difficult (Osofsky, 1982). All the stresses of assimilating new roles and a new family member are present. Gay or lesbian parents may suffer an identity loss as they no longer fit squarely into minority culture and are seemingly moving toward the mainstream, that is, a primarily heterosexual parenting culture. A firm gay or lesbian identity may be disarmed during this transition. The dominant culture generally assumes parents are heterosexual. Issues of invisibility, not fully fitting in anywhere, and the loss of the simple prechild identity emerge for parents at this time. Gay and lesbian parents must forever straddle two contradictory worlds: the gay and lesbian community, where children are still somewhat of an anomaly, and the heterosexual world of families, where reactions to one's homosexuality can still be a wild card.

This dichotomy may not be felt until the preschool and school-age years (Martin, 1993). Childhood events such as co-ops, ballet classes, schools, scouts, and soccer seem to present an endless chain of opportunities to either "come out" or remain "in the closet." There are pros and cons with every disclosure or lack of it. Heterosexuals sometimes have difficulty understanding this dilemma. Straight friends might comment, "I don't tell Jeffery's soccer coach that I am straight, why should you worry . . ." The dynamic tension of this latency phase centers around the child's need for the mainstream and the parent's preservation of a separate homosexual identity. Most parents opt to put their child's needs first throughout the life cycle. One parent described his dilemma when his son wanted to join the Boy Scouts. "I knew I could never be a pack leader as out as I was in the community. But still Michael wanted to be in Tiger Cubs. I explained to him that it was a homophobic organization. We had one of those little chats. Michael said, 'Dad, you know I'm not a bigot but I really like the camping and the uniforms.' So here I was a gay man who wrote checks out to Act Up and AIDS Project Los Angeles and I found myself writing out a check to Boy Scouts of Greater Los Angeles." Another parent explained the same issue this way. "I told Scott that this was an organization that believed Jack and I were not good role models for children. I would no more let him join that organization than I would let him join a white supremacy organization." Sometimes being a parent is in contradiction to being a homosexual. Gay and lesbian parents of school-age children are wise to pick their battles, giving in on issues that are important to the child and holding firm on decisions that would truly erode the healthy homosexual identity.

During the adolescent years, the child's need for conformity with peers is at an all-time high (Adams, 1984). The child's sexuality is emerging. At this time, these two issues combine synergistically and can create friction in formerly solid family relations. Children may distance themselves from their diverse family as they try to find their own identities, which is of course the developmental task of adolescence. Susan and Heather brought their 16-year-old daughter, Erin, into treatment because they felt she was sexually promiscuous. Susan, the biological parent, was dismayed and couldn't understand why a child reared in an open feminist household would have sex with boys she really didn't want to be emotionally involved with. In family sessions, a breakthrough was reached when Erin admitted she was having sex that was neither emotionally or physically satisfying. Alone with the clinician, Erin also admitted why. "I don't want the guys to accuse me of being like them (her lesbian parents) so I have to keep proving it." The clinician served as a bridge here working with the heterosexual daughter to educate her about caring for her emerging heterosexuality. She also worked with the parents so that they understood their daughter's unique and developmental need for differentiation.

At the launching phase, the adult child needs a lot of stability from the parent. The push-pull theme centers around being able to do the work of launching, and still being able to rely on parental support. As the adult child selects a mate, the gay or lesbian parent does well to focus on whether this person is good for their offspring rather than whether the potential mate is homophobic. Generally, a child who has grown up in an alternative family needs a tolerant mate. As Vicki, the daughter of a lesbian put it, "Even though I am straight if I found I was telling a boyfriend about my life and the way I grew up and his eyes started to glaze over in unrecognition, then I felt dismissed, as if my childhood could never be seen or understood."

The adult child who is marrying needs to direct the telling of in-laws about her gay or lesbian parents. As in any family, the child who is marrying should be allowed to make decisions. As one nonbiological lesbian mother put it,

"Kathy was getting married in Russia. She called and told her mother that she didn't want me to come. Her mother was really angry, but I knew Kathy loved me. She told me later that she was almost overwhelmed managing this Lithuanian Catholic family that could barely understand that she was taking their son away let alone that she has lesbian parents. I let Kathy set the pace because I trusted her judgment."

The Parent's Identity Formation

The third prong of the assessment triangle is the parent's own development of a lesbian or gay identity. The classic model of homosexual identity formation is the Plummer model based on his study of gay men (Plummer, 1975). This model depicts a linear journey through three phases: sensitization (where the first possibility of a homosexual identity begins), signification (when the person moves on to identify as a homosexual), and stabilization (when the person commits to homosexuality and adjusts his life accordingly). Cass (1979) refined Plummer's model by further explicating the stabilization phase and Troiden (1979) added to the model by adding a coupling or commitment phase to the model. The model presented in this chapter, though not empirically tested, has been useful in working with families because it considers how family life itself can sometimes shift the emphasis from homosexual identity formation to homosexual identity maintenance. The coevolution of family and homosexuality prompts a cyclical rather than linear journey through the life cycle. The coming out process is ongoing. With growth and change, one is always in a new position in this process. The wheel shown in Figure 4.2 represents the process of lesbian and gay identity development.

Growth toward a complete homosexual identity is an individual, lifelong process. For purposes of discussion here, it is laid out into six general phases. Any developmental model greatly reduces idiosyncratic individual experience and (in the case of this journey) fails to capture the remarkable. This is a nonlinear model because people position themselves differently on this wheel, depending on such variables as whose company one is presently in or what crisis may have recently occurred. For example, a man who has been fairly "out" to himself and others as a homosexual may retreat back into denial (1) at the loss of a relationship, saying it was just that man, not men in general whom he loves. A woman with a well-articulated lesbian separatist (10) identity may move into irrelevancy (16) as she puts on pantyhose to appear in court for a child custody hearing. All the phases on the wheel have equal value. (Denial (1) has its value as a self-pacing mechanism and must be respected.)

Particularly at risk is the homosexual in denial of his or her homosexuality. The self is lost, trying to conform to a social ideal. There may be no conscious awareness (2) of one's sexual difference. Such people are at risk of making choices that take them further away from their life's true path. Often marriage and family originates during the denial phase. People in denial are probably at

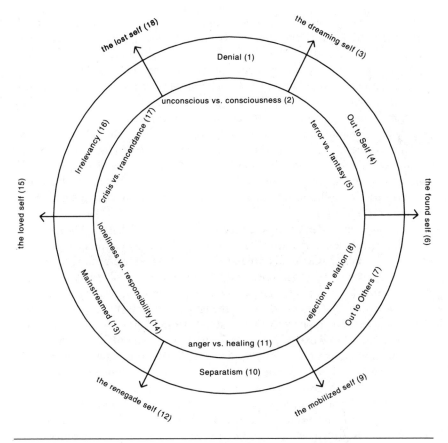

Figure 4.2   A Non-Linear Model of Homosexual Development

risk of unsafe sex, substance abuse, and depression, for the burden of covering this secret within the psyche is heavy (Beane, 1981; Reyes, 1993). No one is held in greater disdain in the gay and lesbian community than the person who is closeted to him- or herself. The memory of the denial phase is so painful to homosexuals who have freed themselves from it that association with a "closet case" is sometimes intolerable. A person trying to parent during the denial phase is likely not operating from a fully operational, evolved position.

The struggle toward consciousness sometimes begins in the dream life of the individual (3). Others may act out sexually yet still deny that they are homosexual. But as people move toward being "out" to themselves (4), the crisis shifts from unconsciousness to fantasy (5). The homosexual person struggles with the emerging homosexual identity without acting on it yet. At the same time, the fantasy, sexual and otherwise, of being fully developed begins to flower. This is a tumultuous time. A parent may not be able to be the solid, stable person his or her child needs. The bumpy developmental transition of the child and the parent's shifting identity can synergize into a conflict of crisis proportions.

As homosexuals begin to be out to others (7), they may swing between rejection and elation (8). The self is found and that is cause for rejoicing; however, all former relationships are in a state of flux as people outside the emerging identity begin to integrate this new information. Family members need time to assimilate the changing relative. Sometimes, the exhilarating momentum of the homosexual overruns the slower pace of family and friends. What looks like rejection may only be the other's process of integrating the data. Family members not familiar with this experience need time. This is particularly true of children for whom this information may also come with the loss of their intact family.

Many gay and lesbian people go through periods of anger and healing (11) in their respective communities. This may be expressed in as quiet a gesture as moving to a more gay-friendly area of the city or as large a gesture as moving to women-owned land, where men and boys are forbidden. The self at this time is mobilizing (9) and politicizing. This is a move toward healing. Like Holocaust survivors, or Vietnam veterans, the homosexual must heal past trauma in the context of a community that understands from within what the person has suffered. This period can be particularly disruptive to family life in that it may not be possible to put the child's needs first. A gay or lesbian family member who is strongly in the separation phase of identity development may benefit from a referral to a gay or lesbian therapist. But the referral process must be a careful one so as not to duplicate historical rejection or abandonment.

During the mainstreaming phase (13), gay or lesbian persons struggle with loneliness versus responsibility (14). They are facing the responsibility of living in the world, yet sometimes this is exhausting, dismissing, and hard. Even the most conservative personality may feel like a renegade (12) simply because homosexuality is still considered somewhat of an anomaly in the main culture.

The irrelevancy phase (16) almost defies expository description. People can move into this phase as a result of transcendence or crisis (19). As one lesbian mother put it, "My daughter was dying, why did it matter to the hospital social worker that I was lesbian?" Sometimes people enter this phase as a result of transcendence. The sexuality is so integrated that it is less important than other components of the person's identity. Gore Vidal expressed this transcendence when he stated, "There was no such thing as a heterosexual person or a homosexual person, there are only heterosexual and homosexual acts" (Harrison, 1990). In irrelevance, the self is accepted (15) or lost (18) depending on the situation. After rape, lesbian women sometimes express a feeling that their lesbianism is irrelevant. This can be dangerous. That is why on the wheel, the irrelevancy phase shares a common boundary with denial (1).

No phase is optimal for childrearing. Each has its conflicts, glories, and pitfalls. It is important for the clinician to know where on this wheel of development the gay or lesbian person positions him- or herself at any given moment.

It is also important in assessing couples and families because when family members are in different positions of identity development, it can be a source of couple and familial conflict.

The three points of the assessment triangle: genesis, life cycle phase, and homosexual identity phase can best be ascertained over time through open-ended questioning in an atmosphere of respect and understanding. More will be said later about the healing nature of the therapist-family relationship.

GENERIC ISSUES COMMON TO ALL GAY AND LESBIAN FAMILIES

Apart from varied family beginnings, family life cycle, and the coming out process, gay and lesbian families have issues and concerns that could be classed as generic, indeed, common to all homosexual families. The clinician is wise to keep these in mind, as well, when treating a family.

Bias and discrimination are a real and constant part of gay and lesbian life (Adelman, 1977). No homosexual who lives in this culture can honestly say he or she has never felt the sting of discrimination. In families, this discrimination can spread to the children. Parents may make choices in service of protecting children from this risk. The issue of bias and discrimination is the wellspring of many of the other generic issues mentioned here as well.

Internalized homophobia is part of all gay and lesbian people (Fein & Nuehring, 1981). It is difficult to love oneself in a culture that promotes hate. This can cripple full development even in the healthiest of people. Internalized homophobia can show itself in the context of treatment no matter how adjusted a person may seem. In families, internalized homophobia often takes the form of perfectionism: "I cheated the gods to get this child, so now I must be a perfect parent." The clinician may remind the person that he or she has every right to be a parent. But the mirror image of the patient's internalized homophobia is the clinician's homophobia, which may manifest in lowered expectation for gay and lesbian parenting. (The therapist's homophobia will be discussed in depth in the Treatment Considerations section of this chapter.) It is a lifelong process to free oneself from the internalized homophobia learned in a culture that does not value the diversity of lesbian and gay people. Homophobia must be recognized and dealt with openly in the therapeutic setting.

Uneven support systems are another by-product of bias. Often gay and lesbian families have emotionally cut off from a family of origin that is not able to support their lifestyle (DeVine, 1983–1984). It is common for gay and lesbian families to have less than adequate vertical support, that is, support reaching back across generational lines within the family. On the positive side however, many gay and lesbian families have greater horizontal support from friends and surrogate family in their community (Warren, 1974). Unlike other minorities who can take refuge in the shared diversity of the family of origin, gay and lesbian people must create new families that share their diversity (Warren, 1974). This affords them greater support of friends during the family years. Though much more common now than a decade ago, children are still a rarity in the gay and lesbian community (Mayadas, 1976). These horizontal families, often with no children of their own, and many also deeply touched by the specter of AIDS seem to take a special joy in the affirmation of these children's lives (Provenzano, 1994).

Social learning theory confirms how powerful a learning agent social modeling is (Bandura, 1969). Children learn roles from their parents. Most gay and lesbian parents grew up in heterosexual households. There is a dearth of same-sex parenting models in the larger culture as well. These families are often creating first-time roles, rules, and rituals. The family clinician can join as a co-architect in the designing of these families "from scratch." Children benefit from referrals to programs that have a social learning component like participating in a program that offers group discussions with children of other gay and lesbian parents (Kirkpatrick, 1987).

Concern about the children's sexual identity still ranks high among the issues that concern gay and lesbian parents (Louis, 1985). Much research documents that there is no significant difference in the sexual identity outcome in gay and lesbian parented children from their heterosexually raised counterparts (Green, 1982; Hoetter, 1981; Louis, 1985).

A final by-product of bias and discrimination is the social experiment of child rearing in the gay and lesbian community. Determined not to let their children suffer the wounds of a culture that has been less than supportive, some gay and lesbian parents dedicate themselves to creating a new world for their children (Weston, 1991). Many of these children do grow up with a greater degree of tolerance for diversity than do children in heterosexual families (North, 1987). They develop coping skills and are less involved in rigid gender roles (Hill, 1981). This is the positive side of the social experiment of parenting. Yet sometimes the natural flow of family life is interrupted by the social experiment. Much like spectatoring during sex, parents who are overly concerned with doing right by all humanity may lose a certain spontaneity in their dealings with their children.

TREATMENT CONSIDERATIONS

Even with all the stresses and issues discussed in this chapter, it does not necessarily hold that simply because one is a gay or lesbian family that therapeutic treatment is indicated (Freedman, 1975). Generally, gay and lesbian families present not because of their sexual identity but because of some problem or problems that likely are unrelated to homosexuality (MacKinnon, 1984–1985). As with any treatment, the clinician does not make an issue unless it is, in fact, an issue for the patient.

Self-disclosure is another treatment consideration. Regardless of one's therapeutic orientation, the gay or lesbian patient does well with some self-disclosure around the issue of sexual orientation (Collins, 1983). The heterosexual therapist can be very healing. Most gay and lesbian people grew up in families with heterosexual parents. Referring a family out to a gay or lesbian clinician may replicate earlier rejection. Because homosexuality (unlike ethnic diversity) is largely invisible, some self-disclosure is useful. Great detail is not necessary here. "I'm heterosexual, but my sister is a lesbian," is enough to place a context around the therapist. Modeling self-disclosure can be a potent intervention (Cramer, 1986). Safety and connection are useful ingredients to any healing relationship (Kahn, 1936). The gay or lesbian family needs to know through what lens they are being viewed.

The clinician may want to examine all biases and fears before taking on a gay or lesbian family. Using a gay or lesbian clinical consultant can be a useful compromise between referral and misunderstanding the diversity. One of the unfortunate manifestations of the therapist's unexamined homophobia is clinical light-handedness (Graham, 1984). When clinicians are heavy-handed, they may move at too swift a pace or use interventions that "get ahead" of the patient's work. Much the opposite can happen in treatment when the therapist has not examined his or her own internalized homophobia. In an attempt to secure the diverse person's trust, one would err not to use the same standards for the gay and lesbian clients as for heterosexuals. This light-handedness could show itself in something like overlooking substance abuse or domestic violence in a lesbian or gay family (Lobel, 1986). Heterosexual families do not have a monopoly on dysfunction. In treating families, clinical light-handedness can manifest as having a double standard for homosexual and heterosexual families.

Although gay and lesbian clients need understanding, it should not come at the expense of the needs of the children. Strong attachment, firm but kind limits, a steady self for the child to differentiate from, valuing the child, healthy boundaries, encouraging growth even when it takes the child in a different direction from that of the parent, all are components of good parenting in any family (Steinhaur, 1983). The child of a lesbian or gay parent has the same developmental needs as the child of a heterosexual parent (Collins, 1983). Attempts to mask conscious or unconscious discomfort with gay and lesbian families by downstaging harmful parenting will likely have a deleterious outcome.

As with all families, the journey of the gay and lesbian family is one of joys and losses. The losses must be explicated and resolved. At the same time, the family can experience great joys. Whether it be the welcoming of a baby or the embracing of one's own true love, there seems to be a special deliciousness because at one time it all seemed so improbable. The gay or lesbian family is a blend of bold and subtle but very human contradictions.

Clinicians who can reach across difference stand to enrich themselves. Gaining confidence in working with families that are nonnormative for any reason will only enlarge our picture of what is normal family process. A celebration of oneness and difference is the reward. As the poet Gerard Manley Hopkins exclaimed, "Glory be to God for dappled things."

REFERENCES

Adams, G. (1984). Ego identity status, conformity behavior, and personality in late adolescence. *Journal of Personality and Social Psychology, 47*(5), 1091–1104.

Adelman, M. (1977). Sexual orientation and violations of civil liberties. *Journal of Homosexuality, 2*(4), 327–330.

Alpert, H. (Ed.). (1988). *We are everywhere.* Freedom, CA: Crossing Press.

Bandura, A. (1969). *Principles of behavior modification* (pp. 133–143). New York: Holt, Rinehart & Winston.

Beane, J. (1981). I'd rather be dead than gay: Counseling gay men who are coming out. *Personnel and Guidance Journal, 60*(4), 222–226.

Bozett, F. (1987). *Gay and lesbian parents.* New York: Praeger.

Cass, V. C. (1979). Homosexual identity formation: A theoretical model. *Journal of Homosexuality, 4*(3), 219–235.

Cass, V. C. (1984). Homosexual identity: A concept in need of definition. *Journal of Homosexuality, 9*(2, 3), 105–126.

Coleman, E. (1981–1982). Developmental stages in the coming out process. *Journal of Homosexuality, 7*(2, 3), 31–43.

Collins, L. (1983). Homosexual and bisexual issues. *Family Therapy Collections, 5,* 82–100.

Cramer, D. (1986). Gay parents and their children: A review of referral and practical implications. *Journal of Counseling and Development, 64*(8), 504–507.

De Cecco, J. (1984). *Bisexual and homosexual identities: Critical theoretical issues.* New York: Hayworth.

DeVine, J. (1983–1984). A systematic inspection of affection preference orientation and family of origin. *Journal of Social Work and Human Sexuality, 2*(2, 3), 7–9.

Erikson, E. (1959). Identity and the life cycle. *Psychological Issues, 1,* 1–17.

Fein, S., & Nuehring, E. (1981). Intrapsychic effects of stigma: A process of breakdown and reconstruction of social reality. *Journal of Homosexuality, 7,* 3–13.

Freedman, M. (1975, March) Homosexuals may be healthier than straights. *Psychology Today, 8*(10), 28–32.

Goldenberg, I., & Goldenberg, H. (1985). *Family therapy: An overview* (pp. 16–24). Monterey, CA: Brooks Cole.

Gonsiorek, J. (Ed.). (1984). *Homosexuality and psychotherapy: A practitioner's handbook of affirmative models.* New York: Hayworth.

Graham, D. (1984). Therapist's need for training in counseling lesbians and gay men. *Professional Psychology, Research and Practice, 15*(4), 482–496.

Green, R. (1982). The best interests of a child with a lesbian mother. *Bulletin of the American Academy of Psychiatry and the Law, 10*(1), 7–15.

Guth, J. (1978). Invisible women: Lesbians in America. *Journal of Sex Education and Therapy, 4,* 3–6.

Harrison, B. (1990, January 28). Pure gore. *The Los Angeles Times Magazine,* p. 9.

Hill, M. (1981). Effects of conscious and unconscious factors on child-rearing attitudes of lesbian mothers. *Dissertation Abstracts International, 42,* 1608.

Hitchens, D. (1979–1980). Social attitudes, legal standards and personal trauma in child custody cases. *Journal of Homosexuality, 5,* 89–95.

Hoetter, B. (1981). Children's acquisition of sex-role behavior in lesbian mother families. *American Journal of Orthopsychiatry, 51*(3), 536–544.

Hopkins, G. M. (1962). Pied beauty. In R. Aldington (Ed.), *The Viking book of poetry of the English speaking world* (p. 1062). New York: Viking.

Kahn, M. (1936). *Between therapist and client.* New York: Freeman.

Kirkpatrick, M. (1987). Clinical implications of lesbian mother studies. *Journal of Homosexuality, 14*(1, 2), 201–211.

Lobel, K. (Ed.). (1986). *Naming the violence.* Seattle, WA: Seal Press.

Louis, A. (1985). Homosexual parent families: Gay parents, partners, and their children. *Dissertation Abstracts International, 46,* 2789.

MacKinnon, L. (1984–1985). The sexual component in family therapy: A feminist critique. *Journal of Social Work, 3*(2, 3), 81–101.

Margolis, L., Becker, M., & Jackson-Brewer, K. (1987). Internalized homophobia: Identifying and treating the oppressor within. In Boston Lesbian Psychologies Collective (Eds.), *Lesbian psychologies: Explorations and challenges* (pp. 229–241). Urbana: University of Illinois Press.

Martin, A. (1993). *The lesbian and gay parenting handbook.* New York: HarperCollins.

Mayadas, N. (1976). Children in gay families: An investigation of services. *Homosexual Counseling Journal, 3*(2), 70–83.

North, P. (1987). A comparison of adolescent girls raised by lesbian mothers with adolescent girls raised by heterosexual mothers on five personality traits (Doctoral dissertation, Unites States International University). *Dissertation Abstracts International, 48,* O8B.

Osofsky, H. (1982). Expectant and new fatherhood as a developmental crisis. *Bulletin of the Menniger Clinic, 46*(3), 209–230.

Patterson, C. J. (1994). Lesbian and gay families with children. In R. C. Savin-Williams & V. M. Cohen (Eds.), *Understanding diversity among lesbians, gays, and bisexuals: Clinical, developmental, and social issues.* New York: Harcourt Brace.

Plummer, K. (1975). *Sexual stigma: An interactionist's approach.* London: Routledge and Kegan Paul.

Potter, S. (1984–1985). Traditional health care systems and lesbian invisibility. *Journal of Social Work and Human Sexuality, 3*(2, 3), 59–68.

Provenzano, T. (1994, April 5). Ren and Stimpy: Not not gay. *The Advocate,* 56–57.

Reyes, D. (1993, May 6). AIDS is special problem within Latino community. *Los Angeles Times,* 1.

Rowland, R. (1982). The childfree experience in the aging context: An investigation of the pro-natalist bias of life span developmental literature. *The Australian Psychologist, 17*(20), 144–150.

Rowland, R. (1985). The social and psychological consequences of secrecy in artificial insemination by donor programmes. *Social Science and Medicine, 21*(4), 91–396.

Stein, E. (Ed.). (1990). *Forms of desire.* New York: Garland.

Steinhaur, P. (1983). Assessing for parenting capacity. *Journal of Orthopsychiatry, 53*(3), 468–481.

Troiden, R. (1979). Becoming homosexual: A model of gay identity acquisition. *Psychiatry, 42,* 362–373.

Wallerstein, J. (1985). Children of divorce: Emerging trends. *Psychiatric Clinics of North America, 8*(4), 837–855.

Warren, C. (1974). *Identity and community in the gay world.* New York: Wiley.

Weston, K. (1991). *Families we choose.* New York: Columbia University Press.

PART THREE

Challenges to the Family Life Cycle

CHAPTER 5

Aging Problems and Family Solutions

THOMAS H. PEAKE, SUSAN G. ROSENZWEIG, and JEFFREY M. WILLIAMSON

Family clinicians need to proceed with a nonageist respect for both the wisdom some families already possess and the limits of our craft. The senior author was working with an elderly couple and their family—the wife had Alzheimer's disease. In one meeting, the husband asked this disturbing question, "What will we do when the experts are gone?" He then proceeded to answer, telling his wife, his grown children, and the therapist stories of the last years of the couple's own parents. It was a sad, wonderful, and hopeful account of a family's ways of sharing love and meaning beyond death and human limits. This family had and used a transgenerational legacy to cope with and give meaning to a tragic conundrum of aging and illness. Their solutions put into perspective the value and the limitation of science and medicine (Peake, 1993), and the need to work with a family's own strengths. When all the medical and psychological specialists are gone, the family remains.

Families tell us a story on both a personal and a professional level. The stories can be about challenge, identity, tragedy, health, and the cycles of continuity and change throughout life. Bateson (1972) said that change and continuity are two sides of the same coin. Problems, symptoms, and challenges may serve a homeostatic or an evolutionary function. Individual and family oral histories capture the human flavor of these patterns.

On a philosophical level, Alfred Lord Whitehead has suggested, "The art of progress is to preserve order amidst change and change amidst order." Research on individual and family life cycle development describes the transitions and passages through the human seasons. These stage transitions are marked by periods of relative stabilization and periods of change (Costa, Gatz, Neugarten, Salthouse, & Siegler, 1989).

Eric Erikson (1982) elegantly sketched a picture of emotional health and the life cycle in eight stages. In *The Life Cycle Completed,* Erikson suggests the healthiest resolution from each of the eight stages include the following:

The authors thank Jennifer Hughes for her valuable work in the preparation of this manuscript.

(a) hope, (b) will, (c) purpose, (d) competence, (e) fidelity, (f) love, (g) care, and (h) wisdom. His work has also been elaborated by others (Gilligan, 1982; Gilligan & Pollack, 1988; Levinson, 1986).

Families both help and hinder healthy development. The life cycle of families is an important backdrop for the individual's development, and is described in more detail in Chapter 1. Carter and McGoldrick, (1988) describe the predictable family passages well. The two cycles, family and individual, can complement or collide. A family helps define those life seasons, and can also help individuals navigate their lives in more effective and enjoyable ways (Bergston & Schaie, 1989).

LIFE STORIES

Throughout time, the telling of stories, whether by individual reminiscence, family legends, or family secrets is an important way to preserve one's sense of identity across the life span. Several recent authors (Bruner, 1986; Howard, 1989, 1991; Mair, 1989; McAdams, 1985; Polkinghorne, 1988; Sarbin, 1986) have suggested that the development of identity is an issue of "life story construction." With this analogy in mind, psychopathology may be viewed as life's stories gone awry and psychotherapy as exercises in story repair. Creating healthy individual and family narratives may be the key to reduce and prevent pathology. Watzlawich (1984) talks about the importance of constructed meaning or worldviews or "invented realities" that guide individuals and families. Epston and White (1975, 1992) magnify the irony, intrigue, and possibilities of *Literate* (narrative) *Means to Therapeutic Ends,* as a way to understand, value, and even change families and their storied histories and traditions. Similarly, Howard (1989) explains that life stories are largely a constructed reality; stories which both describe our identities and help us cope with our experiences. Pathology can be conceived as stories gone awry. Therapy can be thought of as life story repair.

Health care can sometimes dehumanize people or families by doing clinical histories in contrast to "hearing life stories." Someone must encourage people to tell, understand, and even therapeutically change their life stories. Throughout this chapter, one theme recurs; that emotional and physical health care can promote rather than fragment healthy life stories.

HEALTH AND HEALING

Psychology has much to offer aging and the family, and yet aging and the family might broaden psychology's scope. Healthy aging (at any time in the life span) is a product of physical, psychological, and spiritual dimensions, Victor Frankl (1973) has well stated:

Western humanity has turned from the priest to the doctor. . . . nowadays too many patients come to the medical man with problems which should really be put to a priest.

Patients are constantly coming to us with problems such as, what is the meaning of their lives. It is not that we doctors attempt to carry philosophy over into medicine, although we are often accused of doing so; the patients themselves bring us philosophical problems. . . .

Man lives in three dimensions: the somatic, the mental, and the spiritual. The spiritual dimension cannot be ignored, for it is what makes us human. To be concerned about the meaning of life is not necessarily a sign of disease or neurosis. It may be; but then again, spiritual agony may have very little connection with a disease of the psyche.

. . . I remember my dilemma in a concentration camp when faced with a man and a woman who were close to suicide; both had told me that they expected nothing more from life. I asked both my fellow prisoners whether the question was really what we expected from life. Was it not, rather, what life was expecting from us? I suggested that life was awaiting something from them. (pp. ix–x)

Family clinicians may be in a better position than physicians to discover individuals' and families' spiritual strengths and to promote psychological and spiritual meaning (Abeles & Eisdorfer, 1991). Families have answers in this area whether or not they are well articulated. C. P. Snow (1959), in his often cited work, *Two Cultures,* laments that the two "knowledge cultures" (art and science) speak different languages and rarely converse with each other. Even if they do talk, they do not integrate their knowledge. However, a third culture (often equally separate) exists: spirituality. Psychology and medicine rarely have answers to spiritual questions. Art in the form of life stories may both ask and answer questions about aging. Family stories often carry puzzles, but they also often provide wise answers. Psychology could benefit from the integration of family and life stories.

The guild of mental health care is intertwined with the political and financial entity of medicine (Engel, 1977). Professionals in medical settings will agree that the interaction of mind and body is a crucial aspiration, but good balanced models of mind/body interaction are rare in health-care systems. Any discussion of aging and aging in the family is limited if the effect of health-care systems is not considered. Fortunately, families can help reshape health-care policy. Families with strong values and spiritual resolutions may be well suited to better shape health care and even influence caregivers. Families must contend with our health-care system. American health care has poorly integrated psychological, spiritual, and medical dimensions. Kiesler (1992) argues convincingly that U.S. mental health policy is "doomed to failure" if it only imitates medical health care. The family can help rewrite the story on health, both as an advocate for a balanced integration of physical, psychological, and spiritual health care, and as a resource of wise family solutions to aging dilemmas.

The family has legions to offer healthy development and health care. One offering is that the family is present when all the medical and psychological specialists are gone. Most care for illness is not delivered in hospitals or by professional practitioners but by the family (Kleinman, 1980, pp. 179–202). A family's culture can both wound and heal at any stage in the life cycle. For instance, an individual's developmental needs may be helped or hindered by the family's facility or ineptness at promoting individuation. A family that is too enmeshed or too disengaged makes the life journey daunting. Even researchers' and therapists' notions about the family are shaped by the families from which they come. The sense of continuity and the ability to incorporate challenge, change, and reintegration are the special gifts of families. The family is a contributor to as well as a user of these health dimensions. The most useful task will be to clarify how to promote and integrate the three dimensions of health and healing.

The reciprocal processes whereby aging influences the family and the family influences aging will be examined and subsumed by three main questions:

1. What challenges and problems do the aged and their families face?
2. What are some existing and possible solutions for problems that aging families face?
3. Where do we go from here?

Several innovative directions and models in applied settings will be considered, as will current emphases and future directions in research. The intent is to both broaden the scope of family psychology and also strengthen our understanding of areas that need healing in older people and their families as well as in health and mental health delivery systems. With the aged, the field of family psychology, like the family itself, must balance the sense of continuity and identity with the demands of loss and the challenges to change (Costa et al., 1989; Viorst, 1986). Family psychology offers both old and new ideas to preserve continuity amidst loss, and change amidst continuity.

WHAT CHALLENGES AND PROBLEMS DO THE AGED AND THEIR FAMILIES FACE?

Healthy aging, for the individual or the family, involves three dimensions; the physical, the psychological, and the spiritual. It is useful to think about problems in these same three dimensions.

Physical Dimension

For the older adult, the possible problems involve every organ system. The cardiovascular, pulmonary, gastrointestinal, metabolic/endocrine, musculoskeletal, and the infectious and immune systems provide countless possibilities for things to go wrong. Psychophysiological and psychosocial factors also can cause or exacerbate medical conditions. The complexity can vex patient and physician.

Perhaps equally important as individual medical needs are the inadequacies of our health system. Navigating the American health system takes great stamina, good insurance, or other supportive resources. In our clinical work, older adults tell us horror stories about misunderstanding their treatment as well as failing to get the medical treatment they need (Cohen, 1991).

Medicine can rarely create health by focusing only on curing disease. It is risky to ignore emotional and spiritual aspects of healing. In an often cited article, Estes and Binney (1989) caution about "the biomedicalization of aging." The Western tradition believes that technology and medicine can eradicate sickness and death. If we focus exclusively on the medical technologies, we may overlook the importance of mind and spirit for the healthy self and family. Sickness and an insensitive health system with contradictory values may prevent the preservation of a healthy individual identity.

The value or ethic that health care is a right rather than a privilege ("Borderline Medicine," Public Broadcasting Station, 1992), has become a casualty of our current U.S. system. Numerous writers describe the deficiencies in our health-care system. Near the end of his life, Dr. Seuss (1986) wrote a book called *"You're Only Old Once"* that captures with humor and irony the personal frustration, contradiction, and tragedy of adults' attempts to navigate this system.

The status of older adults in Social Security and national health is precarious and political (Aaron, Kotlikoff, Rother, & Weaver, 1992). The guiding values are not clear. Callahan (1987) and Homer and Holstein, (1990) warn that difficult decisions must be made about health technology resources and who will finance them when funds are limited. Who will be left out if there is no consensus plan for allocation of resources? The senior author had the opportunity to spend a sabbatical studying healthy aging and health care in the United States and the United Kingdom. Both health-care systems are in the midst of change and reform trying to reconsider "What is a right and what is a privilege?" in health care. Both systems cite increased costs without commensurate increased funding. Even though Britain boasts a national health-care system "accessible to all," they are moving toward privatization (market-competitive models of managed care). The U.S. movement seeks health-care access for all, but balks at anything that hints of socialized medicine. The dilemma in both venues is that health care should include prevention, treatment (plus diagnosis), and recovery (or rehabilitation); if funds are limited, however, health costs for prevention and recovery are slighted. Acute treatment for acute disease processes (and sophisticated diagnostic technology) are the highest priority. Medicine must "stop the bleeding." Older adults are often low priority in decisions about allocating services because the expense for prevention and rehabilitation are deemed "wasted" on old people without much future (except, of course, wealthy seniors). Callahan's (1987) book *Setting Limits: Medical Goals in an Aging Society* underlines the need to make proactive ethical decisions about how to allocate medical resources. Too often, the costs are allocated by medical urgency, the fantasies of unlimited entitlement, and biomedical solutions for all problems, or the risk of a form of managed care motivated only by a profit.

The aging individual will confront loss of health through change, loss through the death of friends or family, and loss of independence. Medical afflictions represent losses as well and touch on individual, family, and societal variables. Psychophysiological presentations of stresses aggravating physical ailments and vice versa are more common and more complex in the aged (Williams, 1988). Senile dementias of the Alzheimer type are increasing in epidemic numbers (Cohen & Eisdorfer, 1986; Mace & Rabins, 1991). Other physical problems also contribute to intellectual decline, and the loss of sense of self and loss of independence go along with these failings (Koss, Haxby, De-Carli, Schapiro, & Friedland, 1991). In that respect, dementias produce an interaction of medicine and psychological problems for individual and family.

Alcoholism is increasing among older adults (see Chapter 14). Medication addictions and interaction of medication with physical and psychological infirmities can also compound medical problems. Elder abuse (detailed in Chapter 9) also is an appalling plight and important concern. The preceding represent just a few areas where medical, psychological, and societal problems interact. The ominous medical term "comorbidity" conveys the seriousness of these and other presentations where mind and body can interact dangerously (Gatz & Smyer, 1992). These interactive themes preview the psychological dimension.

Psychological Dimension

In the psychological dimension, adult age-appropriate concerns of intimacy versus isolation, generativity versus stagnation, and integrity versus despair (Erikson, 1982) raise challenging and troublesome questions about the way a person has spent his or her life. When death takes loved ones or when loss of function or independence challenges our lifelong view of ourselves, we feel threatened (Jung, 1963). Many of our treatment strategies for younger people are aimed at working to change the future based on an internal locus of control and a compelling belief in self-determination. These assumptions may not work with seniors. For older adults, the future is shorter, the possibilities of conquering new territories are limited, and physical limitations and other losses at least partially eclipse self-determination.

In a recent article on psychotherapy with older adults, Peake and Philpot (1991) suggest that working with older adults demands four important considerations. *First,* the therapist should have and convey an understanding of developmental issues including family as well as individual life cycles. *Second,* the therapist must evidence a sensitive appreciation of the impact of losses. The way the individual and the family have previously navigated, ignored, absorbed, or acknowledged loss has important implications for the individual's ability to handle current challenges. A *third* consideration for the therapist with older adults is a respect for the complicated interactions of problems in old age. The interaction of physical, psychological, and spiritual dimensions in later years must be understood by our health-care systems as well as by psychotherapists (Knight, 1986). *Finally,* a person's complex identity needs to be preserved through the senior years. Families can be "a veritable weed patch of human foibles" (Moore, 1992) but also can be a saving thread of continuity throughout life. Sharon Kaufman (1986) found that the preservation of a coherent sense of self in the face of physical and psychological losses is the best predictor of psychological and physical resilience for the elderly.

Spiritual and Existential Dimension

A third dimension of health and healing is the spiritual and existential dimension. Psychology and medicine rarely have answers for questions concerning the meaning of life despite these issues' developmental importance for the aged. We know that for many older adults, aging takes away physical capability, depletes financial resources, limits mobility and independence, and calls into question the worth of one's life. Resolutions for spiritual or existential dilemmas may best be addressed by families. Moreover, families have much to teach medicine and psychology about these troubling yet potentially renewing issues. Studies of the family's effect on individuals, stress that multigenerational themes of family values, family traditions, family rituals, family legends, and family love create meaning in the face of sometimes incomprehensible life circumstances (e.g., Minuchin & Nichols, 1992). In the face of loss through conflict or expected and unexpected challenges, families may respond effectively or pathologically. Families may embrace or reject spiritual options. Even where formal religious or spiritual cultures are not part of the family fabric, rituals and traditions evolve in a way that may offer meaning and continuity in life across cultures and across generations (Berman, 1989; Simon, 1989; Baum & Page, 1991). Prest and Keller (1993) urge that family clinicians be sensitive to and encourage spiritual dimensions.

This sketch of the array of problems facing families and the aged has included dimensions of physical, psychological, and spiritual needs. Next, we will consider some ways that families and family clinicians can address these challenges, including existing models, new possibilities, and an overview of some relevant research on the topic of aging and the family.

WHAT ARE SOME EXISTING AND POSSIBLE SOLUTIONS FOR PROBLEMS THAT AGING FAMILIES FACE?

A senior person's family is the natural context for growth and healing. Family relationships are extremely important in later life. Over 70% of the aged live with spouses or relatives (e.g., children, siblings; Walsh, 1988), and 75% of the aged report contact (physically or by phone) with an adult child in the preceding week (Montalvo & Thompson, 1988). Most elderly report preferring to maintain separate households from their children; however, frequent contact and the presence of close emotional ties appears positively associated with emotional well-being (Butler & Lewis, 1983; Streib, 1977) and even longevity (Walsh, 1988). Such findings suggest that the family system is particularly important to the aging individual and the system must confront major adaptational challenges.

It is useful to think of aging as a series of developmental challenges for individuals and their families. The challenges that define aging demand cognitive and emotional changes in the individual. Adjustments in the emotional and adaptive (e.g., information processing and solution generating) processes in family relations are equally crucial. Whether these challenges become an opportunity for growth and transformation, or for loss and regression depends on the success of emotional support and problem solving in past developmental transitions (both family and individual life cycles) and other life stressors, such as illness, divorce, and relocation. Good solutions to earlier problems in life can help current life challenges. Individuals and families usually will apply old strategies or solutions and use familiar patterns of emotional support and problem solving when dealing with new challenges. If these previous negotiations were unsuccessful, then new strategies are needed. Family therapy may help. A family therapist can help a family create new solutions to new problems or old ones never mastered.

Family patterns of adaptation are established to preserve stability, predictability and integration of the family and its members. If established patterns of interaction and problem solving become rigid and inflexible, especially in the face of new demands, such demands will not be mastered. Moreover, patterns of interaction that preclude emotional support and intimacy (e.g., disengaged families) or preclude healthy autonomy (e.g., enmeshed families) can prevent healthy transitions in aging. Assessing the family's patterns of emotional involvement and adaptability (i.e., the ability of the family to change their roles and relationship rules in response to challenges) across the family life cycle is a therapist's first task in helping the aging family.

While individuals and families are faced with demands for change, there is also a tendency for individuals to preserve intrapersonal structures (e.g., continuity theory), and for family systems to preserve their preferred transactions (e.g., family homeostasis) (Atchley, 1989; Papp, 1983). Several aspects of development and family life emerge from these negotiations of change and continuity. These issues include autonomy, connectedness, and innovation (Bergston & Kuypers, 1985). The tensions between autonomy and dependency are present throughout the life cycle and are particularly important when aging involves loss of functioning and increased dependency. The elderly face ambivalence between the increased concern and caretaking that loss causes and the discomfort about dependency on children who once depended on them. Similarly, the children are divided by loyalties to their parents and to their own children; not knowing if they are doing too much or too little for their parents, and if they are ignoring their children. Tensions evolve between being connected to and separate from family members as families negotiate their individual and life cycle transitions. Power, authority, and dominance issues arise from these differences in autonomy and connectedness, and must be negotiated with sensitivity throughout the family life cycle. Bowen's work on cross-generational issues is pivotal on these issues of individuation (Kerr & Bowen, 1988).

Family Developmental Stages

To understand a family's ability to absorb aging changes, one must consider how the family of elders and the family of the child have negotiated their issues of autonomy, connectedness, and innovation across their respective family biographies. Research on individual adjustment and family functioning suggest that flexibility in structure, roles, and responsibilities is integral to successful adjustment to extrafamilial and developmental stress (Walsh, 1988). Mental health professionals can do much to highlight a family's existing adaptive strengths and develop new ones when necessary. A knowledge of the problems of aging must complement the usual family treatment skills.

We consider the tasks of aging to be the last of a series of developmental challenges that affect and define a family. The family's ability, to provide emotional support yet change their transactions to adapt to the changes of aging, depends upon how well previous life stages were navigated. Chapter 1 presented several theories of family development, notably Carter and McGoldrick (1988). In this chapter, these stages are revisited with a specific focus on how various stages impact the elder and the family.

For young adults, *leaving home* marks the transition when they must become responsible both emotionally and financially. To achieve this, they must differentiate themselves as independent of the family of origin, achieve work and financial status, and develop healthy new relationships to meet emotional needs. Young adults may need to consider what emotional adaptive solutions they bring from the family of origin and what style they will create themselves. Difficulty separating from the family of origin, or failure to individuate and develop emotional autonomy can haunt older adults throughout their lives. These issues reappear when later life losses challenge poor individuation. Optimal resolution of this stage is marked by the beginning of individuation (Kerr & Bowen, 1988); a connection to, yet separateness from the family of origin. A sense of autonomy with a confidence about healthy emotional support is the result.

Emotional commitment to a significant other or marriage marks the second stage of the family life cycle. In marriage, spouses bring conflicting patterns of interaction and expectations of intimacy learned in their respective families of origin. Primary areas to be negotiated at this time include establishing boundaries around the spousal subsystem, negotiating relations with in-laws and peers, and balancing the practical aspects of life together while preserving each person's individual differences (Haley, 1980). If intimacy issues and disagreement are poorly negotiated, the stage is set for problems later in the family's and the elder's development. These difficulties are compounded in a society where blended families (remarriages) are common and poor resolution of emotional commitment just gets more complicated.

When children are added to the system, the spouse dyad must create emotional space to incorporate the children, and the spouses must define themselves as part of a new generation with specific responsibilities accompanying child rearing. *Children* create new responsibilities for their parents including nurturance, management, health promotion, fostering of spiritual and psychological values, and increased economic responsibility. While the couple negotiates these new responsibilities, they define their relationship (and their children's) to their respective families of origin. Emotional attachment, promotion of the children's autonomy and maturity, and setting limits are child-rearing issues that, if poorly negotiated, lead to clinical problems then and even worse in later years. This time also marks the beginning of the shift toward joint caring for the older generations.

Launching children from the home or the emancipation of adolescents is the beginning of family relationship patterns for the latter stages of life. At this point, aging individuals must separate emotionally from their offspring and emotionally invest back into their marriage and into new roles. The amount of turmoil experienced during these transitions depends, in part, on how successfully members of the couple negotiated their past marital issues, and how well they renegotiate *a new relationship* with one another given the changes each has absorbed over the years. Ideally, each spouse will view this as a time for companionship and marital sharing. This renegotiation can be extremely difficult if the children had the role of stabilizing the marriage. For example, if a child has been the primary communication focus for the couple, then at emancipation (when the child leaves home), the couple may not really know or communicate with one another. Previous unresolved issues between the couple may reappear, leading to either renewed conflict or a new alliance.

For a single parent, the threat of the child leaving home may signal the beginning of loneliness for the parent and a loss of the familiar parental role. Indeed, the term *"empty nest"* reflects the necessity of aging individuals to devote their energies to new roles and responsibilities or interests.

A common developmental transition that faces the aging individual and the family is retirement. *Retirement* is typically the result of a family decision (Giordano & Beckham, 1983), but forced retirement requires adjustment especially for individuals whose sense of importance was tied to their work (Walsh, 1988). Retirement is particularly difficult when there is no role continuity. Retirement, particularly for men, can precipitate loss of role identity, work-related responsibilities, and relationships. The loss of these roles and relationships, whether from vocational pursuits or child rearing, challenges retirees to find new direction and meaning for their lives (generally) or face stagnation. The financial strain of retirement and the loss of family and friends (if one has to change residences) represent stresses frequently encountered by the elderly.

Fortunately, most couples experience an increase in marital satisfaction after retirement as companionship, mutual caretaking, and mutual enjoyment of friends and activities become more important (Lowenthal, 1977). Changes in role expectations frequently occur as roles become more egalitarian (e.g., husbands become more incorporated or integrated into household responsibilities while women tend to become more assertive and independent) (Gilligan, 1982). Retirement may provide a greater opportunity to enjoy adult children and their offspring. New roles at retirement, however, may conflict with an earlier sense of identity (e.g., household, finances). As the couple renegotiates these new roles and relations, the opportunity for intimacy, generativity, and integrity increase. However, a common lament heard when counseling older couples is the wife's lament, "I married him for better or for worse, but not for lunch." This humor captures the strain of a husband's role change with time on his hands.

The death of a spouse, *widowhood,* is a critical stressor for the elderly. Compared with other life events, it is often the most difficult readjustment (Giordano & Beckham, 1985). The widowed must grieve and eventually accept the loss of his or her spouse. Shared experiences transform into memory and the task of adjusting ensues. Healthy resolution of this loss is marked by interest in new activities and seeking significant others. The loss of functioning or death of a spouse often requires other family members to assume the roles of the deceased. Research suggests that the widowed usually turn to relatives and, especially their children (daughters) for emotional and instrumental support (Bunagin & Hern, 1982). This support, however, may be inadequate if the family system has dealt with previous losses poorly, or if individual members' grief was compounded by unresolved conflict with the deceased or surviving spouse. Support may also be compromised if the designated caretakers are taxed by problems in their respective families.

Often a widower will deal with the loneliness accompanying the loss of a spouse by remarrying. Family support appears particularly important to the success of the marriage, as research suggests a strong association between the children's approval of the marriage and its success (Butler & Lewis, 1982). Remarriage forces the system to engage in new relationships, and members struggle to deal with loyalty and guilt issues generated from the previous marriage. For the remarrying elder, satisfaction with the new marriage appears related to resolution of grief and the ability to negotiate intimacy anew (Balkwell, 1981). Finally, offspring of the elderly may actively encourage parents to establish such a relationship as this may allow the offspring more autonomy and resources to resolve their own life cycle issues (Gelfand, Olsen, & Block, 1978).

A substantial proportion (between 70% and 94%) of individuals over age 65 have grandchildren (Butler & Lewis, 1982; Streib, 1977). *Becoming a grandparent* assists the aged in accepting mortality, solidifying generativity, and positively evaluating his or her life. In addition, becoming a grandparent offers the individual new role opportunities and meaning, and allows for emotional connectedness between generations (Walsh, 1988). Research suggests, however, that the type of interactions occurring between children and their grandparents is strongly influenced by the children's parents' attitude (e.g., facilitative or hindering) toward the grandparents (Robertson, 1975). Problems can arise if grandparents and grandchildren form an alliance against the parents that is precipitated by unresolved conflicts between the grandparents and their offspring (the parent). When the grandchildren become triangulated, the overt conflict between grandparents and their offspring revolves around parenting issues. Similarly, grandparents may become triangulated in their offspring's marital conflicts and may serve as a "safety valve" to defuse conflict in the nuclear family. Conflict also may spring from a poor balance between being supportive and being intrusive in caretaking roles (Walsh, 1988). Thus, the roles that grandparents take toward their grandchildren appear to be defined by systemic processes operating in the family of origin (the aged and their offspring) and the nuclear family (offspring and their children), rather than by the direct choice of the grandparent.

The fear of *illness and dependence* are common concerns for the elderly. Such concerns are legitimate. Research suggests a significant increase in the incidence of depressive disorders, organic brain disorders, and chronic health problems for individuals 65 years of age and older (Gurland, 1976). Given that only 5% of the elderly are institutionalized for their health problems, increased caregiving demands are generally placed on the family. Unfortunately, there are few caregiving guidelines available to families regarding effective management of an impaired elder. One recent exception is the book, *Seven Steps to Effective Parent Care* (Cohen & Eisdorfer, 1993). This is a thoughtful and well-conceived guide for adults caring for their parents. Even as medical and residential institutions assume increasing responsibility for the instrumental caregiving of the elderly, the family is still needed for the provision of emotional support, decision making, and spirituality.

Family Influences on the Effects of Aging

There is a paucity of research about how the family influences the outcome of illness. However, some research suggests that relationships that foster autonomy and minimize the loss of independence tend to limit the psychological distress associated with failing health (Giordano & Beckham, 1985). Although a number of issues become more prominent when serious illness befalls the elderly, increased dependency becomes the foremost concern. Disabled adults' increased dependency on their spouse or children creates confusion and ambivalent expectations for caregivers who must assume the roles and responsibilities lost to the disabled elder. Frequently, the caregiver will respond by overfunctioning and the elder tends to become more dependent. In other words, as caretakers become increasingly "helpful," the disabled elder becomes increasingly incompetent and the potential for maximum recovery becomes reduced. The overfunctioning of the caretaker may be motivated, in part, by the caretaker's avoidance of his or her own anxiety, perception of vulnerability, and personal dependency needs (Walsh, 1988; Stoddard, 1992).

The couple described at the start of this chapter were a great example of a healthy family story for cross-generational problems. That couple shared with their children the loving and humane way they had cared for their own parents at the end of the grandparents' lives. They answered the question, "What will happen to us when the experts are gone?" (in the face of the mother's Alzheimer's disease). They thereby gave their children a model for honor and caring even in the face of death. An ironic Pakistani folktale is worth sharing on this same theme.

> An ancient grandmother lived with her daughter and grandson. As she grew frail and feeble, instead of being a help around the house, she became a constant trial. She broke plates and cups, lost knives, and spilled water. The daughter sent the grandson to buy his grandmother a wooden plate. The boy hesitated because he knew a wooden plate would humiliate his grandmother. But his mother insisted, so off he went. He returned bringing not one, but two wooden plates. "I only asked you to buy one," his mother said. "Didn't you hear me?" "Yes," said the boy. "But I bought the second one so there would be one for you when you get old."
>
> —*Pakistani folktale*

Successful adaptation to these various issues requires a realistic assessment of the disabled elder's capacities and potentials with the goal of preserving the elder's honor and competence. Helping older adults preserve their identity, and enhance their competence through change and adaptation, means the life stories of the individual and the family can be happy ones.

WHERE DO WE GO FROM HERE?

As already mentioned, the problems of aging are *multidimensional* (physical, psychological, and spiritual), and *multisystemic* (individual, family, community, cultural, and political). Some of the more prominent problems facing the aging and the family have already been mentioned. In the physical dimension, a multitude of illnesses are available to hamper and limit the quality of life of the aged. Comorbidity (Gatz & Smyer, 1992); especially the interaction between physical and mental/emotional problems, is common. Older adults are more likely to consult physicians than mental health professionals about their psychological problems when there is a coexisting situation. This preference suggests that the problem of *biomedicalization* discussed earlier is perpetuated not only by the medical and physical health system but by the expectations of the elderly. Gatz and Smyer (1992) point out that psychiatrists in independent practice provide most of the treatment for elder's mental health problems. Psychologists provide only 5.5% of all outpatient mental health services for older adults, suggesting a bias toward the medical approach. Family clinicians are in a position to create new models for helping the aged by learning from these families life stories.

Gatz and Smyer (1992) also note that there is a historic lack of cooperation between the aging network and the mental health system. Antagonism exists between state units on aging and state mental health agencies. These barriers must be overcome, and these agencies must also work in cooperation with state and private sector agencies focusing on physical health and the interaction with psychological factors (Kleinman, 1988). Mental health care need not be bound by limitation of general health care. New models of psychological treatment need to be made available. Informed family clinicians can mobilize and modify family wisdom and resources to make life better for elders and their families.

In a studied presentation, Stokols (1992) stressed the need for a social ecology of health promotion. He notes that past health promotion strategies have emphasized behavioral change rather than environmentally focused interventions. He points out that social, cultural, and family resources can be focused and integrated in a way that counteracts the too narrow biomedicalization trend in treating illness. Prevention and recovery from illness are as important as the acute phase of treatment. Existing resources such as social and family groups, as well as other agencies within the community including religious and community organizations, can be mobilized to augment medical care. Stokols also suggests that health-care systems driven by fee for service do not promote prevention. Whereas the health-care system provides a growing technology for diagnosis and treatment of medical problems, it does not effectively integrate the psychological and spiritual dimensions. The family may be the nucleus of change to ensure prevention, treatment, and recovery are evenly valued. The family can do this by keeping or revising its own health as well as being an advocate for ethical and informed changes in health care.

CONCLUSION

In a way, the sweeping scope of problems in aging appears overwhelming. When we ponder the strategies to combat these difficulties, the task may also seem too large. It is our contention that family clinicians are in a position to understand: the problems in all three spheres of physical, psychological, and spiritual dimensions, as well as to mobilize solutions and resources from the existing cultures and systems that shape the family. The family in turn shapes these cultures and can be either a victim or a moving force to shape better health care.

Earlier, we mentioned the elderly man who asked a rhetorical question about the treatment of his wife with Alzheimer's. "What will we do when the experts are gone?" We think he also highlighted an answer. He talked about the passages, rituals, and traditions of his and his wife's family. He demonstrated a strength in preserving the identity of families across generations and through episodes of physical and psychological loss, stress, and change. Family clinicians have the resources to preserve what is good about the identity of individuals, families, and agencies. The strain of preserving a sense of continuity, when changes are necessary, highlights the paradox of health. Family therapy has models for preserving identity when continuity is called for, and promoting structural change (without threatening the identity, pride, and sense of hope that goes with family development) when change is required.

As with other family issues in considering the problem of aging, it is important to understand developmental stages in individuals and in families. These two cycles often collide and threaten the identity and continuity of the individual or the family. Family clinicians can help identify and mobilize resources in the individuals and families so that the two life cycles can coincide and cosupport.

Families have answers to spiritual questions that medicine and psychology usually cannot provide. The families have a great wisdom about what families and individuals need (Prest & Keller, 1993). When elders and family members have health-care needs, they must be aware that the current health-care system is driven by managed health care, a good idea in principle, but applied in variegated and contradictory ways that often create physical or psychological problems. These problems are unique to the monster of a health care practiced with fractioned goals, contradictory application, and only lip service to a balance of body, mind, and spirit. Families and family clinicians can be advocates to influence a health care that is both "elder friendly" and "family friendly."

Gatz and Smyer (1992) suggest that in the 1990s, most gains in the treatment of the aged will occur in the biomedical arena, rather than in service provision or public policy. They believe that this is because groups other than the elderly are speaking for the needs of older adults. Except where older adults fall within another priority, such as severe mental illness or Alzheimer's disease, it is not likely that the mental health of older adults will be a priority in the 1990s. Family clinicians can influence the face of mental health care for the 21st century. Family psychology is a force that can mobilize families and reeducate the bias that the elderly have about using mental health services. Family clinicians can also learn from families. We can learn the traditions, rituals, and wisdom that families possess about how to heal themselves before the experts arrive—and after "the experts are gone."

REFERENCES

Aaron, H., Kotlikoff, L., Rother, J., & Weaver, C. (1992). Social Security: Invaluable or outmoded? *Modern Maturity: Publication of AARP, 35,* 34–46.

Abeles, N., & Eisdorfer, C. (1991). Educational training recommendations for competence to work clinically with older adults. *The Psychotherapy Bulletin, 26,* 43–44.

Anderson, D. (1988). The quest for a meaningful old age. *The Family Therapy Networker, 12,* 16–23.

Atchley, R. C. (1989). A continuity theory of normal aging. *The Gerontologist, 29,* 183–190.

Balkwell, C. (1981). Transition to widowhood. *Family Relations, 30,* 117–127.

Bateson, G. (1972). *Steps to an ecology of mind.* New York: Ballantine.

Baum, M., & Page, M. (1991). Caregiving and multigenerational families. *The Gerontologist, 31,* 762–769.

Bergston, V. L., & Schaie, K. W. (Eds.). (1989). *The course of later life: Research and reflections.* New York: Springer.

Berman, P. L. (1989). *The courage to grow old.* New York: Ballantine.

Bruner, J. (1986). *Actual minds, possible worlds.* Cambridge, MA: Harvard.

Bunagin, V. E., & Hern, K. F. (1982). Observations on changing relationships for older married women. *The American Journal of Psychoanalysis, 42,* 133–142.

Butler, R. N., & Lewis, M. I. (1983). *Aging and mental health: Positive psychosocial and biomedical approaches* (3rd ed.). St. Louis: C.V. Mosby.

Callahan, D. (1987). *Setting limits: Medical goals in an aging society.* New York: Simon & Schuster.

Carter, E., & McGoldrick, M. (Eds.). (1988). *The changing family life cycle.* New York: Gardner.

Cohen, D. (1991). The subjective experience of alzheimer's disease: The anatomy of an illness as perceived by patients and families. *The American Journal of Alzheimer's Care, 6,* 6–11.

Cohen, D., & Eisdorfer, C. (1986). *The loss of self: A family resource for Alzheimer's disease and related disorders.* New York: Norton.

Cohen, D., & Eisdorfer, C. (1993). *Seven steps to effective parent care.* New York: Putnam.

Costa, P. T., Gatz, M., Neugarten, B. L., Salthouse, T. A., & Siegler, I. C. (1989). *The adult years: Continuity and change.* Washington, DC: American Psychological Association.

Engel, G. L. (1977). The need for a new medical model: A challenge for biomedicine. *Science, 196,* 129–136.

Epston, D., & White, M. (1975). *Literate means to therapeutic ends.* Adelaide, South Australia: Dulwich Centre Publications.

Epston, D., & White, M. (1992). *Experience, contradiction, narrative and imagination.* Adelaide, South Australia: Dulwich Centre Publications.

Erikson, E. H. (1982). *The life cycle completed.* New York: Norton.

Estes, C. L., & Binney, E. H. (1989). The biomedicalization of aging: Dangers and dilemmas. *The Gerontologist, 29,* 587–596.

Frankl, V. E. (1973). *The doctor and the soul.* New York: Vintage.

Gatz, M., & Smyer, M. A. (1992). The mental health system and older adults. *American Psychologist, 47,* 741–751.

Gelfand, O. E., Olsen, J. J., & Block, M. R. (1978). Two generations of elderly in the changing American family: Implications for family services. *The Family Coordinator, 27,* 395–403.

Gilligan, C. (1982). *In a different voice.* Cambridge, MA: Harvard University Press.

Gilligan, C., & Pollack, S. (1988). The vulnerable and invulnerable physician. In C. Gilligan, J. V. Ward, & J. M. Taylor (Eds.), *Mapping the moral domain.* Cambridge, MA: Harvard University Press.

Giordano, J. A., & Beckham, K. (1985, April). *Having a few too many in the later years: An examination of the characteristics of the late-onset alcoholic.* Paper presented at the Southern Gerontological Society 4th Annual Meeting, Atlanta, GA.

Gurland, B. J. (1976). The comparative frequency of depression in various adult age groups. *Journal of Gerontology, 31,* 283–292.

Haley, J. (1980). *Leaving home.* New York: McGraw-Hill.

Homer, P., & Holstein, M. (Eds.). (1990). *A good old age: The paradox of setting limits.* New York: Simon & Schuster.

Howard, G. S. (1989). *A tale of two stories: Excursions into a narrative approach to psychology.* Notre Dame, IN: Academic Publications.

Howard, G. S. (1991). Culture tales: A narrative approach to thinking, cross-cultural psychology, and psychotherapy. *American Psychologist, 46,* 187–197.

Imber-Black, E. (1989). Creating rituals in therapy [Special issue]. *The Family Therapy Networker, 13*(4).

Jung, C. G. (1963). *Modern man in search of a soul.* New York: Harcourt, Brace & World.

Kaufman, S. R. (1986). *The ageless self: Sources of meaning in late life.* New York: Meridian.

Kerr, M. E., & Bowen, M. (1988). *Family evaluation: An approach based on Bowen theory.* New York: Norton.

Kiesler, C. A. (1992). U.S. Mental Health Policy: Doomed to failure. *American Psychologist, 47,* 1077–1082.

Kleinman, A. (1980). *Patients and healers in the context of culture.* Berkeley: University of California Press.

Kleinman, A. (1988). *The illness narratives: Suffering healing and the human condition.* New York: Basic Books.

Knight, B. (1986). *Psychotherapy with older adults.* Beverly Hills, CA: Sage.

Koss, E., Haxby, J. V., DeCarli, C., Schapiro, M. B., & Friedland, R. P. (1991). Patterns of performance, preservation and loss in healthy aging. *Developmental Neuropsychology, 7,* 99–113.

Levinson, D. J. (1986). A conception of adult development. *American Psychologist, 41,* 3–13.

Lowenthal, M. F. (1977). Toward a socio-psychological theory of change in adulthood and old age. In J. Boren & K. W. Schaie (Eds.), *Handbook of the psychology of aging.* New York: Van Nostrand Reinhold.

McAdams, D. (1985). *Power, intimacy and the life story.* Homewood, IL: Dorsey Press.

Mace, N. L., & Rabins, P. V. (1991). *The 36-hour day.* Baltimore: John Hopkins.

Mair, M. (1989). *Between psychology and psychotherapy.* London: Routledge.

Minuchin, S., & Nichols, M. P. (1992). *Family healing.* New York: Free Press.

Montalvo, B., & Thompson, R. F. (1988). Conflicts in the caregiving family. *The Family Therapy Networker, 12,* 30–35.

Moore, T. (1992). *Care of the soul.* New York: HarperCollins.

Munson, C. (Ed.). (1984). Family of origin applications in clinical supervision [Special issue]. *The Clinical Supervisor, 2.*

Neugarten, B. L., & Neugarten, D. A. (1989). Policy issues in an aging society. In M. Storandt & G. Vandenbos (Eds.), *The adult years: Continuity and change.* Washington, DC: American Psychological Association.

Papp, P. (1983). *The process of change.* New York: Guilford.

Peake, T. H. (1993). *Healthy aging, healthy treatment: Telling stories.* Grand Rounds presentation, Dartmouth Medical School/New Hampshire Hospital.

Peake, T. H., & Philpot, C. (1991). Psychotherapy with older adults: Hopes and fears. *The Clinical Supervisor, 9,* 185–202.

Polkinghorne, D. P. (1988). *Narrative psychology.* Albany, NY: SUNY Press.

Prest, L. A., & Keller, J. F. (1993). Spirituality and family therapy: Spiritual beliefs, myths and metaphors. *Journal of Marital and Family Therapy, 19,* 137–148.

Robertson, J. F. (1975). Interaction in three generation families, parents as mediators: Toward a theoretical perspective. *International Journal of Aging and Human Development, 6,* 103–110.

Sarbin, T. R. (Ed.). (1986). *Narrative psychology: The storied nature of human conduct.* New York: Praeger.

Seuss, Dr. (1986). *You're only old once.* New York: Random House.

Simon, R. (Ed.). (1989). Ritual: The hidden resource [Special issue]. *The Family Therapy Networker, 13*(4).

Snow, C. P. (1959). *The two cultures and the scientific revolution.* New York: Cambridge University Press.

Stoddard, S. (1992). *The hospice movement: A better way of caring for the dying.* New York: Vintage.

Stokols, D. (1992). Establishing and maintaining healthy environments. *American Psychologist, 47,* 6–22.

Streib, G. F. (1977). Older people in a family context. In R. A. Kalish (Ed.), *The later years: Social applications of gerontology.* Monterey, CA: Brooks Cole.

Viorst, J. (1986). *Necessary losses: The loves, illusions, dependencies and expectations that all of us have to give up in order to grow.* New York: Ballantine.

Walsh, F. (1988). The family in later life. In E. Carter & M. McGoldrick (Eds.), *The changing family life cycle.* New York: Gardner.

Watzlawich, P. (Ed.). (1984). *The invented reality.* New York: Norton.

Williams, P. R. (1988). *Family problems: Oxford general practice series, #17.* Oxford: Oxford University Press.

CHAPTER 6

Adoptive Families: Are They Nonnormative?

LITA LINZER SCHWARTZ

The primary factor that makes adoptive families nonnormative is that, in most cases, they are composed of persons not related to each other by biology. Spouses in any Western family are usually not biological kin; in adoptive families, however, the children are also not genetically related to the parents or to each other, unlike most other families. A second major factor that differentiates adoptive families is that adopting children is a very conscious decision, unlike the more usual act of procreation. Third, with adoption, the parent-child relationship is created legally by a court. And fourth, three types of principals are involved in adoptive families rather than the usual two, with birthparents adding another dimension to the family picture.

There are other differences as well: Many adoptive families have come into family status somewhat later than couples who conceive their own children; the children arrive at different ages, some at age 2 or 3 days and some already of school age; some adoptive families have members of varied ethnic and/or racial backgrounds; and some adoptive families have ongoing interactions with the children's biological parents, whereas others do not. Not all biological mothers (or fathers) are anxious to reunite with their long-placed children, nor do all adopted children choose to seek their long-gone progenitors.

Not all adoptive families are the same in creation and structure. In this sense, adoptive families have a dimension of diversity in addition to those variations ordinarily found from one family to another. It is this diversity that clinicians must be aware of as they work with adoptive families, as indeed they should attend to the specific characteristics of any client family.

In examining studies of adoptive families, it quickly becomes apparent that in too many cases researchers lump together "adopted children" as subjects without attending to the unique circumstances under which they joined their families. They may also consider all adoptive parents to have come to this role in the same way or for the same reasons. Thus, much of this chapter is arranged in terms of the questions that one of the parties in a therapeutic situation might ask, and some of the answers that might emerge.

AN HISTORICAL NOTE: SHOULD ADOPTION BE "OPEN" OR "CLOSED"?

Prior to the enactment of state laws governing adoption, a married couple, typically in a rural area, might take an unwed pregnant woman into their home, care for her, and then adopt her child, or, alternatively, children of unwed mothers might be placed in an orphanage and then offered out as indentured servants (Sorosky, Baran, & Panner, 1984). By the end of the 19th century, however, abuses of the latter practice led to state regulations of adoption that included both termination of biological parents' rights and sealing of the adoption record. These provisions were based on public policies (Cook, 1992):

> First, confidentiality would ensure privacy and anonymity for the adoptee, as well as for both the natural and adoptive parents. Second, confidentiality would promote unity in the new adoptive family. Third, confidential adoptions would facilitate the adoptive parents' security in their new parental role. Finally, termination of the natural family-child relationship was necessary both to prevent the child from being subject to a conflict of authority and to encourage closer bonding in the adoptive family. (p. 474)

The last argument is probably the one that is still most salient today, at least in those adoptive families where the child comes as an infant.

Proponents of open adoption arrangements, which permit interaction among the three facets of the adoption triangle, on the other hand, have suggested that breaking the relationship with the biological parent(s) "can be detrimental to the child's emotional and psychological well-being and may in fact impede the formation of new relationships in the future" (Cook, 1992, p. 475). The degree of openness can vary from contact with the biological parent(s) prior to and/or at the time of delivery, to contact by mail only, to a regular pattern of visits and possibly even overnight or vacation stays. Where continuing interaction with the biological parents does not interfere with the functioning of the adoptive family as a unit or with the child's development, this argument may have merit, especially with children who are beyond toddler age at the time of adoption or who are adopted by a relative. Another factor to be considered from this point of view is that the option of visitation may encourage unwed mothers, especially young girls, neither to abort the fetus nor to try to raise the child when they are clearly inadequate to the task.

What is generally unmentioned by proponents of open adoption is what might happen in adoptive families where each of two, three, or more adoptees has different biological parents who have contact with the family. The potential for conflicts in these multiple relationships (for there is secondary influence by the parents of one child on the other children as well as on the adoptive parents) increases exponentially (Schwartz, 1993a). In addition:

> Some critics express concern about a child's ability to manage relationships with two sets of parents . . . [or that] adoptive parents or birth parents do not live

up to their contract. Either party may cut off contact or may be erratic in following through on the original agreement. (Rosenberg, 1992, p. 12)

QUESTIONS AND ANSWERS

There are three branches of the adoptive family tree: the biological parents, the adoptive parents, and the adoptee. Any or all of them may appear in a mental health professional's office. Depending on which parties to the adoption are being seen by a therapist, a vast array of questions may come to mind.

In the case of the biological parents, what was the biological mother's state of mind during and after her pregnancy? To what extent was her decision to release her baby for adoption a reflection of her relationship with her own parents? Did she weigh whether two adoptive parents were better for her child than one biological parent? Was the biological father aware of the pregnancy and/or the decision to place the child for adoption? Has either biological parent continued to mourn the loss of the child over the years, perhaps hoping for a magical reunion when the child becomes an adult?

In the case of prospective adoptive parents, to what extent has their infertility intruded on their marriage? Have they both been able to accept their inability to perpetuate their families' genetic heritage or does this remain a source of covert mourning throughout their lives? Was the decision to adopt a wholehearted one on both their parts? Do their families accept and support the adoption? Does it matter to the couple, or their families, whether the adoption is transracial, transnational, interreligious, infant, or older child?

As for the adoptees, do they feel conflict between the psychological bonds with their adoptive parents and the biological ones with their birth parents? Does this contribute to acting-out behavior, withdrawal, or anxiety? Rosenberg (1992) suggests that testing the limits occurs more often "where a child has been traumatized by separation (prior to the adoption) and then becomes compelled to effect rejection and abandonment again and again through provocative behavior. He repeats the trauma in an effort to master it" (p. 76). If adoptees entertain thoughts of finding their biological parents, do they feel disloyal toward or rejecting of their adoptive parents as a result? As adults, should they pursue a reunion if the birth parent does not want one? Is open adoption better for them than the more traditional confidential arrangement?

As an Adoptee, How Do I Feel?

The answers to the previous questions vary by family and even within a family, with additional factors entering the picture at different developmental stages of the adoption. A helpful analysis of the emotional conflicts that arise is contained in Rosenberg's (1992) approach to developmental stages in the adoption life cycle. These conflicts are in addition to those delineated by Erikson (1950).

The first tasks, whether the adoptee is a neonate or older, are to deal with the trauma of separation from the birth parent(s) and to establish bonds with the adoptive parents, to develop a sense of trust. If the child is old enough at the time of separation to recognize his or her early caretakers, the trauma tends to be greater and the fear of renewed separation, now from the adoptive parents, may persist for years.

In both biological and adoptive families, young children often fantasize that their "real" parents are members of royalty, or famous in some field. This is a fairly common wish when they are angry with their adoptive parents. According to Rosenberg (1992), however:

> For the fantasy to be effective for the adopted child, it must include some overriding and powerful explanation for the loss of the [biological] parents, that is, an explanation that in no way compromises their perfection. It must be entirely someone else's fault that the child is no longer with them. (p. 99)

In some cases, peers may exaggerate adoption as being "different," a status that disturbs any child. As school-age children, the earlier separation anxiety may reappear as they seek to establish their self-esteem, even as they deal with having been "abandoned" earlier, and try to affirm the permanency of the family in which they are being raised (Rosenberg, 1992, p. 196).

As adopted children approach adolescence, they, like their peers in biological families, wonder, "Where did I come from?" For some adopted children, the usual explanation of procreation is often insufficient, even with added information about the circumstances of the adoption. They wonder about which parent they look like, what strengths and weaknesses they may have inherited, whether they carry genes that will predispose them to physical or emotional illness. The development of a sense of identity may raise additional questions, beyond those asked by most adolescents, because of the duality of their background. Some female adolescent adoptees may attempt to resolve their feelings about sexuality, identity, and relationships with their adoptive parents by identifying with their birth mother and changing their behavior "in the direction of the imagined behavior of the birth mother, often toward more rebellious and sexual activity. Simultaneously, the young woman is giving a major test to the values of the adoptive parents, as well as to the strength of the adoptive attachment" (Reitz & Watson, 1992, p. 183). The typical separation-individuation of late adolescence may also create greater anxiety in some adoptees (and their adoptive parents) than it does in some biological children, again depending on how well they have moved toward an integration of their biological and psychological aspects of identity.

> As adopted people begin searching for mates, they are likely to have more interest and curiosity about their own genealogy. . . . Potential mates and their families may have concern about the adopted one's hereditary base and may express similar interest. . . . How much does the unknown matter to them? (Rosenberg, 1992, p. 83)

Not all adoptees or their prospective families-by-marriage are troubled by this equally, as much depends on the individual's earlier resolution of these questions.

For the young mother-to-be who is adopted, and sometimes the prospective father who is an adoptee, the pregnancy may stir up a variety of feelings. On the one hand, the expected baby represents biological kin, a novel experience. On the other hand, the pregnancy may rearouse the questions of earlier years about the individual's own biological roots, and about the promiscuity, maturity, and other characteristics of the biological parents.

Why Did My Mother Give Me Up?

There are several reasons a biological mother would choose to place her child for adoption. This may vary according to *when* she was pregnant, that is, the calendar years of the event, as well as with her more individual characteristics.

Looking back to the pre-1970s era, for example, unwed motherhood was generally not acceptable to society in general or to individual families. Pregnant girls typically were sent away from home, often to maternity residences operated by social welfare agencies such as the Salvation Army. They were expected to release the illegitimate child for adoption shortly after his or her birth and then to resume the path to their adult lives. This was seen as the best alternative for the girl (and her family), and for the baby, who would have a chance for a loving family and a wholesome life. Most adoptions were supervised by social service agencies, although some were handled privately by physicians and attorneys in the "grey market" (no extra fees to the intermediary) or "black market" (extra "placement" fees to the intermediary).

In more recent years, the number of unwed adolescent pregnancies has climbed to more than one million per year, with about half of these resulting in live births (Kalmuss, Namerow, & Bauer, 1992). One rarely sees reference to illegitimacy today, and it is generally recognized that the circumstances of the pregnancy and birth are not attributable to the baby as in the past. Indeed, as Anne Brodzinsky (1990) points out, the highly moralistic attitudes of the past have declined over the past two decades. Most of the girls who have live births tend to keep the baby, and even those from middle- or upper-class families are less often regarded as a disgrace to their families. In many cases, these are cases of "babies bearing babies," which is rarely desirable for either mother or child. Too often, the girls have little pre- or postnatal care, lack parenting skills, leave school, have too few marketable skills (or are too young) to obtain a decent job, and they and the baby, who also may lack medical care, skimp by living on welfare checks. An alternative to this dismal picture, for both mother and child, is to place the baby for adoption. Barth (1987) found, however, that these young mothers had rarely been given much information about adoption as an option. When they were, they tended to be "reasonably positive" about the possibility of open-adoption practices.

Another view is that some young women who have concluded that they cannot raise their baby, but who are opposed to abortion, choose placement of the child as not only the most viable option but also one that has positive aspects. Rosenberg (1992) found that they "feel gratified by the belief that they are providing both life for their child and a child for a longing couple" (p. 23). This altruistic decision is similar to that voiced by some young women who have chosen to become surrogate mothers (Schwartz, 1991). Even as they make this decision, however, grief may be experienced relevant to the separation, and it may not be resolved for some time if counseling support is withdrawn at the time that the baby is surrendered to others.

Data cited by Donnelly and Voydanoff (1991) indicate that fewer than 4% of unintended live births to adolescents are released for adoption. Kalmuss, Namerow, & Bauer (1992) using a different source, cite the figure at 5%. Significant differences between those who kept their babies and those who did not were found in several areas. Demographically, the "releasing" mothers were more often young adolescents, white, had better educated mothers, were not on welfare, and were attending school and earning good grades (Donnelly & Voydanoff, 1991, pp. 406–407). They also had higher educational expectations than the girls who kept their babies. They tended to have more realistic perceptions of the responsibilities of parenting and awareness of alternatives to parenthood, as well as stating that *their* mothers would prefer adoption. A key factor in their decision appears to be greater overall emotional maturity in perspective. That is, apart from the demographic factors and a generally favorable attitude toward adoption, the younger mother who places her child for adoption tends to

> expect that raising a child now would be a commitment she would likely regret, to think that parenting as an adolescent would not be much fun. . . . She is likely to have thought a lot about what she will be doing in the future, plans to continue her schooling, and believes that ideally women should become mothers in their 20s. (p. 408)

She is also more likely to have been a victim of sexual abuse, or to have become pregnant as a result of sexual abuse than is her peer who opts to keep her child.

A study of 527 unmarried mothers, ages 13 to 21, by Kalmuss, Namerow, and Bauer (1992), similarly reported that most of those who placed their child for adoption (41% of their sample) were white and that they and their families had not been on welfare. The fact that 75% of the subjects were living in maternity residences, as the authors were careful to point out, may be related to their decision. In addition, this slightly older sample had a higher level of education than those in the Donnelly and Voydanoff study; 52.8% of those releasing their babies already were high school graduates, and it was the older girls and young women rather than the younger ones who placed their babies rather than keeping them. Kalmuss et al. found that more than half of those who chose adoption "reported little or no regret about their decision (56%). Moreover, more than three-quarters of the relinquishers stated that they would make the same pregnancy resolution decision again (78%)" (1992, p. 89).

What about My Biological Father?

In most cases of adoption, the biological father is not married to the biological mother, and sometimes may not even be aware that she is pregnant. Often he is an adolescent, possibly a school dropout or unemployed. Depending on age, ethnic background, social class, and numerous other factors, he may or may not admit to fatherhood if he is aware of the pregnancy or birth. Under these circumstances, because there is less certainty about who is a child's biological father, absent DNA testing, it may be very difficult for an adopted child to identify him. As a result of several legal decisions and state laws in the past two decades, however, he must consent to the adoption if he is identified, can be located, and has asserted his role in rearing the child in a timely fashion (Atwater, 1989). This has provoked both legal difficulties and withdrawn adoptions in recent years (Schwartz, 1983, 1986, 1993b).

Under the Uniform Parentage Act of 1987, "It has been deemed essential that the potential rights of the unknown or unascertained father be terminated in order to protect the adoption" (Atwater, 1989, p. 273, n. 38). Cases where the father may not have known of the existence of his child until months or more than a year later but requests custody promptly on learning he is a father, thus over-turning an adoption placement, have been the cause of mixed court rulings (Atwater, 1989; Hevesi, 1992; Schwartz, 1983, 1986, 1993b). To some judges, the biological relationship is paramount; to others, the child's "best interests" have first priority.

Why Did We Choose to Become Adoptive Parents?

Again, one must look at the era in which a couple decided that they wanted to become parents through adoption. Until the 1970s, this was one of the few alternatives available to the infertile couple. The other two principal alternatives were remaining childless or becoming foster parents. Thus, opting for adoption was a deliberate decision based on accepting an unwanted reality—the couple's infertility. Daly (1990) found, however, that not all couples felt that all attempts to resolve the infertility problem had to have failed before they could consider adoption as a road to parenthood. Rather, 28% of his subject couples had concurrent processes, "continuing to hope for a biological child while committing themselves increasingly to becoming adoptive parents" (p. 487). To them, the key issue after several years of frustration was to become parents.

Apart from all the pain and stress engendered by years of medical treatment, insensitivity on the part of family and friends about the lack of pregnancy as evidenced by their questions and their conversation, and the self-doubts arising about one's masculinity or femininity, opting to adopt someone else's biological offspring was, and is, a major decision (Schwartz, 1991). (Some couples who already have biological children also choose to adopt children for a variety of reasons.) Sometimes this was an option discussed with the couple's parents in an effort to obtain guidance and a sense of how accepting they would be of adoption. In one case, for example, the wife's grandmother, a very religious woman, conveyed via her daughter that adoption was a "mitzvah," a good deed. At the same time, the husband's parents were neutral to negative in their attitude toward the impending adoption. Confronting such conflicts and resolving them became yet another part of the decision-making process for the couple. Infertility support groups such as RESOLVE, a comparatively recent phenomenon, may also play a role in the couple's transition to prospective adoptive parenthood (Daly, 1988).

Having decided to adopt, the couple then had to decide whether to work with an adoption agency or to seek private adoption. They often found agency caseworkers intrusive in their questions about the most intimate as well as the most routine details of their lives. Biological parents did not (and do not) have to worry about their grades on an eligibility scorecard with respect to age, income, religion, outside interests, and housing as is true for prospective adoptive parents. Being placed on a long waiting list, or worse, being told that they did not meet the agency's criteria, turned many couples toward private adoption. In some cases, no agency served the community in which they lived. Today, these factors may also incline couples toward adopting an older child instead of an infant because of the shortage of infants available for adoption, toward transracial or transnational adoption, or toward adoption of a child with special needs (physically, emotionally, or mentally handicapped). In this last case, the child may well need mental health assistance regardless of whether he or she is in a biological or an adoptive family.

Once the adoption is completed, in what ways do the couple respond to the child? Is there a "distancing" because of the lack of biological ties, or is the child accepted and loved as their own from the outset? Is there, at some deeply subconscious level, continued mourning for the biological child the couple never had? Does one of the partners continue to wonder about "what *our* child would have looked like"? If so, does this thought intrude on the parent-child relationship?

Can Nontraditional Adoptions Work?

The number of healthy white infants available for adoption, as has been noted, has declined markedly in recent years because of the availability of early abortion as an option and because of the change in society's attitudes toward unwed parents and their offspring. There is also a shortage of adoptive families in nonwhite groups, while overseas, there is an abundance of children in need of families as an alternative to foster care or group homes. This has led to an increase in transracial and transnational adoptions by white individuals and couples, as well as to increasing adoptions of special needs children. The transracial and transnational adoptions are frequently opposed by groups of the child's biological heritage.

In the case of Native Americans, there is anxiety within the tribes that children adopted by non-Indians will lose their cultural heritage and ethnic identity, and that the tribes will lose the strengths of the younger generation (Schwartz, 1991). The tribes have already seen the damage done to some of their youth by education at boarding schools off the reservation that seek to prepare their students for the larger society. As a result, they have pressed for laws that would make transracial adoptions of their children difficult, if not impossible. One of these is the Indian Child Welfare Act of 1978 which gave first preference to Native American families and tribes in the adoption of American Indian children (Howard, 1984).

Similarly, the National Association of Black Social Workers has fought adoption of black children by white parents, alleging that this has negative effects on the child's development and cultural identity. In some studies, however, the findings suggest that "the deleterious consequences of delayed placement are far more serious than those of transracial adoption" (Silverman & Feigelman, 1981, p. 535).

As in other adoptive situations, age at the time of adoption appears to be the principal critical factor in the child's adjustment. Consider, for example, that in fiscal year 1989, 36.6% of children whose adoptions were finalized in 23 reporting states were aged 6 to 12 years and another 9.1% were 13 to 18 years old (Tatara, 1993). To counteract undesirable delays, the Senate Judiciary Committee, in October 1993, approved legislation "forbidding federally funded agencies from denying adoptions solely because the adoptive parents' race is different from the child's" (Glazer, 1993, p. 1043). As two authors of a book on adoption and foster care wrote, "The truth is that a young life is a terrible thing to waste, and children of color left in limbo while waiting for same-race parents are doomed to a life without roots" (McKelvey & Stevens, 1994, p. 152).

Arrangements for adoption of children from other countries involve United States' laws as well as those of other countries. Under our immigration laws, the child may qualify for immigration benefits as an orphan, if specific conditions are met (U.S. Dept. of Justice, 1990).

Elizabeth Bartholet (1993), a Harvard lawyer, mother of one biological youth and now a single parent, has provided a close look at the difficulties (and costs) with which she was confronted in adopting two young children in Peru. The bureaucratic snarls that caused her months of anxious residence in Lima typify the problems faced by many prospective adoptive parents at the transnational level. Laws change after their arrival in Rumania or Korea or somewhere in Latin America; they are taunted as "buyers" of children even as official hands are held out for baksheesh; and while they wait for the official seals on a mountain of documents, the would-be adoptive parents care for and come to love a baby who may or may not come home with them.

On the other hand, when the child arrives in the United States, parents need to be aware that there may be more social response to the child's skin color than to his or her national or cultural origins (Essa & O'Neil, 1989; Wardle, 1990). The postinfant child has a new language to learn as well as the task of acculturating to a totally different environment. That behavior and/or academic problems may develop is not surprising, although sometimes the difficulties arise from unrealistic expectations of school personnel (Essa & O'Neil, 1989). The risks may be greater for older international adoptees (Verhulst, Althaus, & Versluis-Den Bieman, 1990), as is the possibility that they may have suffered from malnutrition and minimal or abusive caregiving in their earlier years.

The Adoption Assistance and Child Welfare Act of 1980 was directed toward finding adoptive placements for special needs children who were in foster care (Glazer, 1993; Groze & Rosenthal, 1991, p. 67). These would be children who have sensory handicaps or other chronic medical problems, who are mentally retarded or learning disabled, or who have social or emotional disorders. They tend to be difficult to place in adoptive homes and, for that reason, to be older when they are eventually adopted. Their adoptive parents must not only be aware of their needs and prior experiences, but also must be prepared to deal with ongoing problems and the prevention of additional ones.

Groze and Rosenthal (1991) specifically studied the outcome of adoptions of these children by single parents, approximately 15% of a larger sample. The largest identified group of adopted children in the study tended to be mentally retarded girls, while the single parents were more often black and female, with the single women older than adoptive mothers who were part of a couple, and with lower incomes than adopting couples. They perceived the overall impact of the adoption as mostly or very positive significantly more often than did the two-parent families. There was no difference in educational functioning between children from single- or two-parent homes, and those "who had experienced group-home or psychiatric placement prior to adoption managed particularly well in single-parent adoptions" (Groze & Rosenthal, 1991, p. 75). Although the single-parent adoptive family is even more nonnormative than the adoptive family in general, Groze and Rosenthal suggested that this is a positive alternative that placement agencies may have overlooked.

Should I Search for My Biological Parents?

Traditionally, adoption records have been sealed. Since the 1980s, however, several organizations, most notably Concerned United Birthparents (CUB), have sought to overturn that policy in the interest of reuniting children with their biological mothers and occasionally with their biological fathers. Members of CUB "insist that were it not for coercive and insensitive adoption practices, coupled with a lack of family support, they would have been able to parent the children to whom they gave birth" (A. Brodzinsky, 1990, p. 299). CUB and similar organizations have made the community more aware of the emotional trauma that adoption represents for some birthparents, a trauma that can warrant mental health intervention. They provide a positive answer to the question of a search for birthparents.

From the viewpoint of adoptive parents, however, there is a question of the benefit to adopted children in opening the records (Geissinger, 1984). As of 1992, only Kansas, Hawaii, and Alaska had opened adoption records, although several other states have opened registries that enable the two parties to be reunited if all parties to the adoption agree (Morgan, 1992). Some of the groups involved in questioning adoption policies and practices believe that both biological parents and adoptees must agree to a meeting, whereas others insist that it is the adoptee's right to know his or her parents whether or not the latter want to be located. This raises an additional question: In the event of differing desires, whose rights should prevail?

There are certainly legitimate reasons to seek reunion, or at least for the child to obtain some information about his or her biological parents. These reasons tend to center on medical data, both for their own benefit and for the children they themselves may have, although other adopted children may want to know whom they resemble or what their ethnic heritage is; or they hope "to heal the wound caused by the separation [from the biological parents], and thereby to provide a more authentic base for living their lives" (Andersen, 1988, p. 19).

Are Adopted Children More Likely to Have Problems?

Over the years, many studies have suggested that adopted children are over-represented in clinical populations (Brodzinsky & Schecter, 1990; Kirk, 1964). Their perspective is either that nature outweighs nurture in the behavior of adoptees, as several studies based on Scandinavian populations suggest, or that the fact of adoption creates such tensions in the adopted child that acting-out or other abnormal behavior occurs. Indeed, David Brodzinsky (1990) found that a common thread connecting the problems of adoptees and their families "is that adoption is experienced as *stressful* by many children and parents and, consequently, results in a variety of coping efforts, some of which are successful in handling the stress and others which are not" (p. 4). However, it is unclear in the text of the study whether the stress is caused by the adoption status or by the relinquishment that preceded it. When the coping efforts are inadequate to handle the stress, seeking help to learn more effective strategies should be perceived as a constructive move rather than necessarily as an indication of pathology. On the other hand, Brodzinsky (1993), after an extensive review of relevant literature, concluded, "The way children view their adopted experience and cope with it may be tied to the feedback they receive about their adoptive status from the society in which they live, the peers with whom they have contact, and most important, the specific family in which they are reared" (p. 162).

Inasmuch as many adoptive parents are well educated and are aware of the difficulties faced as youngsters develop, they seem to be more ready to seek professional help when problems arise than is true of the general population. This can account for some of the disproportionate share of adoptees in clinical populations, although even so these numbers represent only a small minority of adoptees.

If adoptees represent 1% to 2% of children under age 18, which the Brodzinskys and colleagues use as a working assumption, then a 5% rate of adoptees in outpatient mental health settings, 8% to 15% of children in inpatient centers, and 5% to 7% of children in the special education population (Brodzinsky &

Steiger, 1991) indeed constitutes overrepresentation. One key question has to be whether those classified as neurologically impaired, perceptually impaired, or emotionally disturbed were placed as healthy, young infants, or at a later age. Another question relates to the point in the child's development when the need for special education became apparent (before school entrance or after).

Few of the studies differentiate between the child adopted as a healthy infant and the one adopted at a later age, perhaps after one or more foster home placements or as a special needs child who was already troubled at arrival in the adoptive family. Few of the studies consider, also, the attitude of the adoptive parents toward seeking counseling or therapy when there is a problem. Prior experience with a social service agency, or with support groups, may predispose them to seek help when they have a concern with which they cannot deal. In much of society, however, there is still a negative attitude toward psychotherapy, as if seeking help is an admission of defeat rather than a constructive and positive act.

What about Disrupted Adoptions?

Rare but real, there are adoptive families that cannot seem to "work" no matter how much effort is expended or therapy sought. In some cases, deliberately or not, the couple was not informed by the placement intermediary that the child was a "crack" baby, or was abused by biological or foster parents. In other instances, for one reason or another, psychological bonding simply does not occur and an intolerable situation results for all parties. The adoption may be disrupted before it is legally finalized or at some other point. In general, courts perceive adoption as a lifetime commitment and will rarely overturn a completed adoption except in cases where there was deliberate misrepresentation or concealment of facts by an agency (Hayes, 1992). California enacted a mandatory disclosure law in 1974 to require agencies to release known medical information on adoptees, but this law (and those in other states) still does not differentiate between newborns and older children (Dickson, 1991). Prior history on the latter is particularly important, as we have seen, because of the potential negative effects of earlier experiences on them.

Disrupted adoptions are painful for everyone involved. The children lose the hoped-for acceptance by a family (although, if old enough to be aware of it, they may have expected rejection at the same time) and also the benefits of consistent caregiving, which is important to their healthy psychosocial development (Elbow & Knight, 1987). For the adoptive parents, a disrupted adoption tends to have negative impact on their self-esteem in addition to the loss of the hoped-for child, the loss of their roles as parents if they have no other children, and the need to work their way through the several resulting stages of bereavement and grief.

In a review of studies of adoption disruption by Festinger (1990), a few factors emerged as predictive of negative placement outcomes. One was age: The child who was older at the time of adoption placement tended to be in the disruption group more often than younger children. The average number of earlier foster placements, as well as placement in a group facility, also militated against a successful outcome. Serious problem behaviors at the time of placement, some resulting from prior placements and others related to medical conditions, were more frequent in disrupted adoptions, especially when the adoptive parents had great difficulty coping with the problems. Those who had been more psychologically bonded to their families of origin, typically older children, "may even have viewed adoption as an act of disloyalty," according to Festinger (p. 210). Demographic characteristics of the adoptive parents, and the presence of biological children in the home (and their age, sex, and race), presented no conclusive evidence suggesting positive or negative outcomes of adoption. In situations where the placing agency provided inadequate or inconsistent support services at the time of and subsequent to the placement, there was a also greater tendency for disruption, again especially with the older children.

A different aspect of disrupted adoption, though not always identified by that term, occurs when biological parents withdraw consent for the adoption. This appears to occur more often in independent adoptions than in agency adoptions. This was seen in the 1993 case of "Baby Jessica," (Schwartz, 1993b) and the 1995 case of "Baby Richard," (Associated Press, 1995) and represented a severe rupture of the children's stability and the psychological bonding that had already occurred between them and their would-be adoptive parents. The negative impact on the adults was apparent on national television; the long-term effects on these children can only be hypothesized.

The adoptive parents in such situations certainly experience the sense of loss and the grief mentioned earlier and may need to confront these with professional help. Elbow and Knight (1987) have suggested a "good-bye ceremony" to provide a sense of closure, but this would seem more appropriate where the child is not an infant or where there are other children, adoptive or biological, in the home. On the legal front, Dickson (1991) has proposed modifications in existing California law that would require the birthmother (or birthparents) to give irrevocable consent closer to the time of adoption placement, thus providing some reduction in the risk to adoptive parents.

Explaining the disruption of an adoption to very young "siblings" may be overwhelming to the grief-stricken parents, resulting perhaps in a minimal explanation and subsequent repression of the entire event for many years. This would be especially true where a biological parent had withdrawn consent to the adoption, which could evoke very threatening questions to the adoptive parents from another child as to why his or her parents did not similarly reclaim him or her. Rather than have the remaining child(ren) feel a renewed sense of rejection, the parents may simply not discuss the matter ever again.

RECOMMENDATIONS

In counseling pregnant adolescents, it seems important to make them more aware of alternatives to early parenthood such as higher educational achievement and better career opportunities. This assumes the existence of community programs that offer the needed medical care, social services, educational programs, legal advice, and job training to support a decision to choose an alternative. Some such programs have been funded by the Office of Adolescent Pregnancy Programs, and others have been developed by local community efforts, possibly involving interagency cooperation (Donnelly & Voydanoff, 1991). One program, in Billings, Montana, specifically targets unmarried teen fathers in an effort to teach them the realities of parenting, financial responsibility, and the value of completing their education ("Local look," 1994).

Kalmuss, Namerow, and Bauer (1992) similarly stress the importance of educational aspirations and achievement for teenage mothers, which can be conveyed to them by school counselors as well as social workers and mental health therapists:

> Insofar as aspirations are related to educational attainment, becoming a teenage mother may decrease the number of years of schooling a young woman ultimately completes by lowering her aspirations. Diminished educational attainment, in turn, has implications for occupational attainment, income, and dependence on public assistance. (p. 89)

Although counseling of the unwed mother is needed if she is to make an appropriate decision for her future and the child's, it is also apparent that continued counseling is appropriate if she decides to place the child for adoption. She is entitled to grieve, rather than being advised simply to put this behind her and out of her mind. As with any other loss, there may be a need for professional help in dealing with this type of bereavement and in focusing on reorganization of her life even as she works through her grief (A. Brodzinsky, 1990).

With the adoptive parents, it may be relevant to the presenting problem to discover whether they reject, deny, acknowledge, or insist on any differences distinguishing their family and biological families. A continuum of recognition of "differences" appears to be more realistic than an "either-or" perspective as has been suggested by Kirk (1964), Di Giulio (1987), and others. These views of their families, or "coping strategies" as Kirk (1964) called them, certainly affect the adoptees' self-image as well as their relationships with the adoptive parents. Kaye (1990) suggested, however, that a strategy in which "The more problems they had had, the *more* the parents and children attributed those problems to adoption and the *more* they thought about the birthparents" might be an attempt to cope with the problems, but that it was hardly an adaptive strategy (p. 137). He warns professionals working with adoptive families "to recognize that a sprinkling of distinguishings amid many assurances of normalcy is probably healthy and accurate, rather than label all such assurances as 'rejection of differences' in a pathological sense" (p. 141).

In cases of transracial or some transnational adoptions, of course, it would be impossible to deny the fact of adoption. However, counseling may be warranted for children who are confused about their ethnic identity or are finding it difficult to cope with the prejudice and hostility of peers or others. Adoptive parents in these cases may seek counseling on how best to deal with the race and culture issues. Indeed, they may even seek guidance prior to entering into such an adoption, if only to prevent as many problems as possible.

If clients have experienced a disrupted adoption, on the other hand, they have other concerns. They will need to work through feelings of grief and bereavement if the biological parent(s) reclaimed the child, feelings of anger at the intermediary where they had been inadequately informed of the child's problems, and/or feelings of inadequacy or failure as parents if they had been unable to meet the child's needs.

In this complex world, it behooves all parents to raise their children so that they develop into resilient and responsible adults. What characterizes such a person? Flach (1988) described the resilient personality, and some of its elements that are particularly relevant in the rearing of nonbiological children, suggest goals that the clinician can help the adoptive parents meet:

> A *strong, supple sense of self-esteem.* This has to begin with building a sense of trust and attachment from the start of the relationship (Howe, 1992), but may take extra effort as many adopted children feel, at least at times, as if they must have had little worth to their biological parents.
>
> A *high level of personal discipline and a sense of responsibility.* Assertive youngsters, especially adolescents, may require extra assistance in light of what they perceive as irresponsibility on the part of their biological parents.
>
> *Insight into one's own feelings and those of others, and the ability to communicate these in an appropriate manner.* To the degree that the parents know of the difficulties that caused the biological parents to place their child with someone else, such information may be tactfully shared, with the suggestion that the child "put on their shoes" to gain insight into the biological parent(s)'s thinking and subsequent decisions.
>
> *Focus, a commitment to life, and a philosophical framework within which personal experiences can be interpreted with meaning and hope, even at life's seemingly most hopeless moments.* This is important for everyone, but perhaps especially so for adopted children who may have been moved from home to home to yet another home. Parents may ask these children to reflect on what they have learned in the several families with which they have lived over time, and what the relative stability of the adoptive home has meant to them.

CONCLUSION

The answer to the title question has to be equivocal. Adoptive parents confront the same joys and trials of child rearing that biological parents face. They are usually as proud of or as anxious about their children as are any biological parents. In addition, however, they have "ghosts" hovering in the background—the biological parents—who may emerge with some frequency in an open adoption, who may be actively sought as the adolescent approaches adulthood, or who may forever remain somewhere "out there." To some degree, the effects of their ghostly presence vary with the era in which the child was adopted, with the parents' perception(s) of their chosen role, and with the relationship that has developed over time between the adoptee and his or her adoptive parents. In addition, the parents may have their own unresolved feelings about infertility, adoption, and genetic predispositions versus the environment they provide.

It is essential that therapists and counselors, when meeting with one member group of the adoption triangle, ascertain whether their clients are seeking help because of the adoption factor in their lives or for more ubiquitous reasons of the life cycle. It is not the professional's role to create new problems by urging reunion of biological parents with their offspring as a solution to the parents' more mundane problems, nor is it appropriate to emphasize the adoption aspect where the adoptee has dyslexia and needs to learn techniques to deal with that problem. On the other hand, acting-out behavior on the part of an early adolescent may be related to identity-seeking that, although perfectly normal behavior at this age, becomes more complex in the adoptive family and should be treated in that context when appropriate.

The stance to be taken by clinicians should be to regard the client(s) first as part of a family and only secondarily to deal with adoption issues as they are relevant to the functioning of the family members as individuals and as a family unit. It is no more appropriate to make unwarranted assumptions about the nonnormative nature of adoptive families' concerns than it is to jump to conclusions about the dysfunctional qualities of biological or remarried families without adequate supporting evidence. On the positive side, therapists can do much to reassure clients that many of the questions they raise are perfectly normal, as are many of the problems they face. As always, the goal is to help the client toward a more fulfilling life and to deal with life's challenges in the healthiest possible way for that client.

REFERENCES

Andersen, R. S. (1988). Why adoptees search: Motives and more. *Child Welfare, 67,* 15–19.

Associated Press. (1995, May 1). Adoptive parents hand over boy in 4-year custody fight. *The New York Times,* p. A13.

Atwater, M. W. (1989). A modern-day Solomon's dilemma: What of the unwed father's rights? *University of Detroit Law Review, 66,* 267–296.

Barth, R. P. (1987). Adolescent mothers' beliefs about open adoption. *Social Casework, 68,* 323–331.

Bartholet, E. (1993). *Family bonds: Adoption and the politics of parenting.* New York: Houghton Mifflin.

Brodzinsky, A. B. (1990). Surrendering an infant for adoption: The birthmother experience. In D. M. Brodzinsky & M. D. Schecter (Eds.), *The psychology of adoption* (pp. 295–315). New York: Oxford University Press.

Brodzinsky, D. M. (1990). A stress and coping model of adoption adjustment. In D. M. Brodzinsky & M. D. Schecter (Eds.), *The psychology of adoption* (pp. 3–24). New York: Oxford University Press.

Brodzinsky, D. M. (1993). Long-term outcomes in adoption. *The Future of Children, 3*(1), 153–166.

Brodzinsky, D. M., & Schecter, M. D. (Eds.). (1990). *The psychology of adoption.* New York: Oxford University Press.

Brodzinsky, D. M., & Steiger, C. (1991). Prevalence of adoptees among special education populations. *Journal of Learning Disabilities, 24,* 484–489.

Cook, W. (1992). Open adoption: Can visitation with natural family members be in the child's best interest? *Journal of Family Law, 30,* 471–492.

Daly, K. (1988). Reshaped parenthood identity: The transition to adoptive parenthood. *Journal of Contemporary Ethnography, 17,* 40–66.

Daly, K. (1990). Infertility resolution and adoption readiness. *Families in Society, 71,* 483–492.

Dickson, J. H. (1991). The emerging rights of adoptive parents: Substance or specter? *UCLA Law Review, 38,* 917–990.

Di Giulio, J. F. (1987). Assuming the adoptive parent role. *Social Casework, 68,* 561–566.

Donnelly, B. W., & Voydanoff, P. (1991). Factors associated with releasing for adoption among adolescent mothers. *Family Relations, 40,* 404–410.

Elbow, M., & Knight, M. (1987). Adoption disruption: Losses, transitions, and tasks. *Social Casework, 68,* 546–552.

Erikson, E. K. (1950). *Childhood and society.* New York: Norton.

Essa, E. L., & O'Neil, L. (1989). The school and transracially adopted children. *Educational Leadership, 46*(5), 77–79.

Festinger, T. (1990). Adoption disruption: Rates and correlates. In D. M. Brodzinsky & M. D. Schecter (Eds.), *The psychology of adoption* (pp. 201–218). New York: Oxford University Press.

Flach, F. (1988). *Resilience: Discovering a new strength at times of stress.* New York: Fawcett Columbine.

Geissinger, S. (1984). Adoptive parents' attitudes toward open birth records. *Family Relations, 33,* 579–585.

Glazer, S. (1993, November). Adoption. *The CQ Researcher, 3,* 1033–1055.

Groze, V. K., & Rosenthal, J. A. (1991). Single parents and their adopted children: A psychosocial analysis. *Families in Society, 72,* 67–77.

Hayes, S. W. (1992, April). Sending children back. *ABA Journal, 78,* 88.

Hevesi, D. (1992, October). Court denies father's late request to overturn adoption. *The New York Times,* p. B6.

Howard, M. (1984). Transracial adoption: Analysis of the best interests standard. *Notre Dame Law Review, 59,* 503–555.

Howe, D. (1992). Assessing adoptions in difficulty. *British Journal of Social Work, 22,* 1–16.

Kalmuss, D., Namerow, P. B., & Bauer, U. (1992). Short-term consequences of parenting versus adoption among young unmarried women. *Journal of Marriage and the Family, 54,* 80–90.

Kaye, K. (1990). Acknowledgement or rejection of differences? In D. M. Brodzinsky & M. D. Schecter (Eds.), *The psychology of adoption* (pp. 121–143). New York: Oxford University Press.

Kirk, D. (1964). *Shared fate.* New York: Free Press.

"Local look." (1994, March). *NEA Today, 12*(7), 7.

McKelvey, C. A., & Stevens, J. E. (1994). *Adoption crisis: The truth behind adoption and foster care.* Golden, CO: Fulcrum.

Morgan, P. (1992, June). The searchers. *Applause,* 24–25.

Reitz, M., & Watson, K. W. (1992). *Adoption and the family system.* New York: Guilford.

Rosenberg, E. B. (1992). *The adoption life cycle: The children and their families through the years.* New York: Free Press.

Schwartz, L. L. (1983). Contested adoption cases: Grounds for conflict between psychology and the law. *Professional Psychology, 14,* 444–456.

Schwartz, L. L. (1986). Unwed fathers and adoption custody disputes. *American Journal of Family Therapy, 14,* 347–355.

Schwartz, L. L. (1991). *Alternatives to infertility.* New York: Brunner/Mazel.

Schwartz, L. L. (1993a). The interaction of field theory, family systems theory, and children's rights. *American Journal of Family Therapy, 21,* 267–273.

Schwartz, L. L. (1993b). What *is* a family? A contemporary view. *Contemporary Family Therapy, 15,* 429–442.

Silverman, A. R., & Feigelman, W. (1981). The adjustment of black children adopted by white families. *Social Casework, 62,* 529–536.

Sorosky, A. D., Baran, A., & Panner, R. (1984). *The adoption triangle: Sealed or open records: How they affect adoptees, birth parents and adoptive parents.* Garden City, NY: Anchor Press/Doubleday.

Tatara, T. (1993). *Characteristics of children in substitute and adoptive care: A statistical summary of the VCIS National Child Welfare data base.* Washington, DC: American Public Welfare Association.

U.S. Department of Justice, Immigration and Naturalization Service. (1990). *The immigration of adopted and prospective adoptive children.* Washington, DC: U.S. Government Printing Office (M-249Y).

Verhulst, F. C., Althaus, M., & Versluis-Den Bieman, H. J. M. (1990). Problem behavior in international adoptees: II. Age at placement. *Journal of the American Academy of Child and Adolescent Psychiatry, 29,* 104–111.

Wardle, F. (1990). Endorsing children's differences: Meeting the needs of adopted minority children. *Young Children, 45*(5), 44–46.

PART FOUR

Impact of Unusual Events on Families

CHAPTER 7

Families of People with Mental Illness

DIANE T. MARSH, HARRIET P. LEFLEY, and JUNE R. HUSTED

Particularly since the 1980s, there have been significant developments in theory, research, and practice concerned with families of people with serious mental illness. Serious mental illness includes schizophrenia, major depressive disorder, bipolar disorder, schizoaffective disorder, delusional disorder, panic disorder, obsessive-compulsive disorder, and other persistent and disabling conditions. Many factors have influenced these changes, including (a) deinstitutionalization, which has resulted in a mental health system that is as much family-based as community-based; (b) greater recognition of the legitimate rights and needs of families; (c) new evidence regarding the biological substrate of serious mental illness; (d) documentation of the devastating impact of serious mental illness on families; (e) increasing acknowledgment of the family's positive contributions and expertise; (f) availability of effective family-oriented intervention strategies; (g) national initiatives that mandate the involvement of consumers and families; and (h) the consumer-advocacy movement, which has moved families into more assertive, informed, and involved roles.

This larger context has important implications for clinicians, who are facing new opportunities, assuming new roles, employing new modes of working with families, applying new models for professional practice, and developing new intervention strategies.

A SYSTEMS APPROACH TO PROFESSIONAL PRACTICE

General systems theory offers a unique vantage point for professional practice with families of people who have mental illness. Reflecting the concept of hierarchic and integrative levels, a systems perspective facilitates the movement from one level of analysis to another and acknowledges the inherent interdependence among levels. With respect to the familial experience of serious mental illness, for example, it is essential to focus on the levels of the ecological system, the family system, family subsystems, and individual family members.

At the highest level, an ecological systems perspective views individuals and families as embedded in a larger sociocultural matrix. Such a broad perspective is essential in working with these families, whose experience with mental illness is etched by the larger society. Society defines the nature of mental illness and applies diagnostic labels, determines social priorities and mental health policies, establishes the locus and form of treatment, and creates the climate in which families come to terms with the illness. There is increasing recognition of the value of an ecological perspective for conceptualizing the familial experiences of disability (e.g., Seligman & Darling, 1989); of chronic health problems (e.g., McDaniel, Hepworth, & Doherty, 1992); and of serious mental illness (e.g., Marsh, 1992a).

Moving to the level of the family system, the expertise of clinicians prepares them to understand the impact of serious mental illness on families and to assist families in coping with this catastrophic event. In response to their relative's illness, as Lefley (1989) has discussed, family members are subject to a powerful subjective burden, which consists of the personal suffering of family members in response to their relative's illness, and to an objective burden, which refers to the reality demands that confront the family. The subjective burden often includes a range of intense emotions, such as anger, guilt, and despair; a grieving process related to the loss of the mentally healthy family member they knew and loved prior to the illness; symbolic losses concerned with hopes, dreams, and expectations; the experience of chronic sorrow as the tragedy of mental illness is woven into the familial tapestry on a continuing basis; an emotional roller coaster that results from the characteristic pattern of remission and relapse; and empathic pain as they share in their relative's suffering. Here are the words of one mother:

> The problems with my daughter were like a black hole inside of me into which everything else had been drawn. My grief and pain were so intense sometimes that I barely got through the day. It felt like a mourning process, as if I were dealing with the loss of the daughter I had loved for 18 years, for whom there was so much potential. That daughter was now lost to me, and I had to adjust to another one who was mentally ill, who might need a lifetime of care, and who was not going to survive in any meaningful sense. (Marsh, 1992a, p. 10)

Components of the objective burden include the need to cope with symptomatic behavior, with crisis intervention and caregiving responsibilities, with family conflict and strain, with the mental health system, with social stigma in the larger society, and perhaps with the criminal justice system. The following woman, whose mother had schizophrenia, describes the impact of the illness on her family:

> Mental illness is a ravaging, devastating disease, which disrupts a family, probably more than any other. I remember my mother crying a lot, being hostile a lot, and family members trying to convince her to go to the hospital. It is a financial strain on the family and disrupts interpersonal relationships. It often isolates the family because of the stigma and the family member's inappropriate social behavior. (Marsh & Dickens, in press)

As this family member conveys, the assault on the integrity of the family system presents many potential risks, including the risk of family disruption and stress, of failure to balance the needs of all family members, and of family disintegration. As with any catastrophic event, however, there is the potential for families to demonstrate competence and mastery, to strengthen family bonds, and to change in constructive and adaptive ways. This woman grew up with a brother who had schizophrenia:

> My husband once asked me how it was possible that I evolved unscathed from my upbringing with a mentally ill brother. It never occurred to me that as a family we should have fallen apart. To me my brother's illness was just a fact, like Daddy went to work on Monday mornings. It was okay for him to be that way, and it was okay for us to be happy. It was simple—you love your family, you care for each individual, you respect each other. It always felt solid, it felt right. (Marsh & Dickens, in press)

Shifting to the level of family subsystems, a differentiated approach to professional practice offers clinicians many opportunities to meet the varying needs of parents, spouses, siblings, and children. The impact of the mental illness on individual family members depends partly on its timing in the life spans of the individual and the family and on the characteristics of the illness itself (see Marsh, 1992a; Rolland, 1994). For example, because of their developmental status, young family members are particularly vulnerable to the adverse consequences of a relative's mental illness (Marsh & Dickens, in press). The disability of a family member functions as an "energy sink" that consumes energy needed for normal development (Bubolz & Whiren, 1984), deflecting young family members from their expected course.

The following woman has a brother with schizophrenia. She talks about the impact of his mental illness on her own life:

> I became the perfect child to spare my parents any more grief. I was forced to become responsible. In many ways it forced me to accomplish things in my life I might not have otherwise done. But I have spent my life trying to run away from this problem. Feeling guilty and helpless, the unending sorrow for not being able to help. I have not felt entitled to be happy most of my adult life. (Marsh & Dickens, in press)

From a developmental perspective, the presence of mental illness in the family may undermine the acquisition of basic trust during infancy, the development of peer relationships and academic skills during childhood, and the establishment of a secure sense of identity during adolescence. A child who is confronted from birth with parental mental illness may be vulnerable to all these risks. This early exposure to mental illness may result in a residue of "unfinished business" from childhood and a reduction in the energy available for the tasks of adulthood. For example, in response to two national surveys (Marsh et al., 1993), adult siblings and children reported that their earlier experience with the mental illness of a close relative had a significant and often negative impact on their self-concept, on their career, on their adult relationships, on their marriage and childrearing, and on their family responsibilities.

This woman carried a dual legacy into adulthood, having grown up with the mental illness of both a parent and a sibling:

> I have spent the last 25 years trying to find confidence, love, acceptance. I am extremely sensitive and weep easily. I avoid intimacy but crave it desperately. I want more friends but fear to trust. I took on a role of peacemaker at a young age and developed some exceptional coping skills: problem solving, soothing, getting along with difficult people, and intellectual searching. I am a doer and a fixer but paid a price. (Marsh & Dickens, in press)

Finally, at the level of individual family members, clinicians need to acknowledge the unique biological subsystems and psychosocial experiences of each member of the family. In summary, then, clinicians who work with families of people who have mental illness can enhance their effectiveness by assuming an ecological systems orientation that acknowledges the importance of the larger context in which the family system is embedded, by a family systems orientation that delineates the impact of this nonnormative event on the family as a unit, by a family subsystems orientation that acknowledges the experiences and needs associated with particular roles within the family, and by an individual orientation that recognizes the singular reality of personal lives. Here is one man's depiction of the impact of mental illness on his own life. He has experienced the serious mental illness of a mother and three siblings, including a brother who committed suicide:

> It was like a large cloud moved over our heads and everyone was paralyzed for years. This mental illness business affected all aspects of my life—self-esteem, trust, intimacy, hope, and emotional development. I lost my ability to feel for many years. Loss of hope, helplessness, confusion, powerlessness. We needed professional understanding and validation of our experience. (Marsh & Dickens, in press)

NEW ROLES FOR CLINICIANS

Professional practice with families of people who have mental illness offers many roles for clinicians. These include traditional roles as providers of clinical services, including individual, marital, family, and group therapy. An earlier generation of clinicians was often exposed to conceptual models that incorporated assumptions of family pathogenesis or dysfunction and that mandated treatment of all members of the family. As we will discuss, these unverified assumptions often had an adverse impact on family-professional relationships and on family members, including young siblings and children. Two siblings relating their experiences:

Even a few years ago, blame was placed on mothers and dysfunctional families. As an adolescent, I blamed myself for my brother's disease. The most helpful professionals presented the facts of schizophrenia in a nonjudgmental way. Families need education and support. . . .

I heard what doctors said about childrearing and mother's rejection causing the illness. I still have a lot of anger toward the mental health professionals who made everything even more difficult, pouring salt in wounds. (Marsh & Dickens, in press)

In fact, as is the case for all families, families of people with mental illness vary along a continuum of competence. Some families demonstrate mastery in fulfilling all their functions; others experience difficulty in solving even minor problems; and most families fall someplace in the middle of the continuum. Accordingly, clinicians need to avoid making general assumptions about families and to evaluate each family on its own terms. For the majority of family members who do not need traditional treatment, clinicians can assume constructive roles as providers of nonclinical services, such as educational programs and support groups, and as family consultants. As Bernheim (1989) has discussed, family consultants can offer expertise, skills, and advice to families, who maintain primary responsibility for determining their own goals and implementing decisions. She notes that consultation can result in a range of outcomes, including a decision to decline further services or to receive nonclinical or clinical services, singly or in combination. Consumer satisfaction is the central outcome variable in family consultation.

Wynne, Weber, and McDaniel (1986) have discussed the rationale for a consultative model for working with families and other systems, defining consultation as the process in which a consultee seeks assistance from a consultant to identify or clarify a concern or problem and to explore options available for problem resolution. The authors cite six advantages of systems consultation: (a) the nature of the problem is not prejudged; (b) the meta position of the consultant offers advantages for assessment of system issues; (c) consultation facilitates the reframing of problems; (d) consultation can emphasize health, strengths, and positive resources; (e) collaborative relationships between consultant and consultee can be readily established; and (f) a consultant role offers a base for flexible shifts to alternative professional roles.

NEW MODES OF FAMILY-PROFESSIONAL RELATIONSHIPS

As Lefley (1994) has discussed, until relatively recently, relationships between mental health professionals and the families of people with serious mental illness were informed primarily by variables that were both structural and ideological. Structural variables included the isolation of people with serious mental illness and their long-term stay in state hospitals; years of living in a remote institution rendered these family members marginal to the family system. Ideological variables included the prevailing theories of family patho-genesis and the therapies derived from their basic assumptions. In response to these variables, clinicians became the patient's protector and, in many cases, the family's antagonist.

On a more subtle but equally powerful level, family-professional relation-ships have also been influenced by Western value orientations that seek causes and solutions to most of life's problems in human agency, particularly in envi-ronmental experiences. In the case of serious mental illness, these experiences were assumed to involve family dynamics. Based on the unverified premise that psychotic systems would cease when they were no longer needed to sustain a dysfunctional family system, family members were often catapulted into fam-ily therapy, sometimes lacking informed consent (McElroy, 1990). In one study, for example, 50% of parents of children and adolescents with serious emotional disturbance reported that they had been required to participate in family therapy as a condition for receiving treatment for their child (Marsh, Koeske, & Schultz, 1993). Family members who encounter this type of family therapy often experience frustration when their expressed needs for informa-tion, support, and illness management are ignored (Hatfield, 1983).

Fortunately, professional attitudes and behaviors have gradually been changing, chiefly as a result of the proliferation of biological and genetic re-search findings that led to modifications in etiological theory. Indeed, the 1980s witnessed a transformation in relationships between families and pro-fessionals, reflected in a zeitgeist for more favorable attitudes, cognitions, and alliances (Lefley, 1989), and in an emphasis on "building bridges" between the two groups (Backer & Richardson, 1989). The new modes of family-professional relationships are essentially collaborative partnerships designed to build on the strengths and expertise of all parties; to respect the needs, desires, concerns, and priorities of families; to enable families to play an active role in decisions that affect them; and to establish mutual goals for treatment and rehabilitation. There is much recognition of the value of a col-laborative mode for professional practice (e.g., Lefley & Johnson, 1990; Marsh, 1992a; Peternelj-Taylor & Hartley, 1993).

The following mother affirms the value of a more collaborative approach with family members:

> When I went to the hospital out there, it was really a different system. It was wonderful to have some doctor call me in and tell me about my son's illness, ex-plain everything, give me choices, and tell me what he thought was the best, all the whys and ifs. I wanted to know how to deal with the grief and pain and tur-moil in my life. I also wanted answers to why the system worked as it did. (Marsh, 1992a, p. 2)

A useful way of thinking about family-professional relationships is in terms of an institutional alliance with families that is designed to meet the needs of all family members and to complement the therapeutic alliance that is established with the mentally ill relative for purposes of treatment (see Grunebaum & Friedman, 1988). Reflecting a family systems perspective, an institutional alliance can assist families in providing maximum support to the recovering client (Bernheim, 1982); can offer essential understanding and support to family members (Stewart, 1984); and can enhance their own problem solving, competence, and self-esteem (Goldstein, 1981).

In offering suggestions for professionals who work with families, this sibling mentions the barrier of confidentiality:

> A major problem in the mental health system is the exclusion of relatives under the guise of client confidentiality. Involve them! Acknowledge them and their grief, their loss, anger, and frustration. They are hungry for information. Help them separate the person from the disease. Give them concrete ways to deal with their realities. Do not blame. (Marsh & Dickens, in press)

In fact, there are many ways to meet the needs of all members of the family while honoring the principle of confidentiality, including use of release of information forms designed specifically for family members (see Figure 7.1).

NEW MODELS FOR PROFESSIONAL PRACTICE

The new models for professional practice with families emphasize their strengths, resources, and competencies, which traditionally have received little acknowledgment. Two such models will be discussed: a competence paradigm and a coping and adaptation framework.

A Competence Paradigm

A competence paradigm for professional practice with families offers a constructive alternative to the pathology paradigm that has often guided professional practice in the past. As indicated in Table 7.1, competence and pathology paradigms differ in many respects.

In contrast to a pathology paradigm, a competence paradigm offers a developmental model that views families as competent or potentially competent; that emphasizes their positive characteristics; that regards professionals as enabling agents and families as collaborators; that has as its goal the enablement and empowerment of families; that assumes an ecological systems framework; and that employs an educational services model. A competence paradigm provides a comprehensive framework that subsumes some elements of a pathology paradigm. For example, a competence paradigm acknowledges the possible presence of competence deficits, as well as the value of professional intervention designed to help families correct these deficits.

CONSENT TO RELEASE CONFIDENTIAL INFORMATION TO FAMILY MEMBERS

NAME: _____ DOB: _____ SS#: _____

I hereby request and authorize (SPECIFY AGENCY) _____
to release verbal information regarding me to the individual(s) listed below. I understand that the purpose
of this release is to improve communication between the above-named agency and the individual(s) listed
below and to assist in my treatment. Treatment began at this agency on (SPECIFY DATE)_____.

****

I hereby request and authorize you to release the information indicated below to the following individual(s)

(SPECIFY NAME/RELATIONSHIP): _____

You have my permission to release verbally the following information:

    ___ Name of Case Manager   ___ Name of Therapist(s)
    ___ Service Plan   ___ Treatment Program(s)
    ___ Medication   ___ Treatment Plan
    ___ Scheduled Appointments   ___ Discharge Plans
    ___ Admission to/Discharge from Any Facility

    ___ Other (SPECIFY): _____

                    _____

****

I understand that this gives my consent for the verbal release of information to the individual(s) listed
above. I also understand that this allows the above-mentioned individual(s) to provide information to my
therapist or case manager.

THIS CONSENT WILL REMAIN IN EFFECT UNTIL I GIVE WRITTEN REVOCATION.

_____	__/_____	_____	__/_____
Witness #1	Date	Client	Date
_____	__/_____	_____	__/_____
Witness #2	Date	Parent/Legal Guardian	Date

(Second witness needed if client is unable to give verbal consent.)

---

*Adapted from a form developed by the Allegheny County Mental Health/Mental Retardation
Program, Pittsburgh, PA.

Note: From "Working with Families of People with Serious Mental Illness" by D. T. Marsh, 1992.
In *Innovations in Clinical Practice: A Source Book,* L. VandeCreek, S. Knapp, and T. L. Jackson
(Eds.), Vol. 11, pp. 389–402, Sarasota, FL: Professional Resource Press. Copyright by Professional Resource Press. Reprinted with permission.

Figure 7.1   Release of Information Form*

A competence paradigm offers many advantages for clinicians (e.g., Marsh,
1992a; Masterpasqua, 1989). The paradigm fosters the development of alliances between families and professionals; facilitates the identification, assessment, and enhancement of the competencies that are relevant to coping
with serious mental illness; encourages more precise theory and research concerned with families; provides a blueprint for designing, implementing, and

TABLE 7.1   A Paradigm Shift in Professional Practice with Families

Pathology Paradigm	Competence Paradigm
Nature of Paradigm	
Disease-based medical model	Health-based developmental model
Families Viewed as	
Pathological, pathogenic, or dysfunctional	Competent or potentially competent
Areas of Emphasis on	
Weaknesses, liabilities, and illness	Strengths, resources, and wellness
Role of Professionals	
Practitioners	Enabling agents
Role of Families	
Clients or patients	Collaborators
Basis for Assessment	
Clinical typologies	Competencies and competence deficits
Goal of Intervention	
Treatment of family pathology or dysfunction	Enablement and empowerment
Modus Operandi	
Provision of psychotherapy	Enhancement of coping effectiveness
Systemic Perspective	
Family systems	Ecological systems
Service Model	
Authoritarian model	Educational model

From "Working with Families of People with Serious Mental Illness" by D. T. Marsh. In *Innovations in Clinical Practice: A Source Book,* L. VandeCreek, S. Knapp, and T. L. Jackson (Eds.), Vol. II, p. 391, 1992, Sarasota, FL: Professional Resource Press. Copyright 1992 by the Professional Resource Exchange. Adapted by permission.

evaluating professional services; improves the service system for people with mental illness; and promotes the empowerment of families. Our research with family members has provided much evidence for the potential competence of families under conditions of severe stress.

For example, this 34-year-old woman has a brother with bipolar disorder. Her family has served as a cornerstone of his support system and facilitated his recovery:

> He lived at home, and we offered him a comfort zone that kept him out of the hospital. I tried to always maintain patience and to gain understanding, to be stable and calm. I helped my brother maintain his reality contact. I never forget that it could have been me. He has had the security of home and the support of his family. We are proud of his progress. We helped him to find his own way to become a valuable member of society. (Marsh & Dickens, in press)

A Coping and Adaptation Framework

In addition to a competence paradigm, there are additional conceptual models that can facilitate the design, implementation, and evaluation of services for families (see Lefley & Wasow, 1994). As Hatfield and Lefley (1987) have discussed, a coping and adaptation model also focuses on the strengths, resources, and adaptive capacities of families. The serious mental illness of a close relative is a catastrophic event for families. As is the case for other catastrophic stressors, such as serious physical illness or developmental disability, families who are coping with serious mental illness undergo a process of adaptation.

Hill's (1949) ABCX model of family stress offers a useful framework for conceptualizing this adaptation process. More recently, the Double ABCX model has been formulated to reflect the family's adaptation through time (see Figley, 1989). In her discussion of the familial experience of disability, Wikler (1986) has provided an overview of the ABCX model. The ABCX schema includes four components: *A,* family life events; *B,* family resources; *C,* family appraisal of the event; and *X,* family adaptation. The model assumes that familial adaptation to a member's disability is a complex process that is influenced by family life events, resources, and appraisal. Figure 7.2 depicts the application of the ABCX model to the familial experience of serious mental illness.

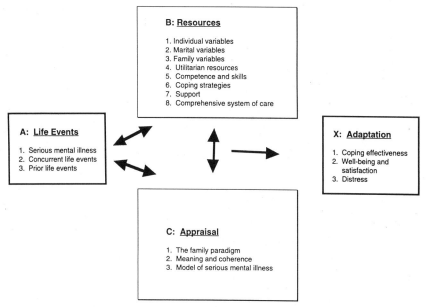

From "Services for Families: New Modes, Models, and Intervention Strategies," by D. T. Marsh, 1994. In *Helping Families Cope with Serious Mental Illness,* H. P. Lefley & M. Wasow (Eds.), New York: Harwood Academic Publishers. Copyright by Harwood Academic Publishers. Reprinted with permission.

Figure 7.2   The ABCX Model

As applied to the familial experience of mental illness, the ABCX model incorporates research concerned with coping and adaptation (e.g., Kessler, Price, & Wortman, 1985; Matheny, Aycock, Pugh, Curlette, & Cannella, 1986); with familial stress (e.g., Figley, 1989); with the familial experience of developmental disability (e.g., Frey et al., 1989); and with the familial experience of serious emotional disturbance in children and adolescents (Marsh, in press). Although the model has a number of limitations (e.g., Walker, 1985), there is empirical support for the value of the ABCX model in conceptualizing the familial process of adaptation to stress and in enhancing the coping effectiveness of families (e.g., Orr, Cameron, & Day, 1991). Each of the four components of the ABCX model will be discussed briefly.

Family Life Events (A)

In this context, the first component of the ABCX model is family life events, including (a) the serious mental illness itself, (b) other concurrent life events, and (c) prior life events. Family life events are those present and past occurrences that are potential stressors for family members. As we have noted, there is much evidence that the mental illness of a close relative has a devastating impact on the entire family. The overall context of familial stress also includes concurrent life events that may increase family distress, as well as prior events that may have depleted family resources.

Family Resources (B)

The second component, family resources, includes the following: (a) individual variables (wellness, self-esteem, self-efficacy, beliefs, commitments); (b) marital variables (status, satisfaction, roles, consensus); (c) family process variables (boundaries, hierarchical organization, family homeostasis, information processing, differentiation, emotional climate); (d) utilitarian resources (educational level, family income); (e) competencies (cognitive, behavioral, affective, social); (f) coping strategies; (g) support (informal, formal); and (h) a comprehensive system of care. An extensive literature is available for many of these variables (see Marsh, in press), including valuable work with the familial process of coping and adaptation (e.g., Hatfield & Lefley, 1987; Zipple & Spaniol, 1987b).

Family Appraisal (C)

The third component is family appraisal, which is the collective set of beliefs about the stressor that may or may not make it traumatizing for a particular family (Figley, 1989). As represented in the transactional model of stress, a life event becomes stressful only after it has been appraised as threatening (Singer & Davidson, 1991). Family appraisal can be described in terms of the following variables: (a) the family paradigm, which consists of the underlying assumptions about reality that are shared by all family members and that guide their construction of reality (Reiss & Klein, 1987); (b) meaning and coherence, which is the family's sense of significance in the event (see Thompson &

Janigian, 1988); and (c) the family's model of serious mental illness (e.g., interpersonal, biological, diathesis-stress).

Terkelsen (1987) has discussed the variables that can influence the familial process of appraisal in the case of serious mental illness, including the extent of involvement in primary caregiving; the models of causation, symptoms, and outcomes assumed by family members; and the particular circumstances and attributes of individual family members. Family appraisal affects other aspects of the familial experience of mental illness, including the feelings of guilt and helplessness experienced by family members (Terkelsen, 1987), and their attitudes and caregiving patterns (Chesla, 1989).

Family Adaptation (X)

The final category is family adaptation, which comprises (a) coping effectiveness (with the serious mental illness, with other adaptive demands); (b) sense of well-being and satisfaction; and (c) level of family distress.

Implications for Services

The ABCX model provides a useful framework for conceptualizing services for families, with the goal of improving family adaptation. Family adaptation is likely to be enhanced by services that increase resource availability and utilization (e.g., coping skills workshops, a support group, improved services for their relative), or that alter family appraisal in positive ways (e.g., by educating families about serious mental illness). In essence, intervention strategies that improve family resources and appraisal are also likely to have a constructive impact on family adaptation.

This woman has a sister with schizophrenia. She talks about her own needs as a young family member and the resources that would have facilitated her adaptation process:

> As a child I needed concrete explanations of what was going on. The family needed support, not blame, from my sister's [professional] caregivers. Siblings need help with their fear of becoming mentally ill themselves, help sorting out ordinary adolescent emotions, and help with their relationship with the sibling. I still feel ashamed—the stigma was internalized as something wrong with me. (Marsh & Dickens, in press)

INTERVENTION WITH FAMILIES

A number of general considerations should guide clinicians in their work with families of people who have mental illness. First, consistent with the new modes and models of professional practice that have been discussed, the overarching objective of professional practice is to empower families in achieving mastery and control over the circumstances of their lives, including the mental illness of their relative. Accordingly, clinicians should offer services in a manner that acknowledges the strengths, resources, and expertise of families, that provides opportunities to strengthen family functioning, and that promotes a sense of intrafamilial mastery and control (see Dunst, Trivette, & Deal, 1994).

Second, family consultants can assist families in making an informed choice regarding their use of available services. The goal is to provide an optimal match between the needs, desires, and resources of particular family members and the services that are available. A full continuum of services for families includes nonclinical services designed primarily to offer education and support, and clinical services designed to offer various forms of psychotherapy. Professional consultants should inform family members about the nature and purpose of specific nonclinical and clinical services; about the potential benefits, risks, and costs of these services; about the risks of forgoing the services; and about the available alternatives.

Third, recommendations for family members should be based on an ecological perspective that considers relevant variables at the levels of the social system, the family system, family subsystems, and individual family members. Shifting from the family system to family subsystems, for example, it is important to offer services not only to parents of people with mental illness, but also to spouses, siblings, and children, whose experiences, needs, and coping resources may differ significantly as a function of their family roles (e.g., Marsh & Dickens, in press).

Fourth, recommendations should also be informed by relevant research findings. For instance, there is empirical evidence that nonclinical services, such as educational programs and support groups, are a valuable resource for family members who are coping with the mental illness of a close relative (e.g., Lefley, 1987). There is also evidence of the benefits of clinical intervention, which can assist family members in resolving their emotional burden. In a national survey of adult siblings and children of people with serious mental illness (Marsh et al., 1993), over three fourths (77%) of respondents reported that they had received psychotherapy (primarily individual therapy); a majority (63%) rated the therapy as very or extremely helpful. Thus, family consultants should inform family members regarding the full range of available nonclinical and clinical services.

Fifth, once family members have made an informed choice regarding their use of services, clinicians should make appropriate referrals. Families may elect to receive a single service offered in a clinical setting or in the community; may pursue complementary services, such as an educational or psychoeducational program led by professionals and a family-facilitated support group in the community; or may decline or defer their use of services. Following the initial decision regarding service utilization, clinicians should remain available to families, because their needs and desires may change. For example, some families may benefit from services on an as-needed basis, particularly during crises or periods of inpatient treatment for their relative.

Finally, in addition to their general expertise, clinicians need to develop specific expertise in the areas of serious mental illness, family experiences and needs, and effective intervention strategies. There are many resources available for clinicians who wish to enhance their effectiveness in working with this population. These include training manuals (e.g., Bisbee, 1991; Meisel & Mannion; 1989; Zipple & Spaniol, 1987b); books (e.g., Bernheim & Lehman, 1985; Hatfield, 1990; Lefley & Wasow, 1994; Marsh, 1992a); chapters and articles (e.g., Bentley & Harrison, 1989; Kuipers, 1991; Lam, 1991; Zastowny, Lehman, Cole, & Kane, 1992); and videotapes (e.g., Marsh, 1993; Weisburd, 1991).

The following parent offers some suggestions for professionals who work with families:

> Deal first with the problem which the family identifies as the problem and then go from there. Try to help the family for their own sake (and that in turn will help the ill person). Do not assume that family members are ill themselves on the basis of the way they behave. It is most likely a reaction to the illness. If it becomes evident that family members are also ill, refer them for treatment. Do not confuse treatment for an illness with helping someone respond to the illness of a relative. If you were helping family members deal with a terminal illness like cancer in a loved one, the way you approached them would be different from the way they would need to be approached if they had cancer and needed treatment for the illness. The same applies with mental illness. (Marsh, 1992a, p. 195)

NONCLINICAL SERVICES FOR FAMILIES

Families who are coping with the serious mental illness of a close relative have a number of essential needs, including their needs for information about mental illness and community resources, for skills to cope with the illness and its consequences for family members, and for support for themselves. Nonclinical services can meet many of these needs. As Zipple and Spaniol (1987a) have discussed, nonclinical programs may be primarily educational, skills-oriented, or supportive. Alternatively, a multimodal program can be designed to fulfill all these functions.

A comprehensive program of nonclinical services should include the following: (a) a didactic component that provides information about serious mental illness and the mental health system; (b) a skills component that offers training in communication, conflict resolution, problem solving, assertiveness, behavioral management, and stress management; (c) an emotional component that provides opportunities for grieving, sharing, and mobilizing resources; (d) a family process component that focuses on the impact of mental illness on the family unit and on individual family members; and (e) a social component that increases utilization of informal and formal support networks.

Educational programs and support groups are two examples of effective nonclinical strategies.

Educational Programs

The professional literature provides many descriptions of educational programs for families (e.g., Moller & Wer, 1989), as well as empirical evidence for the value of such programs (e.g., Abramowitz & Coursey, 1989). Most of these programs have been offered to parents of adult children with mental illness. As this woman asserts, however, young family members also have a compelling need for information. She grew up with a father who had schizophrenia.

> Children need to be given information just as much as adults. When I was a child I wished my father had cancer or something I could understand, because no one seemed able to explain it to me. Hence I got all sorts of zany ideas on my own. Find a good counselor, join the National Alliance for the Mentally Ill, and read everything on the subject that is written for your age group. (Marsh & Dickens, in press)

As illustrated by the 10-week educational program outlined in Table 7.2, such programs should cover a range of topics. These include an overview of the program; family-professional relationships; serious mental illness and its treatment; managing symptoms and problems; the family experience; stress, coping, and adaptation; enhancing personal and family effectiveness; and community resources.

TABLE 7.2   Ten-Week Educational Program for Families

Week 1. Nature and Purpose of Program
Introductions; overview of agency program; written survey of family needs and requests

Week 2. Family-Professional Relationships
Establishing collaborative partnerships; roles and responsibilities; communication

Week 3. Serious Mental Illness I
Diagnosis; etiology; prognosis; treatment

Week 4. Serious Mental Illness II
Symptoms; medication; diathesis-stress model; recent research

Week 5. Managing Symptoms and Problems
Positive symptoms; negative symptoms; specific problems

Week 6. The Family Experience
Family burden and needs; life-span perspectives; family system and subsystem issues

Week 7. Stress, Coping, and Adaptation
Dealing with a catastrophic stressor; enhancing coping effectiveness

Week 8. Enhancing Personal and Family Effectiveness I
Behavior management; conflict resolution; communication; problem solving

Week 9. Enhancing Personal and Family Effectiveness II
Stress management; assertiveness; meeting personal and family needs

Week 10. Community Resources
Consumer-advocacy movement; community support system; appropriate referrals

From *Families and Mental Illness* (pp. 182–183) by D. T. Marsh, 1992, New York: Praeger. Copyright 1992 by Diane T. Marsh. Adapted by permission.

Clinicians who work in an institutional setting might offer an education program for families whose relatives have been hospitalized with a diagnosis of serious mental illness. The general structure of the program can be modified to meet the needs of specific providers, diagnostic groups, and populations (e.g., Marsh, 1992a; Marsh et al., 1993). Many resources are available for clinicians who wish to offer educational programs for family members (e.g., Hatfield, 1990; Zipple & Spaniol, 1987b).

Support Groups

Families who are confronted with serious mental illness often feel stigmatized by the larger society and alienated from their usual channels of social support. Under these circumstances, involvement in a support group can be beneficial (e.g., Hatfield & Lefley, 1987). Support groups for families can offer opportunities to mobilize resources and resolve their emotional burden in a protected and nurturing environment; to obtain information about mental illness, coping strategies, and community resources; and to move into roles as effective advocates. Many resources are available for clinicians who wish to offer support groups for families (e.g., Weisburd, 1991). When support groups are offered in clinical settings, professionals can serve as facilitators or as cofacilitators with family members. Professional-family member cofacilitation offers a model of collaboration for participants and increases the likelihood that they will find the group responsive to their needs.

Additional Nonclinical Services

In addition to educational programs and support groups, clinicians can offer other nonclinical services to family members. These include educational seminars focusing on specific topics, skills-oriented workshops, a crisis group, a drop-in center for family members, an advocacy group, written materials, a newsletter, multifamily groups, and forums that utilize professional and community resources. To ensure the usefulness of nonclinical programs, clinicians should solicit the input of family members as such programs are designed and implemented. Moreover, many provider-based programs can benefit from the involvement of family members as consultants, as presenters, and as facilitators or cofacilitators with professionals.

Family-Facilitated Services

Increasingly, family members themselves have become providers of nonclinical services (e.g., Burland, 1991), often through local affiliates of the National Alliance for the Mentally Ill (NAMI). In lieu of duplicating those services in professional settings, clinicians can assist families by making referrals to existing support groups in the community. Clinicians may also wish to offer consultation to family support groups and to present programs on specific topics.

The following family member participated in an educational and support group offered through the Siblings and Adult Children (SAC) Council of NAMI. She talks about the value of the group in her own life:

> The first SAC meeting changed my life. The group has been like a beacon, providing me with information, support, and understanding. I am learning to set limits, to say no, to live apart, to have a happy, well-adjusted life—and not to feel guilty about it. I still feel responsible for "saving" my family, but it is set within realistic perimeters. Most importantly, I know that I am not alone in this. (Marsh & Dickens, in press)

CLINICAL SERVICES FOR FAMILIES

Clinical services also offer a valuable resource for some family members, who may benefit from psychotherapy designed to assist them in resolving problems that are reactive to their relative's mental illness or in addressing other mental health problems that may have been precipitated or exacerbated by current stress. More generally, the feelings of anguish and demoralization often experienced by family members may be diminished through psychotherapy, which offers potential improvements in interpersonal functioning, in self-esteem and self-confidence, in satisfaction, in mastery and competency, and in level of distress (Strupp, 1989).

Consistent with the changes in family-professional relationships that have been discussed, clinical services should be offered in a manner that fosters family-professional collaboration and family empowerment (e.g., Combrinck-Graham, 1990; Hoffman, 1990; Simon, McNeil, Franklin, & Cooperman, 1991). Once a family member has chosen to participate in psychotherapy, the family consultant can employ a process of differential therapeutics to ensure selection of the most appropriate form of treatment.

In our research with adult siblings and children, more than three-fourths reported they had received personal therapy as a result of their relative's illness. Most of these family members found it very helpful, as affirmed by the following 50-year-old woman, who grew up with a mother who had schizophrenia. Even decades after her initial encounter with mental illness, she found therapy worthwhile.

> It wasn't until I sought therapy for anxiety upon my divorce that I began to understand some of the dynamics of my family and myself. The mental illness [in my family] profoundly changed my life. I have missed much, have just begun to recognize what has been lost or even never realized. It has taken me a long time to finally face the original problem. Therapy opened doors to my self and answered many puzzling questions. (Marsh & Dickens, in press)

Differential Therapeutics

Clarkin and his colleagues (1992; Frances, Clarkin, & Perry, 1982) have delineated the field of differential therapeutics, describing the process for selecting the most effective form of treatment for particular individuals. They distinguish between two levels of treatment planning: the macro level, which includes five dimensions (setting, format, strategies and techniques, duration and frequency, and medication); and the micro level, which involves modifications of therapeutic strategies in light of the client's problem complexity, coping style, and reactance level. The authors also differentiate between the final goals of therapy, which are to alleviate the symptoms and conflicts for which assistance was sought, and the mediating goals of therapy, which are hypothesized to be related to the initial symptoms and conflicts.

Based on the discussion of Clarkin and his colleagues (1992), the process of differential therapeutics can be fruitfully applied to professional practice with families of people who have serious mental illness. The following topics will be examined: format, strategies and techniques, and duration and frequency.

Format

Treatment format determines the number of individuals who will be present and defines the interpersonal context of the intervention. Alternative formats include individual, marital, family, and group treatment. Given the diversity among family members, each of these formats has potential value. Many clinicians have discussed the relative indications and contraindications for the various formats (e.g., Frances et al., 1984; Marsh, 1992a). For example, individual intervention is appropriate when psychological issues are most prominent, and group intervention when there are pressing needs for social support (Toseland, Rossiter, Peak, & Smith, 1990).

Similarly, marital therapy may be beneficial when preexisting marital problems have been exacerbated by current stress. Family therapy is appropriate when there are significant difficulties in communication or problem solving, when the family is unable to cope adequately with the mental illness of the family member, or when successful treatment of an individual requires the involvement of other family members. All of these formats also pose potential risks, including the risk of scapegoating or isolation in individual therapy, the loss of autonomy and privacy in family therapy, and the neglect of pressing individual issues in group therapy. The following family member attests to the potential value of several therapeutic formats:

> Family therapy occurred in a hospital setting during the initial hospitalization. It seemed mostly an opportunity for the psychiatrist, social worker, and psychiatric nurse to observe family interactions and may have been helpful in our son's treatment. Individual and marital therapy [were] helpful in resolving problems which were exacerbated by the serious mental illness of my son. Trying to change is never easy, but overall it was helpful. (Marsh, 1992a, p. 199)

Strategies and Techniques

Strategies and techniques are the technical interventions used by the therapist to induce change. At the macro level of treatment planning, clinicians should employ the strategies and techniques likely to meet the expressed needs of families of people with mental illness, including their needs for information about mental illness and its treatment, for effective coping skills, for support for themselves, and for resolution of their emotional burden.

Their theoretical orientations strongly influence the strategies and techniques employed by clinicians. There are numerous biological, psychological, systems, and multidimensional models. All these conceptual models have potential value for conceptualizing serious mental illness. In fact, in light of the complexity of the area, a biopsychosocial model appears to offer the most useful framework for understanding and treating serious mental illness. In connection with services for families, psychological models are likely to be beneficial in addressing issues of loss and mourning, in treating the depression that is sometimes experienced by family members, and in developing a sense of meaning and coherence in the event (Marsh, 1992a). Systems models are helpful in dealing with the impact of mental illness on the family system and on family subsystems. Technical eclecticism, with its emphasis on the potential value of the full range of strategies and techniques, offers a data-based approach that can increase therapeutic efficacy with families (see Norcross & Newman, 1992).

Duration and Frequency

Duration and frequency pertain to the way the treatment is embedded in time. Clarkin and his colleagues (1992) discuss three treatment forms that vary along these dimensions: (a) crisis intervention, which is an intense, timely, brief, and goal-directed treatment designed to resolve a crisis of major and urgent proportions and of recent onset; (b) brief therapy, which is characterized by an established time limit, clear and limited treatment goals, and an active therapist; and (c) long-term psychotherapy, which is appropriate for problems that are ingrained, complex, and extensive.

As we have noted, families of people with mental illness are likely to vary along a continuum of competence and to exhibit a range of competencies and competence deficits. In fact, any preexisting problems in these families are likely to be exacerbated by the severe and chronic stress that accompanies a member's mental illness. Thus, depending on the circumstances of particular families and family members, each of these treatment forms may be appropriate. Family members may benefit from crisis intervention designed to reduce the risk of imminent harm, from brief therapy designed to provide assistance during periods of their relative's relapse or inpatient treatment, and from extended therapy designed to resolve severe problems in multiple areas of functioning.

Here is the account of an adult child who benefited considerably from long-term therapy. Her mother has schizophrenia:

> I sank into an 8-year depression. My mother's illness completely interrupted my life. Her illness progressed, and I found myself isolated and powerless in dealing with it. My mother would not agree to see a doctor. The establishment

repeatedly told me that there was nothing they could do unless my mother wished help. She didn't. I've been in therapy for 11 years now. That's the only good result I can see coming out of this tragedy. (Marsh & Dickens, in press)

Psychoeducation

Especially since 1985, there has been a proliferation of psychoeducational interventions designed for families of people with mental illness (e.g., Anderson, Reiss, & Hogarty, 1986; Falloon, Boyd, & McGill, 1984; Kuipers, Birchwood, & McCreadie, 1992; Lam, 1991). Although the terms *education* and *psychoeducation* are sometimes used interchangeably, the two approaches differ in some important respects. As we have discussed, educational programs are a nonclinical form of intervention to meet the needs of families for information about mental illness and its treatment, about caregiving and management issues, about the mental health system and community resources, and about family coping and adaptation.

In contrast, psychoeducational programs have been offered predominantly as a form of clinical intervention to enhance the family's ability to cope with serious mental illness (including schizophrenia and the affective disorders) and to reduce the risk of relapse. Researchers have demonstrated the greater risk of relapse among individuals with mental illness who return to family environments characterized by a high level of expressed emotion, which is operationalized as critical comments, hostility, and emotional overinvolvement. There is also empirical evidence that psychoeducational programs designed to lower an initially high level of expressed emotion in families can result in reduction or delay of relapse. Following her review of the relevant literature, Lefley (1992) has concluded that, despite the limitations of research concerned with expressed emotion, the findings are important in highlighting the adverse impact of overstimulating or high-demand environments on individuals who have the core information-processing deficits of serious mental illness. Rather than representing a family variable, expressed emotion appears to reflect the importance of environmental stress across a wide range of settings (e. g., Drake & Osher, 1987).

Family components of psychoeducational programs generally include (a) an empathic, validating, nonblaming, task-oriented alliance with the family; (b) comprehensive family assessment (e.g., the Camberwell Family Interview); (c) education about mental illness and its management; (d) training in specific skills and competencies (e.g., problem solving, communication); (e) family treatment designed to lower expressed emotion; and (f) contact with other families. Psychoeducational programs typically include additional components for the family member with mental illness, such as education about mental illness and its management, emphasis on medication compliance, and training in social skills. Psychoeducational programs offer a potentially valuable intervention strategy for families because such programs are designed to foster collaborative family-professional relationships and to meet many essential family needs (e.g., Fox, 1992).

On the other hand, because psychoeducational programs are offered as an adjunct to the treatment of the relative who has mental illness, such programs may not meet the needs of particular families, including those who are low in expressed emotion or who do not function as primary caregivers (the majority of families in both instances). In addition, there is sometimes a pejorative quality to the term "high-EE family" that recalls the earlier phrase "schizophrenogenic mother." Finally, psychoeducational programs often fail to acknowledge the strengths, resources, and expertise of families, as well as the importance of the larger sociocultural context.

No Treatment

When consulting with families of people with mental illness, clinicians should initially consider no treatment as the prescription of choice. Reflecting the principle of least intervention (Thompson, 1990), clinical services should be provided only when a genuine need exists. It is important not to overprescribe therapy for problems that a family may be able to resolve without professional assistance or that may be transitional in nature (Lewis, 1989). Clarkin and associates (1992) distinguish among three groups who might be considered for no treatment, including those likely to improve without treatment (e.g., those suffering from acute stress, but with a history of effective functioning and coping); those who are at risk for a negative response to the treatment itself (e.g., due to the nature of the treatment or the disorder); and those who are at risk for failing to respond to treatment (e.g., due to poor motivation). Accordingly, a recommendation of no treatment is appropriate for family members who have a history of effective functioning and are likely to improve on their own (or with nonclinical intervention). A recommendation of no treatment also avoids the risk of negative treatment effects.

Negative Treatment Effects

The literature describing clinical practice with families of people who have serious mental illness suggests that the potential for negative treatment effects is relatively high among family members. For example, there is the risk of adverse effects when clinicians inappropriately assume that families are pathogenic or dysfunctional (e.g., Carr, 1990; Drake & Sederer, 1986; Terkelsen, 1983). Such assumptions are likely to add to the subjective burden of family members and to undermine family-professional relationships. The following woman has a brother with schizophrenia. She talks about her own experience in therapy with a clinician who held families accountable for the mental illness:

I was 16 when my 14-year-old brother had his first psychotic episode. He was hospitalized for most of my adolescence. His illness was the most devastating

episode of my entire life. I was ashamed, I was afraid, I was confused. I was involved in family therapy sessions that put the blame on the family. It was awful.
(Marsh & Dickens, in press)

In addition, there are risks when family therapy is mandated as a condition for
treating the relative who has mental illness (see Marsh et al., 1993) because families may not see themselves as needing or wanting treatment (Grunebaum &
Friedman, 1988), and may object to being treated as the "unidentified patient"
(Bernheim, 1989). Such general prescriptions of therapy are also in conflict with
the ethical principle of informed consent and with the process of differential
therapeutics, which is designed to provide the optimal match for particular family members. The account of this mother suggests that the psychodynamic therapy she received was a relatively poor match for her needs:

> I feel now that it was a mistake to get into therapy, that the costs outweighed the
> benefits. In many respects, there was a poor match between what I wanted and
> needed and what psychotherapy offered. I was not mentally ill and did not need
> treatment or analysis. The usual interpretations were largely irrelevant to my
> concerns, and I had no need to deal with my mother at that point in my life. Nor
> was it constructive for me to become a patient or to become involved in a pro-
> cess that seemed to emphasize my vulnerability and to drain my energy. I needed
> to feel healthy and strong and intact, the very things that were undermined by
> what happened in therapy. The last thing I needed was to be treated as if I were
> the problem instead of my daughter. (Marsh, 1992a, p. 204)

Finally, the available evidence indicates that the most compelling needs of
families are for information, skills, and support. Thus, family members may be
poorly motivated for therapy that focuses on intrapsychic or intrafamilial phenomena during a period of depleted resources, and such therapy may be experienced as irrelevant or intrusive. Many of these families may find nonclinical
services a better match for their needs.

When clinical services are provided to families of people with mental illness, the risk of negative treatment effects can be minimized by family consultation, which ensures that family members have made an informed choice
regarding their use of services, and by differential therapeutics, which mandates consideration of the expressed needs and concerns of families.

Treatment Planning

Practitioners who offer clinical services to family members of people with
mental illness should be guided by a number of considerations. As we have discussed, these include new modes and models for professional practice, the literature concerned with family experiences and needs, the principle of informed
consent, the relative value of nonclinical and clinical intervention, the process
of differential therapeutics, and the risk of negative treatment effects.

In addition to these general considerations, a number of treatment goals are
appropriate for family members, including provision of support, enhancement

of coping effectiveness, reframing of personal and familial experience, and expression and resolution of the emotional burden. Bernheim's (1982) supportive family counseling illustrates an approach that is likely to be beneficial to many family members. In addition, clinicians should be sensitive to the unique experiences and needs of individual family members, such as young family members.

Finally, consistent with the general psychotherapy literature, the central consideration is the quality of the therapeutic alliance that is formed with family members. A constructive therapeutic alliance is likely to be promoted by a respectful and empathic attitude toward families, an understanding of their phenomenological reality, an effort to meet their expressed needs, and a goal of family empowerment.

All members of the family are profoundly affected by the mental illness of a close relative. As the following sibling affirms, clinicians can offer valuable assistance to family members and support them in coping with this catastrophic event:

I was so depressed and lonely. I even thought of suicide. For many years, I looked for answers for my brother's problems, never realizing I had to find myself first. I had to leave home to survive. I have—being in therapy, learning I'm okay. I'm now married and successful in my job as an elementary guidance counselor. I am what I wanted to be—a caring, nurturing person. (Marsh & Dickens, in press)

REFERENCES

Abramowitz, I. A., & Coursey, R. D. (1989). Impact of an educational support group on family participants who take care of their schizophrenic relatives. *Journal of Consulting and Clinical Psychology, 57,* 232–236.

Anderson, C. M., Reiss, D. J., & Hogarty, G. E. (1986). *Schizophrenia and the family.* New York: Guilford.

Backer, T. E., & Richardson, D. (1989). Building bridges: Psychologists and families of the mentally ill. *American Psychologist, 44,* 546–550.

Bentley, K. J., & Harrison, D. F. (1989). Behavioral, psychoeducational, and skills training approaches to family management of schizophrenia. In B. A. Thyer (Ed.), *Behavioral family therapy* (pp. 147–168). Springfield, IL: Charles C. Thomas.

Bernheim, K. F. (1982). Supportive family counseling. *Schizophrenia Bulletin, 8,* 634–641.

Bernheim, K. F. (1989). Psychologists and families of the severely mentally ill: The role of family consultation. *American Psychologist, 44,* 561–564.

Bernheim, K. F., & Lehman, A. F. (1985) *Working with families of the mentally ill.* New York: Norton.

Bisbee, C. (1991). *Educating patients and families about mental illness: A practical guide.* Gaithersburg, MD: Aspen.

Bubolz, M. M., & Whiren, A. P. (1984). The family of the handicapped: An ecological model for policy and practice. *Family Relations, 33,* 5–12.

Burland, J. (1991). *The Journey of Hope Family Education Course*. Poultney, VT: Alliance for the Mentally Ill of Vermont.

Carr, A. (1990). Failures in family therapy: A catalogue of engagement mistakes. *Journal of Family Therapy, 12,* 371–386.

Chesla, C. A. (1989). Parents' illness models of schizophrenia. *Archives of Psychiatric Nursing, 3,* 218–225.

Clarkin, J. F., Frances, A., & Perry, S. (1992). Differential therapeutics: Macro and micro levels of treatment planning. In J. C. Norcross & M. R. Goldfried (Eds.), *Handbook of psychotherapy integration* (pp. 463–502). New York: Basic Books.

Combrinck-Graham, L. (1990). Developments in family systems theory and research. *Journal of the American Academy of Child and Adolescent Psychiatry, 29,* 501–512.

Drake, R. E., & Osher, F. C. (1987). Using family psychoeducation when there is no family. *Hospital and Community Psychiatry, 38,* 274–277.

Drake, R. E., & Sederer, L. I. (1986). The adverse effects of intensive treatment of chronic schizophrenia. *Comprehensive Psychiatry, 27,* 313–326.

Dunst, C. J., Trivette, C. M., & Deal, A. G. (Eds.). (1994). Strengthening and supporting families. Volume 1: Methods, strategies, and practices. Cambridge, MA: Brookline.

Falloon, I. R. H., Boyd, J. L., & McGill, C. W. (1984). *Family care of schizophrenia.* New York: Guilford.

Figley, C. R. (1989). *Helping traumatized families.* San Francisco: Jossey-Bass.

Fox, P. (1992). Implications for expressed emotion therapy within a family therapeutic context. *Health & Social Work, 17,* 207–213.

Frances, A., Clarkin, J., & Perry, S. (1984). *Differential therapeutics in psychiatry: The art and science of treatment selection.* New York: Brunner/Mazel.

Frey, K. S., Greenberg, M. T., & Fewell, R. R. (1989). Stress and coping among parents of handicapped children: A multidimensional approach. *American Journal on Mental Retardation, 94,* 240–249.

Goldstein, E. G. (1981). Promoting competence in families of psychiatric patients. In A. N. Maluccio (Ed.), *Promoting competence in clients: A new/old approach to social work practice* (pp. 317–341). New York: Free Press.

Grunebaum, H., & Friedman, H. (1988). Building collaborative relationships with families of the mentally ill. *Hospital and Community Psychiatry, 29,* 1183–1187.

Hatfield, A. B. (1983). What families want of family therapists. In W. R. McFarlane (Ed.), *Family therapy in schizophrenia* (pp. 41–65). New York: Guilford.

Hatfield, A. B. (1990). *Family education in mental illness.* New York: Guilford.

Hatfield, A. B., & Lefley, H. P. (Eds.). (1987). *Families of the mentally ill: Coping and adaptation.* New York: Guilford.

Hill, R. (1949). *Families under stress.* New York: Harper & Row.

Hoffman, L. (1990). Constructing realities: An art of lenses. *Family Process, 29,* 1–12.

Kessler, R. C., Price, R. J., & Wortman, C. B. (1985). Social factors in psychopathology: Stress, social support, and coping processes. *Annual Review of Psychology, 36,* 531–572.

Kuipers, L. (1991). Schizophrenia and the family. *International Review of Psychiatry, 3,* 105–117.

Kuipers, L., Birchwood, M., & McCreadie, R. G. (1992). Psychosocial family intervention in schizophrenia: A review of empirical studies. *British Journal of Psychiatry, 160,* 272–275.

Lam, D. H. (1991). Psychosocial family intervention in schizophrenia: A review of empirical studies. *Psychological Medicine, 21,* 423–441.

Lefley, H. P. (1987). Impact of mental illness in families of mental health professionals. *Journal of Nervous and Mental Disease, 175,* 613–619.

Lefley, H. P. (1989). Family burden and family stigma in major mental illness. *American Psychologist, 44,* 556–560.

Lefley, H. P. (1992). Expressed emotion: Conceptual, clinical, and social policy issues. *Hospital and Community Psychiatry, 43,* 591–598.

Lefley, H. P. (1994). An overview of family-professional relationships. In D. T. Marsh (Ed.), *New directions in the psychological treatment of serious mental illness* (pp. 166–185). Westport, CT: Praeger.

Lefley, H. P., & Johnson, D. L. (Eds.). (1990). *Families as allies in treatment of the mentally ill.* Washington, DC: American Psychiatric Press.

Lefley, H. P., & Wasow, M. (Eds.). (1994). *Helping families cope with serious mental illness.* Newark: Harwood Academic Publishers.

Lewis, W. (1989). How not to engage a family in therapy. *Journal of Strategic and Systemic Therapies, 8,* 50–53.

McDaniel, S. H., Hepworth, J., & Doherty, W. J. (1992). *Medical family therapy: A biopsychosocial approach to families with health problems.* New York: Basic Books.

McElroy, E. (1990). Ethical and legal considerations for interviewing families of the seriously mentally ill. In H. P. Lefley & D. L. Johnson (Eds.), *Families as allies in treatment of the mentally ill* (pp. 173–183). Washington, DC: American Psychiatric Press.

Marsh, D. T. (1992a). *Families and mental illness: New directions in professional practice.* New York: Praeger.

Marsh, D. T. (1992b). Working with families of people with serious mental illness. In L. VandeCreek, S. Knapp, & T. L. Jackson (Eds.), *Innovations in clinical practice: A source book* (Vol. 11, pp. 389–402). Sarasota, FL: Professional Resource Press.

Marsh, D. T. (Writer and narrator). (1993). *Shattered dreams* [Videotape]. Harrisburg, PA: Alliance for the Mentally Ill of Pennsylvania.

Marsh, D. T. (in press). Families of children and adolescents with serious emotional disturbance: Innovations in theory, research, and practice. In C. A. Heflinger (Ed.), *Families and mental health services: Policy, services, and research.* Newbury Park, CA: Sage.

Marsh, D. T., & Dickens, R. M. (in press). *Troubled journey: Siblings and children of people with mental illness.* New York: Tarcher/Putnam.

Marsh, D. T., Koeske, R. D., & Schultz, K. (1993). Services for families: A NAMI CAN survey. *Innovations & Research, 2*(4), 53–54.

Marsh, D. T., Dickens, R. M., Yackovich, N. M., Wilson, J. M., Leichliter, J. S., & McQuillis, V. A. (1993). Troubled journey: Siblings and children of people with mental illness. *Innovations & Research, 2*(2), 17–28.

Masterpasqua, F. (1989). A competence paradigm for psychological practice. *American Psychologist, 44,* 1366–1371.

Matheny, K. B., Aycock, D. W., Pugh, J. L., Curlette, W. L., & Cannella, K. A. (1986). Stress coping: A qualitative and quantitative synthesis with implications for treatment. *Counseling Psychologist, 14,* 499–549.

Meisel, M., & Mannion, E., (1989). *Teaching manual for coping skills workshops* (rev. ed.). Philadelphia: Mental Health Association of Southeastern Pennsylvania/The T.E.C. Network.

Moller, M. D., & Wer, J. E. (1989). Simultaneous patient/family education regarding schizophrenia: The Nebraska model. *Archives of Psychiatric Nursing, 3,* 332–337.

Norcross, J. C., & Newman, C. F. (1992). Psychotherapy integration: Setting the context. In J. C. Norcross & M. R. Goldfried (Eds.), *Handbook of psychotherapy integration* (pp. 3–45). New York: Basic Books.

Orr, R. R., Cameron, S. J., & Day, D. M. (1991). Coping with stress in families with children who have mental retardation: An evaluation of the Double ABCX model. *American Journal on Mental Retardation, 95,* 444–450.

Peternelj-Taylor, C. A., & Hartley, V. L. (1993). Living with mental illness: Professional/family collaboration. *Journal of Psychosocial Nursing, 31,* 23–28.

Reiss, D., & Klein, D. (1987). Paradigm and pathogenesis: A family-centered approach to problems of etiology and treatment of psychiatric disorders. In T. Jacobs (Ed.), *Family interaction and psychopathology* (pp. 203–255). New York: Plenum.

Rolland, J. S. (1994). *Families, illness, and disability: An integrative treatment model.* New York: Basic Books.

Seligman, M., & Darling, R. B. (1989). *Ordinary families, special children: A systems approach to childhood disability.* New York: Guilford.

Simon, C. E., McNeil, J. S., Franklin, C., & Cooperman, A. (1991). The family and schizophrenia: Toward a psychoeducational approach. *Families in Society, 72,* 323–333.

Singer, J. E., & Davidson, L. M. (1991). Specificity and stress research. In A. Monat & R. S. Lazarus (Eds.), *Stress and coping: An anthology* (3rd ed., pp. 36–47). New York: Columbia University Press.

Stewart, R. P. (1984). Building an alliance between the family and the institution. *Social Work, 29,* 386–390.

Strupp, H. H. (1989). Psychotherapy: Can the practitioner learn from the researcher. *American Psychologist, 44,* 717–724.

Terkelsen, K. G. (1983). Schizophrenia and the family. II. Adverse effects of family therapy. *Family Process, 22,* 191–200.

Terkelsen, K. G. (1987). The meaning of mental illness to the family. In A. B. Hatfield & H. P. Lefley (Eds.), *Families of the mentally ill: Coping and adaptation* (pp. 128–150). New York: Guilford.

Thompson, A. (1990). *Guide to ethical practice in psychotherapy.* New York: Wiley.

Thompson, S. C., & Janigian, A. S. (1988). Life schemes: A framework for understanding the search for meaning. *Journal of Social and Clinical Psychology, 7,* 260–280.

Toseland, R. W., Rossiter, C. M., Peak, T., & Smith, G. C. (1990). Comparative effectiveness of individual and group interventions to support family caregivers. *Social Work, 35,* 209–217.

Walker, A. J. (1985). Reconceptualizing family stress. *Journal of Marriage and the Family, 47*, 827–837.

Weisburd, D. (Producer). (1991). *The facilitator. Part 1. A support group* [Videotape]. Sacramento: California Alliance for the Mentally Ill.

Wikler, L. M. (1986). Family stress theory and research on families of children with mental retardation. In J. J. Gallagher & P. M. Vietze (Eds.), *Families of handicapped persons: Research, programs, and policy issues* (pp. 167–195). Baltimore, MD: Brookes.

Wynne, L. C., Weber, T. T., & McDaniel, S. H. (1986). The road from family therapy to systems consultation. In L. C. Wynne, S. H. McDaniel, & T. T. Weber (Eds.), *Systems consultation: A new perspective for family therapy* (pp. 3–15). New York: Guilford.

Zastowny, T. R., Lehman, A. F., Cole, R. E., & Kane, C. (1992). Family management of schizophrenia: A comparison of behavioral and supportive family treatment. *Psychiatric Quarterly, 63*, 159–186.

Zipple, A. M., & Spaniol, L. (1987a). Current educational and supportive models of family intervention. In A. B. Hatfield & L. P. Lefley (Eds.), *Families of the mentally ill: Coping and adaptation* (pp. 261–277). New York: Guilford.

Zipple, A. M., & Spaniol, L. (1987b). *Families that include a person with a mental illness: What they need and how to provide it. Trainer Manual.* Boston, MA: Boston University Center for Psychiatric Rehabilitation.

CHAPTER 8

Trauma and the Family

MARY BETH WILLIAMS

Case Example

Miriam is a 44-year-old woman who runs a day-care center in her home. Her husband Jerry works nights. The couple has two children, Margaret, 20, and Jim, 17. Miriam has a history of severe sexual abuse which began at age 3 and involved at least 10 different perpetrators. She has worked through all of the abuse except that by her father and is "stuck" because she does not want to see him as a perpetrator. Her husband was very supportive during her early years of healing. As she has become more independent, though, he has been forced to give up his caretaker role and has begun to examine his own history of physical abuse by his father and sexual abuse by his two older brothers. He has become extremely angry and, in a passive-aggressive manner, has sabotaged therapy. He has taken Miriam to medical doctors when she has stomach problems that are body memories and has blamed the therapist for those problems. Miriam has also begun to purge herself with laxatives as she deals with the abuse because she feels dirty from what her father did to her.

Miriam is exceptionally angry at her husband because he has begun to "forget" to pay bills, passive aggressively discourages her from getting her driver's license (so she can be independent and get to therapy without his driving her) because all the overdue and bad check charges have taken the money that was to be used for her driving instruction. He constantly explodes and takes his anger out on the children. Miriam is also a ritual abuse survivor and her son Jim raises snakes in the house, even though he knows it is against his mother's wishes. Jerry buys mice for the snakes to eat but, if the snakes get out of their cages, he screams and yells at Jim for upsetting his mother. Their daughter Margaret sits at home for all but 3 hours a day when she works at a local restaurant. She wants to go to community college but refuses to work the hours necessary to earn her tuition. Her parents constantly threaten to "kick her out" but then do nothing. She smokes in the house, even though her mother has allergies.

Miriam wants to end the marriage if "things do not change." She has begun to pay the bills, taking away another of her husband's control mechanisms. Jerry attends a partners' group but refuses to get individual therapy. Initially, Miriam and Jerry appeared to be emotionally connected but that connection has become fragile, if not nonexistent. The future of their relationship, and Miriam's ability to participate in therapy, is guarded.

Families are systems made up of individuals who attempt to interact together in expected ways in circular patterns rather than in strict, linear cause-and-effect connections (Blevins, 1993). They are governed by rules and have boundaries that define which ideas and things are included in the family and at what level of intimacy (Hoopes, Fisher, & Barlow, 1984). Families try to maintain a steady state; however, trauma interrupts that state and the routine of the system. When a traumatic event occurs to a family member, the event signals the family system that it is in some kind of danger. Although the direct trauma may involve one or more members, other family members can also become traumatized by association and chiasmal transmission of the trauma (Blevins, 1993; Catherall, 1992; Figley, 1989).

When a family member experiences events either outside the range of normal, human experience or perceived to be devastating, the individual may develop a posttraumatic stress disorder (DSM-IV; American Psychiatric Association [APA], 1994). Posttraumatic stress disorder (PTSD) is a specific pattern of intrusive and avoidant behaviors, emotional responses, and cognitions, accompanied by physiological components of the disorder. The diagnostic criteria for PTSD are shown in Figure 8.1. Traumatic events wound the individual victim and impact basic cognitions and assumptions of safety, benevolence, and predictability in the world (Janoff-Bulman, 1992). These events also modify bodily responses including central nervous system functioning, behaviors, relationships, emotional reactivity, and spirituality.

WHAT HAPPENS IN THE TRAUMATIZED FAMILY?

Posttraumatic stress disorder in a family is not confined to the primary victim or victims. Instead, it has ramifications throughout the family and frequently exhibits itself in a similar pattern of secondary posttraumatic stress (STS) in other family members. In the case example at the beginning of this chapter, the children have become hypervigilant and watchful, expecting to see angry outbursts from their parents or flashback reenactments. Partners, as in this case example, may become codependent, while neglecting personal healing and expressing resentment to the partner and the therapist when that partner heals and upsets the family system.

Secondary PTSD may be the result of caring too much, particularly if the nondirectly traumatized family members themselves are overinvolved in the healing process. In other cases, exposure to the trauma of the victim triggers memories and symptoms of personal traumas. In the case example, the daughter Margaret, after observing her mother's regression to a 4-year-old alter who had been molested by an older brother, suddenly revealed that she had recently been date raped. She had not shared this trauma previously with anyone.

When one or more family members are exposed to a traumatic event, a variety of symptoms may be seen. The family may emphasize negative self-attributions and blame the victim for any system change. The family may see

A. The person has been exposed to a traumatic event in which both of the following were present

   (1) the person experienced, witnessed, or was confronted with an event or events that involved actual or threatened death or serious injury, or a threat to the physical integrity of self or others

   (2) the person's response involved intense fear, helplessness, or horror. **Note:** In children, this may be expressed instead by disorganized or agitated behavior

B. The traumatic event is persistently reexperienced in one (or more) of the following ways:

   (1) recurrent and intrusive distressing recollections of the event, including images, thoughts, or perceptions. **Note:** In young children, repetitive play may occur in which themes or aspects of the trauma are expressed

   (2) recurrent distressing dreams of the event. **Note:** In children, there may be frightening dreams without recognizable content.

   (3) acting or feeling as if the traumatic event were recurring (includes a sense of reliving the experience, illusions, hallucinations, and dissociative flashback episodes, including those that occur on awakening or when intoxicated). **Note:** In young children, trauma–specific reenactment may occur

   (4) intense psychological distress at exposure to internal or external cues that symbolize or resemble an aspect of the traumatic event

   (5) physiological reactivity on exposure to internal or external cues that symbolize or resemble an aspect of the traumatic event

C. Persistent avoidance of stimuli associated with the trauma and numbing of general responsiveness (not present before the trauma), as indicated by three (or more) of the following:

   (1) efforts to avoid thoughts, feelings, or conversations associated with the trauma

   (2) efforts to avoid activities, places, or people that arouse recollections of the trauma

   (3) inability to recall an important aspect of the trauma

   (4) markedly diminished interest or participation in significant activities

   (5) feeling of detachment or estrangement from others

   (6) restricted range of affect (e.g., unable to have loving feelings)

   (7) sense of a foreshortened future (e.g., does not expect to have a career, marriage, children, or a normal life span)

D. Persistent symptoms of increased arousal (not present before the trauma), as indicated by two (or more) of the following:

   (1) difficulty falling or staying asleep

   (2) irritability or outbursts of anger

   (3) difficulty concentrating

Figure 8.1   Diagnostic Criteria for 309.81 Posttraumatic Stress Disorder

(4) hypervigilance

(5) exaggerated startle response

E. Duration of the disturbance (symptoms in Criteria B, C, and D) is more than 1 month.

F. The disturbance causes clinically significant distress or impairment in social, occupational, or other important areas of functioning.

Specify if:

Acute: if duration of symptoms is less than 3 months

Chronic: if duration of symptoms is 3 months or more

Specify if:

With Delayed Onset: if onset of symptoms is at least 6 months after the stressor

Note: From *Diagnostic and Statistical Manual of Mental Disorders, Fourth Edition* (p. 428), 1994, Washington, D.C.: American Psychiatric Press, Inc. Copyright 1994 by the American Psychiatric Association. Reprinted with permission.

Figure 8.1   *(continued)*

the victim of the situation in a linear, black-white manner and attribute blame (e.g., if the victim had only done a specific act to avoid the trauma, the event would not have happened). The family may ignore the context of the trauma and believe that any symptoms of distress lie totally within the victim and are therefore unexplainable and uncontrollable. The family may become less open and flexible and lessen its use of humor and change patterns of intimacy (L'Abate, 1986). Dysfunctional rules of relationships (e.g., avoid conflict, avoid any hint of responsibility, do not discuss feelings openly) may become the norm to help powerless family members gain a sense of control.

When one or more members of a family have been traumatized, the emotional bonds of the family may be challenged or even shattered and open discussion of the trauma frequently does not occur. As the traumatized individual exhibits symptoms of a posttraumatic stress reaction (PTSR) or PTSD, other family members may pull away and have less desire to stay connected as a family unit. The family may create rigid norms and rules by which the trauma is avoided or repressed. In many instances, all family members are not included in this rule setting. Flexibility in the family becomes less, and a willingness to compromise and give to one another frequently lessens or even disappears (McCubbin & McCubbin, 1989).

Figley (1983) identified a series of characteristics of families who cope best with trauma. These families:

- Accept the occurrence of the stressor.
- Focus on the systemic impact of the trauma.
- Move toward mobilization with flexibility rather than get stuck on blame and scapegoating.

- Are tolerant of change and each other.
- Are committed to one another and show feelings and affection openly.
- Communicate openly.
- Have a high level of cohesion and like to be with one another.
- Have flexible roles and allow nontraumatized family members to take on more duties or become caretaker(s) to the victim/survivor.
- Are able to access resources both within and outside the family, as needed, and do not isolate themselves.
- Do not respond with violence and anger.
- Do not turn to substance abuse (or self-abuse) to self-soothe, modulate feelings, or show control and power.
- Take part in social activities around them.
- View sexuality as an expression of intimacy.

In reality, though, many traumatized families do not have these resources or abilities. Families are expected to support each other in times of need. If one individual has been severely traumatized, others frequently do attempt to provide support and tend to that individual's needs. However, in the process, as their own needs frequently remain unfulfilled, they often become overwhelmed, angry, and unavailable as well as depressed, withdrawn, and exhausted. In addition, when the traumatic event has been a secret in the family, disclosure of the secret can have a widespread, dangerous impact (Imber-Black, 1993). As Pittman (1993) noted, when private things are made public, the revealing of the secret frequently leads to problems.

If the primary victim is an adult who does not heal or work through the trauma and continues to have PTSD symptoms over time, the spouse may withdraw, the children may leave the family, and that survivor may decompensate. In other instances, sensing the impact of the trauma on the family, the primary victim may isolate or numb out and avoid the trauma so that the family may continue to exist as a unit, denying his or her own need to heal.

Niles (1990) noted that typical reactions of traumatized families include problems in relationships including lack of intimacy and emotional numbing; withdrawal from social contact; angry outbursts; placement of pressure on the survivor to return to the former homeostasis; verbal abuse and substance abuse. Trauma may impact the ego development of other family members in areas of competency, safety, trust, identity information, assumption of personal power, self-esteem, and intimacy (McCann & Pearlman, 1990; Williams, 1990).

Rosenthal, Sadler, and Edwards (1987) noted that families of trauma survivors may develop a series of symptom patterns that include:

- Symptoms of secondary PTSD.
- Boundary distortions leading to separation, lack of intimacy, or enmeshment.

- Somatization of rage and grief.
- Mistrust of the outside world.
- Parentification of children.
- Encouraged family avoidance that becomes the norm.
- Ambivalent feelings toward the victim/survivor.
- Profound need for social support.
- Various behaviors that encourage individual and familial numbing, including substance abuse.
- Feelings of guilt.
- Self-destructive behavior.
- A strong need for each member to be in control.
- Attempts to meet the needs of others at one's own expense.
- Frequent attempts to control the behavior of other members in the family as well as self-behavior.

Individual Posttraumatic Reactions

What makes one traumatic event more devastating in impact than another to an individual? Rosenthal, Sadler, and Edwards (1987) noted that certain specific aspects of a catastrophe had an impact. These included having little or no time to prepare, feeling a lack of control and helplessness, experiencing a sense of loss, spending an interminable time in crisis, experiencing disruption and destruction as well as danger and life threat, having exposure to death and destruction, acknowledging the existence of inherent moral conflict, assuming the role of victim during the trauma, and having a large proportion of the community impacted (rather than an individual personal crisis). In other words, when the traumatic event is unexpected, when the individual(s) involved have little or no time to prepare, when those individuals are exposed to a greater degree of death and grotesqueness, and when they experience numerous losses, their reactions will be more severe. Traumatic events put demands on the coping abilities of the individual family member. These coping abilities, in turn, depend on the level of individual flexibility, skill, self-esteem, prior experience with trauma, prior history of trauma, developmental level, and ability to utilize family resources (Bell, 1993).

Spousal/Partner Reactions

The spouse and/or partner of a trauma survivor is impacted both directly and indirectly. Partners can react to survivors with denial, suspicion, anger and rage, or depression and withdrawal (Graber, 1991). For example, Jerry has begun to sabotage therapy and has reacted with anger as his role as caretaker has been negated. He has "forgotten" to pay bills and blames the therapist for his wife's physical symptoms as she deals with parental abuse.

Spouses are not always aware of the existence of a trauma history in the lives of their partners and therefore are unaware of why partners react as they do (e.g., in a sexual relationship). This is particularly true in the cases of spouses of persons dealing with previously repressed memories of child sexual abuse. Miriam did not reveal any of her abuse history until approximately 7 years ago. She had repressed the extent of the abuse and has been very reluctant to deal with the memories and the accompanying emotions that overwhelm her, particularly during a sexual act. Miriam and Jerry established patterns of interaction for their marriage that have been significantly challenged since her trauma history has emerged. Miriam has begun to realize that many of her husband's behaviors, as well as his intense anger, remind her of her father. Her PTSD symptoms tend to regulate distance and intimacy. When she becomes strong, Jerry reacts with anger and passive aggressive attempts to control her healing. Miriam then is triggered by him and steps back from the work of therapy that needs to be done. Yet the memories continue to flood and she becomes more overwhelmed. Her husband then is able to reestablish his caretaking role as she decompensates (Zabukovec & Moore, 1993). It is even possible that Miriam was drawn to Jerry because of reenactment and trauma bonding in that he shares qualities of her perpetrators when he is angry and manipulative (Nair, 1993).

Gilbert (1995) noted that providing support to one's spouse can lead to symptoms in the other spouse. Hearing (or not hearing) the stories of the trauma can lead to feelings of helplessness, hopelessness, rage, and impotence in that spouse (Monahon, 1995). Jerry, hearing of Miriam's rapes by her brother-in-law, expressed initial homicidal thoughts and fantasies that he quickly brought under control. Matsakis (1988) found that female partners of Vietnam veterans came to believe that they themselves were experiencing symptoms of PTSD. They felt lonely and socially isolated, and had problems coping with their husbands' hyperreactivity, emotional numbing, and verbal abuse. They frequently overfunctioned and repressed their own anger out of fear. Hankin, Abueg, Gallagher-Thompson, and Murphy (1993) found that interpersonal difficulties in Vietnam veterans' families included problems with self-disclosure, family cohesion, sexual intimacy, and expression of affection and aggression. In fact, these authors noted that some symptoms of PTSD are expressed entirely and only within intimate relationships. Coughlin and Parkin (1987) also noted that female partners appeared to mimic symptoms of their veteran husbands.

In cases of rape trauma, normal marital patterns frequently are disrupted. Miller, Williams, and Bernstein (1982) noted that husbands had problems understanding, providing emotional support to, and making a commitment to their wives after rape. Many husbands felt powerless, helpless, and uncertain as to the future of their relationship. When Jerry felt the relationship threatened, as the case example indicates, his reaction was to encourage Miriam to quit therapy. When she did not, he convinced her primary physician to order her to terminate and to refuse to authorize more insurance visits. The physician then referred Miriam to a therapist of the physician's own choosing. This therapist never contacted the original therapist about the history, nor would the physician return phone calls to discuss the family pathology.

Gilbert (1995) noted that there are two primary reasons for the development of secondary traumatic stress in spouses. The first centers around the need in the family for a stable relationship that will be understood and that does not change. The second centers around the emotional connection and desire to help the spouse resolve or escape from the impact of the trauma. There may be yet a third reason: The spouse may want to avoid dealing with his or her own trauma and may use the survivor as a reason to exist, thereby avoiding personal issues.

Partners are frequently called on to perform almost superhuman duties. They are expected to be compassionate, flexible, resourceful, patient, and have incredible awareness of their own needs and limits, as well as those of the survivor (Davis, 1991). They are frequently called on to deal with crisis situations in the survivor, including self-mutilation attempts and suicide threats or gestures. The potential for developing a secondary posttraumatic stress reaction or disorder during this coping process exists and needs to be brought into awareness.

Traumatic Reactions in Children Whose Parents Are Victims

Much of the research describing children's reactions to parental victimization comes from the Holocaust literature (Danieli, 1981). Klein-Parker (1988) found that children of Holocaust survivors had intense, yet somewhat superficial, relationships with parents that had become more personal over the years. Parent and child were deeply attached and interdependent. Children of Holocaust survivors believe they need to shield their parents from painful present experiences by covering up or concealing their own feelings; therefore communication between generations is often ambiguous and indirect.

Danieli's (1994) assessment of countertransference reactions in therapists who deal with trauma applies to children's reactions as well. Children of trauma survivors often express horror at hearing the stories of their parents' victimizations. They frequently have nightmares of those events, even when they have never been told of them directly. The feel shame when they think about what the parent had to do to survive and frequently become mournful and tearful. At other times, they may refuse to listen to stories or even acknowledge the parents' traumas. Instead, they distance themselves and may even run away or threaten suicide.

These children may feel a sense of alienation within their families. Children of traumatized parents may choose to escape into personal isolation including emotional distance and/or geographic distance when possible (Nair, 1993). They deal with a variety of issues when parents have histories of trauma and are displaying PTSD. They may have to fear abandonment or the possibility of having to endure traumatic reenactment of flashbacks. They may express confusion about the trauma itself and what happened. Yet, asking questions may lead to further reenactment or rage outbursts. The potential nonavailability of the parent may lead to feelings of lack of nurturance, or they may fear bringing friends home or having sleepovers because of uncertainty about how the parent will behave. Matsakis (1988) found that the children in her study of families of Vietnam veterans internalized the low self-image of their fathers. Their major difficulties were in emotional areas: They reacted with fear and anxiety and with stifled anger through repression or allowed it to erupt in aggression or self-mutilation. They frequently distanced themselves from the parent, particularly if the parent had little or no energy. They tended to relive the experiences of the survivor and to exhibit their parents' symptoms. Matsakis (1988) concluded that these children need to talk with other children and share feelings but they do not need exposure to every gory detail of parental abuse or trauma.

Children are secondarily impacted by their parents' traumas because secondary traumas can also affect parenting ability and lead to depression and anxiety. Armsworth, Mouton, DeWitt, Cooley, and Hockwerda (1993) found that adult trauma survivors, as they attempt to parent, are often afraid. They have problems with discipline and feel helpless, overwhelmed, numbed, and detached. They may be unable to express emotions or provide nurturing. Issues of control for them are strong: They may overcontrol as a compensatory measure and/or may undercontrol and be impulsive and abusive. Parenting skills may be weak or absent if they themselves were inappropriately parented or were abused by that parent. In addition, they may also feel inadequate and may have difficulties with closeness and intimacy. Furthermore, they may seek to isolate themselves and family members, preventing healthy contacts with outsiders who might be potential support systems. However, as Albeck (1994) observed, it is not yet known which specific parental experiences and beliefs are critical in the transmission of trauma to the children.

The impact of parental trauma is not always negative. In fact, it can be positive (e.g., leading a child to choose a career in the helping professions as a social worker or psychologist). Children can build bonds of closeness with parents through understanding and empathy. Imagining themselves in the parent's place during the trauma is a way to feel connected that frequently is not pathological. This transposition of trauma helps children focus on the same challenges to meaning that their parents faced as each family member perceives his or her own rendition of what happened and its impact (Salston, 1994).

Traumatic Reactions in the Family When the Child Is a Victim

When a child in a family experiences a traumatic event, others in the family constellation are also impacted. In some cases, the event may trigger memories of similar traumas in the lives of the parents. The pain experienced by the child affects everyone including siblings who may feel ignored if all the attention is given to the victim. The victim, in turn, may feel guilt if he or she takes responsibility for the trauma or may be anxious, fearful, worried, depressed, or in shock. Siblings may feel abandoned, jealous, and distressed (Monahon,

1993). The parents may have problems coping with day-to-day life activities and may develop secondary PTSD. Seeing their child traumatized may shake their belief systems to the core. If the trauma resulted in the death of a child, mourning and bereavement may be particularly intense and devastating. Parents frequently feel helpless and ask how a traumatic event could have happened to their child. If the event was the result of their negligence or was a crime of violence perpetrated by them, their guilt may be particularly great.

In many instances, traumas involving children leads to family and marital distress including conflict, distancing, separation, and divorce (Marsh, 1992; Monahon, 1993; Monahon, 1995). For example, giving birth to a seriously ill or premature infant can cause secondary reactions in (a) the mother who feels responsible for giving birth early or having a traumatic delivery; (b) the father who must deal with the birth and the ill child while the mother recuperates; and (c) siblings who suddenly must be cared for by others as the parents turn their attention to the new sibling, grandparents, and others (Chapter 11 deals in more detail with such dynamics).

Parents may become preoccupied with the trauma and need to retell it frequently. They may have flashbacks of the trauma or imagine what the child endured (e.g., if the child was injured or killed in a situation away from the home, such as a school hostage situation or school disaster). Parents may try to cope with the trauma either by minimizing or exaggerating the extent of the child's reactions.

If the family is to recover, parents need to model positive coping, encouraging open processing of the traumatic events and accompanying feelings, cognitions, somatic reactions, and behavioral consequences. They need to give children honest, accurate explanations of what happened and why, as well as normalize symptoms that occur as an aftermath of the trauma. It is important that parents and children alike understand all aspects of traumatic reactions including the role of triggers, self-destructive behaviors, dissociation, dreams and nightmares as reenactments, compulsions, anxiety, self-image difficulties, and shame and guilt.

Matsakis (1988, 1992) and Monahon (1993) offer similar suggestions to parents and family members of traumatized children. It is important to adjust expectations of the child; to respect and hear the child's fears and repetitious retelling or replaying of the traumatic event; to educate the child about the normalcy of a posttraumatic stress reaction; to protect the child against reexposure to the trauma, even through repetitious play. Parents need to expect some difficult behavior while they maintain family routines as much as possible.

Children who have been traumatized need physical outlets for potential aggressive feelings. Any distorted misunderstandings of events that they may have need to be corrected by parents as well. It is also important for parents to give the children positive messages about healing, focusing on strengths in the child and in the family. Finally, parents need to recognize any problems in their own coping patterns and deal with the development of secondary PTSD, should it occur.

ASSESSMENT OF THE FAMILY

A thorough assessment of family dynamics, strengths, and weaknesses is necessary before the clinician devises a treatment plan. However, as Carroll, Foy, Cannon, and Zwier (1991) noted, any family evaluation must examine the history of each member beyond the current relationship as well as the extent of distress in each member. Figley (1989) noted that family patterns of cohesion, adaptability, interpersonal social skills, and conflict resolution skills need to be identified. The clinician should also ascertain the history of the marital relationship and the degree of marital as well as familial satisfaction.

Carroll, Foy, Cannon, and Zwier (1991) also suggested that an assessment of the family sequelae of trauma includes examination of the current status of the trauma survivor, the family's understanding of PTSD and symptomatology, the family's readiness and motivation to cope with traumatic sequelae in the survivor and themselves, and current levels of family skills of problem solving and conflict resolution. As a therapist, I utilize a number of psychometric measures to assess the status of the family, including belief system inventories (Williams, 1990), the Myers Briggs Personality Inventory, and learning style inventories.

It is also important to assess how stress has been handled in the family in the past, including patterns of substance use and abuse, physical abuse and battering, self-mutilation, spending addictions, eating disorders, and others. In other words, assessment must determine whether or not the family is a safe place in which the trauma work can be done. Family strengths as well as weaknesses and client/family member fragility need to be identified, as do social support networks. Figley (1989) believes that assessment needs to include a family history of traumas, the present status of each family member, the level of commitment of each member to the healing process, the degree to which the traumatic event(s) impact the family, the chiasmal impact of the trauma, communication skills and relationship skills, the level of blame, and the availability of resources both in and outside the family.

In the case described at the beginning of this chapter, Jerry is a recovering alcoholic with 14 years of sobriety. Miriam has turned to laxatives to purge herself of her badness and remove memories (and any trace of her father as well as her own dirtiness) from her body. She is having serious gastrointestinal problems. The greater Jerry's anger, the more she turns to the laxatives to rid herself of what she perceives is the cause of his upset. Assessment indicates that Miriam is not ready to handle intense memory work while her husband is so angry, especially since he is not in therapy himself. His enabling and manipulating behaviors that attempt to keep Miriam "sick" and a victim continue to help him avoid dealing with his own issues. Yet, as Miriam heals in spite of him, his issues have become more obvious and he has resorted to sabotaging the therapeutic relationship. Consultation with his Partner Group therapist indicates that he has been dishonest and manipulative about family dynamics and his role in the situation. He tells his group that his wife wants to quit therapy and that she does not want him to have therapy because there is no extra money to pay for it. In reality, he fears facing his own history and does not want to give up his remaining control over his wife. However, he is unable to share his own feelings with the group. Sharing of assessments between therapists has led to a more complete understanding of family dynamics and motivations.

Assessment must also take cultural factors and the role of culture in a particular family into account. Culture helps to define what constitutes a traumatic event in a family. It is important to assess cultural views of fate, personal responsibility, time, locus of blame/shame/control, resource availability, patterns of communication, patterns of intimacy, social support, and degree of guilt and anger (Erickson, 1989; see also Chapter 2).

When an individual or individuals are traumatized, the assumptions of those persons and others around them are challenged. They no longer are invulnerable to "bad things" and life is no longer only positive and understandable (Janoff-Bulman, 1992). Likewise, the beliefs of those family members who are exposed to the trauma survivor are also impacted as they attempt to place meaning on symptoms that they observe or deduce. For example, if children do not understand what is happening during a flashback, they may derive their own interpretations of events that have nothing to do with the actual traumas being reenacted.

In many instances, children and partners/spouses may, themselves, have unexplained memories of traumatic events that have happened to the primary trauma victim. Clinical experience confirms that this can happen: Children of abuse survivors have confided the content of dreams that depict abuse experiences of their mothers in vivid, accurate fashion. The mothers are shocked to learn "what their children have seen" in their minds and insist that they have never shared their experiences with the children.

If a survivor discusses the effects of trauma with the family, his or her private world is made public and the revelation tends to defy or at least challenge other family members' assumptions of a safe world. Yet, to find meaning in an event, there must be public witness (Jay, 1991).

For these reasons, assessment also needs to include an identification of the personal meaning of the trauma to each family member and how much any resultant change in personal meaning impacts daily life. Assessment of theories of causation of the trauma, including assessment of locus of control is important to include. This part of the assessment attempts to identify how family members make sense of events or make them predictable (Bell, 1993).

TREATMENT

For a family to heal, family treatment must occur. The primary survivor first must focus on personal healing and the individual family members must also have therapy to work on their own issues. The secondary survivors (family members of the primary survivor) have to deal with their own personal adjustment, particularly if they have trauma histories. They might also focus on how the primary survivor's healing impacts the family relationship.

As Carroll et al. (1991) note, the most appropriate therapeutic approach appears to be a combination of individual, couple, family, and other conjoint sessions. Many times, individuals must resolve personal traumas before they can address relationship issues (Graber, 1991). Ideally, the family becomes a healing environment that acknowledges and validates the experiences, emotions, and other phenomenological reactions of the survivor (Nair, 1993).

In this type of therapy, the definition of who is the client varies according to the needs presented. In the case example, Miriam is the focal point of healing in this family. Family sessions including Jerry are frequent, but he has been repeatedly encouraged to get his own therapist. He is reluctant to do so and confines his personal healing time to within the Partners' Group. However, his anger is spilling over into this group and he is having outbursts. The children have attended only a few sessions, generally only after a family blowup has occurred and threats by Jerry toward the children (to move out, get rid of snakes, etc.) have been made. Neither child is willing to participate in individual therapy.

In some cases, when partners of primary survivors are healthy and are not dealing with their own trauma histories and issues, treatment centers primarily on supportive functions. Partners and children are then encouraged to talk to the survivor, letting the survivor know what is "OK" to hear. They also need to know when to "back off" in a quest for information so that emotions in the survivor do not become overwhelming. In addition, they need to know what meaning the trauma has had to the survivor and in the survivor's life.

Figley (1989) states that the first step to helping a traumatized family is to help them notice that a trauma has occurred and that the event is having a traumatic impact on the family. Next, it is important to help individuals recapitulate what happened during the trauma while asking a series of questions: "What happened? Why did it happen? Why did . . . respond as he [she] did? Why has . . . acted like . . . since? If it happened again, could I cope?" Next, the therapist helps family members work through traumatic memories and any accompanying conflicts.

Parents of child survivors need to develop a family context in which the trauma can be discussed, remembered, and processed. This context is one of safety and involves, as much as possible, maintenance of a routine and stability. Helping the child with feelings, listening to the child's experiencing, and dealing with traumatic play are major tasks of the parents and other involved family members.

The therapist can offer assistance to family members to help them to deal with the primary survivor as well as their own posttraumatic stress reactions. The therapist may provide education about PTSD, help with skills acquisition in areas of communication, negotiation, conflict management, problem solving, assertiveness, behavioral management, and stress management, and help them discern more of their own secondary traumatic reactions and how these reactions impact family relationships.

Educating all members of the family about PTSD and secondary PTSD is essential. Knowledge is an extremely important coping tool and adds to feelings of empowerment and control. Families must face the truth about what has impacted them and the ramifications of the traumatic event. Families need access to information and psychoeducation as well as assistance in developing other appropriate coping tools. Education about the PTSD diagnosis and sharing of that diagnosis with the family can be a positive therapeutic intervention, particularly if the diagnosis depathologizes the survivor (Chapter 15 presents therapeutic modalities, including psychoeducation, that may be useful to these families).

Limit setting within the family and clarification of realistic roles and rules in relationships empower both victims and secondary victims (other family members; Williams, 1991). Rules need to be overt, appropriate, flexible, and healthy, leading to communication and cooperation among family members. Rules need to fit the family system and need to be attainable. Ideally, rules are positive in tone, promoting openness and individual differences, while confirming each member's self-worth. Survivors may need to learn to confine flashbacks to specific places or times so that children are not traumatized by them.

Families may be helped to communicate their priorities and needs for having, doing, and being to one another. If one of the goals is to build intimacy, then treatment can be designed to help members learn to be close to one another while maintaining clear boundaries of identity, as well as establishing trust, and regulating self-disclosure and commitment (Hovestadt & Fine, 1987). The building of intimacy often involves teaching trauma survivors and their families how to play with each other (Williams, 1991). Families of survivors of trauma, as well as the survivors themselves, need to learn a variety of expressive, empathic, conflict resolution, negotiation, self-change, and maintenance skills as part of the therapeutic process (Hardley & Guerney, 1989).

A major component of therapeutic work with the family centers around how much knowledge of the trauma is to be shared. Victims generally have a desperate need to be heard and, when silenced through direct or indirect messages, feel exposed, condemned, and shamed. A consequence of shame is the wish to disappear and withdraw (Jay, 1991). In this process, children, parents, and therapist together need to determine when to include children, particularly young children, in sessions. In some instances, however, children will be too young to comprehend what is occurring or has occurred or may not be competent enough (e.g., emotionally disturbed, learning disabled) to participate in the therapeutic process.

Part of this process, and a major aspect of treatment, is to build awareness of what is happening and has happened within the family. This building of awareness includes the development of the knowledge of the trauma history of the family as a whole and its individual members, and may actually be the development of an information-processing mechanism that leads to communication between family members (L'Abate, 1986). Sharing of gory details of a traumatic past, however, is not always necessary nor wise for children to hear.

This is particularly true if the children are vulnerable to further traumatization or sensitive to the type of material that would be presented.

If meaning in the family has been challenged or distorted as a result of the traumatic experience, then family members need help to clarify their personal views of how to explain away the trauma. If family members blame themselves or one another inappropriately, then reattribution of that blame needs to occur through cognitive-behavioral techniques including decatastrophizing, fantasizing of consequences, examining the advantages and disadvantages of maintaining the belief, self-instruction, distraction, thought stopping, and other techniques (Freeman & Zaken-Greenberg, 1989).

Other goals of therapy are to make the family a safe place; build trust among family members while stabilizing those who are out of control; and promote self-disclosure and other forms of communication. In addition, the therapist helps to empower individual members and the family system as everyone works through the traumatic event (Figley, 1989).

Family-oriented treatment often includes grief work and crisis intervention within the systems context. Family members must be stabilized before they can begin to work through the traumatic material. Dealing with traumatic events neutralizes the trauma, but only after events and emotions are attached or reattached. Victims and their families are taught to monitor and modify self-talk and dissociative reactions. Social skills training often comes later, as does the identification and/or creation of family resources and the assignment of a new sense of meaning to the traumatic event while attempting to correct cognitive distortions.

One way to find new meaning in a traumatic event is to conduct a healing ritual (Catherall, 1992). Rituals involve symbolism and may help people change a self-image or may be utilized to help persons bring closure to an event or a life. Rituals need to be planned and implemented as a family for them to be successful in resolving some of the loss that trauma brings. For example, to establish safety with their home, the family in the case example brought in a priest to bless the house and identify unsafe objects that might trigger flashbacks. With great reluctance, the children "gave up" certain records and tapes (but not the snakes) that described Satanic abuse, as well as occult-oriented reading materials. Jerry agreed to read potentially distasteful sexually oriented books and magazines in private and removed them from the bedroom.

Therapists who deal with trauma and secondary trauma need to have a model of healing in practice that specifies their basic assumptions as well as the processes of their therapeutic approach (Worell & Remer, 1992). Many models contain a series of steps or stages (Figley, 1985; Scurfield, 1994; Williams & Sommer, 1994). All these models stress the necessity for family stabilization, for creation of safety before the trauma work begins, the need for trauma memory recovery and emotional processing, the need to assign meaning to the event, and the development of social skills before termination occurs.

The therapist who works with traumatized families often functions as a case manager, leading members to appropriate persons and resources. Multiple intervention in trauma families is important, if possible, and if resources and financial assets are available. A combination of individual therapy and group therapy for each partner, couples therapy, family therapy, and other therapies as indicated (e.g., art therapy, body work, movement therapy), although an expensive treatment protocol, is more successful than are scattered individual interventions. Whatever the style or model of treatment used, goals need to include limit setting, clarification of roles and rules, creation of a routine in the home or reestablishment of a routine, education about PTSD, education about communication skills and conflict resolution skills, and the use of appropriate touch.

IMPACT OF FAMILY WORK ON THE THERAPIST

Trauma work is difficult and has a secondary impact on the therapist as well (Danieli, 1994; Munroe, 1994). McCann and Pearlman (1990) have coined the term "vicarious traumatization" and Figley (1994) refers to the impact as "compassion fatigue." Working with traumatized individuals can challenge the therapist's belief systems of safety, trust, power, esteem, and intimacy. Therefore, it is important to have a support network available to use to talk over cases and process secondary trauma in the therapist. Therapists must constantly bear witness to the pain their clients experienced and, in doing so, they run the risk of taking on that pain or shutting off that pain. Through self-attention, therapy when needed, and consultation on a regular basis, therapists can minimize these inevitable effects.

CONCLUSION

What will occur in the case that has been presented? If Jerry has his way, treatment may terminate or Miriam may transfer to another therapist and have to build a new therapeutic alliance. Miriam feels hurt, angry, and frustrated. If she complies with her husband's wishes and temper outbursts, she is again a victim. On the other hand, she is not willing to sacrifice her marriage to remain in therapy. If termination at this time is truly in her best interest, then the caring therapist will suggest other potential referrals, express a willingness to cooperate and consult with a new therapist, and wish her a healing journey. This type of flexible, patient, open response by a therapist provides a model for problem solving and may result in family and individual growth in the long run. A focus on the family needs at this time, rather than on Jerry's or Miriam's individual traumas, may help all family members to redefine roles, examine the meanings of their symptoms and actions in a new light, and may lead to the establishment of more productive patterns of behavior. The goal of work with the traumatized family is to reestablish a steady state in spite of the trauma history and traumatic event(s), while minimizing negative transference and countertransference reactions and, at the same time, providing empathic support. That work is challenging; yet its rewards are many as families can and do heal.

REFERENCES

Albeck, J. H. (1994). Intergenerational consequences of trauma: Reframing traps in treatment theory—a second-generation perspective. In M. B. Williams & J. F. Sommer, Jr. (Eds.), *Handbook of post-traumatic therapy* (pp. 106–125). Westport, CT: Greenwood Press.

American Psychiatric Association. (1994). *Diagnostic and statistical manual,* (4th ed.). Washington, DC: Author.

Armsworth, M. W., Mouton, S., DeWitt, J., Cooley, R., & Hockwerda, K. (1993, October). *Intergenerational effects of incest on parenting skills, abilities and attitudes.* Paper presented at the 9th annual meeting of the International Society for Traumatic Stress Studies, San Antonio, TX.

Bell, D. B. (1993). How deployment stress was reduced among families during Operation Desert Shield/Storm. In D. Mangelsdorf (Ed.), *User's Conference Manual* (pp. 106–110). San Antonio, TX: D. Mangelsdorf.

Blevins, W. (1993). *Your family, your self: How to analyze your family system to understand yourself and achieve more satisfying relationships with your loved ones.* Oakland, CA: New Harbinger.

Carroll, E. M., Foy, D. W., Cannon, B. J., & Zwier, G. (1991). Assessment issues involving the families of trauma victims. *Journal of Traumatic Stress, 4*(1), 25–40.

Catherall, D. R. (1992). *Back from the brink: A family guide to overcoming traumatic stress.* New York: Bantam.

Coughlan, K., & Parkin, C. (1987). Women partners of Vietnam vets. *Journal of Psychosocial Nursing, 25*(10), 25–27.

Danieli, Y. (1981). Families of survivors of the Nazi Holocaust: Some short and long term effects. In C. D. Spielberger, I. G. Arason, & N. Milgram (Eds.), *Stress and anxiety* (Vol. 8). New York: McGraw-Hill/Hemisphere.

Danieli, Y. (1994). Countertransference and trauma: Self-healing and training issues. In M. B. Williams & J. F. Sommer, Jr. (Eds.), *Handbook of post-traumatic therapy* (pp. 540–550). Westport, CT: Greenwood.

Davis, L. (1991). *Allies in healing: When the person you love was sexually abused as a child.* New York: Harper/Collins.

Erickson, C. A. (1989). Rape and the family. In C. R. Figley (Ed.), *Treating stress in families* (pp. 257–289). New York: Brunner/Mazel.

Figley, C. R. (1983). Catastrophes: An overview of family reactions. In C. R. Figley & H. I. McCubbin (Eds.), *Stress and the family. Vol. 2: Coping with catastrophe* (pp. 3–20). New York: Brunner/Mazel.

Figley, C. R. (1985). From victim to survivor: Social responsibility in the wake of catastrophe. In C. R. Figley (Ed.), *Trauma and its wake: The study and treatment of post traumatic stress disorder* (pp. 398–415). New York: Brunner/Mazel.

Figley, C. R. (1989). *Helping traumatized families.* San Francisco: Jossey-Bass.

Figley, C. R. (1994). Compassion fatigue workshop. Charleston, SC: International Association of Trauma Counselors annual conference.

Freeman, A., & Zaken-Greenberg, F. (1989). A cognitive-behavioral approach. In C. R. Figley (Ed.), *Treating stress in families* (pp. 97–121). New York: Brunner/Mazel.

Gilbert, K. R. (1995). Spouses and secondary traumatic stress. In C. R. Figley (Ed.), *Trauma and its wake III: Secondary traumatic stress syndromes.* New York: Brunner/Mazel.

Graber, K. (1991). *Ghosts in the bedroom: A guide for partners of incest survivors.* Deerfield Beach, FL: Health Communications.

Hankin, C. S., Abueg, F., Gallagher-Thompson, D., & Murphy, R. T. (1993, October). *Caregiver stress: Conceptualizing adaptation of partners of PTSD combat veterans.* Paper presented at the 9th annual meeting at the International Society for Traumatic Stress Studies, San Antonio, TX.

Hardley, G., & Guerney, B. G. (1989). A psychoeducational approach. In C. R. Figley (Ed.), *Treating stress in families* (pp. 158–181). New York: Brunner/Mazel.

Hoopes, M. H., Fisher, B. L., & Barlow, S. H. (1984). *Structured family facilitation programs.* Rockville, MD: Aspen Systems Corporation.

Hovestadt, A. J., & Fine, M. (Eds.). (1987). *Family of origin therapy.* Rockville, MD: Aspen.

Imber-Black, E. (1993, May–June). Ghosts in the therapy room. *Family Therapy Networker, 17*(3), 18–29.

Janoff-Bulman, R. (1992). *Shattered assumptions: Toward a new psychology of trauma.* New York: Free Press.

Jay, J. (1991, November/December). Terrible knowledge. *The Family Therapy Networker, 15*(6), 18–29.

Klein-Parker, F. (1988). Dominant attitudes of adult children of Holocaust survivors toward their parents. In J. P. Wilson, Z. Harel, & B. Kahana (Eds.), *Human adaptation to extreme stress: From the Holocaust to Vietnam.* New York: Plenum.

L'Abate, L. (1986). *Systemic family therapy.* New York: Brunner/Mazel.

McCann, I. L., & Pearlman, L. (1990). *Trauma and the adult survivor.* New York: Brunner/Mazel.

McCubbin, M. A., & McCubbin, H. I. (1989). Theoretical orientations to family stress and coping. In C. R. Figley (Ed.), *Traumatic stress in families* (pp. 1–43). New York: Brunner/Mazel.

Marsh, D. T. (1992). *Families and mental illness: New directions in professional practice.* New York: Praeger.

Matsakis, A. (1988). *Vietnam wives: Women and children surviving life with veterans suffering post traumatic stress disorder.* Kensington, MD: Woodbine House.

Matsakis, A. (1992). *I can't get over it: A handbook for trauma survivors.* Oakland, CA: New Harbinger.

Miller, W. R., Williams, A. M., & Bernstein, M. H. (1982). The effects of rape on marital and sexual adjustment. *American Journal of Family Therapy, 19,* 147–159.

Monahon, C. (1993). *Children and trauma: A parent's guide to helping children heal.* New York: Lexington Books.

Monahon, J. (1995). Treating secondary trauma in caregivers. In C. R. Figley (Ed.), *Trauma and its wake III: Treating secondary traumatic stress.* New York: Brunner/Mazel.

Munroe, J. (1994). *Self care of the therapist: Preinstitute workshop on ethical issues and trauma.* Chicago, IL: 10th Annual Meeting of the International Society for Traumatic Stress Studies.

Nair, M. S. (1993). *Techniques for recovering memories of incest and other painful life events.* Long Beach, CA: Author.

Niles, D. (1990, Summer). PTSD: Family implications. *International Association of Marriage and Family Counselors Newsletter, 1,* 2.

Pittman, F. (1993, May–June). No hiding place. *Family Therapy Networker, 17*(3), 30–37.

Rosenthal, D., Sadler, A., & Edwards, W. (1987). Families and post-traumatic stress disorder. In D. Rosenthal (Ed.), *Family stress* (pp. 81–96). Rockville, MD: Aspen.

Salston, M. (1994). Clinical treatment of survivors of homicide victims. In M. B. Williams & J. F. Sommer, Jr. (Eds.), *Handbook of post-traumatic therapy* (pp. 129–145). Westport, CT: Greenwood.

Scurfield, R. R. (1994). War-related trauma: An integrative, experiential, cognitive and spiritual approach. In M. B. Williams & J. F. Sommer (Eds.), *Handbook of Posttraumatic Therapy* (pp. 179–204). Westport, CT: Greenwood.

Williams, M. B. (1990). *Williams-McPearl Belief Scale.* Santa Barbara, CA: Dissertation Instrument.

Williams, M. B. (1991, June). Clinical work with families of MPD patients: Assessment and issues for practice. *Dissociation, 4*(2), 92–98.

Williams, M. B., & Sommer, J. F. (1994). *Handbook of post-traumatic therapy.* Westport, CT: Greenwood.

Worell, J., & Remer, P. (1992). *Feminist perspective in therapy: An empowerment model for women.* New York: Wiley.

Zabukovec, J., & Moore, R. (1993). *Couples group therapy for chronic posttraumatic stress disorder.* Paper presented at the 9th annual meeting of the International Society for Traumatic Stress Studies, San Antonio, TX.

CHAPTER 9

Families Affected by Domestic Violence

MICHELE HARWAY, MARSALI HANSEN, B. B. ROBBIE ROSSMAN, ROBERT
GEFFNER, and IRENE DEITCH*

This chapter considers the various forms of intimate violence that occur in the home. For most people, home is where they are safe from the violence that plagues our society. By contrast, for survivors of spouse abuse, child abuse, or elder abuse, home is where they are most at risk from violence perpetrated by a loved one. We will discuss each of these forms of abuse and describe interventions that practitioners can make.

SPOUSE ABUSE: A CRITICAL CONCERN IN THE TREATMENT OF FAMILIES

Spouse abuse has long been recognized as underreported by those who endure it and frequently missed in the assessment of presenting problems by therapists (Hansen, Harway, & Cervantes, 1991). Therapists often fail to address abuse and instead attempt to address concerns more readily accessible to intervention, such as communication difficulties between partners (Hansen, Harway, & Cervantes, 1991; Harway & Hansen, 1993). Spousal abuse affects large numbers of women while failing to be recognized and treated. Koss (1990) reports that spousal abuse occurs in 28% to 33% of married couples; Koss also reports that among dating couples, dating violence occurs in 50% of the cases.

Recent high profile cases include that of O. J. Simpson, currently on trial for murdering his exwife. During the pretrial publicity, a lengthy and substantial history of spousal violence was reported. The case detailed a classic relationship of frequent battering, sometimes with severe injuries that required hospitalization and instances of repeated police intervention, followed by relatively superficial treatment (the case involved a few sessions with a psychotherapist on the telephone). This example highlights the relatively ineffectual police involvement, the limited psychotherapeutic interventions made in most cases, and

---

* The section on spouse abuse was written by Michele Harway and Marsali Hansen, the section on child abuse by B. B. Robbie Rossman and Robert Geffner, and the section on elder abuse by Irene Deitch.

the continued danger a battered woman may be in, even after her marriage has ended.

Feminist family therapists have long held that inequities in the societal view of women are to blame for the relative inattention to this growing social problem and for the ineffective interventions by police, legal systems, and clinicians. These inequities are the focus of perspectives presented in the growing body of feminist family therapy literature (Goldner, 1985; Hare-Mustin, 1978).

According to this literature, society views women as having less value than men and condones violence in the home while tolerating far less violence toward strangers. Spousal abuse is seen as "a family issue" (Archer, 1989; Mugford, Mugford, & Easteal, 1989) and an experience that is highly exaggerated by its recipient. The recipient is perceived as someone who must have done something to deserve the abuse. This view affects the type of help that a battered woman can expect from others; family members are likely to urge her to "try harder," friends and clergy may tell her that it is her duty to make her marriage work, police and legal representatives are likely to underplay and discount the danger she is in, and psychotherapists may attribute to her at least partial blame for the violence. Among women who are repeated victims of violence (where police intervention is required), 65% have been prior recipients of counseling, and most do not return for a second visit because the therapist never even asked about the violence (Goodstein & Page, 1981).

Battering is much more common among couples seeking marital counseling than previously believed. Holtzworth-Munroe, Waltz, Jacobson, Monaco, Fehrenback, and Gottman (1992) sought nonviolent control groups for a study of spousal abuse. Psychotherapists were asked to identify nonviolent maritally distressed couples from among their clientele. Depending on the sample, 55% to 56% of the supposedly nonviolent men reported having been violent toward their wives.

All these factors—the high prevalence rates of spousal violence among the population in general and among those presenting for marital counseling in particular, the tendency of battered women not to return for treatment if the first contact with a clinician has been unsatisfactory, and the historical blaming of the victim by the clinician—suggest that awareness needs to be raised among psychotherapists and that more training is needed. The remainder of this section will highlight some issues of assessment and treatment of battered women, batterers, and their children. These issues are detailed at greater length in Hansen and Harway (1993) and in Harway and Hansen (1994).

Assessment of Spousal Violence

The identification of domestic violence in couples presenting for couples counseling, in battered women seeking individual treatment for a whole constellation of symptoms, and in families where the child may be the identified patient presents special challenges for clinicians. Most clients are unlikely to present the violence as the reason for seeking therapy and may in fact, experience considerable shame such that the violence is never voluntarily brought up. The battered woman is typically in denial about her circumstances and may in fact resist the battered woman label. In addition, the woman may fear increased violence from her partner if she describes abuse to a third party, particularly if such a disclosure is made in the presence of her spouse (Giles-Sims, 1983; Pressman, 1989; Walker, 1984). The batterer is likely to come into therapy as part of a maritally distressed dyad, while unlikely to present for individual therapy of his own volition. Often the woman has gone to considerable lengths to convince her spouse to enter treatment. Both partners may believe that the therapist will be able to help the woman prevent the conflicts that they believe result in the abuse (Hansen, 1993). Therapists may also feel a need to engage both partners in treatment and may inadvertently collude with the man against his wife in the joining process. Couples work is likely to be ineffective and may in fact be dangerous to the woman due to the psychological pattern of abuse, which includes controlling by fear, demeaning comments that result in impaired self-esteem, and projection of responsibility for maintaining the violent interactions. Separating the couple for assessment and treatment is widely recommended (Cook & Frantz-Cook, 1984; Goldner, 1992; Hansen, 1993). Once separated, asking direct questions of each partner about conflict resolution (Pizzey, 1974; Pressman, 1989; Walker, 1979) is an important part of the intake, as is ascertaining degree of commitment to the relationship.

A thorough assessment prior to beginning treatment is particularly important in cases of suspected spousal abuse. Battered women typically present with a constellation of trauma-related symptoms (Harway, 1993; Hotaling & Sugarman, 1986). Improper identification of the abuse may lead instead to treatment of a battered woman for an anxiety disorder, borderline personality disorder, or any other diagnosis which shares common symptoms with the sequelae of abuse.

Men who batter often have a charming persona which they present outside of the home. Identifying the violence through an assessment of the man's presenting issues will, as a consequence, rarely be fruitful. Instead, O'Neil and Egan (1993) indicate that abuse should be considered when the man presents with rigid, sexist, or restrictive gender role conceptions, restrictive emotionality, and a focus on power and competition issues.

Children exposed to battering in the home suffer from both short-term and long-term effects. Moreover, as many as 30% to 60% of children who witness abuse are victims of abuse themselves (Hughes, 1982; Straus, Gelles, & Steinmitz, 1980). Children who witness abuse are reported to develop a wide range of symptoms including emotional arousal, distress, increased aggressiveness, school performance drop, depression, and anxiety (see Berman, 1993 for a review of studies). The possibility of violence in the home must always be considered when children are symptomatic because the presenting symptoms are the same as for other situations negatively impacting children. This topic will also be explored in greater detail in the section on child maltreatment later in this chapter.

Treating Spousal Violence

Treatment with clients where violence is a concern must always address safety issues first. Safety plans are needed both for women and their children (Fleming, 1979; Pizzey, 1975; Register, 1993; Walker, 1979) and behavioral rehearsal of safety plans is critical (Ganley, 1981; Neidig & Friedman, 1984; NiCarthy, 1982).

Harway and Hansen (1994) describe a treatment model for working with battered women, which includes a crisis intervention phase (assessing for the existence of violence, assessing the danger the woman is in, educating the woman about battering and validating her experience, and developing and practicing a safety/danger management plan), a short-term counseling phase (working on empowerment, developing independent living skills and attitudes, and helping the woman grieve the loss of the idealized relationship) and finally a long-term counseling phase (healing the past, developing trust, and working from a trauma recovery model to heal resulting psychological problems).

Therapists have a special challenge to remain sensitive at all times to the contributing factors because battered women are reluctant, with good reason, to leave their relationship. Economic concerns are very real for these women (Aguirre, 1985; Hart, 1993; Strube & Barbour, 1983) and therapists who fail to address these economic realities may find that their clients return multiple times to the abusive relationship. Moreover, many batterers threaten to harm their spouse if she threatens leaving, and in fact, the risk of fatality or serious injury increases when the woman does leave (Browne, 1987; Sonkin, Martin, & Walker, 1985). Women who state that they are afraid to leave because their husbands have threatened to kill them if they do are voicing very real fears (Bernard, Vera, Vera, & Newman, 1982; Dutton, 1988; Saunders & Browne, 1990). The battered woman's fear needs to be validated and addressed by the therapist. The clinician cannot afford to remain a neutral third party because therapeutic work with this population may require consultations with experts including shelter personnel, people in the legal system, and victim services. Unfortunately, research indicates that many therapists are reluctant to conceptualize therapeutic interventions that involve this expanded view of treatment (Harway & Hansen, 1993). In addition, in ensuring that a battered woman continues in treatment, it is important for the therapist to acknowledge that the batterer has many positive characteristics which are valued by his spouse and which enhance her commitment to the relationship. These characteristics need to be recognized and addressed by the clinician if therapy is to be effective (Hansen & Goldenberg, 1993).

In working with batterers, it is important to remember that men who present for treatment are not likely to disclose violence in their relationship, especially men who seek therapy to salvage a relationship. Most batterers do not enter treatment voluntarily but instead are brought into therapy by their spouses or are court-ordered (Segel-Evans, 1994). Those men tend to project the responsibility for the violence onto their victims claiming that "the bitch deserved it" and to minimize the violence. The recognition of the seriousness of the act and accepting responsibility for it are important first steps in treatment (Jenkins, 1990). During the crisis intervention phase, these acknowledgments are made at the same time as the batterer receives education about violence and violence control, begins to identify feelings, learns socially acceptable ways of channeling those feelings, and develops a danger management plan (Harway & Hansen, 1994). During the short-term counseling phase, learning to orient power into socially acceptable channels, doing shame and guilt work and exploring feelings of abandonment are the major tasks to be accomplished. Finally, in the long-term counseling phase, healing the abuse of the past and developing relational skills with other men and women and with the spouse are the focus of treatment. This work is best accomplished in a group setting with adjunctive individual therapy (Harway & Evans, in press). It is also important for the therapist to recognize that physical abuse may be preceded by psychological violence or control, or even that some men may cease their battering but continue their abusive behavior. A therapist's inquiry about violent behavior, in the latter cases, could well yield a response of "No, I don't get physically violent," when in fact abusive behavior, sometimes of a terroristic nature may continue (Edleson & Syers, 1990; Tolman & Bhosley, 1990). Finally, an important fact is that not all treatment approaches have been equally effective with batterers (Gondolf, 1993) nor are all batterers good candidates for treatment (Jacobson, 1993).

CHILD MALTREATMENT: CONSEQUENCES AND INTERVENTION

In this portion of the chapter, the focus is on child sexual and physical abuse and neglect, which comprised 15%, 25%, and 48% of reported child abuse cases, respectively, during 1990–1991 for the 21 states with comparable abuse reporting categories in the 1991 Fifty-State Survey conducted by the National Committee for Prevention of Child Abuse (NCPCA, 1992). In the following section, we briefly review research on physical and sexual maltreatment of children and adolescents, and then highlight some of the issues and techniques considered in the treatment of abuse victims and their families. The reader is also referred to recent summaries of symptomatology associated with these types of child maltreatment (e.g., for sexual abuse, see Finkelhor, 1990; Hanson, 1990; Kendall-Tackett, Williams, & Finkelhor, 1993; for physical abuse, see Hansen, Conaway, & Christopher, 1990; Malinosky-Rummell & Hansen, 1993; Wolfe, 1987; for witnessing of parental violence, see Berman, 1993; Harway & Hansen, 1994; Jaffe, Wolfe, & Wilson, 1990). A few short-term (e.g., Gomes-Schwartz, Horowitz, Cardarelli, & Sauzier, 1990) and long-term (e.g., Erickson, Egland, & Pianta, 1989) longitudinal studies have been conducted.

Effects of Maltreatment

Children's difficulties that have been linked to physical and sexual maltreatment have been understood in several ways: as disruptions of the parent-child relationship and other developmental processes (Cicchetti, 1989); as inappropriate behaviors learned in the context of the abuse setting and inappropriate parenting (Wolfe, 1987); and as trauma reactions that may crystallize into enduring behavior patterns (Rossman, 1993; Wolfe & Jaffe, 1991). All these models have unique features to add to our understanding of maltreatment. Considered together, they reflect the broad-based disruption of normal development that can accompany abusive treatment. However, several factors appear to influence an abuse victim's symptomatology: age of abuse onset; age of the child when assessed; gender; intensity and duration of abuse; sources of support for the child; and other child and family factors. For example, Zwiney and Nash (1988) found girls sexually abused prior to age nine showed more cognitive and emotional disruption on Rorschach protocols than girls abused later.

The manner in which symptomatology is expressed may also change with age such that physically abused school-age children may be seen as rambunctious, but in adolescence are considered delinquent (Malinosky-Rummell & Hansen, 1993). In addition, Terr (1991) argues that single-event trauma may be associated with somewhat different symptomatology than repeated trauma. It is not surprising that no single pattern of symptomatology emerges consistently with all physical or sexual maltreatment victims.

Looking first at physical abuse and neglect, a careful longitudinal study of maltreated preschoolers who were physically abused, emotionally abused, physically neglected, or emotionally neglected (Erickson, Egland, & Pianta, 1989), showed the physical neglect group to be the most cognitively disadvantaged, and the emotional neglect group to have the highest levels of aggressive and disruptive behaviors. The physical abuse group was generally doing more poorly than the nonabused control group but was not always different from or worse than other maltreatment groups. The physically abused children by age 6, however, were notable for their aggression and acting-out, impulse and affect regulation problems, and poor school performance. At age 6, the researchers identified a group of sexually abused children within their sample who were characterized by their anxiety, attentional problems, and need to be close to teachers. Other studies have also identified cognitive deficits for neglected children. Severely neglected children, aged 3 through 8 years, showed greater overall cognitive difficulties than physically abused, generally neglected, and nonmaltreated children (Fox, Long, & Langlois, 1988), and abused adolescents evidence school learning difficulties (Malinosky-Rummell & Hansen, 1993).

Studies examining the impact of physical abuse and neglect on social functioning have produced mixed results. Although some investigations (e.g., Jaffe, Wolfe, Wilson, & Zak, 1986) found no differences in social competencies of abused children, other research (e.g., Hoffman-Plotkin & Twentyman, 1984; Main & George, 1985) has suggested that abused children are more socially withdrawn, less prosocial, and express fewer positive emotions during social interactions than nonabused peers.

Emotional development also appears to be at risk (Hansen et al., 1990). For physically maltreated children, levels of internalizing behaviors including depression are elevated, self-esteem and body image are lower, and aggressive and self-destructive behaviors, including substance abuse and suicide, are heightened (Malinosky-Rummell & Hansen, 1993). Externalizing and aggressive/impulsive behavior problems often accompany physical maltreatment (Jaffe et al., 1986), in addition to other types of problems such as enuresis, and attentional deficits (Hansen et al., 1990). In a recent study, Trickett (1993) replicated the finding of poorer cognitive maturity, social problem solving, and greater behavior problems for 4- to 11-year-old physically abused children. They found instances where aspects of the child-rearing context (e.g., family environment and child-rearing beliefs and behaviors) were more predictive of functioning than abuse status, emphasizing the co-occurrence of abuse with family and parent dysfunction. Aggressive problems seem to carry forward with about 20% of abused children becoming delinquent compared with a 5% base rate in the population (Lewis, Mallouh, & Webb, 1989). Teens with such abusive backgrounds exhibit more violence in treatment situations (e.g., Cavaiola & Schiff, 1988), and in dating or extrafamilial relationships, and carry out nonviolent crimes (Garbarino & Plantz, 1986; Reuterman & Burcky, 1989).

Sexual abuse victims also show cognitive difficulties in terms of both distortions on projective instruments (Leifer, Shapiro, Martone, & Kassem, 1991; Zwiney & Nash, 1988), and school functioning (Browne & Finkelhor, 1986). Several features of their symptomatology suggest that there are problems with social development. These include withdrawal, low self-esteem, and inappropriate sexual behaviors or promiscuity. Emotional development and regulation also seems disrupted as reflected in higher levels of fear and anxiety, including PTSD syptomatology, and greater depression and internalizing symptomatology. Behavioral difficulties are also noted in self-destructive behaviors, delinquent, aggressive, and illegal acts, and running away. Conte and Schuerman (1987) compared 4- to 17-year-old sexual abuse victims with a community group and found abuse victims to have significantly greater problems with body-image/self-esteem, withdrawal, aggression, concentration, depression, fear, and PTSD symptoms. Gale, Thompson, Moran, and Sack (1988) studied children referred to a community clinic, some with emotional and behavioral problems only, some with physical abuse, and some with sexual abuse. Inappropriate sexual behaviors and lower noncompliance discriminated sexual abuse victims from the other groups, whereas depression, aggression, anxiety, and withdrawal were among behaviors that did not. As compared with conduct-disordered boys, sexually abused boys (aged 3-12 years) were higher on sexual problems and lower on aggression and externalizing problems (Friedrich, 1988). In another comparison of 3- to 12-year-old nonabused, sexually abused, and psychiatric outpatient children, Friedrich (1988) reported that sexually abused children were highest of the three groups on sexual problems, but were between the outpatient and nonabused children on levels of hyperactivity, aggression, and externalizing dimensions.

Kendall-Tackett et al. (1993) noted that examining symptomatology by age group was useful in identifying patterns that were somewhat more cohesive. For preschoolers, the most common sequelae were anxiety and PTSD symptoms, sexually inappropriate behaviors, and internalizing and externalizing problems. School-age children tended to show fear, aggression, hyperactivity, nightmares, school problems, and regression. Adolescents were more likely to show depression, withdrawal, self-injury through substance abuse or suicide, illegal acts, and running away. Although long-term longitudinal studies have not been done, Kendall-Tackett et al. noted that some symptoms appeared regularly across age in cross-sectional studies even though their form of expression might have changed: depression, sexualized aggression or behaviors (though less common during school age), and antisocial behaviors. Sexual abuse of girls also may be linked to changes in the usual timing of puberty and associated hormonal changes, such that early sexual abuse may lead to earlier maturation (Trickett & Putnam, 1993). In sum, sexual and physical abuse and neglect are associated with delays or distortions in one or more developmental systems, and there are many individual differences among victims and abusive families.

Interventions

Abuse interventions typically involve several components: assessment of child and family functioning, especially with regard to ongoing family violence and the protection of the child following disclosure, the availability and cooperativeness of the child's support system (parents, sibs, extended family, teachers, etc.), and need for out-of-home placement; and medical examination of the child to rule out or treat injuries or medical conditions such as malnourishment (Azar & Wolfe, 1989). There are additional treatment issues for maltreated children. One is the desirability of telling such children they have been abused. Some advocate awareness for all victims (e.g., Ney, 1987), whereas others (e.g., Weinbach & Curtiss, 1986) argue that this awareness may not be useful depending on the age and circumstances of the child if abuse is no longer a threat. Second, decisions need to be made about whether deficits should be regarded as behavioral disorders, or components of the trauma process, or both (Conte, 1990; Rossman, 1993). Third, the developmental level of the victim must be considered in terms of how much behavior and play (as opposed to language and talking) can be emphasized in treatment, and the level of complexity of understandings and emotional reactions that can be assumed (Geffner, Barrett, & Rossman, in press).

Stages through which treatment proceeds include crisis intervention and initial assessment at the time of the disclosure, short-term intervention, and long-term therapy (Bell & Chance-Hill, 1991). The goals of crisis intervention and assessment include ensuring the safety of all endangered family members, assessing trauma and distress symptoms, and gathering information about the nature of the abuse. Short-term intervention goals involve continued assessment, psychoeducation about abuse and parenting, and work to enhance competencies of victims and caretakers to deal with the abuse (e.g., skills for anger management and resolution, anxiety management, and social problem solving). Long-term goals include further understanding of abuse as connected to family history and individual issues, personal growth, and plans to avoid recurrence of abuse. Medications (Terr, 1989) or age-appropriate relaxation training can also be used for decreasing distress (Walker, Bonner, & Kaufman, 1988), and intervention may be needed for different types of problems (such as enuresis or cognitive delays).

In addition to the preceding general treatment considerations, intervention programs have been designed specifically for physical and sexual abuse. Many of the programs for physical maltreatment have targeted the parent(s) for intervention, with special attention to cultural and subcultural factors that may be involved (Hansen et al., 1990). Some general treatment considerations are maximizing the generalizability of interventions to increase program maintenance; using a multidisciplinary team approach with medical, educational, legal, and psychological personnel in program planning; and increasing compliance with interventions by assessing and dealing with factors that are likely to interfere. Azar and Wolfe (1989) reviewed behavioral techniques used with abusive parents and note key feature in using any of these programs is to engage the parent(s) because the parent(s) may not regard their behavior as inappropriate. They recommend reframing the problem in terms other than the abuse such as child noncompliance, parental stress, or lack of social support, and providing incentives for regular participation. Programs that emphasize parenting skills and self-control training with the reframed goal of better child behavior and parent-child interactions have been used successfully with abusive parents (Wolfe, Sandler, & Kaufman, 1981).

Family therapy, from various perspectives, may be used if it seems safe for the victim(s), the rationale being that family communication or dynamics may support the abuse and need to be changed or abuse will continue (Walker et al., 1988). Lutzker (1984; Lutzker & Rice, 1984) and his colleagues have designed and successfully used "Project 12-Ways," a relatively broad-based program for working with abusive and neglectful families, which addresses health and safety issues; parent training; parent stress management, self-control, social support, financial management, and job training; and development of needed competencies and skills in the child. Justice and Justice (1990) describe another multiple system program for abusive families. Although many of these programs emphasize work with caretakers, physically maltreated children are also likely to need help with the following issues: building nonaggressive relationships with and trust in others; regulation of anxiety, anger, and depression; increasing competence and self-worth; remediating cognitive delays; and, social interaction skills and social problem solving. These needs can be addressed with individual treatment, specialized groups, and educational remediation through the schools. Yoshikawa's (1994) review of interventions to prevent delinquency stresses the importance of both early child educational efforts and supportive family interventions. The strategy allows one to avoid the partial solution of working only with parents or only with children (Graziano & Mills, 1992).

Intrafamilial or extrafamilial sexual abuse also constitutes a family crisis. Distress levels are likely to be high for victims and caretakers. If the abuse is intrafamilial, Figley (1988) argues that more time and skill are needed in treatment because these families are likely to have been abusive longer, have developed maladaptive coping devices, and have difficulties with social support, skills, and trust. Since sociocultural, family, and child factors are thought to contribute to the abuse, most approaches to sexual abuse are multiple system approaches (e.g., Trepper & Barrett, 1986), whether or not they view the abuse as a systemic family problem. Interventions may occur with individuals, parent-child dyads, couples, and the family. Because research suggests that a child's relationship with a supportive adult is one of the more powerful predictors of recovery, it seems critical to involve all potentially supportive adults in intervention (Conte & Schuerman, 1988). The positive effects of adult support may be implicated in the 18-month follow-up finding of diminished emotional distress in 55% of sexual abuse victims, although all received initial crisis intervention, and 35% received additional treatment (Gomes-Schwartz et al., 1990).

A number of interventions have been devised specifically for sexual abuse. Barrett (in Geffner, Barrett, & Rossman, in press) describes a three-stage treatment program for working with incestuous families. Her goals for Stage 1 include case management, assessment of involved parties, reduction of family denial, the perpetrator taking responsibility for the abuse, the family agreeing on a treatment plan, and the development of a safe context and trusting relationship with the therapist. Individual and multiple-person sessions may be involved at this stage. At Stage 2, specialized therapy groups that only include other victims (or perpetrators, etc.), and sessions for other involved parties (e.g., sibs, couples, or extended family) may be useful. At Stage 3, the major issue is preventing recurrence of the abuse by identifying perpetuating factors and instituting needed changes. Giarretto (1982) also presents a program with multiple components, and Knittle and Tuana (1980) describe the use of groups with adolescent victims. It is likely that child sexual abuse victims will need to deal with at least the following issues: the degree to which they can trust relationships and count on the support of others; the extent to which they feel helpless, traumatized, and depressed; and, maladaptive coping strategies like denial or dissociation that have developed to help them withstand repeated abuse.

SILENT SUFFERERS: DOMESTIC VIOLENCE AND THE ELDERLY

The least discussed form of family violence is elder abuse. The elderly are the fastest growing segment of the population with an estimate that by the year

2050, the over-65 group will triple (Tatara, 1990; Tomes, 1993). A majority of the "oldest-old" (75 and over) will be women. Perceptions, definitions and interpretations of what constitutes mistreatment may differ between victim and victimizer, between agencies and state legislatures, and between various cultural groups and ethnic groups (Holtzworth-Munroe & Arias, 1993; Hudson, 1989; Moon & Williams, 1993).

Despite the myth that families of older people are uncaring, unconcerned, and unavailable, 80% of the caregiving is performed by family members, usually adult children or spouses, and only 5% of the elderly are institutionalized (Hugh, 1991; Pritchard, 1993). The circumstances of the caregiving situation and the quality of that relationship, however, require scrutiny.

Data indicate an alarming rise in the prevalence of elder abuse (Tatara, 1990). The 200,000 reported cases of elder abuse are far from an accurate reflection of the reality of the situation. It is estimated that only 1 out of 14 actual cases is reported to the authorities. Most victims are reluctant to report the abuse because most forms of abuse occur within the home and are perpetrated by family members. In 1991, 40% of crimes against women aged 65 and older were committed by family members, friends, or acquaintances. A more accurate estimate of elder abuse may be of two million incidents (National Aging and Resource Center on Elder Abuse, 1990; Stein, 1991; Tatara, 1990, 1991). Pillemer and Finkelhor (1988) studying elder abuse in Boston, found it to occur in more than 3% of the population of over 65. However, they indicate that spouse abuse is more prevalent than abuse of the elder by adult children. They report a similar rate of victimization for both men and women. By contrast, Hwalek (1990) describes the majority of abused elders as being between 60 and 85 years, Caucasian, female, and widowed with male abusers, most of whom were older adults as well. She also found that if the abuser was married to the victim and was an informal caregiver, successful intervention was more likely. The outcome of elder abuse can also be extreme. Statistics released at a Washington News Conference by the Older Women's League (May 5, 1994) reported that the murder rate of women aged 65 and older rose 30% (from 1974), whereas the murder rate of men the same age as women declined 6%. Underrated, underreported, and often unrecognized, elder abuse is a social and political issue. It is also a crime! Tatara (1990), Director of the National Aging Resource Center on Elder Abuse, indicates that elder abuse is an emerging national problem calling for everyone's help. Elder abuse is anticipated to be the problem of the next century.

Nature of Elder Abuse

Several different models have traditionally been presented to help explain elder abuse. These include comparing elder abuse with child abuse, looking at the inherent stresses of the caregiving situation, and blaming the abuse on the aging of the elder. None of these models provides a satisfactory explanation. The use of a model that compares elder abuse with child battering (Utech & Garrett,

1992) has led to stereotypical perceptions of the elderly as helpless, fragile, dependent, and childlike. Efforts to understand the abuse of elders by examining the relationships with family members have further complicated the issues. Familial factors implicated in elder abuse have included caregiver burden and the elderly person's physical and emotional dependency, factors that Pillemer and Finkelhor (1989) dispute. Their case-controlled research does not support caregiver stress or care-recipient physical status as a basis for abuse. Problems of the caregiver are cited as causes of the abusive behavior.

"Aging" has also been targeted as the cause of elder abuse. Representations of the elderly as demented, debilitated, and diseased are said to have negative impacts on caregiving family members (Deitch, 1993; Steinmetz, 1990; Wolf, 1992). All these explanations have resulted in blaming the victim for the abusive situation (Petel et al., 1988; Pillèmer, 1986; Pillemer & Finkelhor, 1989). Older adults are, in fact, a diverse population. Some are indeed frail or ill, whereas others are autonomous and independent. Many are caregivers to their own elderly parents, their spouses, or dependent adult children (Greenberg, Seltzer, & Greenley, 1993). Many are physically and sexually active (Deitch, 1994).

By contrast, several studies by Pillemer and colleagues indicate that characteristics of the abuser may be helpful in understanding elder abuse. Pillemer and Finkelhor's (1989) case-controlled study explored who among the elderly would most likely become victims and found that abuser deviance and dependency were the most significant predictive variables. Pillemer (1986) reported that abusers have mental, emotional, and alcohol and drug-related problems and tend to be dependent on their victims. Pillemer and Suitor (1991) described the abuser as a dependent, cognitively impaired or mentally ill, adult child or spouse. Moreover, Anetzberger (1987) and Breckman and Adelman (1988) determined abuser deviance to be the most important predictive variable.

In a related series of studies, Pillemer and Suitor (1989) investigated violence-proneness among caregivers and identified four highly related factors: caregiving demand, interactional stress, caregiving characteristics, and caregiving contexts. For those caregivers who expressed a fear of violence, interactional stressors caused by disruptive behavior such as wandering, outbursts or embarrassing and assaultive behavior by caregiving recipients were important predictors. Another finding was that spouses were more likely than any other relative to become violent to care recipients and generally, persons with lower self-esteem feared becoming violent. Adult children who return to the nest and those young adults who are incompletely launched are most likely to be psychologically dependent on their elder parents and therefore present a potential risk category. Shared living situations and social isolation are also likely to be risk factors. Living with the care recipient was also positively related to violent feelings. An important outcome of this study is the finding that caregivers who have more violent feelings toward their care recipients are more likely to institutionalize them.

In short, the abuser profile is one in which there is high probability of pathological history, deficient socialization, a history of mental and emotional problems, psychological dependency on the abused, and substance addiction.

Spousal Abuse and the Elderly

Because spousal abuse is more prevalent than any other form of domestic elder abuse (New York City Department for Aging, 1990; Pillemer & Suitor, 1989), spousal abuse must be discussed from the perspective of older adults.

Not all aging couples go off to "Golden Pond." For many that pond is tainted. Because the normative prohibition against child-to-parent violence is stronger than that of spouse-to-spouse violence (Hwalek, 1990; Pillemer & Finkelhor, 1989; Pillemer & Suitor, 1989), violence by caregiving spouses is more likely than by caregiving adult children or other relatives. Pillemer and Suitor (1989) state that "actual violence by caregivers appears more often to be a form of spousal abuse" (p. 170). The abusing spouse is described as older and having lower self-esteem than the abused (Pillemer & Suitor, 1989).

Elderly spouse abuse may also be seen as a continuation of a long-standing pattern of domestic violence (Sengstock, 1991). Abusive behavior may have begun early in the marriage (Deitch, 1993). Ramsey-Klawsnik (1993) reports that 31% of elderly married women experience violence within the relationship. Physical abuse by older husbands can be just as life-threatening as with younger husbands. Goetting (1989) found that violent tensions in the homes of elders often lead to homicide. In a two-year study of elder abuse conducted by the New York City Department of Aging (1990), a majority of victims were older women (60–99). More than half the perpetrators were men. And spouses were most likely to be involved in physical abuse. Patterns of spousal abuse among the elderly are rarely considered and may go unidentified by the victim; therefore, they are underreported. Tatara (1990) presents substantiated abuse cases showing that the majority of abusers of the elderly in domestic settings are men. In cases of spousal abuse, the likelihood of wives being abused by their husbands is nearly three times greater than that of husbands being mistreated by wives (National Aging Resource Center on Elder Abuse, 1990). Wives who do in fact use violence often are acting in self-defense. On the other hand, Sengstock (1991) examines elder abuse where the wife is the perpetrator. She explains that "reverse spousal abuse" occurs because differential patterns of strength and power in the relationship change. Reverse spousal abuse may also constitute acting-out in retaliation against a spouse who was abusive in prior years.

In a certain number of cases, spousal abuse is a new phenomenon for the older couple. Deitch (1993) describes late-onset spousal abuse (LOSA), in which the eruption of abuse manifests later in life and can be triggered by external stressors (e.g., forced retirement, illness, economic pressure, chemical dependency). For male caregivers, late-onset spousal abuse can also be related to role conflict, skill deficits, diminished capacity, retaliation, dependency issues, or personal pathology. Abuse of power and substance addiction or alcoholism, and at least two major life setbacks, can contribute to late-onset spousal abuse.

More attention to domestic violence by elder spouses is needed to begin to understand the special intervention needs of this population.

Sexual Abuse

Another form of domestic violence found in elders is sexual abuse. National estimates for elderly female rape victims 65 years of age and older were 10 incidents per 100,000 in 1990 (U.S. Department of Justice, 1991). The majority of the sexual assaults are completed by nonstrangers and by men. Holt (1993) in Great Britain, found that, out of 90 cases of "suspected" elder sexual abuse, the ratio of female to male family members who were abused by males was 6:1, with 85% of all victims being 75 or older. Ramsey-Klawsnick (1993) reached similar conclusions.

Sexual abuse is the most hidden form of elder abuse within families, although the extent of sexual abuse in marital or family situations is not known. The lack of information about these forms of abuse does not necessarily mean that they do not exist. Ageist attitudes, specifically that older couples are not sexual beings, may inhibit reporting of sexual abuse incidents. Stereotyping elderly women as sexless and unattractive also contributes to a lack of awareness of domestic sexual abuse (Deitch, 1994). Marital rape is a common form of sexual abuse in later life. Sengstock (1991) reports that sexual malfunction in partners (e.g., impotence, erectile strength, and frequency of ejaculation related to alcoholism, hypertension, and other physical factors), is a contributing factor to sexual abuse. Frustration and the need to prove one's masculinity, sexual power, and control are all significant aspects of sexual abuse. Another form of sexual abuse is adult child to parent incest, which also occurs in persons 65 and older.

Aside from rape, molestation, and incest, there are other forms of sexual abuse of older women by family members. They may include exhibitionism, voyeurism, displaying pornography, using victims to produce pornography or allowing others sexual access to victims (Ramsey-Klawsnik, 1993). Because rapes and other types of sexual abuses are particularly difficult to substantiate in this population, investigations of sexual assault of women over 65 years of age are virtually nonexistent and physical symptoms, body language, and verbal cues of sexual abuse may go unnoticed (Ramsey-Klawsnik, 1993).

The impact of sexual abuse on the elderly is no less traumatic than for younger people. Self-blame, social stigma, shame, and fear of not being believed lead to nonreporting of cases. Recovery from this trauma is a slow process for the victim. Ramsey-Klawsnick (1993) offers guidelines and suggestions for interviewing suspected victims of sex abuse, as does Harway (1992), who recommends the need for well-trained therapists working in this area of domestic violence.

Issues of Cultural Diversity

Elder abuse needs to be considered in a cultural context. Whether abuse is perceived, whether an abused elder seeks help, to whom elders go for assistance, are all influenced by cultural background, ethnicity, and religious beliefs. For example, in Israel, elder abuse is more "acceptable" if it occurs in families "within the context of a caring relationship" (Neikrug & Ronen, 1993, p. 17) than if the abusive person is a nonfamily member. Moon and Williams (1993) in their cross-cultural study on the meaning of elder mistreatment looked at African American, Korean American, and Caucasian American subjects. Each group was shown a series of vignettes involving "elder conflict situations." Recognition of abuse patterns differed for each group, as did the help-seeking behavior.

To counter stereotypes and generalizations that professionals may have about each group served, education and training are essential. Familiarity with cultural attitudes about family violence, the elderly, and the utilization of social services is important (Long, 1986; Stein, 1991; Wolf, 1994).

The use of paraprofessionals whose culture is similar to the population served could be most effective in education for public awareness as well as in sensitizing law enforcement, criminal justice, and social service agencies. Practitioners need to reformulate their understanding of elder abuse so that it accurately reflects the perception and identification of abusive behavior in the elderly client's cultural system. Researchers and practitioners need the insight of older persons representing various cultural groups (Hernandez, 1991; Moon & Williams, 1993).

Mandatory Reporting and Safety Planning

As the issue of elder abuse has come to the attention of the public, it is also being taken more seriously by the legal system. At the present, protection for elders varies by state and by jurisdiction. At a national level, Title VII of the Older Americans Act seeks to increase the quality of life and general welfare for vulnerable adults by directing state agencies to advocate on behalf of those who are most socially and economically vulnerable (National Association and Resource Center for Elder Abuse, 1994). At the state level, mandatory reporting systems are in place in some states "whereby government agencies must report suspected elder abuse, i.e., those received from agencies, complaints by molested people, and other referrals. Other states have voluntary reporting programs" (Tatara, 1990, p. 7). In California, for example, mental health professionals are required to report elder abuse if there is visible evidence of abuse (e.g., bruises, lacerations). Reports are made to the Department of Social Service.

In other jurisdictions, adult protective services have been established to oversee those elderly who have been declared incompetent or incapable of acting on their own behalf. In some locations, elders with physical or mental disabilities, are considered vulnerable and therefore protected. In Arizona, elder abuse statutes are grouped with child or vulnerable adult laws. However, many other areas, including Great Britain, have no mandatory reporting laws (Holt, 1993).

Other agencies may intervene in cases of reported elder abuse. Competency evaluation may determine the extent to which agencies make decisions for client placement. The criminal justice system can follow up with the decision to prosecute the abuser (Douglass, 1988; New York City Department of Aging, 1990;

Simon, 1992). Temporary hospitalization and protection orders can be issued if the victim is determined to be functionally disoriented subsequent to a pattern of abuse. Competency hearings for the purpose of providing protection to an abused elder suggest that mandatory reporting of abuse is a more complicated process than it initially seems. Even though the client's safety and well-being may be threatened by an abusive family member, mandatory reporting may not lead to the best outcome for the client. When the recommendations of the legal and social service agencies are in conflict with the judgment of the abused, the victim's dignity and free choice are threatened. Whereas abused children are not capable of determining what is in their best interest, elders have the right to privacy and to remain in their homes, both of which are threatened when abuse is suspected. Fearing that they will be institutionalized if abuse is detected, many elders may choose to put up with the abuse rather than having to deal with the negative repercussions. Using physical force or threats of placement of an abused elder into an institution, even a good nursing home, may also lead the elder to deny that abuse ever occurred. Unfortunately, both choices only intensify feelings of helplessness, hopelessness, and powerlessness. As a consequence, abuse charges are often dropped because of victims' failure to follow through and because reporting and investigative processes are ineffective. The right to refuse to bring charges against the abuser, whether perceived as a foolish decision or a rational choice, is ultimately preserving the elderly victim's autonomy and independence (Deitch, 1993) because mandatory reporting services may worsen the situation they were supposed to improve.

Planning for safety of abused elders may require searching for appropriate shelter. In the cases of battered women, there is inadequate housing available on an emergency basis for elders in danger; although in planning for the safety of the victim the abuser must be separated from the victim, especially if the abuser is evaluated as pathological (Kosberg, 1988). Safe havens and elder shelters (where they exist) are examples of emergency shelters available to victims of elder abuse. Safety planning may be in the form of immediate placement, hospitalization, temporary relocation with other family members or friends, or placement in an elder shelter. In New York City, "A Safe Place" provides shelter for the abused elderly. In Manhattan, "Safe Haven" is a shelter specifically for abused elderly. Other situations may require referral to an existing shelter for battered women.

Therapists assisting their clients with a safety plan are advocating for them. This involves informing elders of their rights, telling them of available community resources, helping them negotiate through the law enforcement system, and supporting their clients' efforts in the decision-making process. This will be discussed at greater length under intervention strategies.

Treatment Issues

Sadly, few clinicians elect to work with issues of domestic violence and the elderly, although with the "graying of society," increased incidence of elder spousal abuse is anticipated. Nonetheless, treatment for domestic violence of the elderly requires knowledge, skill, and sensitivity.

As with other forms of domestic violence, assessment is key in working with abused elders. The existence of spousal or familial violence against an elder must be ascertained first, a difficult endeavor given the tendency of elders to camouflage the abuse for fear of retaliation by the abuser. It must be determined which elders are at risk in their families. Family boundaries, deviance of the caregiver, history of abuse, dependency, alcoholism, and drug abuse are all precursor factors that need to be carefully assessed in early sessions. The client may be asked to describe a recent family crisis. The clinicians should ask direct questions about the form of abuse, the frequency, and the severity and ask how family members have resolved their conflicts.

When it is clear that there has been abuse, a family history must be secured. Determination must be made regarding the relationship of the abuser to the victim; the involvement of drugs and alcohol; the etiology of abusive behavior; the extent of social isolation of the elder; the degree and nature of cognitive, emotional, and behavioral limitations of the abuser and the abused; judgment and competency issues of the abused; and finally the frequency, severity, and type of abuse. Mental health practitioners will need to assess the level of cognitive functioning of the elder, which may require ordering a neuropsychological examination. If there is cognitive impairment, the clinician will need to determine how recent or long-standing it has been, and whether the patient is medicated. Moreover, it will be important to determine the level of cognitive functioning related to the victimization.

Symptoms associated with sexual victimization may be present or reported. Ramsey-Klawsnick (1993) lists symptoms of possible elder sexual abuse:

- Genital or urinary irritation, injury, or scarring.
- Presence of sexually transmitted disease.
- Intense fear reaction to an individual or to people in general.
- Nightmares, night terrors, sleep disturbances.
- Extreme upset when bathed or changed.
- Self-destructive activity or suicidal ideation.

"Therapists must be alert to the patient who sometimes makes a 'coded' disclosure, which is a hint rather than a direct statement of sexual victimization" (Ramsey-Klawsnick, 1993, p. 9).

Many elderly victims remain silent out of fear, shame, guilt, self-blame, protectiveness of family member, and isolation. In other situations, there may be denial or lack of recognition of the abuse due to cultural and ethnic values and beliefs (Hernandez, 1991).

Emergency room personnel, physicians, and dentists who are alert to the injuries and bruises initiate referrals. Delay in seeking treatment, doctor-hopping, and previous reports of falls, cuts, or accidents are indications of possible elder abuse. Those elders suffering from depression must be evaluated for the possibility of victimization. Building a therapeutic alliance with an elder abuse victim through trust and respect takes time. Working through the client's resistance to accepting the label of abuse is integral to the therapeutic process.

A number of resources for clinicians working with abused elders have recently been developed. The Mount Sinai Victim Services Agency Elder Abuse project (Fall, 1988) published guidelines for detection, assessment, and intervention for patients over 60 years of age who are abused by family members. It includes community resources in the five boroughs of New York City. This is an invaluable reference for professionals working with suspected cases. "The Staircase Model" (Breckman & Adelman, 1988) provides a tool for assessment and care management planning with elder abuse victims. They describe three levels each with stages. The first level is *victim reluctance,* where intervention can only provide emergency assistance and information. The second level is *recognition,* lessening of denial and self-blame and wanting to share it. The intervention at this point might include counseling and support groups. The third level *rebuilding* involves developing a support system, reshaping identity, and seeking life style alternatives. Craig (1994) refers to three stages of working through issues of elder abuse as "naming," identifying the abusive behavior; "blaming," identifying the abuser rather than accepting the blame, and "claiming," reestablishing the right to a quality of life that is violence-free.

Pilot projects to use mediation in the screening of domestic elder abuse are being developed by the American Association of Family Conciliation Courts. Elder mediation, if used in early stages of domestic conflict shows great promise to prevent elder abuse.

Interventions with abused elders vary broadly because victims and abusers are so diverse. Knowledge of the dyadic dynamics will determine the nature of treatment and recommendations.

Therapist Issues and Recommendations

To be effective in working with elders, mental health professionals need to explore their own biases against older adults. Knowledge of developmental and clinical issues of aging is essential. Moreover, knowing that for elders, abuse has little to do with aging, but more to do with shifts of power is important. Knowing whether the abuse is of recent onset (late-onset spousal abuse) or of longer duration will have implications for treatment. In the case of sudden onset of abuse, early intervention may correct the problem, if the victim becomes aware of the changes. Treatment must validate the elder abuse victim and work to empower him or her.

Recommendations

Training

Psychotherapists working with elder issues need expertise in family violence, spousal abuse, and sexual abuse. Their training must include knowledge of developmental, clinical, gerontological issues. Furthermore, psychotherapists need to examine their own biases toward the elderly, toward diverse cultural and ethnic populations, and toward gender issues.

Assessment

Staff training of mental health and hospital workers will result in early recognition of elder abuse—leading to referral for treatment of trauma by a skillful therapist (Harway, 1992). Other assessment issues include determining the degree of social isolation of the elder. Pillemer (1985) has identified this as a risk factor in elder abuse. An important intervention here is to encourage and facilitate an active social network. Psychotherapists can make referrals of their at-risk clients to senior centers, religious and social clubs, and community organizations. Social support, a confidante or a peer group, can reinforce the message that abuse is unacceptable and illegal behavior. Encouraging involvement in community programs or in volunteer work or enrollment in educational courses can also interrupt a pattern of isolation (Toseland, Rossiter, & Labeque, 1989; Wolf & Pillemer, 1994). Recommending independent living or congregated or shared housing with cohorts can also enhance the quality of life and family relationships (Johnson & Troll, 1994; Troll, 1993). Because the demands of a dependent elder can extend over 5 or 6 years, they may far exceed the special assistance the average family can provide (Douglass, 1988). Living arrangements with relatives may increase the risk for violence (Pillemer & Suitor, 1989, 1991).

Therapists need to evaluate the nature of the patient's depression to determine whether it is a reaction to elder abuse. Although therapists are urged to ask patients direct questions regarding violence at the same time, the patient's right to privacy and self-determination needs to be respected. Clinicians must also be cautioned not to force removal from the home.

Treatment and Intervention

In cases involving domestic violence, intervention must include appropriate referrals for abuser services. Psychotherapy with the abuser is also necessary. Treatment with family therapists rather than incarceration of elder male batterers is recommended. Participation in self-help groups can be helpful. Teaching the abuser alternative strategies for dealing with the elder, including pragmatic ones such as exploring other housing arrangements, should be considered. In cases where drug addiction and/or alcoholism play a role in the violent behavior, the substance abuse must also be treated—fewer than 5% of the 20% who have substance abuse problems receive treatment for the substance abuse (Hwalek, 1990).

Another alternative treatment that is worthy of attention is mediation. It is providing another encouraging approach to dealing with elder abuse. Craig (1994) proposes this voluntary, noncoercive process as "providing minimal social intervention and contributing to the prevention of elder abuse at early stages of relational conflicts between elders and their caregivers" (p. 83).

Therapists need to provide education and training programs dealing specifically with recognition and treatment of older victims of sexual abuse. Training programs in family therapy must include courses in gerontology and in domestic violence and the elderly.

Community programs and projects must be developed to raise awareness of domestic violence and the elderly (Foelker, Holland, Marsh, & Simmons, 1990; Wolf & Pillemer, 1994). Telephone hotlines should be available for emergency "on call" crisis counseling and contact with "suspected" elder abuse victims. Additionally, the American Medical Association's guidelines for identification of abuse of the elderly must be better publicized.

CONCLUSION

Intimate violence is an area that is now recognized as being a serious social problem. Clinicians have a responsibility to educate themselves about the symptoms of the three forms of abuse discussed in this chapter: spousal abuse, child abuse, and elder abuse. Assessment is key to survivors obtaining the proper intervention and support. Working with spousal abuse presents special challenges to therapists because of the danger that faces the domestic partners and the intense denial system that the partners present with. Interventions with abused children vary based on the age and developmental status of the child. In working with abused elders, clinicians need to be alert to stereotypes about the older adult and must recognize their own limitations when the victim is reluctant to report the abusive family member.

Finally, psychotherapists who work with domestic violence of all types must go beyond the confines of their offices to avail themselves of appropriate community resources for abused and abuser.

REFERENCES

Aguirre, B. E. (1985). Why do they return? Abused wives in shelters. *Social Work, 30,* 330–354.

Anetzberger, G. (1987). *The etiology of elder abuse by adult offspring.* Springfield, IL: Charles C. Thomas.

Archer, N. H. (1989). Battered women and the legal system: Past, present, and future. *Law and Psychology Review, 13,* 145–163.

Azar, S. T., & Wolfe, D. A. (1989). Child abuse and neglect. In E. J. Mash & R. A. Barkley (Eds.), *Treatment of childhood disorders* (pp. 451–489). New York: Guilford.

Bell, C. C., & Chance-Hill, G. (1991). Treatment of violent families. *Journal of the National Medical Association, 83,* 203–208.

Berman, P. (1993). Impact of abusive marital relationships on children. In M. Hansen & M. Harway (Eds.), *Battering and family therapy: A feminist perspective.* Newbury Park, CA: Sage.

Bernard, G. W., Vera, H., Vera, M. L., & Newman, G. (1982). Till death do us part: A study of spouse murder. *Bulletin of the American Academy of Psychiatry and the Law, 10,* 271ff.

Breckman, R., & Adelman, R. (1988). *Strategies for helping victims of elder abuse.* Newbury Park, CA: Sage.

Brown, A., & Finkelhor, D. (1986). Impact of child sexual abuse. A review of the research. *Psychological Bulletin, 99,* 66–77.

Browne, A. (1987). *When battered women kill.* New York: Free Press.

Cavaiola, A. A., & Schiff, M. (1988). Behavioral sequelae of physical and/or sexual abuse in adolescents. *Child Abuse and Neglect, 12,* 181–188.

Cicchetti, D. (1989). How research on child maltreatment has informed the study of child development: Perspectives from developmental psychopathology. In D. Cicchetti & V. Carlson (Eds.), *Child maltreatment: Theory and research on the causes and consequences of child abuse and neglect* (pp. 377–431). New York: Cambridge University Press.

Conte, J. R. (1990). Victims of child sexual abuse. In R. T. Ammerman & M. Hersen, *Treatment of family violence: A sourcebook* (pp. 50–76). New York: Wiley.

Conte, J. R., & Schuerman, J. R. (1987). Factors associated with an increased impact of child sexual abuse. *Child Abuse and Neglect, 11,* 201–211.

Conte, J. R., & Schuerman, J. R. (1988). The effects of sexual abuse on children: A multidimensional view. In G. E. Wyatt & G. J. Powell (Eds.), *Lasting effects of child sexual abuse* (pp. 157–170). Newbury Park, CA: Sage.

Cook, D. R., & Frantz-Cook, A. (1984). A systemic treatment approach to wife battering. *Journal of Marital and Family Therapy, 10,* 83–93.

Craig, N. (1994). Elder mediation: Can it contribute to the prevention of elder abuse and the protection of the right of the elder and their carers. *Journal of Elder Abuse and Neglect, 6*(1).

Deitch, I. (1993, August). *Alone, abandoned and assaulted: Elder abuse and the family.* Paper presented at 101st convention American Psychological Association, Toronto, Canada.

Deitch, I. (1994, Fall). Attitudes toward sex and the elderly family member. In M. Tallmer (Ed.), *Sex and the elderly.* New York: C. Thomas.

Douglass, R. L. (1988). Domestic mistreatment of the elderly. Towards prevention. Washington, DC: Criminal Justice Services, American Association of Retired Persons.

Dutton, D. G. (1988). *The domestic assault of women: Psychological and criminal justice perspective.* Boston: Allyn & Bacon.

Edleson, J. L., & Syers, M. (1990). The relative effectiveness of group treatments for men who batter. *Social Work Research and Abstracts, 26,* 10–17.

Erickson, M. F., Egland, B., & Pianta, R. (1989). The effects of maltreatment on the development of young children. In D. Cicchetti & V. Carlson (Eds.), *Child maltreatment: Theory and research on the causes and consequences of child abuse and neglect* (pp. 647–684). New York: Cambridge University Press.

Figley, C. R. (1988). Post-traumatic family therapy. In F. M. Ochberg (Ed.), *Post-traumatic therapy and victims of violence* (pp. 83–110). New York: Brunner/Mazel.

Finkelhor, D. (1990). Early and long-term effects of child sexual abuse: An update. *Professional Psychology: Research and Practice, 21,* 325–330.

Fleming, J. B. (1979). *Stopping wife abuse: A guide to the emotional, psychological, and legal implications for the abused woman and those helping her.* Garden City, NY: Anchor.

Foelker, S. A., Holland, J., Marsh, M., & Simmons, B. (1990). A community response to elder abuse. *The Gerontologist, 30,* 560–562.

Fox, L., Long, S. H., & Langlois, A. (1988). Patterns of language comprehension deficit in abused and neglected children. *Journal of Speech and Hearing Disorders, 53,* 239–244.

Friedrich, W. N. (1988). Behavior problems in sexually abused children: An adaptational perspective. In G. E. Wyatt and G. J. Powell (Eds.), *Lasting effects of child sexual abuse* (pp. 171–191). Newbury Park, CA: Sage.

Gale, J., Thompson, R. J., Moran, T., & Sack, W. H. (1988). Sexual abuse in young children: Its clinical presentations and characteristic patterns. *Child Abuse and Neglect, 12,* 163–170.

Ganley, A. L. (1981). *Court-mandated counseling for men who batter: A three-day workshop for mental health professionals (Participants' manual).* Washington, DC: Center for Women's Policy Studies.

Garbarino, J., & Plantz, M. C. (1986). Child abuse and juvenile delinquency: What are the links? In J. Garbarino, C. J. Schellenbach, & J. M. Sebes (Eds.), *Troubled youth, troubled families* (pp. 41–54). New York: Aldine de Gruyter.

Geffner, R., Barrett, M. J., & Rossman, B. B. R. (in press). Family approaches to domestic violence and sexual abuse: Techniques and controversies. In R. H. Micksell, D. D. Lusterman, & S. H. McDaniel (Eds.), *Family psychology and systems therapy: A handbook.* Washington, DC: American Psychological Association.

Giarretto, H. (1982). A comprehensive child sexual abuse treatment program. *Child abuse and neglect, 6,* 263–278.

Giles-Sims, J. (1983). *Wife battering: A systems theory approach.* New York: Guilford.

Goetting, A. (1989, Autumn). Patterns of martial homicide: A comparison of husbands and wives. *Journal of Contemporary Family Studies, 20,* 341–357.

Goldner, V. (1985). Feminism and family therapy. *Family Process, 24,* 31–47.

Goldner, V. (1992). Making room for both/and. *Family Therapy Networker, 16*(2), 54–61.

Gomes-Schwartz, B., Horowitz, J. M., Cardarelli, A. P., & Sauzier, M. (1990). The aftermath of child sexual abuse: 18 months later. In B. Gomes-Schwartz, J. M. Horowitz, & A. P. Cardarelli (Eds.), *Child sexual abuse: The initial effects* (pp. 132–152). Newbury Park, CA: Sage.

Gondolf, E. (1993). Treating the batterer. In M. Hansen & M. Harway (Eds.), *Battering and family therapy: A feminist perspective* (pp. 105–118). Newbury Park, CA: Sage.

Goodstein, R. K., & Page, A. W. (1981). Battered wife syndrome: Overview of dynamics and treatment. *American Journal of Psychiatry, 138,* 1036–1044.

Graziano, A. M., & Mills, J. R. (1992). Treatment for abused children: When is a partial solution acceptable? *Child Abuse and Neglect, 16,* 217–228.

Greenberg, J. S., Seltzer, M. M., Greenley, J. R. (1993). Aging parents of adults with disabilities: Gratifications and frustrations of later life caregiving. *The Gerontologist, 33*(4), 542–550.

Hansen, D. J., Conaway, L. P., & Christopher, J. S. (1990). Victims of child physical abuse. In R. T. Ammerman & M. Hersen (Eds.), *Treatment of family violence: A sourcebook* (pp. 17–49). New York: Wiley.

Hansen, M. (1993). *When battering ends in divorce: Interventions with family members— The children*. Symposium presented at the annual midwinter conference of Division of Family Psychology, San Diego, CA.

Hansen, M., & Goldenberg, I. (1993). Conjoint therapy with violent couples: Some valid considerations. In M. Hansen & M. Harway (Eds.), *Battering and family therapy: A feminist perspective* (pp. 82–92). Newbury Park, CA: Sage.

Hansen, M., & Harway, M. (1993). Directions for future generations of therapists. In M. Hansen & M. Harway (Eds.), *Battering and family therapy: A feminist perspective* (pp. 227–251). Newbury Park, CA: Sage.

Hansen, M., Harway, M., & Cervantes, N. N. (1991). Therapists' perceptions of severity in cases of family violence. *Violence and Victims, 4,* 275–286.

Hanson, R. K. (1990). The psychological impact of sexual assault on women and children: A review. *Annals of Sex Research, 3,* 187–232.

Hare-Mustin, R. T. (1978). A feminine approach to family therapy. *Family Process, 17,* 181–194.

Hart, B. J. (1993). The legal road to freedom. In M. Hansen & M. Harway (Eds.), *Battering and family therapy: A feminist perspective* (pp. 13–29). Newbury Park, CA: Sage.

Harway, M. (1992, Summer). Training issues in working with violent families. *Family Violence and Sexual Assault Bulletin, 8*(2), 18–20.

Harway, M. (1993). Battered women: Characteristics and guilts. In M. Hansen & M. Harway (Eds.), *Battering and family therapy: A feminist perspective* (pp. 42–53). Newbury Park, CA: Sage.

Harway, M., & Evans, K. (in press). Working in groups with men who batter. In M. P. Andronico (Ed.), *Men in groups: Realities and insights*. Washington, DC: ACA Books.

Harway, M., & Hansen, M. (1993). Therapist perceptions of family violence. In M. Hansen & M. Harway (Eds.), *Battering and family therapy: A feminist perspective* (pp. 42–53). Newbury Park, CA: Sage.

Harway, M., & Hansen, M. (1994). *Spouse abuse: Assessing and treating battered women, batterers and their children*. Sarasota, FL: Professional Resource Press.

Hernandez, G. (1991). Not so benign neglect: Researchers ignore ethnicity in defining family caregiving burden and recommending services (Letter to the editor). *The Gerontologist, 31*(2), 271–272.

Hoffman-Plotkin, D., & Twentyman, C. (1984). A multimodal assessment of behavioral and cognitive deficits in abused and neglected preschoolers. *Child Development, 55,* 794–802.

Holt, M. G. (1993). Elder abuse in Britain: Meeting the challenge. *Journal of Elder Abuse and Neglect, 5*(1).

Holtzworth-Munroe, A., & Arias, I. (1993). *Family violence and sexual assault bulletin, 9*(3), 22–25.

Holtzworth-Munroe, A., Waltz, J., Jacobson, N. S., Monaco, V., Fehrenbach, P. A., & Gottman, J. M. (1992). Recruiting nonviolent men as control subjects for research on marital violence: How easily can it be done? *Violence and Victims, 7,* 79–88.

Hotaling, G. T., & Sugarman, D. B. (1986). An analysis of risk markers in husband to wife violence: The current state of knowledge. *Violence and Victims, 1*, 101–124.

Hudson, M. (1989). Analysis of the concepts of elder mistreatment, abuse and neglect. *Journal of Elder Abuse and Neglect, 1*(1), 5–27.

Hugh, M. (1991). A new myth about families of older people. *The Gerontologist, 37*(5), 611–618.

Hughes, H. M. (1982). Brief interventions with children in a battered women's shelter: A model preventive program. *Family Relations, 31,* 495–502.

Hwalek, M. (1990). Intervention effectiveness. Detroit, MI: SPEC Associates.

Jacobson, N. (1993, October). *Domestic violence: What the couples look like.* Paper presented at the annual convention of the American Association for Marriage and Family Therapy, Anaheim, CA.

Jaffe, P. G., Wolfe, D. A., & Wilson, S. K. (1990). *Children of battered women.* Newbury Park, CA: Sage.

Jaffe, P. G., Wolfe, D. A., Wilson, S. K., & Zak, L. (1986). Similarities in behavioral and social maladjustment among child victims and witnesses to family violence. *American Journal of Orthopsychiatry, 56,* 142–146.

Jenkins, A. (1990). *Invitations to responsibility.* Adelaide, SA, Australia: Dulwich Centre Publications.

Johnson, C., & Troll, L. (1994). Constraint and facilitation for friendship in later life. *The Gerontologist, 34*(1), 79–87.

Justice, B., & Justice, R. (1990). *The abusing family* (rev. ed.). New York: Plenum.

Kendall-Tackett, K. A., Williams, L. M., & Finkelhor, D. (1993). Impact of sexual abuse on children. A review and synthesis of recent empirical studies. *Psychological Bulletin, 113,* 164–180.

Knittle, B. J., & Tuana, S. J. (1980). Group therapy as primary treatment for adolescent victims of intrafamilial sexual abuse. *Clinical Social Work Journal, 8,* 236–242.

Kosberg, J. (1988). Preventing elder abuse: Identification of high risk factors prior to placement decisions. *The Gerontologist, 28*(1), 43–50.

Koss, M. P. (1990). The women's mental health agenda: Violence against women. *American Psychologist, 45,* 374–380.

Leifer, M., Shapiro, J. P., Martone, M. W., & Kassem, L. (1991). Rorschach assessment of psychological functioning in sexually abused girls. *Journal of Personality Assessment, 56,* 14–28.

Lewis, D. O., Mallouh, C., & Webb, V. (1989). Child abuse, delinquency, and violent criminality. In D. Cicchetti & V. Carlson (Eds.), *Child maltreatment: Theory and research on the causes and consequences of child abuse and neglect* (pp. 707–721). New York: Cambridge University Press.

Long, K. A. (1986). Cultural considerations in the assessment and treatment of intrafamilial abuse. *Journal of Orthopsychiatry, 56*(1), 131–136.

Lutzker, J. R. (1984). Project 12-Ways: Treating child abuse and neglect from an ecobehavioral perspective. In R. F. Dangel & R. A. Polster (Eds.), *Parent Training: Foundations of research and practice* (pp. 260–293). New York: Guilford.

Lutzker, J. R., & Rice, J. M. (1984). Project 12-Ways: Measuring outcome of a large in-home service for treatment and prevention of child abuse and neglect. *Child Abuse and Neglect, 8,* 519–524.

Main, M., & George, C. (1985). Responses of abused and disadvantaged toddlers to distress in age mates: A study in the daycare setting. *Developmental Psychology, 21,* 407–412.

Malinosky-Rummell, R., & Hansen, D. J. (1993). Long-term consequences of childhood physical abuse. *Psychological Bulletin, 114,* 68–79.

Moon, A. C., & Williams, O. (1993). Perception of elder abuse and help seeking patterns among African-American, Caucasian-American and Korean-American elderly women. *The Gerontologist, 33*(3), 386–395.

Mount Sinai Victims Services Agency. (1988, Fall). *Elder mistreatment, guidelines for health care professionals: Detection, assessment and intervention.* New York: New York City Elder Abuse Project.

Mugford, J., Mugford, S., & Easteal, P. W. (1989). Social justice, public perceptions, and spouse assault in Australia. *Social Justice, 3,* 103–123.

National Aging Resource Center on Elder Abuse. (1990). Elder abuse—questions and answers: *An information guide for professionals and concerned citizens.* Washington, DC: Author

National Aging Resource Center on Elder Abuse. (1994). *Bulletin.* Washington, DC: Author

National Committee for Prevention of Child Abuse. (1992, April). Current trends in child abuse reporting and fatalities: The results of the 1991 annual fifty-state survey. (Working Paper Number 808). Englewood, CO: National Committee for Prevention of Child Abuse.

Neidig, P. H., & Friedman, O. H. (1984). *Spouse abuse: A treatment program for couples.* Champaign, IL: Research Press.

Neikrug, S., & Ronen, M. (1993). Elder abuse in Israel. *Journal of Elder Abuse and Neglect, 5*(3), 1–19.

New York City Department for the Aging. (1990, February). *Elder Abuse, a profile of victims served by the New York City Department for the Aging.* New York: Author

Ney, P. G. (1987). The treatment of abused children: The natural sequence of events. *American Journal of Psychotherapy, 41,* 391–401.

NiCarthy, G. (1982). *Getting free: A handbook for women in abusive relationships.* Seattle, WA: Seal.

O'Neil, J. M., & Egan, J. (1993). Abuses of power against women: Sexism, gender role conflict, psychological violence. In E. Cook (Ed.), *Women, relationships and power: Implications for counseling* (pp. 49–78). Alexandria, VA: ACA Press.

Parks, S., & Pilisuk, H. (1991). Caregivers burden: Gender and psychological costs of caregiving. *American Journal of Orthopsychiatry, 61*(4), 501–508.

Pepper, C. (1985). Elder abuse, a national disgrace. Opening statement at the hearings before the U.S. House of Representatives Select Committee on Health and Long-term Care. Washington, DC: U.S. Government Printing Office.

Petel, M., Cesserta, M., Hutton, A., & Lund, D. (1988). Intergenerational conflict: Middle aged women caring for demented older relatives. *American Journal of Orthopsychiatry, 58*(3), 405–417.

Pillemer, K. (1985, Fall). Social isolation and elder abuse. *Response, 2*–4.

Pillemer, K. A. (1986). Risk factors in elder abuse: results from a care-control study. In K. A. Pillemer & R. S. Wolf (Eds.), *Elder abuse: Conflict in the family* (pp. 239–263). Dover, MA: Auburn.

Pillemer, K. A., & Finkelhor, D. (1988). The prevalence of elder abuse: A random sample survey. *The Gerontologist, 28*(1), 51–57.

Pillemer, K. A., & Finkelhor, D. (1989). Causes of elder abuse: Caregivers stress vs. problem relatives. *American Journal of Orthopsychiatry, 59*(2), 179–187.

Pillemer, K. A., & Suitor, J. J. (1989). Violence and violent feelings: What causes them among family caregivers (Social Sciences). *Journal of Gerontology, 47*(4), S165–S172.

Pillemer, K. A., & Suitor, J. J. (1991, January). Sharing a residence with an adult child: A cause of psychological distress in the elderly? *American Journal of Orthopsychiatry, 61*(1), 144–148.

Pizzey, E. (1974). *Scream quietly or the neighbors will hear.* Short Hills, NJ: Ridley Enslow.

Pizzey, E. (1975, December). Battered wives, Chiswick women's aid: A refuge from violence. *Royal Society of Health Journal, 95*(6), 297–298, 308.

Pressman, B. (1989). Wife-abused couples: The need for comprehensive theoretical perspectives and integrated treatment models. *Journal of Feminist Family Therapy, 1,* 23–43.

Pritchard, M. (1993). Dispelling some myths. *Journal of Elder Abuse and Neglect, 5*(2), 27–36.

Ramsey-Klawsnik, H. (1993). Interviewing elders for suspected sexual abuse: Guidelines and techniques. *Journal of Elder Abuse and Neglect, 5*(1), 73–90.

Register, E. (1993). Feminism and recovering: Working with the individual woman. In M. Hansen & M. Harway (Eds.), *Battering and family therapy: A feminist perspective* (pp. 93–104). Newbury Park, CA: Sage.

Reuterman, N. A., & Burcky, W. D. (1989). Dating violence in high school: A profile of the victims. *Psychology: A Journal of Human Behavior, 26,* 1–9.

Rossman, B. B. R. (1993, August). Children in violent families: Treatment issues and techniques. Paper presented at the meeting of the American Psychological Association, Toronto, Canada.

Saunders, D. G., & Browne, A. (1990). Domestic homicide. In R. T. Ammerman & M. Herson (Eds.), *Case studies in family violence* (pp. 379–402). New York: Plenum.

Segel-Evans, K. (1994). *Treatment issues for men who batter.* Paper presented at the Midwestern Convention of Divisions 29, 42, and 43 of the American Psychological Association, Scottsdale, AZ.

Sengstock, M. (1991). Sex and gender implications in cases of elder abuse. *Journal of Women and Aging, 3*(2), 25–43.

Simon, M. (1992). An exploratory study of Adult Protective Services Programs' repeat elder abuse clients. Washington, DC: Public Policy Institute, American Association of Retired Persons.

Sonkin, D. J., Martin, D., & Walker, L. E. A. (1985). *The male batterer: A treatment approach.* New York: Springer.

Starr, B., & Weiner, M. B. (1986). *The Starr-Werner report on sex and sexuality in the mature years.* New York: McGraw-Hill.

Stein, K. F. (1991). Elder abuse and neglect: a national research agenda. Washington, DC: National Aging Center on Elder Abuse.

Steinmetz, S. K. (1990). Elder abuse myth and reality. In T.H. Brubake (Ed.), *Family relations in later life.* Newbury Park, CA: Sage.

Straus, M. A., Gelles, R. J., & Steinmitz, S. U. (1980). *Behind closed doors: Violence in the American family.* Garden City, NY: Anchor/Doubleday.

Strube, M. J., & Barbour, L. S. (1983). The decision to leave an abusive relationship: Economic dependence and psychological commitment. *Journal of Marriage and the Family, 45,* 785–793.

Tatara, T. (1990). *Elder abuse in the United States, an issue paper.* Washington, DC: National Aging Resource Center on Elder Abuse.

Tatara, T. (1991). *Summaries of national elder abuse data: An explanatory study of state statues.* Washington, DC: National Aging Resource Center on Elderly Abuse.

Terr, L. C. (1989). Family anxiety after traumatic events. *Journal of Clinical Psychiatry, 50,* 15–19.

Terr, L. C. (1991). Childhood trauma: An outline and overview. *American Journal of Psychiatry, 148,* 10–20.

Tolman, R. M., & Bhosley, G. (1990). The outcome of participation in a shelter-sponsored program for men who batter. In D. Knudsen & J. Miller (Eds.), *Abused and battered: Social and legal responses.* New York: Aldine de Gruyter.

Tomes, H. (1993, July). In the Public Interest. *Monitor,* Washington, DC: American Psychological Association.

Toseland, R. W., Rossiter, C. M., & Labeque, M. S. (1989). The effectiveness of three group intervention strategies to support family caregivers. *American Journal of Orthopsychiatry, 559*(3), 420–429.

Trepper, T., & Barrett, M. (1986). *Treating incest: A multiple systems perspective.* New York: Haworth Press.

Trickett, P. K. (1993). Maladaptive development of school-aged, physically abused children: Relationships with the child-rearing context. *Journal of Family Psychology, 7,* 134–146.

Trickett, P. K., & Putnam, F. W. (1993). Impact of child sexual abuse on females: Toward developmental, psychobiological integration. *Psychological Science, 4,* 81–87.

Troll, L. (1993, March). Studies of the old-old (over 85) American population and their families. Paper presented at the 5th International Interdisciplinary Congress on Women, San Jose, Costa Rica.

U. S. Department of Justice. (1991). Uniform Crime Reports, 1990. Washington, DC: U.S. Government Printing Office.

Utech, M., & Garrett, L. (1992, September). Elder and child abuse: Conceptual and perceptual parallels. *Journal of Interpersonal Violence, 7*(3), 418–428.

Walker, C. E., Bonner, B. L., & Kaufman, K. L. (1988). *The physically and sexually abused child: Evaluation and treatment.* New York: Pergamon.

Walker, L. E. A. (1979). *The battered woman.* New York: Harper & Row.

Walker, L. E. A. (1984, August). *The battered woman syndrome study. Psychological profiles.* Paper presented at the Second National Conference for Family Violence Researchers, Durham, NH.

Weinbach, R. W., & Curtiss, C. R. (1986). Making child abuse victims aware of their victimization: A treatment issue. *Child Welfare, 65,* 337–346.

Wolf, R. S. (1992). Victimization of the elderly. Elder abuse and neglect social and psychological gerontology. *Review in Clinical Gerontology, 3,* 269–273.

Wolf, R. S. (1994). *Elder abuse and cultural diversity considerations: A brief look at the research.* Washington, DC: National Resource Center on Aging.

Wolf, R. S., & Pillemer, K. A. (1994). What's new in elder abuse programming? Four bright ideas. *The Gerontologist, 1*(34), 126–129.

Wolfe, D. A. (1987). *Child abuse: Implications for child development and psychopathology.* Newbury Park, CA: Sage.

Wolfe, D. A., & Jaffe, P. (1991). Child abuse and family violence as determinants of child psychopathology. *Canadian Journal of Behavioral Science, 23,* 282–299.

Wolfe, D. A., Sandler, J., & Kaufman, K. (1981). A competency-based parent training program for abusive parents. *Journal of Consulting and Clinical Psychology, 49,* 633–640.

Yoshikawa, H. (1994). Prevention as cumulative protection: Effects of early family support and education on chronic delinquency and its risks. *Psychological Bulletin, 115,* 28–54.

Zwiney, D. A., & Nash, M. R. (1988). Sexual abuse in early versus late childhood: Differing patterns of pathology as revealed on the Rorschach. *Psychotherapy, 25,* 99–106.

CHAPTER 10

Impact of the Environment on Families: Urbanicity's Unique Opportunities and Challenges

JANIS V. SANCHEZ-HUCLES

"Whereas opinion on the evil or benefits of the city on psychological well being abound, data supporting either view are hard to come by" (Simons, 1987, p. 64). Current stereotypes of urban settings summon images of crime, violence, unemployment, poverty, high population density, and inadequate resources. Although these images of the city have a basis in fact, behavioral scientists recently have attempted to clarify what is myth and what is reality in urban settings, how these environments impact the lives of their citizens, what constitutes risk as well as resiliency factors in cities, and what some of the potential benefits are of living in urban centers.

Behavioral scientists have been slow to study the impact of urban environments on human behavior. Krupat (1980) has speculated that too many behavioral scientists have focused their attention within the individual rather than on how individuals, groups, or families may be affected by their external environment. The tragic murder of Kitty Genovese wherein 38 people watched but refused to help, stimulated empirical investigations of the impact of urban environments on human behavior (Milgram & Hollander, 1964). Interestingly, it is the much publicized prevalence of crime and violence in the cities today that is again leading scientists to examine urban centers. Part of the impetus to study urban environments more carefully and to respond to the needs of its residents derives from the widening recognition that we in society are increasingly interdependent. It is no longer possible to pretend that the problems of inner cities can be ignored by citizenry who do not reside in cities. Parnell and Vanderkloot (1991) have noted that urban settings may serve as weather vanes for society, and as once stable communities decline in the inner city, this infection may spread with implications for other residential settings. Careful analyses of the impact of urban environments must be undertaken to develop effective programs that maximize opportunities and minimize problematic outcomes for urban dwellers.

This chapter describes the impact of the urban environment on today's families. A brief history of the forces that have created urban environments will be described as well as some of the salient characteristics of families in cities. An overview of both environmental stressors and resources will be detailed. A particular focus will be placed on several major problem areas that families in cities have been forced to confront including poverty, juvenile delinquency and incarceration, violence, gun use, and gangs. Following the discussion of challenges that families face in the urban environment, interventions will be described that show promise in helping families to handle their stress more adaptively. All too often, portraits of inner-city life focus only on deficiency, failure, and negativity without explaining how the majority of inner-city children grow up to be healthy and productive adults with an array of strengths honed by their challenges (National Center on Education in the Inner Cities, 1994). As therapeutic interventions are described, strategies that utilize the resources of families in the urban setting will be highlighted. A final discussion will summarize current strengths, weaknesses, and challenges therapists face in the provision of services to families in urban settings.

THE DEVELOPMENT OF CURRENT URBAN ENVIRONMENTS

In 1990, approximately one third of the United States population resided in cities with populations above 50,000 (Zero Population Growth, 1993). Half of these 488 cities had poverty rates that exceeded the national average of 13%, and the 25 largest cities had populations of at least 50% ethnic minorities (Greater Washington Research Center, 1993). The current population density in urban areas has evolved over the past century.

The rise of large-scale factory production in the United States following the Civil War was accompanied by the massive migration of rural residents to growing metropolitan areas. Industrial centers required a specialized labor force that led to the growth of the middle class. Immigrants from Europe and Asia provided a large supply of low-salaried, unskilled workers to operate machinery under oppressive conditions (Knox, Bohland, & Shumsky, 1983). Advances in transportation and technology that produced the telephone and the automobile helped to make urban dwellers more mobile. The vitality of urban centers is closely tied to the productivity of its industries and factories. The growth of cities continued until the 1960s with the advent of deindustrialization and the exodus of major corporations. The relocation of industries outside major urban centers led to higher rates of unemployment for those unable to relocate with their former job opportunities. Middle-class individuals were, however, able to emigrate from cities to suburbs. Walker and Small (1991) note that many of the families that left the inner city had previously functioned as community leaders and role models. Today many urban residents find that crime and drugs, unemployment, deteriorating services and physical structures, and low morale and community spirit have transformed their communities.

Anderson (1990) reports that another loss in many urban settings is the relationship between "old heads" and young boys. Old heads are upstanding individuals who believe in family, church, and work and who help socialize young men into the roles of good citizens and strong family members. As these old heads lost their jobs, they also lost their prestige and were replaced by flashy drug dealers with a get-rich-quick orientation. The community also has seen a decline in the female old heads who served as community mothers. These women used to give advice and help mother and discipline children. But these women now face an overwhelming number of children who are unsupervised, impoverished, and in need of care and protection.

Peterson (1985) asserts that race appears to play a central role in the "pace and direction of urban change" (p. 12). Between 1960 and 1975, the higher the percentage of African Americans in a city, the higher the rate of Caucasian migration to the suburbs (Bradbury, Downs & Small, 1982). As families with financial means left the inner city, remaining residents were increasingly diverse with respect to culture, ethnicity, race, and language (Ponterrotto, 1990). These diverse families however often shared the burdens of poverty, unemployment, family disintegration, limited education and job skills, and increasing feelings of hopelessness and powerlessness (Walker & Small, 1991; Wilson, 1980).

The impact of race can be further perceived in the process of gentrification that reshaped the inner city from the 1970s onward. Young, predominantly Caucasian professional couples bought vacated homes for their antique value and for the opportunity to be closer to work and leisure activities. Often these residents or speculators were able to renovate and improve their property, receive revitalized public services, and gain the interest of public servants. As the value of their property increased, however, lower income, long-term residents of these communities could no longer afford increased rental fees and were often forced to move to more rundown neighborhoods. Hence tensions often exist between lower and higher income urban dwellers.

Families that reside in urban centers face a variety of challenges ranging from basic survival issues to how to establish firm boundaries in the face of their complex physical and social environments. Most urban families have a commitment to support and nurture family members in a variety of family constellations including one or more members, a grandparent or multigenerational family members, a single parent, and family members with various sexual orientations (Smilkstein, 1978). Benson (1987) has documented that urban families can be characterized as more likely than nonurban families to consist of one family member, to have mothers as single parents, small size, adolescent parents, parental children, ethnic minority status, and less visible males.

Due to the greater anonymity afforded by cities, special populations and marginalized groups gather in greater numbers in cities and may have different family structures and networks. These groups include: runaways; gays, lesbians, and bisexuals; and the homeless (Strelnick & Gilpin, 1987). Cities have also historically attracted immigrant families from all over the world and have borne the responsibility to help integrate and socialize these families into the mainstream of American culture.

One of the newest developments in urban environments is the recognition that residents, particularly children, are increasingly vulnerable to experiencing posttraumatic stress disorder as a result of their exposure to chronic and unpredictable stress and violence (Garbarino, Dubrow, Kostelny, & Pardo, 1992). How this long-term chronic violence may impact the social development of children is unclear. Hill (as cited in Rodriguez, 1992) notes that children in these environments may demonstrate emotional blunting, distancing, psychic numbing, repression, depression, anxiety flashbacks, and nightmares.

The families that have come to the attention of professional caregivers are often viewed as multiproblem families because they experience crises and emergencies as well as the consequences of the long-term effects of poverty, inadequate resources, exposure to violence, and family disorganization. Because the problems of inner-city families can be so pervasive, there has been a tendency to regard this population as outside the scope of mental health practitioners. This perception has only increased feelings of isolation, alienation, and marginalization for these families.

Urban families face a variety of environmental stressors including crowding and high population density; substandard housing; health risks such as pollution, lead poisoning, and violence; stimulus overload; economic disinvestment; and community disorganization. As a result, these residents are vulnerable to inadequate municipal resources to meet their needs and ensure their safety and well being (Otte, 1987; Simons, 1987).

Despite the real stressors that exist in urban environments, research has also begun to document the resources that characterize cities as well. In contrast to the misperception that people in cities do not help each other, a number of studies have demonstrated that the exchange of help in urban areas is a frequent and important activity (Warren, 1969, 1977). Meaningful relationships are constructed in neighborhoods, places of worship, and on the basis of shared religion, ethnicity, and interests (Simons, 1987). It is perhaps because many urban families do not live near relatives and have low incomes and limited mobility that neighbors become important sources of support. There is also evidence that diverse sources of social support available to families in urban settings can make them more resistant to stress than families in rural settings (Brown & Prudo, 1981; Prudo, Brown, Harris, & Dowland, 1981) and that urbanites, unlike rural dwellers, give, receive, and expect more help from friends than from relatives (Amato, 1993). One explanation may be that the complex and rapidly changing environment of cities fosters the development of flexible and stress-resistant strategies for some urban families (Simons, 1987). Families in cities can also benefit from an abundance of local agencies and services, access to public transportation, the availability of medical and health facilities, and the rich cultural resources of the metropolis (Liang & Warfel, 1983). The use of self-help groups, vocational training, rehabilitation, team counseling, and consultation approaches have all developed in part to serve the needs of families in the inner city (Kesselman, Sullivan, & Cohen, 1987).

As family therapists have studied the normal crises of family development and the impact of ethnicity, they have become aware that unique cultural adaptations of families can provide these families with increased resiliency. Practitioners and theorists are beginning to move away from the perspective that difference in family structure, parenting practices, and coping styles are inherently pathological and have begun to realize that these differences reflect in fact adaptive and ecologically viable survival strategies (Bronfenbrenner, 1979; Ogbu, 1985). Extended family networks, religious and ethnic pride, and cultural customs and traditions can promote feelings of empowerment, stability, and resourcefulness in many of the diverse families in urban settings (Boyd-Franklin, 1989; Kelly, Sanchez-Hucles, & Walker, 1993; McGoldrick, Pearce, & Giardano, 1982).

THERAPY WITH URBAN POOR FAMILIES

Poverty is a central risk factor for urban families characterizing 50% of the children living in these families (Moynihan, 1986). It is linked to substandard housing, education, job opportunities, health care, and limited personal choices (Jenkins, 1990). The problems that these families face can lead to feelings of discouragement and powerlessness due to increased vulnerability to infant mortality, child abuse, educational disability, imprisonment, homelessness, substance abuse, chronic mental illness, unplanned and single parenthood, and family fragmentation (Inclan & Ferran, 1989; Jenkins, 1983; Kantor, Peretz, & Zander, 1984). As federal, state, and municipal services are negatively impacted by budgetary problems, therapists are facing large numbers of these multiproblem families who seek guidance and support. Traditional individual, linear, and psychodynamic models of therapy have not proven to be as responsive to the needs of these families as have multilevel systemic models that include a working knowledge of the societal contexts of these families (Parnell & Vanderkloot, 1991).

Poverty can have differential impacts on urban families. When the poverty is overwhelming, daily survival as well as future planning can be problematic. The strengths and adaptive coping strategies of significant adults and family members can mediate the impact of poverty. Children who have supportive family structures that enhance self-esteem and physical, emotional, and educational attainment show resiliency (Parnell & Vanderkloot, 1989; Powell, 1983). The poor are also heterogeneous with regard to whether they are chronically or temporarily unemployed or part of the working poor. They differ with respect to their current level of functioning, how many generations of poverty the family may have endured, and their ethnicity, culture, and family structure (Hines, Richman, Maxim, & Hays, 1990).

As Aponte (1991) noted, few therapeutic models address both emotional problems and societal ills such as poverty. Historically, the family therapy movement simply substituted family dynamics for individual dynamics as the core of dysfunctional behaviors. The community mental health movement, in its attempt to develop coordinated health care programs for inner-city residents for crisis intervention, began to include the ecosystems of families and to experiment with network therapy and multisystem collaboration. Auserwald (1983) articulated the need for a coordinated system of health care and mental health that would respond in an integrated way to family needs and in which problems would be analyzed in the larger context of the family's functioning. He stressed that sociocultural information should be collected from network meetings involving family members, extended kin, and other support systems that were involved with the family. This therapy was designed to be proactive and meet families' needs by making home visits, using collaboration, working with interdisciplinary teams, and creating new services if current ones were insufficient (Auserwald, 1983).

Minuchin, Montalvo, Guerney, Rosman, and Schumer (1967) developed the structural model of family therapy to meet the needs of the poor. This model was elaborated on by Aponte (1979) to include the social ecology of the community that poor families had to navigate. Aponte characterized these families as underorganized because although these families had rules, organization, and structure, these mechanisms were not strong enough or flexible enough to withstand the constant assault on their integrity due to their impoverished status.

Family therapists have consequently become aware that applying systems theories to the repertoire of behaviors shown by families enmeshed in poverty is a major challenge. We can develop insignificant and Band-Aid approaches or we can devote ourselves to developing "interventions that count" (Kantor, Peretz, & Zander, 1984, p. 60). To be effective in this undertaking requires therapists to understand the contributing factors of racism, denied economic opportunity, unsafe environments, and bureaucratic obstacles to receiving services. This quest to develop effective interventions with the poor has been made more daunting in the face of the perceived failure of antipoverty programs in the 1960s and 1970s and the lack of impact of the conservative approach of the 1970s and 1980s (Edelman, 1987; Inclan & Ferran, 1989).

A cadre of family therapists have begun to delineate strategies that are effective in working with the urban poor. At the foundation of this work is the belief that this therapy should be holistic and ecologically oriented: Families should be understood within their cultural, historical, social, and economic contexts, and solutions should target the intersection of the needs these families have within society (Aponte, 1985).

Interventions with these families typically include the phases of referral and intake, engagement, assessment, implementation of the therapy, and finally, collaboration, consultation, and evaluation. Agreement also seems to exist in the literature that work with these families should be multisystemic (Aponte,

1979; Auserwald, 1968; Boyd-Franklin, 1989; Minuchin, 1974). The multisystems model is designed to impact a variety of levels including the individual, family, marital dyad, extended family, and outside systems.

STRATEGIES FOR THERAPISTS WORKING WITH URBAN POOR FAMILIES

Therapists working with urban poor families must themselves be flexible and improvisational in responding to the unique needs of these families (Parnell & Vanderkloot, 1989). Although the problems of these populations seem overwhelming, it is important for therapists to convey immediately to these families the clear message that by working together, concrete progress can be made in crisis resolution. As Hines et al. (1990) noted, although family therapy cannot be a cure-all, it can empower these families in recognizing the sources of their crisis and in maximizing their options for effective problem solving. Therapists must understand how severe daily survival challenges are to these families. It is also important for therapists to recognize and support adult caretakers in their attempts to parent children effectively, albeit with less finances, resources, and options than those enjoyed by wealthier parents. Therapists must extend an attitude of unconditional positive regard (Carter, 1982) and reinforce parental efforts while recognizing that these parents are often doing the best that they can. It is also important that the therapists treat parents with respect so that the children and extended family members can view the parents as effective change agents by observing the therapists' interactions with parents.

Treatment Teams

A great deal of agreement exists in the field that work with the urban poor is facilitated by the use of therapeutic teams that either match clients in race or ethnicity or are at least sensitive to these issues and are well oriented to the neighborhoods that these families live in. The team approach is significant for a variety of reasons. First, work with these families can be overwhelming, time consuming, emotionally draining, and frustrating. If therapists treating these families become isolated professionally, they may show signs of the posttraumatic stress disorders found in these families. Individual therapists exposed to a steady diet of families with overwhelming odds and with opportunities for only circumscribed success can eventually feel anxious, depressed, and helpless themselves. The team approach makes these side effects less likely as team members support and ground each other. Second, the resources of additional therapists also increases brainstorming about effective strategies and interventions and makes it more likely that family members will find a therapist to align with.

Referral and Intake

There is a consensus that the intake process should be inclusive. All vital family members, kin, friends, and relevant community agencies should be included, for as Auserwald (1983) noted, the process of intake can have a profound impact on the structure of the intervention.

A significant number of poor families interact with therapists in the context of a family crisis. In urban environments, these crises can vary from problems at school or work to situations of violence, abuse, incest, runaways, or contact with the criminal justice system. The first challenge of the therapist team is to assess the meaning the crisis has for the family. Certain crisis situations actually give the family an opportunity to come together and function collaboratively (Walsh, 1981).

Therapists need to be prepared to deal with families who are in crisis and who may be resistant because of being referred by other social services as well as with families who refer themselves for therapy when their already precarious equilibrium ceases to function.

Typically, in poor urban families, the behavior of the identified patient precipitates therapy. Bowen's (1978) metaphor of an undifferentiated ego mass describes the amoebic quality of some of these family systems characterized by limited or absent boundaries and little self-differentiation. Therapists strive to develop relatedness and self-differentiation in an attempt to focus on present, not past, issues.

Therapists must function as change agents within the family as well as establish relationships with community services and resources. The key ingredient to the success of the intervention with these families is the relationship that is established between the family and the therapists. This relationship, not techniques, promotes healing and empowerment (Clark, Zalis, & Sacco, 1982).

Assessment Issues

In the assessment phase of therapy, family therapists utilize trigenerational genograms, with observations of verbal and nonverbal behaviors, tracking who are involved in defining and maintaining behavior patterns and understanding the family's relationship to the larger social systems in the community (Parnell & Vanderkloot, 1989). Therapists also try to identify the family strengths and weaknesses and to document the family's highest level of functioning. Additional information is sought on employment histories, immigrant status, educational levels, and previous mental health treatment.

After data are collected, it is important to reframe information in a manner that gives the family members a sense of confidence that problems can be solved. Weiner-Davis, de Shazer, and Gingerich (1987) have indicated that therapists can sometimes ask for and utilize any pretreatment change that can occur in families prior to their first appointment. Focusing on any pretreatment changes creates a positive sense of expectancy for the therapy process. Therapists must also gather information as to the possible resources and abilities the family has and their potential to mobilize any outside support.

An essential issue for therapists is to gain insight into the organizational structure of the family. Extremes of rigidity or disorganization in the family structure are usually associated with greater vulnerability to harm from a crisis. Families that are organized with clear family rules, roles, and responsibility have proven to be more stress resistant in crisis situations (Schaefer, Briesmeister, & Fitton, 1986).

Heterogeneity of Families

From the assessment of family strengths and weaknesses, different family constellations emerge. Several theorists believe that the "passive poor" constitute the largest group of poor families (Auletta, 1982; Inclan & Ferran, 1989). These are families with multiple agency involvements over time and long-term welfare status; they often have medical and health complications as well. Most of the therapeutic interventions in the literature focus on these families and strategies are directed toward increasing these families' proactive and adaptive coping mechanisms and eradicating their pervasive sense of helplessness, hopelessness, and dependency. Cognitive therapies, network approaches, and community advocacy are all part of the ecological model that is designed to empower these families (Aponte, 1985; Imber-Black, 1986). Whereas the passive poor form a type of silent majority in the cities, it is the "traumatized poor" (Inclan & Ferran, 1989)—the substance abusers, the chronically mentally ill who are in and out of hospitals, and the homeless who have riveted public attention in recent years. These individuals are perceived to present visible evidence of the urban blight that impedes the redevelopment of urban centers. Although these redevelopment efforts are supposedly designed to help some inner-city problems, too often it appears that the true goal of these efforts is to relocate these traumatized poor to create inviting middle-class enclaves in urban centers. The problems for the traumatic poor are particularly intransigent and will not be the focus of this chapter precisely because groups such as the homeless typically do not engage in therapy. Grassroots groups such as the Black Muslims, Spanish Jehovah's Witnesses, the Black Panther Party, and the Young Lords have persevered in trying to reclaim these traumatized individuals whose needs have not been met by traditional mental health sources (Inclan & Ferran, 1989).

Clark, Zalis, and Sacco (1982) describe a variation of the passive poor that they refer to as "low income culturally deprived" (LICD) families. These families were believed to be too challenging to Minuchin's (1974) structural model because they were unable to function at the basic level of providing nurturance to their children. The parents in these families were characterized as deficient in their ability to convey rules, and provide healthy structures and boundaries for the family. These parents were hostile, rejecting, abusive, and neglectful. Hence Minuchin's ideas about joining the family, and repairing and modifying their structure may not be viable goals. Therapy for these families must focus on developing firm boundaries for the family and a sense of relatedness.

Families may not fall neatly into one of the three previously described categories. Many of these families, however, violate the assumptions of traditional family therapists such as Satir (1967), Haley (1976), and Whittaker & Lieberman (1964) because they resist entering family therapy, do not initiate therapy through a phone call, and are unresponsive to setting and keeping regular appointments at the therapist's office. Families seeking therapy who call for appointments and who meet regularly at the therapist's office are already well organized and high-functioning families (Clark, Zalis, & Sacco, 1982).

Engagement and Resistance

A central issue for family therapists with urban poor families is the process of engagement. Many of these families are ambivalent to, if not, resistant about involvement. Therapy may not be seen as potentially effective, there may be little faith in therapists, solving problems on one's own may be a traditional cultural value, and seeking help may be perceived as being weak, especially for many of the males in these families who are already battling issues of proving their masculinity according to mainstream standards.

Because many poor families have a history of no-shows, several therapists recommend greater use of the telephone or a home visit to begin to engage the family in treatment (Aponte, 1991; Boyd-Franklin, 1989; Clark et al., 1982; Hines et al., 1990). Often resistance is an important strategy used by the family to help them negotiate a way to help direct, plan, and implement their treatment (Parnell & Vanderkloot, 1991). If the resistance continues during treatment, it may be a strong indication that the therapist's intervention is inappropriate or ineffective (Imber-Black, 1988a).

Therapeutic Interventions

The multisystems approach has been further developed into a two-tiered, home-based model (Aponte, 1991). In this intervention, home-based family therapy is provided to families in a manner designed to be maximally responsive to their needs. In addition, multiple family groups are organized in the community to provide mutual support to families, to facilitate skill in dealing with community agencies, and to teach families how to advocate collectively as a group.

Another intervention for families involves the therapist's creating letters that paradoxically describe therapeutic failures. These letters congratulate the family on how challenging and overwhelming their problems are and prescribe the probable defeat of the therapist's efforts. This strategy promotes feelings of closeness and success in families and changes their role from victim to rescuers (L'Abate & Far, 1981).

A therapeutic intervention that can be used effectively to engage urban families is the "cultural story" (McGill, 1992). In this technique, therapists help family members develop a story of their unique family problems set in the context of society's norms with regard to gender, ethnicity, class, race, and age. These stories are designed to document the history of the family and its important issues, themes, and lessons.

Imber-Black (1988b) and Friedman (1988) have noted the successful use of rituals in family therapy with urban families. Asking families to become aware of and encouraging their use of rituals, can help these families negotiate transitional issues such as marriage, death, divorce, moves, or imprisonment. Several therapists are particularly impressed with rites of passage programs that focus on developing emotionally healthy adolescents. Some of these programs involve outward bound activities (Gavazzi & Blumenkrantz, 1993). Other programs utilized in the African American community are highly ritualized, long-term programs that teach inner-city adolescent boys and girls their cultural history and the roles and responsibilities they are expected to assume in their larger interdependent community.

A very promising intervention, multiimpact family therapy, has been implemented by Hines et al. (1990). This intervention was designed to meet the unique needs of inner-city, poor, multiethnic families. Families who elect this treatment option have the opportunity to meet with a team of therapists in an extended single-session format. A minimum period of 6 hours is devoted to hypothesizing, assessing, developing, and implementing intervention strategies for these families. This process has been successful in promoting a rapid joining between the family and the therapist team, providing a concentrated therapeutic impact, decreasing problems associated with frequent scheduling of sessions and minimizing the risks of no-shows and cancellation of appointments.

Therapy with urban poor families needs to be responsive to the realities that these families face. Therapy must be affordable, practical, immediate, brief, time limited, and focused on prioritized needs. The focus in treatment is not so much to promote insight as it is to facilitate structural shifts in families and promote adaptive behavior acquisition. Symptoms and identified patients function to alert therapists to areas of rigidity, disorganization, or maladaptive interactions (Szapocznik & Kurtines, 1989).

An important feature of work with urban poor families is offering flexible mental health services. Home visits appear to be successful in minimizing financial, organizational, and transportation barriers. Also, having therapist team members available for drop-in home visits and appointments with short lead times fit the less routinized more crisis-oriented schedules of many of these families.

Using Family Resources

Precisely because urban poor families often must overcome overwhelming obstacles, it is difficult at times for therapists to direct their attention to the resources that these families have. At times, therapy can be too oriented toward the pathology of the family or the environment, or the therapist might place undue emphasis on demonstrating his or her expertise. Karpel (1986) however has asserted that successful family therapy is as much related to utilizing family resources as it is to the skill of the therapist.

Many inner-city families show amazing resiliency. Although outsiders to the community tend to focus on the lack of resources, graffiti, crime, and general dilapidation, therapists who have worked with inner-city families have uncovered some of the following strengths: energy and enthusiasm in interactions, valuing relationships; humor, acceptance, persistence, optimism and determination; the ability to recharge through music, dance, and social activities; and strong commitment to spiritual, religious, and moral values (Coles, 1987; Parnell & Vanderkloot, 1989).

Leading therapists have advocated for a resource orientation toward working with inner-city families. Erikson (1967) urges therapists to utilize the untapped knowledge families bring to therapy. Haley (1980) has stressed that we must incorporate the family's input and wisdom in setting and satisfying therapy goals. The Milan orientation to systemic family therapy views families as natural problem-solving groups that can be strengthened (Selveni Palazzoli, Boscolo, Cecchin, & Prata, 1980). Madanes (1980) and Boszormenyi-Nagy and Krasner (1980) emphasize the development of personal relatedness. Madanes uses "pretend" techniques to assist family members in acting out symptomatic behaviors that serve a protective function. Selveni Palazzoli and colleagues (1980) frame problems in relationships as attempts by family members to show loyalty, concern, and protection. Therapists have also begun to utilize extended kin, multigenerational family members, and religious and spiritual resources to assist families in developing adaptive behaviors and strategies (Abbott, Berry, & Meredith, 1990; Boyd-Franklin, 1989; Hines et al., 1990; Hines, Garcia-Preto, McGoldrick, Almeida, & Weltman, 1992).

Collaboration, Consultation, and Evaluation

The multisystem model of family therapy utilizes a collaborative approach throughout the therapy process. Many therapists either invite key individuals from community agencies to family therapy sessions or network with these individuals regularly. If a family is self-referred for therapy, therapists must immediately assess which agencies need to be contacted. Family therapists must often establish working relationships with child protective services, schools, health personnel, and the court systems. Therapists play an important role in helping urban families develop a sense of empowerment rather than intimidation in dealing with community agencies. The goal of this networking is not just to solve immediate problems but to help families develop the skills and competencies to prevent and solve problems on their own in the future.

Clear communication is essential in working with these complex family systems to establish explicit goals and objectives. As the therapy progresses, the therapist must listen for both overt and subtle indicators to assess whether the therapy is on course and, in collaboration with the family, make needed adjustments. Work with these families may end when basic goals are met, but follow-up contacts with the message that these families are welcome to return help increase the chances for long-term success. Increasingly, family therapists are attempting to consolidate the strength of interventions by having families network together in their communities and by using interdisciplinary community-based family support programs (Aponte, 1991; Lightburn & Kemp, 1994). Therapists can evaluate their interventions with families by making sure they have honored the values of the family, dealt directly with the presenting problems, enhanced the efficacy of the family structure, and increased the family's ability to effectively utilize its resources and those of its community.

JUVENILE DELINQUENCY

The family therapy movement has had a significant impact on how delinquency is understood. Whereas there was a historical practice of focusing on what was pathological in the delinquent, family therapists focus on the meaning of the delinquent's behavior in the context of the family. Many believe that delinquency is simply a way of organizing action. A corollary belief is that all family members play a role in maintaining the behavior of the delinquent (Johnson, 1983). In fact, many theorists believe that delinquent behavior has an adaptive function by identifying family disturbances and prompting family reorganization (Haley, 1980). Parents are often puzzled by those delinquents who are cooperative, easygoing, and respectful at home but break rules when in school or in the broader community. These families may be at a particular loss in terms of knowing how to alter their children's behavior.

The behaviors that are classified as delinquent range from status offenses such as truancy and running away to index offenses, which include murder, rape, robbery, and assault. The Juvenile Justice and Delinquency Prevention Act of 1974 required that youth committing status offenses not be jailed as delinquent. Yet this law was ambiguous as to how these youth should be treated (Schneider, 1984; Simeone, 1985). Despite the lack of clarity with regard to treatment, it is imperative that effective interventions be created for adolescent juvenile delinquents for the following reasons: (a) male adolescents disproportionately commit a high percentage of violent crime, (b) delinquent behavior in adolescents tends to be maintained through adulthood, (c) serious juvenile delinquents seem to repeat violations that adversely affect the life of their community (Henggeler & Borduin, 1990).

Family interventions appear to offer promising results in working with juvenile delinquents. Several theorists have concluded that maladaptive parenting strategies and family relations, poor cohesion, and limited positive communication are implicated in the development of delinquency (Patterson, 1986; Rodick, Henggeler, & Hansen, 1986; Snyder & Patterson, 1987). Another consistent and strong predictor of delinquent behavior is involvement with delinquent peers (Elliott, Huizinga, & Ageton, 1985). Individual factors that appear to be correlated with delinquent behavior include social skill deficits (Dishion, Loeber, Stouthamer-Loeber, & Patterson, 1984), impulsivity (Camp & Ray, 1989), poor problem-solving skills (Henggeler & Borduin, 1990), and academic problems (Wilson & Hernstein, 1985).

Multisystemic approaches based on family systems, have shown success in helping parents develop adaptive management skills, disengaging youth from negative peers, and strengthening positive bonds with the school and community agencies (Haley, 1976; Minuchin, 1974).

Several model programs have been successful in reducing inner-city juvenile delinquency in adolescents using a multisystemic approach (Brunk, Henggeler, & Whelan, 1987; Culbertson, 1990; Haapala & Kinney, 1988; Henggeler et al., 1986; Miller & Prinz, 1990). These programs are aimed at changing the adolescent's interactions with the systems of family, peer, and school by utilizing information on child development, cognitive behavior therapy, and problem-focused interventions (Kendall & Braswell, 1985).

Implementing multisystemic therapy with delinquent adolescents requires a series of interventions. Family therapists must engage the family in treatment and clarify their roles with respect to both the family and the court system. It is usually essential for the therapist to establish an appropriate working relationship with the probation officer. The first sessions are designed to assess the resources and liabilities of the family and to begin to understand the family's structure and functioning. It is recommended that family sessions be held at the family's residence to defuse resistance, allow the family to function in a familiar setting, to maximize the potential for behavior replication, and to affirm the family by showing the therapists' willingness to plan an intervention that is convenient and responsive to their needs.

The first session involves validating the importance of all family members and soliciting their input as to the presenting problems and what changes they would like to see as a result of therapy. It is especially important for the therapist to align with parents to establish a positive working relationship and to help the parents and other family members see the parents as effective family leaders.

Subsequent interventions include strengthening the parents' ability to supervise, emotionally support, and help achieve educational goals for their adolescent. Parents who are overwhelmed with work, child care, or other psychological or physical problems may require the assistance of other community agencies before they have the energy or motivation to engage in the treatment process.

It is also recommended that individual work be conducted with adolescents to begin to develop the social and cognitive skills to improve in school and to disengage from the negative impact of peer culture. Sometimes, family therapists meet with the adolescent and his or her peer group to assess the impact of the peer group on the identified patient. In some cases, therapists have been successful in promoting community interventions to benefit the peer group such as jobs or job training, sports, or recreational activities. To cement the effectiveness of multisystemic therapy in urban environment, parents are taught how to work collaboratively with the school and with community systems. Families are also encouraged to attend support groups with other families with delinquent adolescents. These groups can be effective in providing guidance, support, and a normalization experience for parents (Henggeler & Borduin, 1990).

Other therapeutic strategies in the literature include breaking down family triangles, predicting crises as the family system changes and is restructured, allowing juveniles to have a time-out period with a close relative or friend rather than being institutionalized, building cohesion and cooperation by strategically utilizing court threats that the therapy is the last alternative before a residential setting is imposed, and helping families develop or use existing resources to function effectively (Henggeler & Borduin, 1990).

The success of multisystemic approaches with juvenile delinquents has been empirically validated and offers a significant avenue for allowing juveniles to remain in their family while helping the family to function more adaptively. These programs represent optimistic alternatives to residential, out-of-home incarceration for juveniles in terms of long-term financial as well as emotional costs (Haapala & Kinney, 1988; Henggeler, Melton, & Smith, 1992).

INCARCERATION IN FAMILIES

As the field of family therapy starts to find successful alternatives to residential penal institutions for juvenile delinquents, they are also confronted with the reality of working with families in which a parent is incarcerated. The separation due to a prison sentence creates emotional, social, psychological, financial, and interpersonal problems not just for the incarcerated but for his or her entire family (King, 1993). However, family therapists have not been actively involved in addressing this problem, which is a crisis for inner-city families, especially African American families, as African American males comprise between 46% and 58% of prison populations across the United States (U.S. Department of Justice 1989, 1991).

Among incarcerated individuals, 70% were supporting two or more persons at the time of their conviction, which means that an economic crisis for the family unit is usually precipitated when a person is imprisoned (King, 1993). Spouses of the inmate are vulnerable to feelings of loneliness, depression, and anger (Brodesky, 1974), and children typically feel abandoned and may manifest difficulty eating, sleeping, and doing schoolwork, and may show evidence of increased aggressiveness (Sack, 1977).

Families with an incarcerated member need positive male and female role models, support groups, clinical services, and community-based family life education programs to help them develop insight into their past and present problems and to learn effective utilization of their resources.

GUNS, VIOLENCE, AND GANGS

Poverty and inner-city residence combine to form key environmental risk factors for violence victimization (Fingerhut, Ingram, & Feldman, 1992), and urban adolescents in particular show higher rates of fighting, carrying of weapons, and witnessing violence than found in national norms. In the category of injury-related deaths, homicide is the second leading cause of death for children and adolescents across all ethnic groups and adolescents and young men aged 15–35 are the most likely perpetrators and victims of homicide at the hands of friends and acquaintances (Christoffel, 1990; Report of the Secretary's Task Force on Black and Minority Health, 1986; Rodriguez, 1990).

As Hammond and Yung (1993) note, low income alone is not responsible for the violence of the inner-city, but the combination of community disorganization, unemployment, population density, and high mobility rates. This section will offer an overview of the problems families face in the inner city with respect to violence, gun carrying, and gangs and the status of interventions to help families face these threats.

Gun Carrying

It was traditionally believed that young people in urban areas carried guns to promote or maintain their status among peers. Recent research however demonstrates that the most significant reasons given by adolescents for carrying weapons are self-protection and self-preservation. Weapon carrying is pragmatically believed to even the odds in the case of an attack (Wright, Sheley, & Smith, 1992). In today's urban centers, where 50% of young children report having seen someone shot or a dead body, police protection appears unpredictable, and the threat of violence or intimidation appears very real, the defensive strategy of weaponry appears to be a viable option to many residents.

Increasingly, the media report episodes of children witnessing or being victimized by shooting, kidnapping, or hostage situations. The long-term effects of these experiences have not been well documented (Rozensky, Sloan, Schwarz, & Kowalski, 1993). There is evidence however, that exposure to these acts of violence is correlated with psychological symptoms associated with posttraumatic stress disorder and may predispose the victims to future revictimization or the use of firearms themselves (Richters & Martinez, 1992).

It has long been recognized that drugs and alcohol are significant risk factors for violence. Alcohol use is related to two thirds of all violent situations. More recently, some evidence has implicated food additives, environmental pollutants, toxic metals and vitamin deficiencies as possible triggers for violence in some individuals, particularly in urban environments (Morales, 1989). It is important to note, however, that the majority of research on violence emphasizes social rather than biological factors as the major determinants of violence.

Two factors that are often correlated with low income—public housing and unemployment—make inner-city families vulnerable to violence or the threat

of violence. Although many prominent citizens often explain that they grew up
in the projects and have made a success of their lives, the projects of today are
very different from those of one or two decades ago. The public housing known
as projects was largely built in the post World War II era and is increasingly becoming unfit for residence due to malfunctioning equipment and little or no
maintenance. Projects have become the breeding grounds for violence, gangs,
and illegal activities. Only residents with the barest of financial resources live
in these projects, where unemployment is rampant.

At particular risk for violence or gang activities are the economically and socially marginal youth who have left or have been expelled from school, who do
not have marketable job skills, and who face a shrinking pool of manufactur-
ing jobs. Many of these youth in the past turned to the military for employment, but they are less successful in gaining jobs in this area as higher quality
applicants are cornering this arena for unskilled workers (Huff, 1989). Poor
employment prospects apparently help lure many inner-city youth into illegal
sources of income (Clowhard & Ohlin, 1960). Inner-city youth can make upward of $3,000 a week selling drugs in contrast to earning minimum wages at
a fast-food restaurant (Morales, 1989).

Gangs

Gangs are a natural result of the same social and economic problems that produce crime, mental illness, substance abuse, homelessness, and multigenerational welfare families who live without the expectation that their lives will
get better (Huff, 1989). For many inner-city youth, gangs compete successfully
with churches, schools, and families to provide sources of affirmation, support, and self-identification. Violence and the threat of violence are om-
nipresent, so urban youth learn to be tough and to turn to gangs as sources of
protection, camaraderie, and adventure. Gangs can provide a haven for working out personal problems and help adolescents' transition into and through
adulthood, as many individuals maintain their gang status past adolescence
(Vigil, 1988).

Typically gang members come from dysfunctional families, and the gang
becomes a surrogate family that provides a sense of belonging, cohesion, continuity, affection, and affirmation for children and adolescents whose own families are not meeting their needs. It therefore seems appropriate that gang
members refer to each other using the terms brother, sister, homeboy or home-
girl, or simply "nuestra familia"—our family.

Although we know some of the risk factors for affiliating with a gang, less
is known about the majority of inner-city families and individuals who do not
become involved with gangs. Little is known about what possible resiliency
factors may characterize these families and their offspring. It has been hypothesized that whereas many inner city youths are exposed to risk factors for
gang membership, perhaps a specific personality type characterizes youths
who join gangs. Jankowski (1991) describes these "defiant individualists" as

competitive, mistrustful, self-reliant, and possessing a survivalist orientation toward a hostile world.

Gangs have long been a feature of urban environments, but they used to be treated with more tolerance by other community members (Horowitz, 1987). These community residents understood that gang membership could sometimes signal a somewhat adaptive strategy to collaborate rather than compete for scarce resources. They could also resonate with certain activities that were seen as affirming, protecting, and celebrating ethnic culture and history and that were responses to societal racism, discrimination, marginalization, and neglect. The increasing violence associated with the use of guns rather than less lethal forms of fighting and the increasing drug trade by gangs have led inner-city residents to be less tolerant and more fearful of gang activities.

Although urban areas often try to minimize or deny problems associated with gangs, the premature deaths of thousands of adolescents and young adults, and increasing reports of car hijackings, drive-by shootings, extortion, rape, robbery, and assault have led urban centers to become involved in gang control efforts. Current strategies are less aimed at rehabilitation and are more oriented toward prevention, deterrence, and control of gang members. Interventions with gang members in the 1950s and 1960s included therapeutic programs that were designed to keep gang members crime free. Today, probation officers are rewarded for their success in helping to convict gang members for crimes (Klein & Maxson, 1989). The majority of interventions described in the literature revolve around criminal justice programs or school-based projects. The rationale for these approaches is to take programs to youths because it is believed that gang members do not respond well to traditional agency approaches (Klein, 1971). These school and criminal justice interventions however do not typically utilize family therapy strategies and do not always reflect a sound ecologically oriented collaboration between the key systems of family, school, and social institutions.

Typical school-based programs that are aimed at decreasing violence and gang membership teach children and adolescents cognitive behavior skills, anger management, focused problem solving, and conflict resolution (Coie, Underwood, & Lochman, 1991; Feindler & Ecton, 1986; Graham & Hudley, 1992; Hammond, 1991; Prothrow-Stith, 1991). Hammond and Yung (1993) have emphasized that given the epidemic of violence in urban areas, it is important not only to have prevention and intervention programs but to design these programs so that they are culturally sensitive and responsive to the needs of the population to be served. Communities are diverse with respect to ethnicity, culture, and problematic behaviors and activities. Gangs vary in terms of the former characteristics as well as gender composition, use of violence, drug use, and how goal oriented their activities are (Sanders, 1994; Thornberry, Krohn, Lizotte, & Chard-Wierschem, 1993). Programs will be most effective when they are specifically geared to the needs of the community.

The Paramount Plan, developed by the Department of Human Services in Paramount, California, reflects a combination of providing a gang prevention curriculum in the schools with community awareness programs with parents. This program discusses violence, drugs, peer pressure, and the impact of gangs on families, and presents alternatives to youth (Ostos, 1991).

A criminal justice based program for gangs in Columbus, Ohio, is housed in the Youth Violence Crime Section and is staffed by 18 police officers. This approach includes aggressive enforcement activities against gang leaders and hard-core members, and prevention activities for marginal and possible new recruits for gangs. This program utilizes the four major gang control functions of intelligence, prevention, enforcement, and investigation. This program also collaborates with schools, courts, the district attorney's office, youth outreach programs, and other community groups (Huff, 1989).

Although the programs discussed represent encouraging developments in curtailing and preventing violence, gangs, and guns in urban environments, more work is needed. Much of the work with gang prevention stigmatizes the gang activities of ethnic minorities but rarely discusses the functioning of predominantly white groups such as skinheads, neo-Nazi groups, and Ku Klux Klan members. There seems to be a strong focus on prevention for nongang members and those who are only marginally involved in gangs but there appear to be few programs that target long-term gang members. A vital key to solving the problems of guns, violence, and gangs has to be eradicating the root causes of these problems: discrimination, unemployment, poor educational attainment, inadequate parenting, and poverty. Perhaps therapists working with families can add their efforts to helping family members repair the individual, social, educational, and economic infrastructures that are currently not serving inner-city residents successfully (Huff, 1989).

CONCLUSION

The worsening conditions of America's cities have had one positive consequence. They have refocused the attention of politicians, public policy experts, and professional service providers on the need to collaborate in developing effective solutions. Literature exists on single problem areas in the inner city such as violence, abuse, addiction, or adolescent pregnancy; however, there is a paucity of material that systematically addresses the interaction between the urban environment and the problems and resources of families. Furthermore, what is generally "known" about urban areas by most of the population is shaped by sensationalized media reports not by the scientific literature. Hence, there are distortions and inaccuracies about cities that most people regard as fact, and there is a tendency to focus only on the pathology of cities without noting their opportunities. This tendency perpetuates the convenient fiction that the struggles of inner-city families are irrelevant to those fortunate enough to live in different neighborhoods. Professionals need to help all communities understand that the violence and destructiveness that result from unemployment, inadequate education, neglect, marginalization, and discrimination, cannot be neatly contained within city limits.

Family therapists have had a tradition of working in urban areas but are only slowly responding to the changing needs and demographics of today's urban families. The strategies that these therapists have begun to develop have shown promise in meeting the needs of multiproblem urban families. More work needs to be done, however, in empirically validating how successful these programs are and for which population. It is essential that therapists recognize the diversity of families in urban areas and develop culturally sensitive strategies that respond to these families' needs.

It is critical that family therapists direct their attention to developing better services for families impacted by or at risk for poverty, delinquency, incarceration, gangs, guns, or violence. The recent political climate has not been receptive to allocating resources for prevention and rehabilitation programs. There appears to be the perception that the money spent to resolve inner-city problems in the 1960s and 1970s was wasted, and since these problems still exist, they are unsolvable or too expensive to be solved and can only be mediated by harsher criminal penalties. Hence we have a climate that is more supportive of building jails and detention centers than developing educational programs, vocational skills, and jobs. Family therapists must meet the challenge of developing effective programs of prevention and rehabilitation and demonstrating the efficacy of these programs both in their reduction of incarceration expenses and by increasing the numbers of productive citizens.

To be a successful family therapist with urban families requires skills in community advocacy. We must help mobilize resources to create programs that eliminate the root causes of the symptoms that we treat. These programs must be specifically designed to reduce poverty, unemployment, poor parenting, discrimination, and inadequate educational skills.

Without question, the job description for therapists working with urban families is a challenging one. These individuals must be knowledgeable about the ecological environment of urban families. They should receive training and supervision to understand their own family of origin issues. These therapists need not be experts on all the diverse issues of gender, sexuality, ethnicity, and culture, but therapists must be held professionally accountable for demonstrating cultural competency. Therapists must also have received supervision around their values and how they relate to their family of origin issues and diverse populations. This type of preparatory work can minimize cultural and value conflicts in the therapy process.

The demands on therapists in metropolitan areas include demonstrating their ability to navigate inner-city neighborhoods, tolerate varying degrees of structure, and utilize flexible appointment times. Work with multiproblem families can make therapists vulnerable to high stress and symptoms of post-traumatic stress disorders. If these therapists are effective, they themselves are also exposed to chronic and unpredictable violence, abuse, life-and-death situations, and high amounts of responsibility without the necessary power to implement rapid change. To help minimize and prevent trauma for themselves, therapists should work as part of a therapeutic team, receive appropriate supervision, and mobilize the resources of community agencies and interdisciplinary collaboration. Therapists can do themselves and inner-city families a service by promoting interdisciplinary community based service centers. These community centers can help families meet their diverse needs quickly and effectively.

Therapists working with families also have the difficult challenge of maintaining a resilient focus in their work. They may sometimes feel that their progress in therapy is slow or nonexistent, and they may accurately perceive that their work with inner-city residents is not highly regarded in today's society. Therapists must possess high levels of commitment and self-reinforcement. They need to maintain or develop a capacity to embrace small victories and recognize that reversing the impact of inner-city problems is slow and tedious work and that the rewards of good work may not be overtly visible until a later time. It is also essential for therapists to identify, study, and document the resources and resiliency factors that they find in these families. It is especially important for us to develop a clearer understanding of not just who joins a gang or becomes a delinquent but who does not join the gang or become a delinquent. We need to find more definitive answers to what characterizes the majority of urban families whose children do not show maladaptive behaviors as we understand the structure and behaviors of these resilient families and family members. We can then develop effective psychoeducational programs to teach other families successful strategies and adaptations to the inner city.

To work as a therapist today with urban families requires that an individual be an excellent therapist as well as an effective community change agent. It is critical that more therapists be trained and recruited to meet the challenges and the potential rewards of working with these families. For the city is not only the pandemonium of Babylon, it also has the splendor of Zion, the city of God (Boulding, 1973). The depressing statistics for cities that we hear so such much about represent real people. For family therapy to flourish and survive, it not only must be relevant to today's world but at the same time must also play a significant role in shaping that world (Mirkin, 1990).

REFERENCES

Abbott, D. A., Berry, M., & Meredith, W. H. (1990). Religious belief and practice: A potential asset in helping families. *Family Relations, 39,* 443–448.

Amato, P. R. (1993). Urban-rural differences in helping friends and family members. *Social Psychology Quarterly, 56,* 249–262.

Anderson, E. (1990). *Streetwise: Race, class and change in an urban community.* Chicago: University of Chicago Press.

Aponte, H. J. (1979). Family therapy and the community. In M. S. Gibbs, J. R. Lachenmeyer, & J. Sigal (Eds.), *Community psychology: Theoretical and empirical approaches* (pp. 311–333). New York: Gardner.

Aponte, H. J. (1985). The negotiation of values in therapy. *Family Process, 24*, 323–338.

Aponte, H. J. (1991). Training on the person of the therapist for work with the poor and minorities. *Journal of Independent Social Work, 5*, 23–39.

Auletta, K. (1982). *The underclass.* New York: Vintage Books.

Auserwald, E. H. (1968). Interdisciplinary versus ecological approach. *Family Process, 7*, 202–215.

Auserwald, E. H. (1983). The gouverneur health services program: An experiment in ecosystemic community care delivery. *Family Systems Medicine, 1*, 5–24.

Benson, J. L. (1987). Family structure and function. In R. B. Birrer (Ed.), *Urban family medicine* (pp. 11–17). New York: Springer-Verlag.

Boszormenyi-Nagy, I., & Krasner, B. (1980). Trust based therapy: A contextual approach. *American Journal of Psychiatry, 137*, 767–775.

Boulding, K. (1973). The death of the city: A frightened look at post civilization. In G. Germiani (Ed.), *Modernization, urbanization and the urban crisis.* Boston: Little, Brown.

Bowen, M. (1978). *Family therapy in clinical practice.* New York: Jason Aronson.

Boyd-Franklin, N. (1989). *Black families in therapy: A multisystems approach.* New York: Guilford.

Bradbury, K. L., Downs, A., & Small, K. A. (1982). *Urban decline and the future of American cities.* Washington, DC: The Brookings Institute.

Brodesky, S. L. (1974). *Families and friends of men in prison: The uncertain relationship.* Lexington, MA: Lexington Books.

Bronfenbrenner, U. (1979). *The ecology of human development: Experiments by nature and design.* Cambridge, MA: Harvard University.

Brown, G. W., & Prudo, R. (1981). Psychiatric disorder in a rural and an urban population: Aetiology of depression. *Psychological Medicine, 11*, 581–599.

Brunk, M., Henggeler, S. W., & Whelan, J. P. (1987). A comparison of multisystemic therapy and parent training in the brief treatment of child abuse and neglect. *Journal of Consulting and Clinical Psychology, 55*, 171–178.

Camp, B. W., & Ray, R. S. (1989). Aggression. In A. W. Meyers & W. E. Craghead (Eds.), *Cognitive behavior therapy with children* (pp. 315–350). New York: Plenum.

Carter, P. (1982). Rapport and integrity for Eriksonian practitioners. In J. Zeig (Ed.), *Eriksonian approaches to hypnosis and psychotherapy.* New York: Brunner/Mazel.

Christoffel, K. K. (1990). Violent death and injury in U.S. children and adolescents. *American Journal of Diseases of Childhood, 144*, 697–706.

Clark, T., Zalis, T., & Sacco, F. (1982). *Outreach family therapy.* New York: Jason Aronson.

Clowhard, R. A., & Ohlin, L. E. (1960). *Delinquency and opportunity: A theory of delinquent groups.* New York: Free Press.

Coie, J., Underwood, M., & Lochman, J. (1991). Programmatic intervention with aggressive children in the school setting. In D. Pepler & K. Rubin (Eds.), *The development and treatment of childhood aggression* (pp. 389–410). Hillsdale, NJ: Erlbaum.

Coles, R. (1987, March). *Moral purpose and the family.* Keynote address to the Family Therapy Networker Symposium, Washington, DC.

Culbertson, J. L. (1990, August). *Clinical child psychology in the 90s: Broadening our scope.* Presidential address to the section on Clinical Child Psychology at the meeting of the American Psychological Association, Boston, MA.

Dishion, T. J., Loeber, R., Stouthamer-Loeber, M., & Patterson, G. R. (1984). Skill deficits and male adolescent delinquency. *Journal of Abnormal Child Psychology, 12,* 37–54.

Edelman, M. W. (1987). *Families in peril: An agenda for social change.* Cambridge, MA: Harvard University Press.

Elliott, D. S., Huizinga, D., & Ageton, S. S. (1985). *Explaining delinquency and drug use.* Beverly Hills, CA: Sage.

Erikson, M. (1967). *Advanced techniques of hypnosis and therapy.* New York: Grune and Stratton.

Feindler, E., & Ecton, R. (1986). *Adolescent anger control.* New York: Pergamon.

Fingerhut, L., Ingram, D., & Feldman, J. (1992). Firearm and nonfirearm homicide among persons 15–19 years of age. *Journal of the American Medical Association, 267,* 3048–3053.

Friedman, E. H. (1988). Systems and ceremonies: A family view of rites of passage. In B. Carter & M. McGoldrick (Eds.), *The family life cycle: A framework for family therapy* (2nd ed.). New York: Gardner.

Garbarino, J., Dubrow, N., Kostelny, K., & Pardo, C. (1992). *Children in danger: Coping with the consequences of community violence.* San Francisco: Jossey-Bass.

Gavazzi, S. M., & Blumenkrantz, D. G. (1993). Facilitating clinical work with adolescents and their families through the rites of passage experience program. *Journal of Family Psychotherapy, 4,* 47–67.

Graham, S., & Hudley, C. (1992). An attributional approach to aggression in African American children. In D. Schunk & J. Meece (Eds.), *Student perceptions in the classroom* (pp. 75–94). Hillsdale, NJ: Erlbaum.

Greater Washington Research Center. (1993). *Poverty rates of U.S. cities.* Washington, DC: Author.

Haapala, D. A., & Kinney, J. M. (1988). Avoiding out of home placement of high risk status offenders through the use of intensive home based family preservation services. *Criminal Justice and Behavior, 15,* 334–348.

Haley, J. (1976). *Problem solving therapy.* San Francisco: Jossey-Bass.

Haley, J. (1980). *Leaving home.* New York: McGraw-Hill.

Hammond, W. R. (1991). *Dealing with anger: Givin' it, takin' it, workin' it out.* Champaign, IL: Research Press.

Hammond, W. R., & Yung, B. (1993). Psychology's role in the public health response to assaultive violence among young African American men. *American Psychologist, 48,* 142–154.

Henggeler, S. W., & Borduin, C. M. (1990). *Family therapy and beyond: A multisystemic approach to treating the behavior problems of children and adolescents*. Belmont, CA: Wadsworth.

Henggeler, S. W., Melton, G. B., & Smith, L. A. (1992). Family preservation using multisystemic therapy: An effective alternative to incarcerating serious juvenile offenders. *Journal of Consulting and Clinical Psychology, 60,* 953–961.

Henggeler, S. W., Rodick, J. D., Borduin, C. M., Hanson, C. L., Watson, S. M., & Urey, J. R. (1986). Multisystemic treatment of juvenile offenders: Effects on adolescent behavior and family interaction. *Developmental Psychology, 22,* 132–141.

Hines, P. M., Richman, D., Maxim, K., & Hays, H. (1990). Multi-impact family therapy: An approach to working with multi-problem families. In G. W. Saba, B. M. Karrer, & K. V. Hardy (Eds.), *Minorities and family therapy*. Binghampton, NY: Haworth.

Hines, P. M., Garcia-Preto, N., McGoldrick, M., Almeida, R., & Weltman, S. (1992). Intergenerational relationships across cultures. *Families in Society: The Journal of Contemporary Human Services, 73,* 323–338.

Horowitz, R. (1987). Community tolerance of gang violence. *Social Problems, 34,* 437–450.

Huff, C. R. (1989). Youth gangs and public policy. *Crime and Delinquency, 35,* 524–537.

Imber-Black, E. (1986). Systems consultation. In L. Wynne (Ed.), *The systemic consultant and human service providers* (pp. 357–374). New York: Guilford.

Imber-Black, E. (1988a). *Families and larger systems: A family therapist's guide to family therapy*. New York: Guilford.

Imber-Black, E. (1988b). Idiosyncratic life cycle transitions and therapeutic rituals. In B. Carter & M. McGoldrick (Eds.), *The family life cycle: A framework for family therapy* (2nd ed.). New York: Gardner.

Inclan, J., & Ferran, E. (1989). Poverty, politics and family therapy: A role for systems theory. In M. P. Mirkin (Ed.), *The social and political contexts of family therapy*. Boston: Allyn and Bacon.

Jankowski, M. S. (1991). *Islands in the streets: Gangs and American urban society*. Berkeley: University of California Press.

Jenkins, H. (1983). A family life cycle framework in the treatment of underorganized families. *Journal of Family Therapy, 5,* 359–377.

Jenkins, H. (1990). Poverty, state, and the family: A challenge for family therapy. *Contemporary Family Therapy, 12,* 311–325.

Johnson, T. F. (1983). Therapeutic interventions in delinquency. In M. R. Textor (Ed.), *Helping families with special problems*. New York: Jason Aronson.

Kantor, D., Peretz, A., & Zander, R. (1984). The cycle of poverty-Where to begin? In J. C. Hansen & B. F. Okun (Eds.), *Family therapy with school related problems*. Rockville, MD: Aspen.

Karpel, M. A. (Ed.). (1986). *Family resources: The hidden partner in family therapy*. New York: Guilford.

Kelly, M. L., Sanchez-Hucles, J. V., & Walker, R. (1993). Correlates of parenting in middle income African American mothers. *Merrill-Palmer Quarterly, 39,* 252–264.

Kendall, P. C., & Braswell, L. (1985). *Cognitive behavioral therapy for impulsive children.* New York: Guilford.

Kesselman, M., Sullivan, C. W., & Cohen, C. I. (1987). Psychiatry and the urban family practitioner. In R. B. Birrer (Ed.), *Urban family medicine* (pp. 117–124). New York: Springer-Verlag.

King, A. E. (1993). The impact of incarceration on African American families: Implications for practice. *Families in Society: The Journal of Contemporary Human Services, 74,* 145–153.

Klein, M. W. (1971). *Street gangs and streetworkers.* Englewood Cliffs, NJ: Prentice-Hall.

Klein, M. W., & Maxson, C. L. (1989). Street gang violence. In N. A. Weiner & M. E. Wolfgang (Eds.), *Violent crime, violent criminals* (pp. 198–234). Newbury Park, CA: Sage.

Knox, P. L., Bohland, J., & Shumsky, N. L. (1983). The urban transition and the evolution of the medical care delivery system in America. *Social Science Medicine, 17,* 37–43.

Krupat, E. (1980). Social psychology and urban behavior. *Journal of Social Issues, 36,* 1–8.

L'Abate, L., & Far, L. (1981). Coping with defeating patterns. *Family Therapy, 8,* 91–103.

Liang, J., & Warfel, B. (1983). Urbanism and life satisfaction among the aged. *Journal of Gerontology, 38,* 97–106.

Lightburn, A., & Kemp, S. P. (1994). Family support programs: Opportunities for community based practice. *Families in Society: The Journal of Contemporary Human Services, 75,* 16–26.

McGill, D. W. (1992). The cultural story in multicultural family therapy. *Families in Society: The Journal of Contemporary Human Services, 73,* 339–349.

McGoldrick, M., Pearce, J. K., & Giordano, J. (Eds.). (1982). *Ethnicity and family therapy.* New York: Guilford.

Madanes, C. (1980). Protection, paradox and pretending. *Family Process, 19,* 73–85.

Milgram, S., & Hollander, P. (1964). The murder they heard. *Nation, 198,* 602–604.

Miller, G. E., & Prinz, R. J. (1990). Enhancement of social learning family interventions for childhood conduct disorders. *Psychological Bulletin, 108,* 291–307.

Minucchin, S. (1974). *Families and family therapy.* Cambridge, MA: Harvard University Press.

Minucchin, S., Montalvo, B., Guerney, B., Jr., Rosman, B., & Schumer, F. (1967). *Families of the slums.* New York: Basic Books.

Mirkin, M. P. (Ed.). (1990). *The social and political contexts of family therapy.* Boston: Allyn and Bacon.

Morales, A. (1989). Urban gang violence: A psychosocial crisis. In A. Morales & B. W. Sheafor (Eds.), *Social work: A profession of many faces* (pp. 413–452). Boston: Allyn and Bacon.

Moynihan, D. P. (1986). *Family and nation.* New York: Harcourt Brace Jovanovich.

National Center on Education in the Inner Cities. (1994). *Building on diversity.* Philadelphia: Center for Research in Human Development and Education.

Ogbu, J. U. (1985). Black education: A cultural ecological perspective. In H. P. McAdoo (Ed.), *Black families* (2nd ed., pp. 169–184). Newbury Park, CA: Sage.

Ostos, T. (1991). Alternatives to gang membership: The Paramount Plan. *Public Health Reports, 106,* 241.

Otte, J. K., (1987). Community resources. In R. B. Birrer (Ed.), *Urban family medicine* (pp. 147–153). New York: Springer-Verlag.

Parnell, M., & Vanderkloot, J. (1989). Ghetto children: Children growing up in poverty. In L. Combrinck-Graham (Ed.), *Children in family contexts* (pp. 437–462). New York: Guilford.

Parnell, M., & Vanderkloot, J. (1991). Mental health services—2001: Serving a new America. *Journal of Independent Social Work, 5,* 183–203.

Patterson, G. R. (1986). Performance model for antisocial boys. *American Psychologist, 41,* 432–444.

Peterson, P. E. (1985). Introduction: Technology, race and urban policy. In P. E. Peterson (Ed.), *The new urban reality* (pp. 1–29). Washington, DC: The Brookings Institute.

Ponterrotto, J. G. (1990). Affirmative action: Current status and future needs. In J. G. Ponterrotto, D. Lewis, & R. Bullington (Eds.), *Affirmative action on campus* (pp. 5–18). San Francisco: Jossey-Bass.

Powell, G. T. (1983). Coping with adversity: The psychosocial development of Afro-American children. In G. T. Powell, J. Yamamoto, A. Romero, & A. Morales (Eds.), *The psychosocial development of minority children.* New York: Brunner/Mazel.

Prothrow-Stith, D. (1991). *Deadly consequences: How violence is destroying our teenage population and a plan to begin solving the problem.* New York: HarperCollins.

Prudo, R., Brown, G. W., Harris, T., & Dowland, J. (1981). Psychiatric disorder in a rural and an urban population: Sensitivity to loss. *Psychological Medicine, 11,* 601–616.

Report of the Secretary's Task Force on Black and Minority Health. (1986, January). (Vol. 5). U.S. Department of Health and Human Services.

Richters, J. E., & Martinez, P. (1992). The NIMH Community Violence Project: I. Children as victims of and witnesses to violence. *Psychiatry, 56,* 7–21.

Rodick, J. D., Henggeler, S. W., & Hanson, C. L. (1986). An evaluation of the family adaptability and cohesion evaluation scales and the circumplex model. *Journal of Abnormal Child Psychology, 14,* 77–87.

Rodriguez, J. (1990). Childhood injuries in the U.S. *American Journal of Diseases of Childhood, 144,* 627–646.

Rodriguez, R. (1992). Understanding the pathology of inner city violence. *Black Issues in Higher Education, 9,* 18–20.

Rozensky, R. H., Sloan, I. H., Schwarz, E. D., & Kowalski, J. M. (1993). Psychological response of children to shootings and hostage situations. In F. Saylor (Ed.), *Children and disasters* (pp. 123–136). New York: Plenum.

Sack, W. H. (1977). Children of imprisoned fathers. *Psychiatry, 40,* 163–174.

Sanders, W. B. (1994). *Gangbangs and drive-bys: Grounded culture and juvenile gang violence.* New York: Aldine de Gruyter.

Satir, V. (1967). *Conjoint family therapy*. Palo Alto, CA: Science and Behavior Books.

Schaefer, C. E., Briesmeister, J. M., & Fitton, M. E. (Eds.). (1986). *Family therapy techniques for problem behaviors of children and teenagers*. San Francisco: Jossey-Bass

Schneider, A. (1984). Divesting status offenses from juvenile court jurisdiction. *Crime and Delinquency, 30,* 347–370.

Selvini Palazzoli, M., Boscolo, L., Cecchin, G., & Prata, G. (1980). Hypothesizing-circularity-neutrality: Three guidelines for the conductor of the session. *Family Process, 19,* 3–12.

Simeone, M. (1985). Group home failures in juvenile justice: The next step. *Child Welfare, 64,* 357–366.

Simons, S. M. (1987). The urban high risk patient. In R. B. Birrer (Ed.), *Urban family medicine* (pp. 62–71). New York: Springer-Verlag.

Smilkstein, G. (1978). The family APGAR. *Journal of Family Practice, 6,* 1231–1239.

Strelnick, A. H., & Gilpin, M. (1987). Family organization and dynamics. In R. B. Birrer (Ed.), *Urban family medicine* (pp. 18–26). New York: Springer-Verlag.

Snyder, J., & Patterson, G. R. (1987). Family interaction and delinquent behavior. In H. C. Quay (Ed.), *Handbook of juvenile delinquency* (pp. 216–243). New York: Wiley.

Szapocznik, J., & Kurtines, W. M. (Eds.). (1989). *Breakthroughs in family therapy with drug abusing and problem youth*. New York: Springer.

Thornberry, T. P., Krohn, M. D., Lizotte, A. J., & Chard-Wierschem, D. (1993). The role of juvenile gangs in facilitating delinquent behavior. *Journal of Research in Crime and Delinquency, 30,* 50–87.

U.S. Department of Justice. (1989). *Correctional populations in the U.S., 1986.* (Office of Justice Programs, Bureau of Justice Statistics Publication No. NCJ-111611.) Washington, DC: U.S. Government Printing Office.

U.S. Department of Justice. (1991). *Race of prisoners admitted to state and federal institutions, 1926–1986.* (Office of Justice Programs, Bureau of Justice Statistics Publication No. NCJ-125618). Washington, DC: U.S. Government Printing Office.

Vigil, J. D. (1988). Group processes and street identity: Adolescent Chicano gang members. *Ethos, 16,* 421–445.

Walker, G., & Small, S. (1991). Aids, crack, poverty and race in the African American community: The need for an ecosystemic approach. *Journal of Independent Social Work, 5,* 69–90.

Walsh, T. C. (1981). Families in Crisis: Relating vulnerability and family functioning to treatment. *Family Therapy, 8,* 105–112.

Warren, D. I. (1969). Neighborhood structure and riot behavior in Detroit: Some exploratory findings. *Social Problems, 16,* 464–484.

Warren, D. I. (1977). The functional diversity of urban neighborhoods. *Urban Affairs Quarterly, 13,* 151–181.

Weiner-Davis, M., de Shazer, S., & Gingerich, W. J. (1987). Building on pretreatment change to construct the therapeutic solution: An exploratory study. *Journal of Marital and Family Therapy, 13,* 359–363.

Whittaker, D. S., & Lieberman, M.A. (1964). *Psychotherapy through the group process.* Chicago: Aldine.

Wilson, J. Q., & Hernstein, R. J. (1985). *Crime and human nature.* New York: Simon and Schuster.

Wilson, W. J. (1980). *The declining significance of race: Blacks and changing American institutions* (2nd ed.). Chicago: University of Chicago Press.

Wright, J. D., Sheley, J. F., & Smith, M. D. (1992). Kids, guns and killing fields. *Society, 30,* 84–89.

Zero Population Growth. (1993). *Children's stress index.* Washington, DC: Author.

CHAPTER 11

Mental Health Approaches to Working with Families with Disabled Children

PATRICIA EDMISTER

Over the past 10 to 20 years, there has been revolutionary movement in the field of early intervention and assistance to handicapped children and their families. It began in 1975 with the passage of Public Law 94-142, commonly called the Education for All Handicapped Children's Act, which guaranteed a free, appropriate public education to all handicapped children, and continued with the more recently passed legislation, Public Law 99-457, the Amendments to P.L. 94-142, passed in 1986, which, among other things extended educational opportunities for handicapped children and their families to those identified with handicapping conditions as early as birth. Public Law 99-457 was especially responsive to current movements in the behavioral sciences and society as a whole, which is now recognizing the need to view individuals within families from a family systems perspective (Beckman, Robinson, Rosenberg, & Filer, 1994). Many models have been developed during the past 5 to 10 years that respond to the awareness of the increased instability of the family and its effects on general social stability (Beckman et al., 1994, Breunlin, Schwartz, & Mac Kune-Karrer, 1992; Bronfenbrenner, 1979). In addition, there has been increased awareness of the stress on all families and families with disabled children in particular, and concern over how to decrease that stress, or at least to make it more manageable.

Families with handicapped or disabled youngsters as members (in this chapter, the terms handicapped and disabled will be used interchangeably) are coping with the stressors placed on them by having to care for a child with special needs that may include medical problems, special child-care requirements, and unusual educational requirements, as well as considerable emotional distress for the family members (Beckman, 1991a; Dyson, 1991; Dyson & Fewell, 1986; Friedrich & Friedrich, 1981). In addition, many of these families feel depression (Breslau & Davis, 1986) and isolation (Gallagher, Beckman, & Cross, 1983). However, it has also been found that not all families experience such effects and, that the effects are influenced by the amount of informal social support received by the parents, and by the extent of the caregiving responsibilities (Beckman, 1991b). Beckman (1993) reported that mothers who received informal support when their disabled infants were very young (3 months) reported significantly less stress when their infants were older (24 months). However, no significant relationships were found at any of the ages examined between formal support (traditionally institutionalized sources such as service providers, agencies, and organizations designed to provide services for individuals with disabilities and their families) and stress reduction. Finally, when Beckman (1991b) studied social support reported by 42 mothers of children with disabilities between 18 months and 6 years of age, asking mothers to rate potential sources of formal support (infant/preschool programs, private physicians, private social workers, counselors/psychologists, etc.), she found a fairly large percentage of parents reporting that specific services were not available or not at all helpful (range was 34% to 78%). Only 6.9% to 36.9% (depending on the specific service) reported that a particular type of formal support was extremely helpful. What seemed to have been the case was that service providers were assuming that most or all the sources of stress evolved from the child and his or her disability, and often failed to look at the *family system* and/or the *social service delivery system* as potential sources of, or contributors to the stress experienced by the family members.

Fortunately, these assumptions seem to be changing as service providers and mental health professionals have become aware that there are many socially constructed difficulties contributing to stress on families with handicapped children. Those professionals have integrated the specific issues related to these families into new and existing family systems models to enable mental health professionals and service providers to be of greater assistance to these families as they cope with life (Beckman, 1993).

USEFUL MODELS FOR VIEWING FAMILIES WITH DISABLED CHILDREN FROM A FAMILY SYSTEMS PERSPECTIVE

Current thinking in the field of family therapy tends to see individuals functioning not only as individuals, but also as members of larger systems within which they interact with other members. Bronfenbrenner's (1979) ecological framework is one way to view these issues. Using this model, the individual is seen as functioning within a series of nested settings with each setting itself embedded in larger settings. It is important for the individual and the therapist to be aware of these various settings, for each contributes to the pressures and, hopefully to the support the individual experiences. Awareness of the impact of the various components can assist the individual, couple, family, and therapist evaluate the strength of each component and then determine which elements are helpful, which are hindrances, which can be changed, and which cannot be changed.

Bronfenbrenner (1979) identified the *microsystem* as the immediate setting of the family in which the individual spends most of his or her time. The *mesosystem* refers to relationships among microsystems. This, for most families, would include relatives, neighbors, and extended family members. The *exosystem* would include larger, relatively concrete social structures and organizations such as agencies, schools, hospitals, and so forth that are part of the larger more formal service system. And finally, there is the *macrosystem,* which includes the larger social context in which the exosystem level services function. This would include the cultural context, the political and economic systems that influence the ways families operate (Beckman, 1993).

Another, more recently developed family systems model is the Metaframeworks model developed by Breunlin, Schwartz, and Mac Kune-Karrer (1990), which has pulled together core ideas from many of the principal schools of family therapy. According to this model, the therapist, in assessing the dynamics of the family's interactions, needs to ask two fundamental questions: How is this family feeling stuck or constrained from solving their problems, and how can the therapist collaborate with the family to identify these constraints and work with the family to help them lift the constraints that prevent them from doing what they want to do?

This model encourages therapists to look within the family at the *bio/psycho/social systems* of the family and its members. To do that, the therapist must be aware of the *actions (behavior), meanings (beliefs, values, attributes), and emotions (shame, fear, guilt, anger, or abandonment)* of family members. In addition, the therapist must also be aware that the "meanings" or the "emotions" of the individual can act as constraints that block "actions."

Breunlin et al. (1992) have identified six core ideas for viewing and working with families. They are: (a) internal processes, (b) sequences, (c) organization, (d) development, (e) culture, (f) gender. These metaframeworks provide a comprehensive view of family functioning by providing a lens through which the therapist can view what is happening in a family.

Internal Processes

Even though we are encouraging working with families with disabled children from a family systems perspective, we must not lose sight that each family member is also an individual. The metaframeworks approach holds that the individual's mind consists of a multiplicity of subpersonalities (called parts) which can either work together or go into opposition with each other (Breunlin, Schwartz, & Mac Kune-Karrer, 1990). This concept is important to keep in mind when working with individual family members who may be wrestling within themselves with conflicting ideas and emotions concerning their handicapped family member. For example, one part of the mind "believes" that all human life is sacred and should be preserved at all cost. Another part of the mind may "say," however, "This child cannot see, hear, process information—is functioning in a vegetative state and is a tremendous drain on the family and society; therefore, he [she] should be allowed to die." Thus, the two parts' intentions differ from each other and are potentially in conflict. Therapists can play a critical role in helping an individual resolve conflict between or among parts by helping the client learn how to control the various parts and keep one part from interfering with the appropriate role of the other part.

Sequences

The concept of *sequences* involves looking at a family's patterns of action and the meanings of those actions. Breunlin et al. (1992) identifies four classes of sequences. *S-1* refers to relatively brief face-to-face interactions including all types of nonverbal behavior. With handicapped children, there are many of these everyday, often delivered nonverbally when a youngster is not able to speak. These often have significant, profound effects on other family members who must respond to demands that need to be met.

S-2 sequences involve longer time periods, usually over a 24-hour span. These interactions reflect the patterns by which the family operates to maintain itself in the world and involves the family routines that enable it to get things done. In today's society, and in particular, in families with a disabled child, family routines are often disrupted and nontraditional in terms of role responsibilities and financial constraints. Thus, there is a vast array of alternative family arrangements. In the Smythe family (not their real name), Jane, a 14-year-old girl with Down syndrome, is functioning at a 7-year-old cognitive level, with speech at about a 3-year-old level. Both her parents must work long hours to meet financial obligations, so her older brother, Dick, 16, takes responsibility for seeing that she gets up and is ready for the school bus. If Jane were 14 and not retarded, Dick would not have that responsibility. If Jane were severely retarded, one of the parents might have had to quit his or her job, or the family would have to hire a caretaker to help with Jane. For other families, such a situation might mean that one parent would have to stay home with the children while the other went to work; then the parents might reverse roles so that the "day-time-stay-at-home" parent would go to work on the night shift. This can have significant impact on the adults' relationship in that they seldom spend time with each other or with the family as a whole.

The S-1 and S-2 behavior patterns, while manifested through interactions in day-to-day living, result from the individual's existence within a larger context of the family's rules and rituals through many generations.

S-3 sequences represent the ebb and flow of family life over longer periods of time, such as several weeks or months. Thus, the S-3s contextualize the S-1s and S-2s. Sometimes it is hard to determine just how the longer S-3 patterns affect family life. With handicapped children in a family, however, the pattern of the school year versus vacation periods is an example. During the school year, the youngster attends a school program for a certain number of hours every day, every week. Family members can count on that time to enable them to do other activities without having to worry about child care. However, on weekends and school holidays, respite care or child care must be provided, and that changes family interactions and dynamics as someone within the family must assume such responsibility. Even when a youngster's condition is so severe that he or she must be institutionalized, current practice encourages families to have the child at home for visits and vacations, so even then, additional responsibility and family dynamics are affected. Thus, the degree of severity, as well as the fact of a handicapping condition, also impacts the family members' responsibility levels.

S-4 sequences, called *transgenerational sequences,* are the patterns that are transmitted from one generation to the next. The multigenerational transmission process, derived from Murray Bowen's work (Bowen, 1978), passes on the value system, rules, and beliefs of the family. These elements are usually derived from the evolution of the family's culture, or they may be idiosyncratic to this particular family (Breunlin et al., 1990). Although it has been found that in many cases events from one generation are repeated in the next and the next generation, it has also been observed that some patterns from one generation may be rejected by the next generation either because they were not found to be useful, or because they were found to be counterproductive. This is very true of many families with handicapped children, although there is no set pattern to the way in which they no longer observe patterns of beliefs from the past. Some families today maintain severely handicapped children in their homes—a practice that in past generations would often not occur because the philosophy then was to institutionalize impaired children, often not even allowing parents to see such children at birth so that no bond or attachment would be formed. However, another practice in the past was to allow less severely impaired children to live at home, but not to attend school, learn a trade, or participate in community activities. Today, because of P.L. 94-142, P.L. 99-457, and other state and federal legislation, all children are entitled to a free, appropriate education and "transition to the world of work" services as appropriate. Thus, new patterns for future generations to follow regarding the competencies and family membership roles of handicapped individuals are being formulated and passed on.

Organization

Organization, or how the family functions in terms of hierarchies and boundaries, is viewed through the concepts of leadership, balance, and harmony (Breunlin et al., 1990). This metaframework looks at how a family problem (symptom) can oppress a system as well as how a problem can be maintained by the constraints imposed by that family's system. Thus, the family is viewed in terms of the parents and children, the children as siblings, the family within the larger community of the children's peers, school, church, neighborhood, work, and so on, and how the boundaries operate. This metaframework examines who holds power over whom and when; who is the leader, when that person leads, who nurtures, and how balance in the organization is maintained. The *rules* defining who participates in the family and how that participation is permitted are also analyzed and interpreted (Breunlin et al., 1990, 1992).

In families with disabled children, the traditional organization patterns are often disrupted. Sibling relationships are often distorted because of the inability of the disabled child to behave in age-appropriate ways. Siblings often have to take on caretaking roles for the disabled child which are atypical in normal family situations. Siblings are often embarrassed or angered by the needs and demands the disabled child places on other members of the family. Siblings often resent the amount of time the disabled child receives from parents (time that the nondisabled child would like to have for him- or herself). Many brothers and sisters of disabled children report that they often are reluctant to bring friends to the house because of embarrassment about their sibling's behavior or condition. Others report that they don't want their parents to bring the disabled child to their after-school sports activities or performances due to their embarrassment. In addition, often the nondisabled siblings have to assume parental responsibilities for the disabled child that they may perceive as unfair and undesired. The caretaking role, the possible embarrassment such a child feels toward the disabled sibling, and the guilt the child feels for those feelings, may affect the youngster's relationships with other family members and with peers.

Some parents report that it is difficult for them to be nurturing and caring for their severely impaired child due to the lack of positive feedback from the child, and due to the ongoing need for constant care with no end in sight. Often, they report, it is difficult to keep the organization in balance both within the family and outside in the community because of the lack of time to do other things with other family and community members. Thus, the family has to reorganize itself around the needs of the disabled child, sometimes to the detriment of others in the family.

Developmental Stages

When looking at developmental considerations in families, two perspectives are considered—the *individual's* developmental stage, and the *family's* developmental stage. Carter and McGoldrick (1989) identify six stages in the family's life cycle:

1. The unattached adult.
2. Joining through marriage—the new couple.
3. The family with young children.
4. The family with adolescents.
5. Launching children and moving on.
6. The family in later life.

Having a disabled child in the family can affect all family members as the family tries to move through Stages 3 through 6, for the presence of this child with the concomitant responsibilities for care (depending of course on the severity of the condition) affects the family members' interactional patterns and may cause the family, or at least some of its members, to become stuck in a particular phase longer than is usual. For example, during Stage 3, the family with young children would ordinarily expect the children to mature, take on additional responsibilities for themselves and each other, and behave in ways befitting their birth order positions. Instead, parents may in fact find that the disabled child, perhaps a firstborn, cannot maintain the characteristics of that position and may be surpassed by the abilities and developmental characteristics of a subsequent child. This raises all kinds of issues for family members, disrupting logical sequences in relationships and having significant effects on the self-esteem of the older child. In addition, a severely disabled child may remain developmentally at an infant or toddler stage, requiring the parents to maintain his or her care at that level, thus not enabling them to move on to other stages in their own lives with the concomitant benefits those future stages bring to each adult member.

Puberty is a critical period in the life of any child. With a severely handicapped child, however, it often brings considerable concern for parents. This stage seems to ignite adverse behaviors in some disabled children who, until this time, may have been manageable in their homes or day-school programs. Because of negative behavior, parents may now need to consider the possibility of residential treatment facilities, which means separations from the child, and trust in the institution. It also may bring about concerns about sexual activity. This is especially true for parents of young women who can now become pregnant and who are often taken advantage of due to their lack of understanding. There is a high incidence of sexual exploitation of mentally retarded and developmentally delayed individuals, both inside institutions and out. In addition, there are difficulties with developmentally delayed females maintaining appropriate personal hygiene at this time of life. Therapists need to be aware of and sympathetic to the parents' concerns, but also be helpful to families by knowing the laws related to sterilization and laws related to the civil rights of handicapped individuals.

Not all approaches to doing therapy with these families take into consideration the family life cycle stage of the family. In contrast, the Metaframeworks model expands the more traditional concept of the family life cycle by building on the premise that development in multileveled organic systems takes place at the biological, individual, relational, family, and societal level (Breunlin et al, 1990). This model also suggests that system actions can be a function of developmental oscillations wherein the identified patient acts older or younger than his or her age. This is an important concept when working with families who have a disabled child, for that child often functions at a much younger age, which can then force others to act at much older ages. This model also shows how developmental problems at one level can constrain development at other levels and thus, contribute to the emergence and/or maintenance of problems.

Culture

Breunlin et al. (1990) point out that it has only been in the past decade that family therapy has begun to recognize the important role that culture plays in the behavior and belief systems of families. For Breunlin, the definition of culture included parameters of ethnicity, race, class, economics, religion, region, and gender. The metaframeworks approach seeks to unify the many ideas concerning culture that have not been integrated in the past.

Hanson, Lynch, and Waymen (1990), in describing the influence of culture on views of child rearing, disability, the family, values, language, and communication, found that most American early intervention programs for handicapped young children and their parents reflect the views of middle-class Anglo-Saxons. This is true also of the assessment instruments used to determine the extent of the handicapping condition, and is reflected in the treatment goals. Smith and Ryan (1987) found that language barriers affect service delivery to these families across the board. Mary (1990) found that service providers who do not address and accommodate to cultural and ethnic diversity often make incorrect assumptions about the reactions of families to the child's disability and, consequently, limit the effectiveness of the intervention program. Beckman and Bristol (1991) point out that economic conditions of a family can also have significant impact on timing and rate of referral of families with developmentally delayed children. They report that infants who come from the lowest income, poorly educated families tend to be identified later for intervention than infants from higher income families. In addition, even once identified, low-income families tend to participate less and drop out sooner than other families. Differences in values, expectations, and needs are frequently not taken into consideration by professionals implementing the programs. Interventionists and all helping professionals must (a) become aware of the extent to which their own professional opinions, reactions, and expectations are driven by cultural values; (b) learn about the values and cultural norms that organize and pattern the families with whom they work; (c) hire culturally diverse staff; (d) demonstrate respect for differing values (Beckman & Bristol, 1991).

Gender

Gender roles and responsibilities have long had a place in consideration of family interactional patterns. Recent social and political events have altered the traditional views of male and female roles and responsibilities within the family as more and more women work outside the home due to desire and economic necessity. In addition, the increase in numbers of single parent and female heads of households has also played a significant role in gender role change.

For families with a disabled child, roles and responsibilities have blended and merged, for often the caretaking responsibilities require that both parents, and frequently siblings, play many roles in caring for the child. In addition, significant expenses associated with the medical and maintenance care of the child may necessitate both parents working outside the home to provide for the family's needs. Unfortunately, too, researchers have found that there is a higher incidence of separation and divorce among families with disabled children, again often necessitating changes in traditional gender roles.

USE OF THIS MODEL

The Metaframework model offers therapists a way in which to conceptualize the family system and then, to develop a comprehensive *blueprint for therapy,* which involves four interrelated clinical processes: hypothesizing, planning, conversing, and reading feedback (Breunlin et al., 1990). The therapist working with the family of a disabled child develops this blueprint, taking into consideration what he or she knows about the family's organizational structure; sequential interactions; developmental levels, both as a family unit and as individuals; the internal processes of each individual; the family's cultural background; and the gender of each member.

The initial action of the therapist is to *hypothesize* about the family, based on intake information. This entails drawing from one or more metaframework, which organizes and categorizes specific information offered by members of the system. *Planning* then takes place to determine how the therapist will proceed based on the guiding principles of one or more of the metaframeworks. *Conversing* is what the therapist says to family members moment-to-moment in session, and *reading feedback* is observing and interpreting the family's responses to the therapist's interventions.

Case:

The Smythe family was referred for therapy because the older child, Dick was becoming somewhat defiant and oppositional in his behavior within the family, although no problems were reported at school or in the community. Parents reported that he was often uncooperative and angry at home, no longer wanting to do tasks which had long been his to do.

The family consists of Dick, 16; Jane, a 14-year-old girl with Down syndrome, functioning at the developmental level of a 7-year-old with the exception of her speech, which is at the 3- to 4-year-old level; mother, Susan, an administrator of nurses at a local hospital, and father, Tom, a professor of English literature at a local college. The family lives in a rural/suburban area outside Los Angeles. The recent earthquake has disrupted travel for both mother and father, adding several hours per day to their commutes. Both parents work full time; Dick is a junior in high school, who has just become licensed to drive and has his own car. Mother works extremely long hours, often going to work at 3 or 4 in the morning so that she can get paperwork done before other staff arrive. Dad leaves for work around 6 o'clock, having started Jane and Dick on their morning activities. Dick is responsible for seeing that Jane finishes her breakfast and is ready for the arrival of the school bus at 7:10 A.M. Jane has her own key and is responsible for taking care of herself after the school bus drops her off around 4 o'clock until someone arrives home around 5:30 P.M.

DEVELOPING THE BLUEPRINT

Pat, the therapist, worked in a collaborative fashion with this family. They explored how the family was being constrained from adjusting and adapting to the developmental needs of a family with one adolescent struggling for independence and a second adolescent, handicapped by Down syndrome, functioning at a much younger age cognitively and behaviorally.

In gathering information about this family, Pat applied each metaframework to the presenting problem and the information obtained through intake. In terms of *organization,* she knew that both parents were very busy, working outside the home, which required that Dick take on family responsibilities (care of Jane that usually would not be required of other adolescents his age). Also, Jane had to take care of herself after school, which would not be unexpected for most 14-year-olds, but is a bit much for one with a cognitive functioning of 7 years of age.

In terms of *development,* Pat saw a family in Stage 4—the Family with Adolescents—yet one of them was developmentally and behaviorally at an earlier stage, and the parents were not able to foresee a time when they would be able to move on to a future stage, due to Jane's developmental delays. Dick, now 16 and driving, might be foreseeing his movement on to a later stage and, Pat hypothesized, might be resenting the organizational structure of the family, which had him caring for his sister at a time when he might want to be out and about with his own peers.

Pat also considered the *gender* metaframework and how its components interacted within the family system; many of the traditional gender roles were blurred in this family because both parents were working full time outside the home. All older members of the family were expected to assist in care of Jane, regardless of gender, and this might be troubling to a young adolescent male in the process of formulating and establishing his own gender identity.

Hypothesizing about this family in terms of *culture,* Pat thought about their name, Smythe, which came from a solid Anglo-Saxon tradition. She hypothesized that they may hold to a traditional value system where all family members care for each other and support each other, which might, given the organizational structure of the family and its developmental level, create some difficulty in terms of *internal processes* in conflict within the individual. This might be particularly true for Dick, who would be a product of the multigenerational transmission of valuing each individual and assisting within the family as needed, in conflict with today's societal norms which say adolescent males should be out and about with their peers, separating from parents and establishing their own identity and relationships with an appropriate amount of freedom from familial duties.

Finally, Pat *hypothesized* that the various *sequences* or interactions among family members would hinge very much on the fact that a handicapped child was a member of this family system, and thus her existence had an impact on sequences at all levels of family members' interactions with each other and within the community at large.

Following completion of her initial hypotheses, Pat began *planning* a course of action for her work with this family.

She determined that she would like to know considerably more about Dick, his internal processes, and his interactions with other family members. At the next session, she asked to spend some time alone with Dick, *conversing* about his role in the family, his goals and expectations for himself, his relationships with his parents, and his perception about what was going on at home. While conversing, Pat was *reading feedback* from Dick. He shared his annoyance that he still had to be responsible for Jane, not only in the morning, but at other times. He indicated that since he could now drive, he didn't mind being asked to run errands and so on for the family, but that it also seemed to have added to his being asked to transport Jane. Dick mentioned that he now had a girlfriend who liked to go with him on his errands, but, Dick said, he didn't particularly like having Jane along. Dick talked about how a long time ago he had felt that he didn't get his fair share of time from his parents but added that he and his dad were now spending some really good quality time together camping and fishing, and that he didn't need his parents as much since he was now more independent and enjoyed his peers. He did say that he sometimes felt guilty being annoyed with Jane, for he "knew she couldn't help being the way she was" and he was grateful that it had "happened to her and not to him," but it still felt unfair and a burden.

Following her session with Dick, Pat met with the parents, discussing, with Dick's permission, how he was feeling and asking them what their expectations were of Dick for the short and long term. They discussed on a general basis the individuation needs of adolescents, but also talked about the specific needs of their family, given the care needs of Jane. Together, in follow-up sessions, the family worked together to develop alternatives to Dick's having to assume so much responsibility, arranging for a neighbor to assist with care, and rearranging Dad's teaching schedule so that he could be more available.

Pat also discussed with Susan and Tom, their own plans for the future; what long-term arrangements they should consider regarding Jane's future, and what Dick's expected involvement would be. Pat put them in touch with an estate planner familiar with establishing trusts and other plans for the disabled. They were already involved with a community organization that provided respite care for families with retarded individuals, and Pat encouraged them to reexamine their priorities to give them some additional adult time to enhance their own relationship.

Over a relatively short time, the family system was working well again and Dick was less oppositional, finding that his parents now had more time to spend with him, and also understood that he needed time away from the family to spend with peers.

PRINCIPLES GUIDING THE PROVISION OF SUPPORT SERVICES

There are many approaches to providing support to families of children with disabilities. Beckman, Newcomb, Frank, Brown, and Filer (1993) describe a model for developing and implementing a flexible system of social support that can be individualized for families. Although it was developed as part of a federally funded project designed for families whose children received services through a local urban infant/toddler program (Project Assist), many of the elements of the approach can be helpful to any mental health professional working with families with disabled children as members.

The project is based on several guiding principles. First, *the family is viewed as a system* (Beckman et al., 1993) where individual members exert influence over each other. Second, *families are the primary decision makers for themselves and their child.* This affects the types of therapeutic approach used, for it needs to include a significant problem-solving/decision-making/training component, as well as a means for supporting the family in making and implementing these decisions. Third, *families are self-defining.* Thus, decisions about who is included are made by the parents, rather than being based on preconceived ideas about who constitutes a family. Fourth, *families' concerns change over time.* Families just entering the service system have very different needs from those whose children are moving on. Fifth, *families vary on multiple dimensions.* This means that diversity is reflected in many ways as indicated in the metaframeworks models of gender, ethnicity, and so on. This, therefore, requires flexibility in how support is provided, the type of support available, the length of time support is provided, by whom it is provided, and how intense the support must be.

Group Support

Shulman (1992) has suggested that groups can be beneficial in providing a system of mutual aid, enabling members to create multiple helping relationships that lessen the sense of isolation felt by many families. This aid is provided through sharing of information, discussing feelings, developing a sense of being "in the same boat," and problem solving in a nonjudgmental context. When planning groups, the therapist must make decisions about the group's composition, timing, and structure based on the group's purpose (Shulman, 1992). Shulman posits frequent meetings of the group in the beginning, weekly for about 1½ hours for 12 weeks, with no new members being added during that time to facilitate group cohesiveness. Content is determined by the participants who identify their needs and set the agenda (Beckman et al., 1993).

Phases of Group Support

There seem to be certain phases common to such groups. In the beginning, the therapists may initiate discussion by asking members about their expectations and topics they would like to consider. This is often a time when participants think about how they will fit into and participate in the group. During the second phase, participants discuss the children's disabilities and their impact on the family. This is the time when members begin to establish the degree of involvement and intimacy they wish to have with the group. This is a critical time for the therapist to make sure that the group is a safe place for all participants and that the group remains nonjudgmental so that feelings can be expressed freely.

In the third phase, participants begin to solidify their relationships with each other and use each other for support, feedback, and problem solving (Beckman et al., 1993). Outside experts may be brought in during this phase to answer questions or provide other information.

The termination phase is often a difficult time for participants as they adjust to a sense of letdown or loss. Sometimes a follow-up group may be formed to continue the existing relationships.

Individual Support

This component involves individual contact with families who may not be comfortable in a group context or may have individual needs that cannot be addressed appropriately through a group model (Beckman et al., 1993). The frequency of contact is determined by the family. Individual support includes both emotional and instrumental support. Emotional support is provided through means such as that outlined in the Metaframework model, providing opportunities to discuss the child, family, or other individual issues. Instrumental support may be provided by assisting parents in developing the child's Individualized Educational Plan (IEP), or, by accompanying the parents to the IEP meeting. It may also include asking the therapist to participate as a member of an interdisciplinary team, working together to determine the most appropriate service delivery plan to meet the needs of the child. Individual support may also involve providing support during crises, helping caregivers sort through divergent information and recommendations, and working with other service providers to link parents with other community services (Beckman et al., 1993). The therapist who chooses to work with families that include a disabled child needs to develop an extensive network of other helping professionals to provide information and resources to these families. Combining group and individual approaches can be useful in providing the maximum intervention assistance during various phases of the family's life cycle.

Therapists who plan to work with these families need to have knowledge not only about family systems and good therapeutic techniques. They must also have sensitivity to what family members go through when they are first confronted with the fact of the diagnosis, and the stages through which family members may progress as they come to grips with that diagnosis and its implications. Although the impact and effect may differ, depending on whether the disability exists from birth, or develops at a later stage as the result of disease, accident, or other type of trauma, family members often experience a range of feelings for which they have few coping skills. Therapy can often serve family members extremely well during this initial phase, if the therapist is aware of what the family is experiencing.

Expectations versus Reality

When expectant parents fantasize about their soon-to-be born baby, most envision a picture-perfect, Parents magazine cover infant with sparkling eyes, 10 fingers and toes, and everything physically and mentally intact. As youngsters grow and develop, parents anticipate a bright future for their youngster, where he or she does well in school, has friends, goes off to college or gets a job, and moves on developmentally to have his or her own family and life successes. Unfortunately, such brightly anticipated events do not always occur as desired. Instead, a child may be born with a physical or mental handicap or disability due to some sort of prenatal insult (e.g., exposure to alcohol or psychoactive substances from the mother) or genetic condition (e.g., Down syndrome, Tay-Sachs disease), or may suffer from trauma at the time of birth (e.g., anoxia—lack of sufficient oxygen). Others may be born intact but suffer from an illness or physical trauma during the early years that changes the course of the child's development from proceeding normally to being slowed down in one or several developmental domains (e.g., physical, emotional, speech/language, cognitive, or sensorial—visually impaired, auditorially impaired), or being altered such that development stops progressing or regresses to an earlier developmental stage. This is especially tragic when the youngster has been proceeding very much on schedule and, due to an accident or illness, is severely affected. In all these situations, the impact on *all* family members, both those in the nuclear family and those in the extended family and even the family's close friends, is extreme (Harris, 1983). In effect, a tragedy equivalent in many cases to a death has occurred. And, as with an unexpected death, few are prepared to deal with the emotional impact.

FACTORS AFFECTING FAMILIAL FEELINGS

Many factors affect how family members respond to the presence of a disabled/handicapped child. These include:

1. The severity of the child's handicap.
2. The social acceptability of the handicap.
3. The socioeconomic level of the family.

4. The culture and ethnicity of the family.
5. The manner in which the parents are informed.
6. The age at onset or age of the child when diagnosed.
7. The gender of the child and gender of the parent.

Severity of the Handicap

When a youngster is identified at birth as having a handicap, the handicap is often quite severe, such that it is noticeable visually or is something genetic that is identified through blood or chromosome testing. Because most parents are not prepared for such an event, their response is often a sense of being overwhelmed (Colen, 1981). Other parents may be informed after their child has entered school that he or she has a learning disability, Attention Deficit/Hyperactivity Disorder (ADHD), or a speech/language impairment. These "Hidden Handicaps"—not easily observed—are often easier for parents to handle, for they seem much less severe and have less impact on the child and family, or so it seems. However, Birenbaum (1971) observed that the prolonged dependency of a severely impaired child sharply alters the roles of parents, who must provide basic physical care and supervision for the child for many years. Whereas normal children grow up and become increasingly independent, freeing their parents of caretaking roles, parents of severely impaired children must continue in this role indefinitely. The presence of this disabled child may diminish the parents' sense of freedom to expand to new domains or may also help parents avoid confronting problems of mature adulthood (Harris, 1983).

For Susan and Tom Smythe, the impact was considerable. At the time of Jane's birth, Susan had four grown children from a previous marriage, and Tom and Susan had 2-year-old Dick. Because of Susan's medical nursing training, she had knowledge about what to expect for the future when the diagnosis of Down syndrome was made. She and Tom, however, had planned for her to resume working outside the home shortly after Jane's birth, with child-care arrangements made for both Jane and Dick. Jane, however, had medical complications related to Down syndrome, and Susan's plan to resume work quickly had to be modified. In addition, there were considerably more expenses than had originally been planned for, and the family had to borrow money and scale back on living expenses. Even though Susan and Tom felt relatively comfortable with the facts of their child's condition, there was a certain amount of grief work that needed to be done to help them adjust to the loss of their "dream little girl."

Social Acceptability of the Handicap

It seems as if certain handicapping conditions are more "socially acceptable" than others and that the degree of acceptability often changes with the times. For example, a diagnosis of autism seems to be more acceptable than one of mental retardation although the child may be functioning in the retarded IQ range in both cases.

A diagnosis of ADHD is more socially acceptable than one of emotional disturbance although sometimes the behaviors are difficult to differentiate. Nowadays, a diagnosis of ADHD is almost something parents seem to be asking for, not only for their children, but also for their adolescents and, in some cases, for themselves (Wallis, 1994).

In today's society, the diagnosis of mental retardation bears less stigma than it did 10 or 20 years ago, due to increased recognition of the strengths and positive characteristics of retarded citizens through television programs such as *LA Law* with its Bennie character, and the TV program, *Life Goes On,* which features a young man with Down syndrome. Some of the fear such individuals used to generate in the general public seems to have lessened, although there is still a great deal of prejudice and fear in some segments of society. Susan and Tom have handled Jane's retardation very well, taking her on family outings and including her whenever possible in their activities. This is possible, in part, due to her calm, socially acceptable behavior, for she is not a demanding or acting-out child.

Socioeconomic Level of Family

Research has shown that there seems to be a greater level of acceptability of handicapping conditions among families in lower socioeconomic strata. This appears to be due in part to somewhat lower expectations, higher levels of accepting children where they are rather than worrying about what they will become in economic terms, and a greater knowledge of "the system" of available services that enables families to find help when needed. Often such families are already connected with social service agencies, welfare, the health departments, and so on, and have social workers or other support personnel available to assist them in finding appropriate resources.

Susan, who was already connected in the medical field, was able to draw on knowledgeable colleagues to help her from the beginning.

Culture and Ethnicity

The family's ethnicity and culture often affect the family's level of acceptance of the handicapped child and his or her disability. Some cultures such as the Chinese, view the occurrence of such an event as one of shame for the family (Hanson, Lynch, & Wayman, 1990; Lynch & Stein, 1987; Mary, 1990). Rather than seek help for the child and family (e.g., assessment and therapeutic intervention from an educational or medical agency), the parents may choose to hide the child and his or her condition from the world, often only introducing the child to these agencies at times such as kindergarten enrollment when all children of a particular chronological age are "introduced."

In some cultures, the mother is blamed for having a less than perfect child, and she may suffer from being shunned by her community for having created such a child. When working with such a family, it is critical that the mental health worker be knowledgeable about the cultural background of the parents and, about the social mores of the culture so that no additional harm comes to those involved. This can thereby lessen any negative impact to the parents' relationship and/or standing in their community and, the child can receive services as quickly as possible.

Manner in Which Parents Are Informed

Fortunately, recently trained physicians are better educated in ways to give frightening or undesirable information to parents. Therefore, parents today are more likely to be informed in a sensitive, caring way, that their child has some type of disabling condition. Often, a mental health professional is on site with the physician at the time of the telling, to be able to provide emotional assistance and information concerning resources available to help the family through the crisis stage. When parents do not receive such assistance, they are significantly less able to comprehend the issue and their possible courses of action, with considerably more potential negative impact on the family a consequence.

Age at Onset or Age of the Child When Diagnosed

Therapists must realize that there is no "easy time" in terms of the age of the child for a family to be informed of a suspected or known handicapping condition. When the diagnosis is made at birth, the family members must mourn the "death" of the anticipated "Perfect Child." When the child has been progressing well according to developmental expectations, and then some sort of illness or trauma occurs, the family must cope with the dramatic change from having a "Normal Child," to having one who suddenly is different, thereby forcing the parents to cope with changing expectations. In the latter case, if the problem is due to an accident or illness, parents often feel guilty if they believe they were neglectful in terms of caring for the health or safety of the child. There also may be blame, if in fact, the problem is due to some sort of irresponsibility or neglect by a family member.

The issues the therapist must deal with when assisting the parents of a young handicapped child are very different from those of the family of an older child (Harris, 1983). The parents of a preschooler are attempting to handle the child's initial diagnosis and the disruption of their dreams for the child they "planned" to have. The parents of the school-age child are coping with educational planning, helping their other children cope with the reality of the handicap and its effect on their lives, and dealing with an ever-increasing discrepancy between the child's physical size and his or her cognitive, interpersonal, and emotional development. If the child is their firstborn, the parents must help the older child cope with having a younger sibling surpass him or her, while they must also be fair to the younger child in acknowledging and praising him or her for accomplishments.

For Susan and Tom, this was not as severe a problem as it often is for other families, because they already had one normal child of their own, and had a good understanding of what the future would bring.

Sex of Child; Sex of Parent

Although it is never easy to accept that a child has a disabling condition, it seems to be especially difficult for a father to accept that reality when it is his son who has the problem, especially when the condition is severe. Many such fathers share that they have difficulty giving up or adjusting the hopes and dreams that they have had for their sons' futures; giving up their plans for "playing ball together, teaching the son about the family business, having their son proudly caring on the family name and family traditions." Again, this was not a significant problem for Susan and Tom, for they had an older son and Susan had several older daughters from her previous marriage. Nevertheless, they both report that they had formed a set of expectations for their youngest daughter prior to her birth which they were now having to adjust to the present circumstances.

Stages of Parental Reactions

Early Stages

In the early stage, when parents have just been informed that their child has a significant disability, there is often severe psychological disorganization. They may feel overwhelmed, frantic, not knowing what to do next. The mother and father may be in conflict over what to do medically for the child; the mother is still influenced by her own condition having just been through childbirth; and the father is concerned not only about the newborn, but also about his wife and, if there are siblings, their care at this time. There may also be blame by one parent or another about actions that took place before the birth of the child, such as the mother having had occasional alcoholic drinks or coffee; the father having exposed the child to secondhand smoke, and so on.

Many logistics also need to be dealt with such as medical care for the child; the possibility that the mother may be in a different hospital from the child, or at home, while the child must remain hospitalized; the need to call relatives and friends with the information about the baby and his or her condition. It is often difficult for the father to know what to say at these times, for the expectation is that he will be calling with good news about the baby's gender, weight, length, and the health of the mother. Instead, he now must share distressing information, much of which he may know little about in terms of severity and prognosis. He may also have trouble explaining what is going on to siblings waiting at home, for they too, have expectations that must be revised.

Middle Stages

During the middle stages of reacting, the parents usually have reached an appropriate level of acceptance of the information and diagnosis, have overcome the initial shock, and have moved on to making decisions about the care of the child and the next steps to take. It is hoped they will not be in denial about the diagnosis, for this can result in a lack of placement in an early intervention program designed to assist the child and family in maximizing the child's strengths and remediating his or her weaknesses. Such placements and programs are mandated by federal law, Public Law 99-457, which specifies among other things, a free educational assessment and appropriate treatment for children aged birth to 3 years who meet criteria to be identified as educationally handicapped. This law also mandates the development of an Individual Family Services Plan (IFSP) that is designed to assist the whole family in meeting the child's and family's needs as warranted by the disabling condition.

Denial of the child's problem can result in the driving inward of any psychological problems the parents should be dealing with in terms of their relationships with each other and other family members. Also, it can result in "Shopping Behavior"—parents shop from one expert to another, looking for a cause and a cure, rather than a way of best coping with the existing disability. Many such families have been taken advantage of by unprofessional practitioners who make unrealistic promises about what will result for the child if only the parents will pay for (or get a local school system to pay for) that practitioner's specialized intervention techniques. This is not to say that parents should not seek out second opinions about their child's condition and prognosis. In fact, seeking a second opinion is often wise, for advances are being made in assisting handicapped individuals daily. However, parents do need to be realistic in their expectations concerning the prognoses for their children, and seek out information from reputable professionals.

The role of the therapist in helping families in this stage is to help them cope with their grief while also assisting them in finding resources to accurately assess their child and determine appropriate early intervention services. This may mean the therapist serving as a case manager, pulling together a multidisciplinary team to assist the child and family in receiving those services in a timely fashion. The therapist should become thoroughly familiar with federal, state, and local laws and regulations for servicing such children and their families. This means connecting with public agencies such as the local health department and public school system, for these are most frequently the agencies providing such services. The therapist will also be helping family members deal with their own issues in terms of relationships, finances, expectations, roles, and time management.

Final Stage

In the final stage, parents have accepted their child's situation, sought out help from appropriate medical and educational agencies, enrolled their youngster in an appropriate intervention program, and are now dealing with planning for the future, as well as coping with the realities of a family life where one of the children happens to be disabled. In this stage, mental health workers can play a vital part by assisting in case management, and helping the family negotiate the myriad professionals involved with the child's care and education. They also can help family members deal with their own emotions about the child and the child's effect on the family's functioning and, assist the parents in maintaining their own relationship and their relationships with their other children. It is important for mental health workers working with such families to be sure to include siblings and grandparents, if available, in the process; they are often left out, yet they too have many feelings that need to be considered and dealt with as the handicapped child's condition and care continue to impact the family.

SPECIAL STRESSORS FACING PARENTS OF HANDICAPPED CHILDREN

Therapists working with families which include a handicapped child must be aware that such families are often faced with situations other families do not encounter, or do not encounter at the same level. These situations include the following stressors.

Added Financial Hardship

Having a handicapped child often places tremendous financial obligations on a family. There may be extreme medical costs, child-care costs, transportation costs, and educational costs well beyond those incurred in normal family situations. Families may need help sorting out expenses, help with handling insurance and third-party payors, and help making decisions about various choices in child care and educational programs where costs are a factor.

For Susan and Tom, Jane's birth and medical condition meant that for a while, Susan was unable to return to work, which created considerable financial hardship, for not only was she not bringing in income, but Jane's medical expenses, in spite of insurance coverage, created a financial drain. When Susan was able to return to work, experienced child care was a necessity, creating a higher child-care cost than had been anticipated.

Actual or Perceived Stigma

There is still considerable prejudice against people with disabilities in our society, with some disabilities being more stigmatized than others. Often people, even those who were friends of the family, seem to shy away from the family as well as the child, as if they were afraid of "catching" the disability.

Mental health professionals must work with family members to give them skills for coping with these reactions. Behavioral techniques such as modeling situations where such reactions might occur are often helpful. Practicing or role-playing responses to those who make disparaging remarks can also be beneficial. Working with siblings to help them deal with teasing, misunderstanding, or misinformed other children can help them cope with having a disabled sibling. Offering sibling group experiences is another technique for helping brothers and sisters cope with the negative attitudes of others. In addition, it lets them know that there are others who experience the same situations and feelings about a handicapped sibling—that they are not alone.

When working with groups of this type, therapists must be careful to not "overtherapize" the group. What has proven most successful is for the group to have fun together; to not emphasize the problems of having a disabled sibling, but to let such feelings or thoughts come out in the normal flow of kids interacting with other kids. Too often, therapists working with children are in a hurry for them to "get your feelings out," rather than to let the youngsters "go with the flow." Good work will be accomplished just by letting them get together in an accepting atmosphere where they feel safe and enjoy being together.

Extraordinary Time Demands

Caring for a handicapped child can often be extremely demanding in terms of time spent on personal care of the child as well as time spent attending classes with the child, transporting to medical appointments, and so on. The difficulties associated with simply feeding children with severe conditions can consume large amounts of time, and if the child requires aspirating, intubating, exercising, or other medical procedures, there is not much time for more customary family activities. Often family members suffer from sleep deprivation, especially if the child has irregular sleep patterns or has apnea (failure to breathe, which will set off an apnea monitor to awaken the caretaker). The lack of free time can also contribute to social isolation for parents from friends, and from participating in family activities with other children. There is not enough time nor, in some cases, available child care for the disabled child, to enable parents and siblings to be active socially in the community.

Mental health providers can help families with these problems by providing information on respite care opportunities, and by connecting the family with parent support groups consisting of parents of children with similar disabilities, where they will often take care of each other's children and feel comfortable with the skill levels of the caretaking parent. In addition, mental health providers can help the parents recognize the need they have as adults, and that their other children have, for some social time together. Often parents become so involved in the care of the disabled child that they forget the importance of having fun together and with their other children. This was one of the problems Dick was acting out in his family, which finally brought the family in for counseling. The therapist's job is sometimes one of giving family members permission to enjoy life away from the care of the disabled, even for only a few moments. This is not to say that there are not rewards or pleasurable moments caring for each child; it is just a different kind of caring in some cases.

Difficulties Managing Behavior

Some disabilities have behavioral problems as an associated component. Often autistic children, and some retarded children, manifest acting-out behaviors because they are operating at a cognitive level where they do not understand the need to follow certain directions or they have no impulse controls and want a desired need met immediately. This can be very distressing to a parent or sibling who may be attending a soccer game or be at the grocery store when the disabled child begins screaming, running, refusing to respond to cautions or requests, or behaves in a dangerous manner. Many siblings request that their sibling not be allowed to come to activities where the child's behavior might cause the sibling embarrassment. With Dick, his embarrassment was most manifest when he was asked to take Jane with him when he was with his girlfriend. Few adolescents like to take any sibling with them in such a situation, much less one who is "different."

The therapist can work with the child and parent on behavior management skill building, and also help the parent hear and understand the needs of the sibling to be allowed a certain amount of freedom from the impact of the handicapped child on his or her world. At the same time, work may need to be done with the sibling on issues of acceptance, with decisions being made among family members as to which activities will include all family members and which can, if logistics of child care can be arranged, exclude the handicapped child. These are important family value issues and can best be worked on through a family therapy approach.

General Feeling of Pessimism about the Future

Frequently, the birth and maturing of a handicapped child instigates feelings of pessimism in family members, for they become very concerned about what the future will hold for the child and for the family who may be coping with considerable debt and child-care concerns. All family members worry about who will care for the child as he or she ages, especially when it is doubtful that the child, as he or she matures into adulthood, will be able to become self-sufficient. This issue often worries siblings: "Will my sister's care become my responsibility? How can I possibly meet her needs and my own?"

As in the case of Dick, Susan, Tom, and Jane, the therapist can be of assistance to family members by helping them find resources such as financial planners and attorneys who specialize in long-term planning for such care. Also, the therapist can work with the siblings and family members around their fears of the future, helping parents understand the concerns that siblings often feel as they hear parents discussing financial and care concerns without a full understanding of what role they are expected to play in the future. Parents sometimes have to be helped to understand that it is not fair to put the burden of future care on siblings when they are too young to understand what it all means. Rather, the therapist should help parents develop strategies to reassure their other children about how care will be provided.

The general pessimism is often reflected in an attitude of "Why try to get ahead—all our resources have to go to meeting medical and educational expenses." Another pessimistic thought pattern is about the family relationships, because within the family, relationships often deteriorate with the pressures of caring for the handicapped child in particular, and all the family members generally. The Smythe family was fortunate that they had a very sound family value system which fostered caring for all family members by all family members. The system just needed some work from the developmental metaframework to assist Susan and Tom with understanding Dick's needs, too.

Intensification of Common Activities, Notions of Fairness—Why Us?—Questioning of Religious Beliefs, Concerns about Death

In addition to general feelings of pessimism about the future and concerns about financial obligations, some parents and family members begin to question some of their basic beliefs about fairness and/or their religious beliefs. Some may say, "How can there be a God who would let something like this happen to good people like us?" Others become very concerned about their own health and safety because of the tremendous demands the child's care makes on the family and ask, "What will happen to everyone in the family if something happens to me?" The therapist must help the family members deal with their anxiety and concerns, allowing them to vent their feelings about fairness and religious beliefs, being very careful not to impose any of the therapist's own belief system on the family.

Therapists need to be aware that some family members may cope best by believing that their God "chose them to care for this child because God knew what special caring people they were; thus, they would be the best caretakers for such a child." Again, therapists must be careful not to deny them their defenses nor to question their logic. Rather, the therapist must be supportive in helping them cope however they choose to do so.

PARENTAL ATTITUDES TOWARD AND INTERACTIONS WITH THE HANDICAPPED CHILD

Therapists must realize that the existence of a handicapped child disrupts the normal interactional patterns within a family. Often, parental expectations of what the child is and is not capable of are distorted or inappropriate. Research has found that parents of less visibly handicapped children (such as learning disabled, speech/language impaired) are apt to overestimate the ability of the child. Parents of children with visible physical handicaps often have lowered estimations of their youngster's intelligence or future performance. These misperceptions can affect the attachment process, especially when the parent distances him- or herself from the child because of thoughts that the child will never amount to anything, or that the child will die and the parent does not want to get too attached. Even with older children, the attachment can be damaged when the child has a more hidden handicap and the parents get angry because they think the child "isn't trying," "is lazy," or "is obstinate and not motivated."

The opposite situation exists when a child has a physical handicap that may suggest to others that the child is cognitively impaired. This is often not the case, yet many people respond to physically challenged individuals as if they were cognitively delayed, thereby not challenging them mentally or not providing them with technological devices to facilitate their intellectual development and their communication opportunities. Augmentative devices have improved dramatically in the past few years, such that individuals with very little or no speech can communicate through use of computers with voice synthesizers attached. Therapists can refer families to the Council for Exceptional Children in Reston, Virginia, for information on where to go to get information on such devices, and many educational programs have such information available about local opportunities.

Temperament of the Child

It is often helpful for the family's therapist to spend time with the family including the disabled child so that the therapist has some personal experience with the child's temperament and behavior and how the parents and siblings react to and handle the behavior.

The child's temperament can influence parental and sibling reactions and interactional patterns, for often handicapped children, depending on the type of condition, do not behave or handle their emotions well, causing parents and siblings to feel embarrassed or incompetent when the child acts out. Often, too, when the child has a hidden handicap and parental expectations are too high, the child may get extremely frustrated and/or the parent may get frustrated and tempers may flare. The therapist must start the work with the family around having reasonable expectations, which means that family members must have accurate information from appropriate assessments of the child to know what is reasonable to expect. If behaviors have already gotten out of hand, behavior modification techniques must be put in place to assist the child in managing behavior. Then, the therapist needs to work with other members of the therapeutic team to assist parents and siblings in implementing the techniques appropriately and consistently.

Role of the Professional Mental Health Provider in Assisting Family Members

The mental health provider can play a critical role in helping families adjust to having a handicapped family member. The first way is to be a member of an interdisciplinary team, working together for the welfare not only of the child but also of the family as a whole. That team would include the therapist, medical personnel, educators, the parents, and the child. They would all keep each other informed as to the child's status through periodic meetings or communications designed to support the family in meeting the child's needs.

The primary tasks of the therapist would be to:

1. Help parents feel more competent and empowered in their parenting role, not just with the handicapped child, but with all their children. This might be accomplished by providing parent training and counseling, referrals to parent training and support groups, and/or providing general information about the handicapping condition itself and referrals for provision of accurate information regarding the condition and available services.

2. Help parents recognize not only the *needs* of their disabled child, but also the *strengths* of that child. Concomitantly, parents would be encouraged also to recognize their own needs and those of their other children and extended family members.

3. Assist siblings, grandparents, and other family members in making adjustments in their lives to accommodate meeting the needs of the handicapped child and to assist parents in the new tasks they encounter in providing care for that child.

4. Encourage parents to be active in pursuit of services for their child by providing resource personnel, referrals to support groups, and information concerning their rights to assistance under various federal and state laws. This may include the therapist participating in IEP conferences to serve as a child and parent advocate in enabling the family to receive appropriate services.

Working with families that include disabled individuals can be an extremely rewarding profession. The association with the family often continues, on and off, over a long period as the family passes through various stages. While certain specific expertise is beneficial, as indicated in this chapter, the most critical component is a caring, accepting, tenacious therapist dedicated to helping families. The rewards will be profound.

REFERENCES

Beckman, P. J. (1991a). Comparison of mothers' and fathers' perceptions of the effect of young children with and without disabilities. *American Journal of Mental Retardation, 95*(5), 585–595.

Beckman, P. J. (1991b, June). *Institutional sources of stress for families of children with disabilities.* Keynote address presented at the Louisiana Conference on Early Intervention, Monroe, Louisiana.

Beckman, P. J. (1993). The service system and its effects on families: An ecological perspective. *Early childhood intervention: Theory, evaluation & practice.* A conference in Bielefeld, Germany.

Beckman, P. J., & Bristol, M. (1991). Issues in developing the IFSP: A framework for establishing family outcomes. *Topics in Early Childhood Special Education, 11*(3), 19–31.

Beckman, P. J., Robinson, C. C., Rosenberg, S., & Filer, J. (1994). Family involvement in early intervention: The evolution of family centered services. In L. J. Johnson, R. S. Gallagher, M. J. LaMontagne, J. B. Jordan, J. J. Gallagher, P. L. Hutinger, & M. B. Karnes (Eds.), *Meeting early intervention challenges.* Baltimore: Paul H. Brookes.

Beckman, P. J., Newcomb, S., Frank, N., Brown, L., & Filer, J. (1993). Innovative practices: Providing support to families of infants with disabilities. *Journal of Early Intervention, 17*(4), 445–454.

Birenbaum, A. (1971). The mentally retarded child in the home and the family cycle. *Journal of Health & Social Behavior, 12,* 55–65.

Bowen, M. (1978). *Family therapy in clinical practice.* Northvale, NJ: Jason Aronson.

Breslau, N., & Davis, G. C. (1986). Chronic stress and major depression. *Archives of General Psychiatry, 43,* 309–314.

Breunlin, D. C., Schwartz, R. C., & Mac Kune-Karrer, B. (1990) The metaframeworks perspective in action. *Family Therapy Case Studies, 5*(2), 9–30.

Breunlin, D. C., Schwartz, R. C., & Mac Kune-Karrer, B. (1992). *Metaframeworks: Transcending the models of family therapy.* San Francisco: Jossey-Bass.

Bronfenbrenner, U. (1979). *The ecology of human development.* Cambridge, MA: Harvard University Press.

Carter, B., & McGoldrick, M. (Eds.). (1989). *The changing family life cycle: A framework for family therapy.* Needham Heights, MA: Allyn and Bacon.

Colen, B. D. (1981). *Born at risk.* New York: St. Martin's Press.

Dyson, L. L. (1991). Families of young children with handicaps: Parental stress and family functioning. *American Journal of Mental Retardation, 95*(6), 623–629.

Dyson, L. L., & Fewell, R. F. (1986). Stress and adaption in parents of young handicapped and nonhandicapped children: A comparative study. *Journal of the Division for Early Childhood, 10,* 25–35.

Friedrich, W. N., & Friedrich, W. L. (1981). Psychosocial assets of parents of handicapped & nonhandicapped children. *American Journal of Mental Deficiency, 85,* 551–553.

Gallagher, J. J., Beckman, P., & Cross, A. H. (1983). Families of handicapped children: Sources of stress and its amelioration. *Exceptional Children, 50,* 10–19.

Hanson, M. J., Lynch, E. W., & Wayman, K. I. (1990). Honoring the cultural diversity of families when gathering data. *Topics in Early Childhood Special Education, 10*(1), 112–131.

Harris, S. L. (1983). *Families of the developmentally disabled: A guide to behavioral intervention.* New York: Pergamon.

Lynch, E. W., & Stein, R. C. (1987). Parent participation by ethnicity: A comparison of hispanic, black and anglo families. *Exceptional Children, 54*(2), 105–111.

Mary, N. L. (1990). Reactions of black, Hispanic, and white mothers to having a child with handicaps. *Mental Retardation, 28*(1), 1–5.

Schulman, L. (1992). *The skills of helping: Individuals, families, and groups.* Itasca, IL: F.E. Peacock.

Smith, M. J., & Ryan, A. S. (1987). Chinese-American families of children with developmental disabilities: An exploratory study of reactions to service providers. *Mental Retardation, 25*(6), 345–351.

Wallis, C. (1994, July 18). Life in overdrive. *Time Magazine,* 44–50.

CHAPTER 12

Families with Chronic Illness and Disability

A. MELTON STROZIER, JR.

A quick look at any family provides an idea of the impact of chronic illness and disability. Who does not have concern about a parent or grandparent in the nursing home; an uncle or aunt with cardiovascular disease; a cousin with hypertension; a close friend with diabetes; a child with asthma; a spouse with arthritis; or an in-law suffering from a stroke? As medical science has become increasingly sophisticated, the good news/bad news scenario for our society is that people are living longer with illnesses that were formerly difficult or impossible to treat, but this longevity often involves living with chronic illnesses or disability. Learning to live with chronic health problems challenges both patients and their families, who must learn with these patients how to eat differently, dress differently, inject insulin, leverage bodies out of bed, cope with mood swings, talk, love, and deal with being a permanent part of the doctor-patient-family triangle (Doherty & Baird, 1987). This chapter provides conceptual frameworks for understanding the impact of chronic illness and disability on the family, and includes suggestions for therapists who wish to help those families in their process.

The central tenets of this chapter are that chronic illness and disability are affecting increasing numbers of persons in our society. Furthermore, these stressful conditions affect not only the patients but also their families. The following pages will describe cases where the impact of chronic illness and disability on family systems result in heroic efforts to cope as well as significant alterations in family system functioning. These alterations in family system functioning are sometimes healthy, sometimes dysfunctional. However, even relatively "healthy" changes in family system functioning are stressful and

I wish to express my appreciation to my friends and colleagues in the Family Practice program for their support and help with this chapter. Special thanks go to Mike Walsh, MD, for his feedback on medical issues and help with computer issues. Thanks also to Clark Gillett, MD, John Bucholtz, DO, and The Medical Center for encouragement and support in this endeavor. Special thanks to my wife Paula for her support and help with the manuscript.

246

frequently call for some form of support. On the other hand, less healthy forms of change in family system functioning call for awareness and intervention on the part of the medical and mental health communities. By providing education, support, and therapeutic intervention, family-oriented therapists can offer significant help to families impacted by chronic illness and disability.

CASE EXAMPLES

Case 1: John and Brenda

Brenda came to see the therapist on referral from her primary care physician, who had diagnosed her as depressed. She wept openly as she described living through nearly 2 years of hell. Her husband, John, had gone into the hospital for a relatively safe surgical procedure. Complications developed, and a hospital visit that was to be a minor event in their family history became a pivotal one, forever changing their way of life. Through 18 months of hospitalizations and crises, Brenda cared for John, who had become unable to care for himself. She gave up a meaningful job and separated from nurturing relationships. Dealing with doctors, nurses, hospital administrators, and insurance companies became her occupation. Because she had little or no experience in financial management, the family was overwhelmed by medical expenses, and they were without a steady income, the family financial resources soon became depleted. When John finally finished his lengthy stays in acute and rehabilitation hospitals, he came home disabled and chronically ill. The impact on his sense of self and emotional well-being was significant. A man that had been at the peak of his career and earning power now spent his days in pain, taking medicine, trying to ambulate from one room to another, and sitting in doctor's waiting rooms. The impact on Brenda was significant, also. She had to deal with the loss of career and friends and the traumatic memories of John's illness.

The breaking point came after John returned home to find that he was not only sick but also destitute. He directed his anger toward Brenda, blaming her for their financial condition. She turned her sense of loss and anger inward (she thought, "You can't be mad at a sick person") and became depressed. When she returned for the second therapy session, she brought John with her. They began to talk openly about the impact of John's illness and disability on both of them and on the marriage. Brenda tearfully asked John why he acted so angry toward her when she had worked so hard and sacrificed so much to keep him alive. John's response was clear and direct: he *did* hate her. He wished he had been allowed to die rather than come home sick, disabled, and destitute. He blamed her for his illness and for his poverty, suggesting that she had been financially irresponsible while he was sick.

Hearing John verbalize feelings that he had only acted out previously was a tremendous help for Brenda. She stopped being depressed and became angry. She strengthened as she stopped protecting John from the financial realities of the costs of his illness and their unemployment. She also shared with him in detail some of the courageous decisions she had made for him while he was delirious or unconscious. The most difficult moment for her had been when the doctors had given up hope. She described standing by his bedside as the priest administered last rites. She also shared her outrage that she had given up everything meaningful in her own career and social circles to attend to John, yet he was ungrateful and angry.

By the end of the first family therapy session none of the issues were resolved, but there was an open line of communication. Each had a better understanding of the stresses and losses experienced by the other. In the sessions that followed, John learned to "own" his feelings about his illness and disability and grieve his losses. He also expressed his appreciation to Brenda for her efforts on his behalf. Brenda grieved her losses, expressed her anger toward John for his treatment of her, and eventually understood and forgave John.

Following their work on communication, grief, understanding, and forgiveness, John and Brenda focused on the parameters of caregiving. For nearly 2 years, Brenda had taken care of John while he was unable to care for himself. Now she found it difficult to avoid telling John what to do, when to do it, and how to do it. She also became consumed with guilt and fear every time she left his side. She spent some of their limited funds to keep a cellular telephone in the car so she could call to check on John even when she went out for a short time. Constant vigilance left her exhausted and resentful, but she was unable to force herself to stop. Though he was becoming stronger and more stable medically, John continued to depend heavily on Brenda. He called her on the car phone if she went too long without checking on him. He asked her to do things for him that he was clearly capable of doing for himself. Yet John resented how dependent he was on Brenda.

A critical point came when they discussed whether John was able to climb stairs by himself. Brenda insisted that he was not able to. John argued that he could. In a flash of anger John lashed out, stating "You're trying to turn me into a cripple!" After reflecting for a moment, Brenda thoughtfully said, "All right, you can take care of yourself then." John became thoughtful also, and replied "Well, sometimes I still need some help with some things." Brenda asserted, "When you need my help, you can ask for it." In that moment, the couple negotiated a communicative, collaborative approach to dealing with John's illness. At the next session, they cheerfully announced that Brenda had gone to the grocery store with the car phone turned off. Both felt a sense of relief from the fusion they had been living with. Brenda and John continued to make good progress in family therapy.

One day, however, the therapist received a message to cancel Brenda and John's next appointment. John was back in the hospital, in crisis once more. A few weeks later, Brenda returned to therapy alone because John was too sick to come. Brenda's sense of despair came and went for weeks as she returned to the role of John's primary caregiver. Eventually John moved out of crisis, but his deterioration progressed. The autonomy that John and Brenda had worked so hard to attain diminished with his increased dependency on her.

This case demonstrates a number of important aspects of the impact of chronic illness and disability on the family. The cyclical process of crisis, response to crisis, stabilization, and renewed crisis is clearly demonstrated. The heroic efforts for survival are evident. In dealing with cases such as this, one marvels at the strength and endurance of the human spirit in the face of prolonged and severe stress, and at the tenacity of the human battle for survival of both life and family. At the same time, the toll illness can exact on individuals and family systems is also evident. The autonomy of both the patient and the caregiver suffers, and husbands and wives may regress into behaviors resembling protective parents and angry children. In terms of therapy, a number of issues are demonstrated:

1. Catharsis is important. Though they may be with the family, medical personnel, friends, and more distant relatives may not have the time or skills to really hear the stories of what the illness was like for the persons experiencing it. The family's therapist provides the *holding environment* in which stories of pain and suffering can be related and worked through.

2. Therapists must possess and call on a variety of skills in the treatment of families impacted by chronic illness and disability. Skills in collaboration with the medical community are essential, both in terms of receiving referrals of this type from physicians, and in terms of providing informed treatment for families with medical issues (McDaniel, Hepworth, & Doherty, 1992). Psychoeducational skills are important, for it is often in *normalizing* these experiences that families are helped to understand and deal with the issues at hand. Grief counseling skills are essential, as families are helped through the process of mourning individual and systemic losses. Family therapy skills that facilitate effective communication are essential, as are skills in negotiating power and control issues, and issues of intimacy and autonomy. Empowerment is an optimal concept. Individual patients are helped to strive for their maximum level of care for self. Families are helped to nurture without smothering, and to promote autonomy without abandoning.

3. The therapist's own ability to understand and accept the metasystemic process is very important. The therapy with families impacted by chronic illness and disability will often mirror the family's process. As the family goes through cycles of crisis, stabilization, and renewed crisis, so does the therapy. The therapist must understand and accept that he or she may work long and hard with a family to effect systemic change, only to find the work vanishing into the jaws of the next medical crisis. The next session after such an episode may well find the therapy process back at the beginning, only this time with new limitations, new pains, and new frustrations. Few things are as important in this type of work as the therapist's patience and persistence, and the ability to hope for the family, even when the family's ability to hope for itself falters.

Case 2: Naomi

Naomi is a 35-year-old single black woman. She has no living father or siblings, no aunts or uncles. Three years ago, she lived by herself. She was divorced and had no children. She had a job that paid well and a meaningful relationship with a male companion. As she drove to work one morning, someone ran a stoplight and broadsided her. Weeks in an acute care hospital were followed by months in a rehabilitation hospital. She is now a semiquadriplegic, with limited use of her hands and no use of her legs. She lives with her elderly mother, and home health-care workers come regularly to turn her, bathe her, and change her.

Naomi was referred for therapy by her primary care physician. He had become frustrated with her frequent visits with complaints that were either imagined or amplifications of symptoms. She was found to be suffering from depression and anxiety, with social isolation, rumination, and sleep disturbance. She reported waking up in the middle of the night having forgotten that she was paralyzed. She would panic about being unable to feel her lower body until she remembered the paralysis. Then she lay in bed weeping until sunrise. When asked what bothered her most she reported that it was her situation with her mother. She felt guilty that her mother as an older person was now stressed by caring for a disabled and dependent daughter. Naomi stated that her greatest fear was what would happen when her mother became unable to care for her or died. She feared being placed in a nursing home at a relatively young age, unable to live independently, with no relatives to visit her or advocate for her. Terrified at this prospect, Naomi stayed in denial about the permanence of her disability, holding onto the hope of complete rehabilitation. One day a hurried doctor blurted, "You'll *never* walk again. Give it up!" She then lapsed into a severe depression and alternated between rehabilitation activities and lethargy. The stress eventually precipitated an illness that required rehospitalization. After discharge, she terminated therapy and maintained denial by focusing all of her attention on symptoms that had no apparent physical cause. This helped her avoid dealing with her fears about the future.

Naomi presents issues for therapy which are in many ways different than those presented by John and Brenda. Her primary caregiver is elderly, so she must draw on outside resources such as home health care for her activities of daily living (ADL). Her family is without even the few financial resources that John and Brenda had. The situation of being a person who is sick, disabled, impoverished, and a minority is a particularly frightening one for her. This is especially so when she considers being institutionalized with no one to advocate for her. Faced with such dim prospects, Naomi handled her fears and anxieties by utilizing denial. When her denial was stripped away, she overcompensated. The resulting illness helped her avoid her fears by focusing once more on her health. Therapy may resume again for her at some point in time, if and when her denial system begins to break down, and/or her mother becomes increasingly frail.

Case 3: Benita and Roberto

Benita was referred by her physician for depression related to her husband's recent disability. After years of marriage, raising children, and working hard, her husband had been able to take early retirement. His plans were to spend his days in the outdoors he loved so much, fishing and hunting, until Benita could retire from her work and travel with him. Shortly after his retirement, he had a stroke. Weeks in an acute care hospital were followed by 3 months in a rehabilitation hospital. When Roberto was discharged from rehabilitation and came home, Benita fell apart. As long as Roberto had been in rehabilitation, she had hoped for a full recovery. When she brought him home, she realized the complete recovery was not going to happen. She started crying uncontrollably when alone. While caretaking, she felt she had to keep a smile on her face. It became important not to let Roberto see how she felt about his disability. Roberto was unavailable for family therapy.

Therapy for Benita initially focused on grief work, allowing her a safe place where she could discuss her sense of loss over what was to have been for her husband and herself. In time, however, Benita began to discuss some of the difficult issues she and her husband encountered as they tried to normalize the nonnormative. A breakthrough occurred when Benita and Roberto argued over a caregiving issue. Benita had to go shopping, and Roberto asked her to wheel his chair outside so he could enjoy the outdoors while she was gone. Because there was a possibility of rain, she refused, fearing he might be left outside with no way to gain shelter. Roberto became angry with her and insisted that he would rather be stuck outside in the rain than inside all the time. Benita left home in a fit of rage. She felt all she did was work to support the family and take care of her husband. Benita could not understand why Roberto was being so difficult to deal with.

In therapy she was able to ventilate her frustration. Then the issue of negotiating with him to find that middle ground where he was adequately cared for but allowed to be as independent as possible was raised by the therapist. She agreed to go back home and discuss options with Roberto. The next week, she stated that they had arrived at a creative solution. Their neighbors were usually home and had volunteered to do whatever they could to help with Roberto's care. Benita and Roberto possessed a remote telephone with a range that reached easily into the backyard. In the future, if Benita was to leave home and Roberto wanted to be outside, they would check to see if the neighbors were home. If so, Benita would wheel Roberto outside and leave the portable phone with him so that he could call for assistance if he needed it.

The next issue to deal with was their teenage daughter, Rose. Rose was the only one of four children left at home. In a time when she wanted to be out of the house and with her friends more often, she found herself staying at home to care for her father. Rose directed her anger and resentment toward Benita, taking care to avoid upsetting Roberto. Benita felt frustrated by her daughter's attitude but also understood it. Work was done on negotiating ways to allow Rose to be with her friends more often, while continuing to provide some caregiving.

Much grief work remained for this family, but they began to move toward normalizing their family life as much as possible. The therapy was individual but family-oriented. Benita did some individual grief work initially. The focus then shifted naturally to family systems work. This demonstrates that the family-oriented therapist has to think creatively to deal with family issues when the person with the illness is not available for the therapy process. Creative solutions may include home visits and therapy sessions in inpatient medical settings. Work with the available family members can be effective, however, if they are coached in techniques that facilitate negotiation and empowerment. Cultural issues also had to be addressed: In Benita and Roberto's culture, it is the task of women to care for the sick without complaint. Adherence to this cultural norm in this difficult circumstance was compounded by social isolation. No other family members lived in the area. The stress and isolation became difficult for Benita to bear.

Case 4: Martha and Sam

Martha and Sam's fourth child developed a rare form of cancer as a preschooler. Sam and the three older children tried to live a normal life while Martha and little Allen spent long periods of time in the children's cancer unit of a research hospital far away. For a year, Allen's life hung in the balance. Then, suddenly, the cancer was declared in remission. The family went from a year-long crisis mode to attempting to resume a normal lifestyle again. Normalcy was not found easily. Martha suffered PTSD-type symptoms with flashbacks. The sounds, sights, and smells of a children's cancer unit invaded her consciousness. She entered psychotherapy to deal with her traumas. Meanwhile, other family members began to show signs of stress reactions. One of the older children developed depression, and began taking medication and going to therapy. Another child developed a rage toward Allen. There even was some concern that she might have physically abused him once.

Finally, the entire family entered therapy together. The cancer, treatment, and separation were dealt with. Martha and Sam had functioned in isolation from each other for a year, both doing what they had to do for the survival of the family, and doing it remarkably well.

As the family therapy progressed, Martha was able to express the feelings of loneliness and isolation she had experienced as she stayed by her son's side through the treatment process. There was unconscious resentment toward her husband for not being there with her during all those difficult times in the hospital. These feelings came out as tension between the couple, which the children sensed. The family tension produced depression, anger, and behavioral acting-out in the children. The resentments had also resulted in Martha becoming less responsive sexually, which further exacerbated the tension between her and Sam.

Family therapy helped Sam express his fears and frustrations. He spoke of how hard it had been for him to stay at home, knowing that his son's life hung in the balance. Sam also spoke of how he was unable to receive the support of the medical team. He was unable to express his feelings to his wife for fear of adding to her burden. Isolated from his son and wife, Sam had bottled up his feelings. He then experienced rejection from his wife on her return. Sam had become depressed.

In family therapy, the older children were also able to express their resentments at losing their mother for a year. They felt ignored by both parents as their younger sibling's struggle for life took priority. Family therapy took place over a year as the family fractured by Allen's illness sought to deal with the hurts of the past, rebuild a viable system in the present, and allow itself to trust in the future.

This case demonstrates processes similar to the other cases in this chapter. However, there are some differences worth noting. One is the impact on the siblings of a sick child. The siblings attempted to deal with their own feelings about the chronic/acute illness in the family by either withdrawing or acting out. The siblings' feelings and behaviors also may mirror the tension in the primary marital dyad. Anger, fear, sadness, and abandonment all may be powerful sequelae of an illness that is both chronic and acute. Not all chronic illnesses are terminal or even necessarily enduring. Yet once "cures" are effected, the family may need time and therapeutic help to reestablish itself into a normal pattern of living. Finally, sometimes multiple methods of treatment and providers are necessary. In this case, medications, individual therapies, and family therapy were all utilized. This necessitated occasional treatment-team meetings between the various therapists.

CONCEPTUAL FRAMEWORKS

In this section, conceptual frameworks for understanding the impact of chronic illness and disability on the family system are discussed. Two of the theories, by Papero (1990) and Minuchin (1974), were not originally written to illustrate the effect of illness on the family, but rather to explain family system functioning and pathology. These theories are described with specific application to the impact of chronic illness and disability on the family, utilizing illustrations from the four case studies. One theory (Rolland, 1984) is specifically offered as a way of understanding the effect of chronic illness and disability on the family. The fourth framework will be quite familiar to most therapists but nonetheless bears repeating in the context of understanding the grief associated with loss of health and subsequent forced systemic change (Kubler-Ross, 1969).

Bowen Family Systems Theory

Murray Bowen's core concept is that of growth via differentiation of the self in the context of the family system (Papero, 1990, p. 45). Bowen knew organisms grow more sophisticated along the phylogenetic scale through the process of cell differentiation and specialization. In an analogous fashion, his view of effective family functioning is based on the idea of the increased differentiation of the self in the context of the system. For Bowen, a primary dyad consisting of two individuals in the process of becoming individuated in the context of their respective family of origins comes together to establish a bond and generate offspring. The children are completely dependent on the parents for nurturance, both physically and emotionally. An infant is "attached or bonded, first to its mother, then to its father and/or other caregivers" (Papero, 1990, p. 33). As the infant is nurtured and grows, however, he or she becomes increasingly aware of self as separate from, though attached to, the family. The maturational process eventually leads the child to develop into an adult who becomes capable of forming a bond with a significant other and developing a mutually respectful, caring crucible that meets the needs of both. The cycle is completed—there is then the capacity to produce and nurture offspring of their own.

If this process occurred unimpeded, all persons would develop into mature, healthy individuals with few psychological or family problems. Such is obviously not the case. Bowen theory holds that a variety of processes contribute to the development of individual and systemic pathology. Adults who lack adequate differentiation of the self may have trouble establishing and maintaining adequate bonds in close relationships. There is difficulty in nurturing partners and children. Partners in relationships with inadequately differentiated pairs struggle with abandonment, intimacy, and power issues. These struggles give rise to anxiety, which further interferes with individuation. The anxiety is apprehended by the children and exerts a centripetal force. As children grow up inadequately differentiated, they may eventually establish similar family systems, and the process is repeated from generation to generation. The ultimate task of the family therapist, then, becomes to intervene in the family process in a way that facilitates differentiation of the self in the context of the family system. It is important to note this distinction: The goal is not differentiation from the family system, but differentiation within the family system.

Bowen defines *emotional cutoff* as an unhealthy state of affairs with negative consequences for differentiation. Other theorists have addressed this same issue. Williamson states:

> . . . while differentiation of the self is a critical step, it is not a satisfactory endpoint in the pursuit of human well-being and personal happiness. For if differentiation of self is held and pursued as an independent and commanding goal in and of itself, then undoubtedly a few people will end up alienated from family." (Williamson, 1991, p. 6).

Taggart (1980) speaks of persons "defining themselves in their families-of-origin" (p. 117).

Much has been written about the concept of healthy growth as differentiation of the self within the context of the family system, and the pathology that develops when this maturational process is inhibited. Less has been written about the impact of external environmental events such as chronic illness and disability on the functioning of the family system and the differentiation of the self. If anxiety presents a centripetal force that retards the process of differentiation (Rolland, 1987), then certainly the anxiety and stress of chronic illness and disability would provide a similar force with similar results.

How does a family system respond to anxiety, according to Bowen? Papero (1990, pp. 45–65) discusses the eight concepts of Bowen's theory, which are:

1. **Differentiation of Self.** Refers to varying degrees of ability to preserve a degree of autonomy in the face of pressures for togetherness. More differentiated individuals maintain a greater degree of ability to retain behavior governed by thinking rather than emotional reactivity. Differentiation of self may be inhibited by one or more of the following mechanisms.

2. **The Triangle.** When anxiety resides in either or both partners of a two-person relationship, a third person may be incorporated in order to reduce tension.

3. **Nuclear Family Emotional Process.** Couples with similar levels of differentiation come together. Increased levels of anxiety may produce attempts to reduce it in four ways: emotional distance, marital conflict, transmission of the problem to a child, or dysfunction in a spouse.

4. **Family Projection Process.** The basic process whereby parental problems can be projected onto children. Parents may overvalue or be overly critical with children.

5. **The Multigenerational Transmission Process.** The family projection process continues from one generation of a family system to the next.

6. **Sibling Position.** Certain trends and patterns of behavior tend to characterize persons occupying a given sibling position.

7. **Emotional Cutoff.** Individuals may attempt to use physical or emotional distance to separate themselves from the anxiety of the family system. This often makes them more vulnerable to other intense relationships.

8. **Emotional Processes in Society.** Society at large may operate according to emotional processes similar to those that govern the family system.

Each of these processes may be seen operating in the family system affected by chronic illness and disability. In Case 4, triangulation is evident at several points. For example, the genogram in Figure 12.1 illustrates the triangle between Martha, Sam, and little Allen.

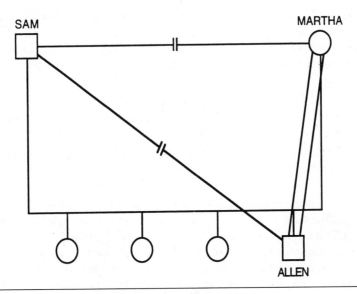

Figure 12.1   Genogram

Anxiety primarily comes from the impact of a chronic illness on this family system. Attempts to manage the anxiety result in a triangle characterized by a *fused* relationship between Martha and Allen and an *emotional cutoff* between Martha and Sam, and Sam and Allen. Other triangles are also present in this system (e.g. the mother/older-child/patient triangle). Here there is a cutoff relationship between the third child and the mother, and a conflictual relationship between the third child and the fourth child. Possibly, this child assumed the role of expressing the anger of the father and the three older siblings toward the mother and the younger sibling for their abandonment of the family.

Other Bowen principles are illustrated in this case. For example, emotional cutoff occurs between Martha and Sam, not because of "the discomfort of attachment" (Papero, 1990, p. 62), but because of the emotionally intense separation forced on the family by the chronic illness. The intensity of the anxiety with respect to the child's struggle for life might have produced emotional cutoff also. Families sometimes tend to handle fears and pain by simply not speaking the unspeakable (Williamson, 1991, p. 199). In Bowen's concept of the nuclear family emotional process, he views couples as handling emotional stress in the relationship by one or more of four methods: emotional distance, marital conflict, transmission of the problem to a child, and/or dysfunction in a spouse. In Case 4, a degree of three of the four methods is demonstrated, from Martha's PTSD and depression (dysfunction in a spouse), to the third child's hostility toward Allen (transmission to a child), to the emotional distance between Martha and Sam.

Minuchin's Structural Approach

Another way of conceptualizing the difficulties imposed on families by chronic illness and disability is by utilizing Salvador Minuchin's structural theory of family system functioning and pathology. Minuchin's (1980, p. 9) three axioms of family system functioning and pathology are:

1. An individual's psychic life is not entirely an internal process.
2. Changes in the family structure contribute to changes in the behavior and inner psychic processes of the members of that system.
3. When a therapist works with a patient or a patient family, his or her behavior becomes part of the context.

Minuchin (1980) states that a family under stress "must be able to transform itself in ways that meet new circumstances without losing the continuity that provides a frame of reference for its members" (1980, p. 52). The continuity that provides a frame of reference for family members is the family system. The family system is *structured* in a *hierarchial* manner. There are subsystems of the family that carry out its various functions (e.g., parental). There are also *boundaries,* which are the rules defining who participates in what part of the family and how. Problems may arise for family functioning when family structures and boundaries are compromised by one of four categories of stressors. Minuchin (1980) identifies medical problems as Category 4, "stresses around idiosyncratic problems" (p. 65). These stresses may be seen as changing family structure and functions in significant ways. For example, in Minuchin's most basic concept of a healthy family system, the family consists of an executive subsystem and a sibling subsystem:

M (executive subsystem)
children (sibling subsystem)

As seen in Case 1 with John and Brenda, a sick spouse may become more dependent and functionally assigned to an infantile role, with the primary caregiver relegated to isolation in the executive subsystem, parentified with respect to his or her spouse:

Parentified Spouse (executive subsystem)
Infantilized Spouse ("sibling" subsystem)

Structurally, this produces a change from the more mature, nurturing egalitarian relationship of two adults to a regressed caretaking relationship in which spouses operate in a parent-child fashion. This produces parental behavior on the part of the caregiver and childlike behavior on the part of the patient.

Dynamically, Minuchin differentiates between system boundaries as *clear* boundaries, *diffuse* boundaries, or *rigid* boundaries. For John and Brenda, part of the problem was that prolonged illness produced not only the structural change of parentification/infantilization, but also the functional change of a more rigid boundary, which made the shift back to a more egalitarian relationship even more difficult.

Other structural and functional changes may occur in systems due to illnesses. In Naomi's situation, an adult was infantilized, reentering a dependent system with her mother. In Case Study 3, Roberto becomes infantilized as the disabled spouse. There is also the parentification of a child who had to become a caregiver. Tension developed between the mother and the child as the child resisted the interruption of his normal centrifugal process. This is an example of the tension that results when chronic illness exerts a centripetal force in a centrifugal stage.

mother/child
father

Therapeutic interventions may also be anticipated from the structural stance. Infantilized patients must be empowered as much as possible. Isolated caregivers must be helped to obtain support and be collaborators with their sick family members. Ways must be found to help parentified children accomplish their normal developmental tasks. Larger social support systems must be called on to provide security for those dependent members of society who have no family advocates.

Kubler-Ross's Theory of Stages of Grief

Elizabeth Kubler-Ross (1969) proposed a classic conceptual framework for the grief process consisting of five stages: denial, anger, bargaining, depression, and acceptance. Whether they use her original model or any of the subsequent elaborations or variations of it, therapists working with families impacted by chronic illness and disability must understand that grief is an inevitable component of the family process. In Cases 1, 2, and 3, the grief of the patients and their families is clearly evident. John (Case 1) grieved the loss of what was, and became stuck in the anger stage. Benita (Case 3) grieved the loss of what was to be, and became caught in the depressed stage. Naomi (Case 2) practiced denial as a primary defense mechanism until it was stripped away, then alternated between bargaining (e.g., doing the rehabilitation exercises to excess) and depression. Eventually Naomi returned to denial by terminating the therapy process and refocusing on aches and pains rather than dealing with the reality of disability. In Case 4, the grief process is seen to turn into a bond rather than a wedge for the family. The family was helped to identify loss, understand the grief process, normalize the feelings associated with grief, and talk about those feelings to each other.

Rolland's Psychosocial Typology of Chronic and Life-Threatening Illness

John S. Rolland (1984, p. 245) proposed a "psychosocial typology of chronic and life-threatening illness" to help the practitioner assess the impact of illness on a patient and their family system along several parameters. Rolland notes illnesses can be categorized in the following ways:

- **Onset.** Acute versus gradual.
- **Course.** Progressive, constant, or relapsing/episodic.
- **Outcome.** Fatal versus shortened life span versus nonfatal.
- **Incapacitation.** Present versus absent.

Utilizing these concepts, Rolland proposes a grid (see Figure 12.2) that provides "a typology with 32 potential types of illness" (p. 251). Additionally, Rolland proposes a *Time Line* that helps to conceptualize the *phases* of an illness (see Figure 12.3). Illnesses can be seen as having crisis, chronic, and terminal phases, with corresponding implications for patients and their families.

An important element of Rolland's typology is that in understanding the impact of illness on a family, it is important for the family therapist not only to know the course of the illness but also the family's *perception* of the course of the illness. A chronic illness that is perceived as terminal might impact a family in different ways than a chronic illness that is perceived as nonfatal.

Finally, Rolland (1987) proposes several key rules for understanding the impact of illness on the family with respect to the family life cycle:

1. Chronic illness exerts a centripetal force on families.
2. If chronic illness occurs during centrifugal periods, it can detract from family tasks (e.g., leaving home).
3. If chronic illness occurs during a centripetal period, it may prolong that period (e.g., child rearing).
4. Normative family needs are generally subordinated to the needs of the chronic illness or the patient.

SPECIAL ISSUES OF WORKING WITH CHRONIC ILLNESS AND DISABILITY

Cultural norms are important in the consideration of ways in which chronic illness and disability impact family systems. Individuals do not function in a vacuum but in the context of a family system. Family systems function not in a vacuum but in the context of a culture that prescribes the rules and norms of the family system. Awareness of special issues related to culture and subculture can facilitate the family therapist's work with families as issues of gender, ethnicity, and class influence and shape the responses of individuals and families to nonnormative events. Many of these issues are addressed ably elsewhere in this volume (especially Chapters 2, 3, and 4), but they will be addressed briefly here in the specific context of the effect of illness on the family.

Gender Issues

Historically, most cultures have identified the woman as the primary caregiver for the family system. This pattern seems to continue today. Many women in this society will spend the majority of their adult years caring for family members: children in the first half, followed by aging and ill parents and spouses in the second half. In her review essay, "Who's Going to Do the Dirty Work?" Ward (1991) looks at three recent volumes on women's roles in the area of managing people's activities of daily living (ADLs) in a society in which more people live longer but with more illnesses requiring more care. In the past, the answer to her rhetorical question has always been women. McGoldrick (1989) points out, "The expectation has been that women would take care of the needs of others" (p. 200).

In three of the four case examples presented in this chapter, women were the primary caregivers. In the fourth, even though the man became the primary caregiver for three children and the household, it was the woman who suspended her career to go with a sick child for treatment. These cases were selected for presentation because they are typical. Cases in which other options were pursued are difficult to find. By raising levels of consciousness about the issue of who gets to do the dirty work, family therapists do not presume to dictate to families who gets chosen as the primary caregiver and why. Therapists

	Incapacitating		Nonincapacitating	
	Acute	Gradual	Acute	Gradual
FATAL				
Progressive		Lung cancer with CNS metastases AIDS Bone marrow failure Amyotrophic lateral sclerosis	Acute leukemia Pancreatic cancer Metastatic breast cancer Malignant melanoma Lung cancer Liver cancer	Cystic fibrosis*
Relapsing			Incurable cancers in remission	
POSSIBLY FATAL SHORTENED LIFE SPAN				
Progressive		Emphysema Alzheimer's disease Multi-infarct dementia Multiple sclerosis (late) Chronic alcoholism Huntington's chorea Scleroderma		Juvenile diabetes* Malignant hypertension Insulin-dependent adult-onset diabetes
Relapsing	Angina	Early multiple sclerosis Episodic alcoholism P.K.U. and other congenital errors of metabolism	Sickle cell disease* Hemophilia*	Systemic lupus erythematosis*
Constant	Stroke Moderate/severe myocardial infarction		Mild myocardial infarction Cardiac arrhythmia	Hemodialysis treated renal failure Hodgkin's disease

	Incapacitating		Nonincapacitating	
	Acute	Gradual	Acute	Gradual
Progressive		Parkinson's disease Rheumatoid arthritis Osteoarthritis		Noninsulin-dependent Adult-onset diabetes
		NONFATAL		
Relapsing	Lumbosacral disc disorder		Kidney stones Gout Migraine Seasonal allergy Asthma Epilepsy	Peptic ulcer Ulcerative colitis Chronic bronchitis Irritable bowel syndrome Psoriasis
Constant	Congenital malformations Spinal cord injury Acute blindness Acute deafness Survived severe trauma & burns Posthypoxic syndrome	Nonprogressive mental retardation Cerebral palsy	Benign arrhythmia Congenital heart disease	Malabsorption syndromes Hyper/hypothyroidism Pernicious anemia Controlled hypertension Controlled glaucoma

* = Early

Source: Reprinted from Rolland, J. S. (1984). Toward a psychosocial typology of chronic and life threatening illness. Family Systems Medicine, 2, 245-62. Reprinted with permission of Family Process Inc.

**Figure 12.2 Rolland's Typology
Categorization of Chronic Illness by Psychosocial Type**

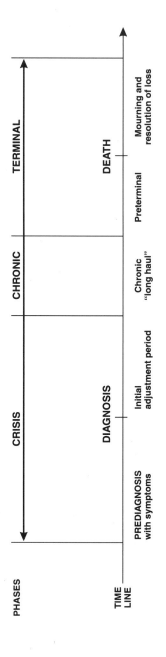

Time Line and Phase of Illness

| PHASES | CRISIS | CHRONIC | TERMINAL |

| TIME LINE | DIAGNOSIS | | DEATH |

PREDIAGNOSIS with symptoms — Initial adjustment period — Chronic "long haul" — Preterminal — Mourning and resolution of loss

Figure 12.3   Rolland's Time Line

Note: From "Toward a Psychosocial Typology of Chronic and Life Threatening Illness." By J. Rolland, 1984, *Family Systems Medicine, 2,* 245–62. Copyright by Family Process, Inc. Reprinted with permission.

must, however, challenge their own assumption that it is always appropriate for the woman to assume this role.

Therapists must also attempt to facilitate families, exploration of this issue, and help families explore options for more egalitarian distributions of the burdens and tasks necessary in the care of a sick family member. In Case 4, Martha and Sam provide a view of some of the special issues facing men in the context of illness in the family. The more traditional tasks of men in this society seem to facilitate emotional isolation (do vs. be; provide vs. nurture; strength vs. tears; career vs. home). Chronic illness and disability in a family tend to exacerbate the emotional isolation of the male caregiver. Sam had the privilege of not having to suspend his career for the care of the sick child. Yet, he cared for three children at home in relative isolation. His pain was compounded because he could not be with his child in his sickness; he could not stand with his wife at his son's bedside to speak with the doctors about his son's condition; and he was isolated from his wife and the comfort they might have been able to provide for each other. In their social groups, people often asked how the mother and child were, but rarely asked how the father and other children were faring.

Another father who assumed the primary caregiver role in the care of his sick child related how the staff in a pediatrician's office expressed dissatisfaction when he and not the mother brought the child in for medical appointments. He described how the doctor and nurses addressed their questions to the mother and ignored him during examinations when both were present, even when the mother referred the medical personnel to him for answers. He eventually entered psychotherapy, stating in his first visit that "I just want *someone* to hear my pain and grief over my child's condition." The gender-sensitive therapist not only will attend to issues of overload for women, but will also attend to issues of unexpressed grief and social isolation for men.

Issues of Ethnicity

Although it is important to avoid generalizations based on ethnic backgrounds, issues that are specifically related to ethnicity should also be a part of the family therapist's awareness. Benita and Roberto, mentioned in Case 3, exemplify some of the issues present in a Hispanic family affected by illness. With a strong norm dictating the wife as the primary caregiver, the cultural expectation that women are to bear such loads without complaint, and in the absence of the traditional support system of female companionship provided by the extended family system, Benita's grief was overwhelming and unexpressed.

Naomi, in Case 2, lived in a housing project with her mother after her disabling injury. The absence of supportive men and extended family promoted the fear of what would become of an institutionalized and impoverished black woman with no one to monitor her care. Naomi lived with this fear nightly. McGoldrick et al. state, "We believe that therapists who appreciate the cultural relativity of family life are in a position to intervene more effectively and that a therapists' own ethnicity influences the helping process" (McGoldrick,

Preto, Hines, & Lee, 1991, p. 546). Ethnic awareness is especially valuable in light of Rolland's assertion that it is not only the illness that impacts a family but the family's interpretation of the illness. The interpretation is influenced by culture.

Nontraditional Family Structures

Families often do not fit the traditional form of mother-father-sister-brother. Single-parent families, stepfamilies, blended families, and other family structures will each have unique strengths and vulnerabilities in dealing with sick members. One single mother with a disabled and chronically ill child demonstrated heroic devotion and care. She dedicated herself to her daughter for almost 8 years. After her daughter's death, the mother saw a counselor for a short period of grief therapy, then stated, "I gave up my life for her. Now it's time for me to live." Naomi's case illustrates a single-mother/adult-child family structure, with the difficulty of knowing the disabled "child" will likely outlive the caregiver. John and Brenda demonstrate a case of an older couple with no adult children in the community to provide support. Martha and Sam are more traditional. However, the dual-profession marriage presented dilemmas related to work they had to deal with as they cared for their sick child. Multigenerational families will likely present more and more challenges in the future. As the life span is extended, grandchildren may end up caring for both elderly parents and grandparents simultaneously.

Nontraditional family systems may be impacted by chronic illness in unique ways. Couples and families who are "not a socially sanctioned family unit" (Roth, 1989, p. 286), or who have alternate lifestyles, may present especially difficult issues. A gay partner may have little or no legal recognition of a relationship in the face of his partner's terminal illness. A lesbian partner who has little access to her companion's family support network may feel isolation and need special support when their relationship is impacted by chronic illness and disability. Cole (1993) found that the sense of isolation and alienation from support systems affects the extended families of AIDS patients. In a study on the families of persons with AIDS, he discovered that most of the families in his study had been active in church prior to their family member's illness. However, when they began caring for the person with AIDS, they often found little support, dropped out of their prior religious activities, and isolated themselves socially.

Spiritual Issues

The faith system of the family may be affected by chronic illness and disability. Fowler (1981) speaks of faith as the process whereby persons create meaning out of their experience, giving them a way to understand the mysteries of life. Rabbi Harold Kushner (1981) wrote *When Bad Things Happen to Good People* as a consequence of the chronic illness and eventual death of his son. He stated that he "was compelled by a personal tragedy to rethink everything I had been taught about God and God's ways" (p. 1). In the stress of raising a child with severe cerebral palsy, the Christian ethicist T. B. Maston (1977) stated:

> Like many of you, I have cried out "Why Suffering?" I have also struggled with the closely related question, "What is God's relation to suffering?" Several years ago I felt I had to find a reasonably satisfactory answer to the preceding question or lose my sanity and/or my faith. (pp. 9–10)

Therapists need sensitivity to the way in which a family constructs meaning for its experience with illness and disability, and how that meaning helps or impairs coping. Especially needed is an awareness that illness can create a crisis of faith.

Sexual Issues

Illness and disability affect a number of aspects of sexual feelings, functions, and behaviors. One couple seen for marital therapy had not had intercourse for 20 years subsequent to the husband's heart attack in his late 40s. They were afraid intercourse would kill him. None of his physicians had ever asked about this area of functioning. The heart attack or stroke patient and their partner may have fears that too much excitement could precipitate another such event. Partners in relationships where one is HIV positive will have to deal with important issues about their sexual activities. Parents of an intellectually challenged child are faced with difficult sexual issues as puberty arrives. The couple in which the man is diabetic may have to deal with erectile dysfunction at some point. The husband of a wife with multiple sclerosis may need to learn new ways of providing stimulation to his partner as the disease progresses and tactile sensitivity is reduced. The therapist working with these persons and partners must be able to inquire effectively as to the impact of illness on sexual desire and functioning. Treatment or referral to an appropriate specialist may be indicated.

RECOMMENDATIONS FOR FAMILY THERAPY WITH FAMILIES IMPACTED BY CHRONIC ILLNESS AND DISABILITY

Exact interventions for family therapy with chronic illness are difficult to recommend because of the varied nature of illnesses and families. Obviously, therapy was different for Sam and Martha with their four children and illness in remission than it was for John and Brenda as an older couple affected by a deteriorating disease. It is possible, however, to make general recommendations for therapists who wish to treat families impacted by chronic illness and disability. The 10 foundational recommendations are intended to guide therapists in preparing themselves for this type of work. Additionally, there are 10 recommendations to provide direction for the therapy process.

Recommendations for the Therapist Treating Families Impacted by Chronic Illness and Disability

1. **Get training in family systems theory and therapy.** When dealing with the family of a person with chronic illness, the family system becomes the patient. Family systems theory provides explanations and insights into the ways stress alters family functioning. Family therapy requires specialized training because it is a different treatment modality with a different set of skills than traditional psychotherapies.

2. **Utilize the biopsychosocial model.** Engel (1977) proposed the biopsychosocial model for understanding human pain and suffering from three levels at once. The idea of looking at illness from biological, psychological, and social perspectives simultaneously has become the norm for family medicine training. Therapists enter the medical world when doing family therapy with chronic illness patients and their families. Thinking of behavioral issues from the standpoint of multiple levels of explanation (Strozier & Armour, 1993) helps the therapist deal with the illness, its psychological sequelae, and the family's systemic issues.

3. **Deal with your own issues around illness and mortality.** Family therapy with chronic illness has a powerful way of pulling out therapists, issues about sickness and death. Therapists can be most effective with families when they have worked through these issues themselves. This helps the therapist empathize effectively as well as deal with countertransference.

4. **Establish collaborative relationships with medical professionals.** Therapists willing to work together with physicians and health-care teams greatly increase their effectiveness. Learning how the medical world functions; learning to speak its language; and building trust and collegiality with physicians so patients and their families can be more effectively treated can be rewarding.

5. **Learn about the illness impacting the family.** Utilize readings, consultations with medical professionals, and information from the patient and family to understand the illness affecting the family. Understanding how certain illnesses and their treatments affect thought and behavior is especially useful. Understanding the caretaking demands the illness places on the family is important also.

6. **Anticipate setbacks and frustrations, both with the illness and the therapy.** Illnesses of the progressive or relapsing/episodic types may be quite frustrating both for the family and the therapy process. It is not unusual to have done effective family therapy so that the family system is stabilized and functioning optimally, only to watch the family destabilize once more with the latest medical crisis. It is helpful to explain this process in advance to the families. The goals of therapy may

include both support in times of crisis and behavioral skills for managing the stress of crisis situations.

7. **Be sensitive to special issues.**
   - *Ethnicity.* What does the illness mean in the context of culture?
   - *Gender.* What gender issues affect the caregiving?
   - *Alternative family structures.* How does chronic illness affect single-parent families, gay relationships, or other nontraditional families differently?
   - *Religion.* What are the beliefs that support or hinder adjustment to chronic illness?
   - *Sexuality.* How does chronic illness affect sexual functioning and relationships?

8. **Get support.** Find a physician or other health-care professional who can serve as a friend, confidante, and consultant on medical issues.

9. **Read about family therapy and medicine.** Authors who are helpful in learning more about family therapy and medicine include Susan McDaniel, William Doherty, Jeri Hepworth, Macaran Baird, Janet Christie-Seely, and Yves Talbot.

10. **Be aware of resources.** Chronic illness can place demands on family systems that require multimodal treatment strategies. Referral to financial counselors, social service agencies, and support groups can be useful.

Ten Recommendations for Family Therapy with Families Impacted by Chronic Illness and Disability

1. **Hear the stories—there is healing in the telling.**
   - *Hear the saga.* Many families have been through so much for so long that they feel overwhelmed by all that has happened to them. A format in which they can tell about illness, hospitalizations, and treatments is important. They often feel that no one else can or will hear them.
   - *Hear the different perspectives.* The experiences may be quite different from the patient to the family, and from one caregiver to another. Each person needs the catharsis of telling his or her own version. Each family member needs to have his or her struggles with the illness heard and understood by the other family members. Misunderstandings can be resolved. Bonds may be formed that will help the family in working together to manage the illness.
   - *Be willing to hear the details.* Much like PTSD victims, some families will have stories to tell that are so horrific that they cannot discuss them with others. Therapists can provide a forum in the therapy

process where families can talk about some of the details of the illness and their related feelings.

2. **Facilitate family communication—there is strength when families discuss the unspoken.** Family therapy can provide the forum for expressing grief, negotiating caregiving tasks, and dealing with difficult issues such as death and dying.

3. **Empower patients and families.**

   - *Help patients assume optimal responsibility for their own care.* A sense of autonomy and control will help the patients feelings about the illness.

   - *Help families avoid the extremes of being overly critical or solicitous.* Both extremes have been shown to impair rehabilitation efforts.

   - *Help families find balance.* The patient should be as autonomous as possible while still receiving the needed care. The family should carry on as normally as possible while still providing the needed care.

   - *Patient/family collaboration is paramount.* Issues impacting the family and their management should be viewed as family issues. The patient and their family together should negotiate the patient's care.

4. **Normalize.**

   - *The grief process.* The process of grieving for loss of health and for the family's former lifestyle is essential. Therapy facilitates the acknowledgment of loss while helping families resolve guilt and shame.

   - *The adjustment process.* Families can function more effectively if they know that the many adjustments that they have to make in lifestyle and environment are a normal and often ongoing part of life with chronic illness.

   - *Fears.* Chronic illness tends to undermine a sense of security. Acknowledging fears and building in reassurances and support can be helpful.

   - *Needs.* Families may need affirmation that it is OK to ask, say no, and negotiate issues.

5. **Facilitate egalitarian distribution of caregiving tasks.** Much stress in the family system may come from one or two individuals assuming a large share of responsibility for caregiving. Family members may not be able to perform all tasks equally well, but tasks can be distributed according to abilities and inclinations so that no one family member gets burned out.

6. **Help family members maintain age-appropriate behaviors and roles as much as possible.**

   - *Patients may become infantilized.* Regressive behavior in the face of illness is common. To minimize the infantilization process, therapists can help patients learn to ask rather than whine or sulk, express anger rather than harbor resentment, negotiate and ask for needs rather than withdraw into depression.

- *Caregivers may become parentified.* They may assume greater levels of responsibility with less time and energy for age-appropriate recreation. Boys may actually be told that with Dad sick they have to be "the man of the family." They may feel that way even if not told. Girls may take on motherly tasks in the face of a mother's illness. Adults may become so consumed with caregiving that they do not take time out for recreation or peer relationships. They may feel guilty if they do so.

7. **Be practical—small helps with ADLs go a long way.** Help the family find concrete ways to deal with activities of daily living. A bar may be installed over a bed so a patient can pull him- or herself up. A pager or cellular phone may give a caregiver more mobility. Neighbors may help with additional support. These are simple and practical ways to help families cope. Families feel trapped when their options are limited—help them explore more options than they might be able to see immediately.

8. **Deal with finances.** For most families, income will decrease while expenses will increase. The opportunity to discuss and grieve this fact of life with chronic illness will be helpful. If the family finds the task of adapting to new financial realities too difficult, family financial counseling should be provided.

9. **Explore issues of meaning and faith.** Rolland has noted it is not only the chronic illness that affects a family, but the way the family views the illness. The meanings attached to issues of illness and mortality can be significant resources for or impediments of a family's coping. Helping the family find meaning in the face of suffering and pain can be a significant help in the management of illness. Resolving toxic feelings can also be critical (e.g., issues of guilt, divine punishment, and blame).

10. **Ask about sexual functioning—treat or refer.** It should not be assumed that anyone has helped the partners deal with issues around their sexual relationship. Often, no one has. It should also not be assumed that sick people are no longer sexual beings, or that geriatric patients and their partners stopped being sexual at a certain age.

CONCLUSION

The therapist choosing to deal with families suffering from chronic illness and disability ventures outside the traditional training of most mental health professions into an area where medicine, psychology, and social systems interface. It may be a realm of insecurity and uncertainty at first. With knowledge, training, and experience, however, the therapist can receive the gratification of helping families struggling with remarkable challenges. The therapist may benefit nearly as much from this type of work as his or her patients do.

REFERENCES

Cole, W. (1993). *Families living with Aids.* Unpublished Doctor of Ministry Research Project, Southern Baptist Theological Seminary, Louisville, Kentucky.

Doherty, W. J., & Baird, M. A. (1987). *Family-centered medical care.* New York: Guilford.

Engel, G. (1977). The need for a new medical model: A challenge for biomedicine. *Science, 196,* 129–136.

Fowler, J. W. (1981). *Stages of Faith.* San Francisco: Harper & Row.

Kubler-Ross, E. (1969). *On death and dying.* New York: Macmillan.

Kushner, H. S. (1981). *When bad things happen to good people.* New York: Avon.

McDaniel, S. H., Hepworth, J., & Doherty, W. J. (1992). *Medical family therapy.* New York: Basic Books.

McGoldrick, M. (1989). Women through the family life cycle. In M. McGoldrick et al. (Eds.), *Women in families.* New York: Norton.

McGoldrick, M., Preto, N., Hines, P., & Lee, E. (1991). Ethnicity and family therapy. In Gurman & Kniskern (Eds.), *Handbook of family therapy, Volume II* (pp. 546–582). New York: Brunner/Mazel.

Maston, T. (1977). *God speaks through suffering.* Waco, TX: Word Books.

Minuchin, S. (1974). *Families & family therapy.* Cambridge, MA: Harvard University Press.

Papero, D. V. (1990). *Bowen family systems theory.* Boston: Allyn and Bacon.

Rolland, J. S. (1984). Toward a psychosocial typology of chronic and life-threatening illness. *Family Systems Medicine, 2*(3), 245–262.

Rolland, J. S. (1987). Chronic illness and the family life cycle: A conceptual framework. *Family Process, 26*(2), 203–221.

Roth, S. (1989). Psychotherapy with lesbian couples. In M. McGoldrick et al. (Eds.), *Women in families.* New York: Norton.

Strozier, A. M., & Armour, M. A. (1993). Family psychopathology. *Contemporary Family Therapy, 15*(1).

Taggart, M. (1980). Salvete et Valete: On saying goodbye to a deceased former parent. *Journal of Marital and Family Therapy, 6*(2), 117–122.

Ward, D. (1991). Review essay: Who's going to do the dirty work? *Journal of Health Politics, Policy and Law,* 823–830.

Williamson, D. S. (1991). *The intimacy paradox.* New York: Guilford.

CHAPTER 13

Families with HIV Illness

JOSEPH M. ROSENTHAL, NANCY BOYD-FRANKLIN,
GLORIA STEINER, and GIL TUNNELL

As we approach the end of the second decade of the AIDS epidemic, the disease remains a worldwide scourge that resists attempts at effective treatment, and does not yet have a cure. Initial optimistic predictions of vaccines and antiviral drugs that would destroy the virus in the body have given way to the daunting biological complexities of a mutating retrovirus's strategies for reproduction and self-protection. What this means is that HIV/AIDS will continue to threaten infected persons and their family members for the foreseeable future, demanding ever more effective psychological and sociological strategies to ensure the preservation and integrity of affected families.

Behavioral and social scientists, researchers, and psychotherapists can all play crucial roles—preventing the uninfected from infection, catalyzing the support of family members for infected persons, safeguarding the mental and physical health of uninfected family members, and preserving the stability and resilience of the millions of American families—and the hundreds of millions of families worldwide—faced with the myriad mysteries and challenges of HIV/AIDS.

As of December 1994, a horrific milestone was reached. More than 440,000 Americans had been stricken with AIDS—acquired immunodeficiency syndrome (Centers for Disease Control [CDC], 1995). One to two million more Americans are estimated to have contracted the human immunodeficiency virus (HIV), some remaining completely symptom-free, many others suffering from a wide variety of symptoms, ranging from mild to severe, yet not showing the clinical profile required for an AIDS diagnosis (CDC, 1990). Although it is unknown how many HIV-infected persons will develop AIDS, it is generally believed that the HIV virus progressively weakens the immune system, eventually rendering all infected persons at risk for some HIV-related disease (Cohen, Sande, & Volberding, 1990).

This chapter addresses the impact of HIV/AIDS on a family system. As used here, the term "family" means a person's intimate social network—a person's current nuclear family, family of origin, lover, family of choice (as in a gay man's community network), or extended blood kin or nonblood kin network. Based on conservative estimates of the number of HIV-infected individuals, the focus, then, is on the concerns, needs, and impact of a staggering number of individuals—the millions of family members of persons with AIDS (PWAs) and HIV-involved people:

- Carlos and Maria were referred for therapy because their usual way of resolving disputes had not been working since Carlos began experiencing physical symptoms associated with HIV. In addition, their 16-year-old daughter had begun acting out.

- Family therapy with Neal and his families of origin and choice was initiated when Neal's mother presented by herself reporting violent fights between herself and her son who had AIDS for over a year.

- The S. family was referred when their physician noticed signs of depression in 8-year-old Julio. Julio's father was a former IV-drug user who had AIDS. Julio's mother was now infected, separated from her husband, and living with her mother who forbade Julio to see his father.

- David and Evelyn came to therapy with their infant daughter and Evelyn's six-year-old by a previous relationship. They asked for help with the "turnaround in (their) lives" since they discovered the baby had AIDS and Evelyn became HIV-positive.

- Joanne and Larry came for therapy with their infant daughter and Joanne's five-year-old son. Larry had just tested positive for HIV and the family was in turmoil following Larry's disclosure to Joanne that he had had affairs with men before their marriage.

- Jim and David were referred by a friend for couples therapy based on escalating fights since Jim contracted HIV-related pneumonia.

In each of these examples, the presence of HIV in a family system presented unique challenges to the physical and emotional health of each member of the family as well as to the structural viability of the family system itself. In each of these cases, an emotional tidal wave threatened to overwhelm the family, threatening the effectiveness of the most important social support system of an individual with HIV/AIDS.

A longitudinal study by Zich and Temoshok (1987) suggests that social support alone may significantly affect the quality of life of people with HIV illness. When someone has HIV disease, family members provide not only a potential social support system but may also act as an advocacy system, home care system, cocounseling system, and spiritual community. Although more research is necessary to identify personal, familial, and larger system factors that facilitate or obstruct the capacity of family members to successfully fulfill these roles without behavioral or emotional dysfunction, a growing corpus of reports from family-oriented therapists has already yielded certain guidelines for the mental health professional interested in maximizing the coping power of families challenged by the presence of HIV.

ASSESSMENT

One tool shown to be highly effective in assessing the many aspects of family logistics and functioning in the face of HIV/AIDS is the multigenerational genogram (Boyd-Franklin, Steiner, & Boland, 1995; Walker, 1991). Genograms allow the identification of family members who might be accessed as resources. A multigenerational genogram also provides a "picture worth a thousand words" which allows for the identification of past and present family structures and dynamics and their evolution, yielding crucial information about how individuals and the system have evolved over the different phases and significant events of the family's life cycle. Cutoffs, inappropriate boundaries or hierarchies, coalitions, alliances, unfinished business, destructive triangles—the myriad obstacles to effective family coping—can then be addressed therapeutically by the mental health professional to access the full resources of the family and offer appropriate interventions.

In the following case example, the use of a multigenerational genogram as the major assessment tool sets up a treatment plan that is appropriate for a family falling apart following the appearance of physical symptoms associated with HIV.

Case Example

Mercedes was referred by her physician after her 8-year-old son Julio began having trouble in school. Mercedes arrived with Julio and her mother, Vanessa. The cotherapists discussed with the family members their reasons for wanting therapy, naturalistically weaving into the discussion some variation of the following questions:

How have things changed in the family since (the HIV test) (the symptoms began)?
Who in the family knows of this situation?
Who is not present today and why?
Who else is available to help out?
What kinds of responses to the crisis have you already tried out?
Are you in agreement as to what to do?
If there are disagreements, how are they resolved?
Who is having the hardest time dealing with the situation?
What feelings do people in the family have/express about the situation?
How have relationships been affected by the situation/disagreements/feelings?
What do you need from each other?
How has the family dealt with illness/crisis in the past?

During the initial session, the genogram in Figure 13.1 was generated.

Based on the genogram-based assessment, the therapy team was able to develop a treatment plan related specifically to the presenting family problems—

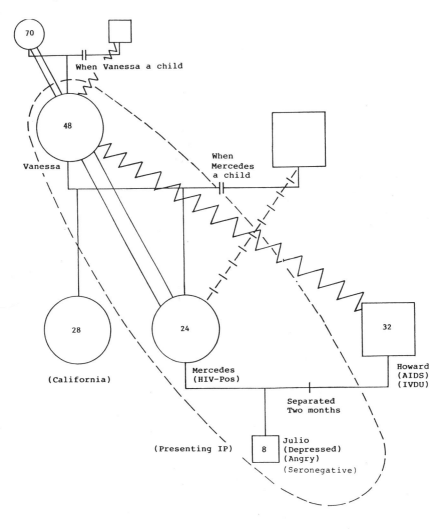

Key to symbols in genogram:

Circle = Male
Square = Female
Straight line = Marriage
Double line = Close relationship
Jagged line = Conflictual relationship
X through a circle or square = Person is deceased
Dotted/Elliptical line around family members = Living together in same household
Two short slashes interrupting a marriage = Divorce
Single short slash interrupting a marriage = Separation

Figure 13.1   Genogram

both as understood initially by the family and as evolved in the assessment—and to hypotheses related to the unique structure, history, and dynamics of this particular family system. Regarding presenting problems, both mother and grandmother focused initially on Julio's acting-out at school and his depression. Following a discussion of Julio's difficulties, the team was able to broaden their understanding via some variation of the preceding questions, starting with, "Is anybody else in the family acting out or depressed?"

The picture that emerged was one of a family torn apart by anger, enmeshment, betrayal, and guilt. Vanessa's anger at her son-in-law for infecting her daughter had led to his extrusion from the family. Because of physical weakness and inability to care for herself and her son, Mercedes had moved in with her mother. Vanessa's rule was that Julio could not see his father. Julio expressed intense hurt and rage toward his mother for agreeing to this plan, then withdrew. Mercedes was conflicted in her feelings toward Howard and also toward her mother who, as a pillar of strength, had always obviated the need for Mercedes to develop her own strength and independence.

With the genogram assessment as a guide, the therapy team developed a treatment plan that related Julio's symptoms to the lack of resolution of emotional conflict between Mercedes and her husband and to Julio's hurt and anger at being kept apart from his father. The family was told that until Mercedes' husband joined the therapy, it would be difficult to understand his part in the stalemate. Without his cooperation, we could not know whether the relationship was, in fact, a viable context for parenting, or whether Mercedes and her mother should be the new parenting team, necessitating some updating of their relationship. Mercedes' dependence on and lack of differentiation from her mother, now exacerbated by the illness, were seen as contributing to structural and hierarchical confusions obstructing the resolution of emotional and political aspects of the present crisis.

The team developed the following treatment plan based on the genogram assessment: (a) Attempt to include Mercedes' husband in the therapy. (Given Mercedes' ambivalence toward her husband, her dependence on her mother, and Vanessa's anger at Howard, this was a challenge that promised delicate therapeutic work.) If Howard attended future sessions, the next goal would be to (b) focus on resolution of emotional and structural issues within the new parenting team of Howard and Mercedes and Vanessa so that the team could work collaboratively to benefit Julio and plan for the future. Whether Howard did or did not attend, subsequent goals would be to (c) empower Mercedes to make her own decisions regarding her relationship with Howard, (d) assist Mercedes and Vanessa in updating their relationship so that Mercedes could develop her own strengths and independent judgment that would be respected by Vanessa, and (e) assist Vanessa in the expression and resolution of her sorrow and anger so that she could understand and honor Julio's need to see his father before he died. A multitude of other crucial logistical and emotional issues could then be addressed (such as Julio's fear of losing his mother) and the family could begin to reorganize itself to deal effectively with the crisis, get additional support, and plan for the future.

For any of these goals to be attained, a seeming infinity of extremely delicate therapeutic issues would need attention. But that is true of any therapeutic encounter. In any case, the genogram assessment had done its work, providing a clear direction for the therapy.

FACILITATING ADAPTIVE RESTRUCTURING

As illustrated in the previous case example, HIV/AIDS often presents complex reorganizational challenges for families. HIV illness may prevent someone from playing the usual role as parent, lover, domestic partner, or breadwinner. Such disruption of the usual role assignments can be frightening and confusing for families whose resilience has depended on a certain structure. Psychologists and other mental health professionals can assist families in understanding and implementing an appropriate reorganization of roles (Boyd-Franklin, Steiner, & Boland, 1995; Macklin, 1989; Walker, 1991). Emotional and functional adaptation of family members may depend on the success of this reorganization.

FAMILY MEMBERS AT RISK

The HIV-involved family member is not alone in his or her need for the family to address these issues and develop adaptive coping and community processes. A decade of therapeutic work with families has shown that family members of HIV-involved persons may also be at risk for emotional difficulties and/or behavioral dysfunction (Frierson, Lippmann, & Johnson, 1987; Macklin, 1989; Walker, 1991). Direct caregivers, especially, are subject to burnout. Direct caregivers need special consideration to prevent a vicious cycle of burnout from destroying a family's stability and emotional cohesion. Caregivers, siblings, parents, children—indeed, all family members—are at risk for a wide range of psychological reactions, including anxiety, depression, anger, guilt at having been spared, fear of infection, anticipatory loss, hopelessness, and helplessness in the face of an unrelenting disease process. Educational, support, and therapy groups can be beneficial for caregivers and other family members (Greif & Porembski, 1988; Kelly & Sykes, 1989; Kreibick, 1995; Pearlin, Semple, & Turner, 1988; Walker, 1991). Oftentimes, caregivers are infected themselves. The needs of infected caregivers, siblings, children, or those with special circumstances are discussed in more detail in later sections.

Often, PWAs reside in different geographic areas from their family members. This may be especially true for gay men who have moved from their families' area to communities with large homosexual populations (e.g., San Francisco, New York City). Recognizing the difficulty people might have in traveling to an unfamiliar place to support a family member with AIDS, a residential hospitality center (Miracle House) has been established recently in at least one city (New York) for the purpose of supporting visiting family members. This center is similar to the Ronald McDonald Houses for family members of severely ill children. In Newark, a similar center has been recently established for family members of HIV-infected and symptomatic children. Therapists need to be aware of such centers and apply their special skills to the success of such endeavors.

All families carry the "unfinished business" of individual hurts, grudges, and confusion. Family therapy can provide a context for the resolution of these issues so that the family can work together collaboratively in dealing with the new challenges posed by the HIV situation. In extreme cases, the interaction of such unfinished business with the guilt or anger experienced by a PWA might lead to extrusion from the family system (often self-initiated), painful isolation, and even premature death. Stigma and shame, fear of contagion, fear of discovery, secrecy, anger at the infected person for "bringing this into the family," and myriad other powerful reactions can tear families apart. In addition, revelations regarding mode of transmission, especially if they involve sexual betrayal and/or drug use, can lead to violence, sudden breakups of marriages, or suicide attempts. Therapists must be skilled in assisting families to discuss these volatile issues in productive rather than destructive ways. Therapists also need to be skilled in assisting families to restructure themselves to reflect the new realities implicit in such revelations.

Therapy that addresses the complex issues involved in family restructuring must explore the role of family attitudes, myths, and history with regard to health and illness, death and dying, sexuality, and medical care. Family attitudes and myths that obstruct an adaptive coping process need to be revealed, examined, and opened up to change through appropriate interventions. Family history needs to be explored with regard to these attitudes and myths because prior events (including those occurring in prior generations) and the meanings attributed to them become the context for the development of family attitudes and myths. The family therapy done with Neal, a gay man dying of AIDS, illustrates these points.

As Neal's health deteriorated, a fierce battle erupted between his mother and his gay friends over Neal's decision to instruct medical personnel to employ no extraordinary life-sustaining measures. Neal's mother castigated his friends as callous and irresponsible for supporting this decision. Neal was caught in the middle, unable to get the cohesive support he needed.

Only after examining her own homophobia and the sexually repressive attitudes of her parents, could Neal's mother begin to accept the possibility of working collaboratively with her son's gay "family of choice." Only after revealing that she secretly blamed her husband's friends for his death three years earlier could she begin to consider that Neal's friends might be trusted to act sincerely and competently on his behalf.

If family members are overly anxious regarding their own risk of infection, they may not be able to play a positive role in the care of the HIV-involved person. Therefore, family members' anxiety regarding casual transmission needs to be assessed and addressed early. Similarly, certain family members may become immobilized by their own sadness or fears for the involved person. Conversely, grandiose feelings or narcissistic rescue fantasies can also obstruct or confuse the family coping process. Family therapy, multiple family therapy, and individual and/or group therapy for family members are all modalities that might allow for the expression and resolution of such feelings.

Family members' ability to play a constructive role may be hampered by a lack of information or by inaccurate information. Mental health and other health professionals can address this issue directly by providing accurate information regarding HIV/AIDS in therapy sessions or by referring family members to publications or groups that provide such information. This issue can also be addressed by developing educational programs for the general public or families of at-risk populations.

Another important focus of family-oriented work is the attribution or discovery of meaning in the pain and suffering of the family (Bateson & Goldsby, 1988; Bellemare, 1988; Boyd-Franklin, Steiner, & Boland, 1995; Sontag, 1989). It is especially important that meanings that can only lead to further pain, such as "this was God's punishment for your father's evil ways" are balanced with more inclusionary and empathic meaning statements.

Sexual Dysfunction and Safer Sex

Sexual dysfunction is a common occurrence in couples where one or both are HIV infected (Leiblum & Rosen, 1989). Sexual dysfunction may be related to a variety of intrapsychic, interpersonal, as well as physical variables, including one or more of the following: guilt or anger about oneself or one's partner having become infected; loss of desire resulting from fatigue, discomfort, fear of contagion, drug side effects; distraction and confusion caused by revelations of stigmatized sexual activity; loss of ability to experience pleasure in the face of inevitable death; diminished sexual self-image due to illness-related physical changes.

While respecting individual and cultural fears and mores, psychotherapists and educators can assist sexual partners to maintain a sex-positive approach in the practice of safer sex (Rampton, 1989). Further research and applied experimentation are needed to develop more effective methods for teaching and learning safer sex practices (Temoshok & Baum, 1990). As new methods are developed, training vehicles for disseminating knowledge and practice of these methods should be devised and emplaced. The urgent need to develop more effective safer sex educational programs cannot be overstated. It also cannot be stressed too emphatically that these interventions need to be tailored to age group, ethnicity, sexual orientation, and socioeconomic status if they are to be most effective. For example, the research of Flaskerud and Rush (1989) comparing the attitudes of African American and Latino women, indicates that prevention programs will be more effective if tailored to fit the beliefs and attitudes prevalent in different ethnic groups. Bracho de Carpio, Carpio-Cedrado, and Anderson (1990) have successfully pilot tested an AIDS education program designed for Latino families and facilitated by Latino family counselors. Belgrave and Randolph (1993) have assembled a volume of the theory and practice of AIDS prevention in the African-American community.

Children

Siblings and children are at increased risk of behavioral and emotional dysfunction. Assessments of siblings and children of HIV-involved persons should lead to appropriate treatment in a variety of modalities: individual therapy, family therapy, group therapy, support groups, play groups. Psychologists and other mental health professionals need to assist families with children at risk for becoming parentless to plan for the child' future. Often, new caretakers must be recruited. The transition must be guided skillfully. Planning for the future of soon-to-be orphaned children is not only essential for the welfare of the children but also assists the most peaceful passing of the dying parent. It is essential that dying persons be included—appropriately to their role in the family—in planning for the future of the family after they are gone. As discussed in detail in the following section, a blend of consultative and therapeutic functions is demanded of the mental health professional if this delicate work is to be successful.

INTEGRATING PSYCHOTHERAPEUTIC AND CONSULTATIVE ASPECTS

Sex and death are two of life's deepest mysteries. HIV/AIDS weaves them together in agonizing tapestries of pain and confusion, demanding of a therapist the utmost in sensitivity and skill. The therapist must be able to assess the relationship between family structure, unfinished emotional business, and family coping styles, and then work toward a salutary restructuring in a delicate way, honoring the intra- and interpersonal forces that push and pull the family in opposite directions, often simultaneously—on the one hand, resisting the pain and confusion associated with change and, on the other, yearning for change and the relief it may provide.

For family therapy with HIV/AIDS to be truly effective and lasting, the therapist must have developed process-oriented skills usually associated with the humanistic or psychodynamic approaches (e.g., tracking, eliciting, and resolving emotional trauma or conflict) as well as the capacity to serve as an expert consultant on family reorganization. Because some approaches to family therapy tend to emphasize one of these functions—psychotherapeutic or consultative—more than the other, successful family work with HIV-affected families often requires an integration of methods, orientations, and theoretical contexts of various schools (Breunlin, Schwart, & Mac Kune-Karrer, 1992). For example, before Vanessa could honor her grandchild's need to see his father (a structural issue), her anger at him would have to be honored, expressed, and put into perspective via elements of process-oriented psychotherapy. Before she would be ready to trust her daughter to act as the mother of her own son (a structural issue related to hierarchies and boundaries), unfinished business between mother and daughter relating to issues of autonomy would also have to be worked with psychotherapeutically.

The demands for such an integrative approach with HIV-affected families also imply a greater attentional and affective flexibility on the part of the therapist. In general, family therapy demands more expansive attentional capacity on the part of the therapist, simply because there are more people and interactions to attend to than in individual therapy. The role of the therapist's attentional flexibility in family work has been considered by numerous authors (Anderson & Goolishian, 1990; Hoffman, 1990; Steinglass, 1978).

The supremely highly charged emotional currents surrounding issues of sexuality and mortality require therapists who work with HIV-affected families to stretch even more in their ability to remain open, responsive, and clear thinking in such an intense atmosphere. The capacity to integrate psychotherapeutic with consultative functions as described earlier also implies an extraordinary degree of cognitive and attentional flexibility. Certain contemplative and meditative practices have been found especially effective in developing such a capacity for radically heightened attention and empathy without cognitive short circuiting or countertransferential boundary confusion. These practices and their relevance for therapist training have been discussed in detail (Rosenthal, 1990, 1992).

SPECIFIC POPULATIONS

Gay Men

Psychotherapists working with gay patients must continuously examine their attitudes toward homosexuality (Isay, 1989). Even therapists who have confronted their own homophobia need to be sensitive to the unique developmental issues faced by homosexuals growing up in a society that has generally outlawed and pathologized their lifestyle (Carl, 1990; Forstein, 1986; McWhirter & Mattison, 1984). More research and training programs are needed with reference to these developmental issues, especially as they related to the impact of HIV/AIDS on the gay community, gay couples, and a nuclear or extended family system with a gay member who is HIV involved. Research and training programs should also be expanded to address the causes and antidotes to familial and societal homophobia. While knowledge about AIDS correlates with more favorable attitudes toward AIDS and those affected by it, simply providing course work may not lead to professional, unbiased care (Green & Bobele, 1994). Contact with actual individuals affected by HIV/AIDS is more effective in reducing homonegative and AIDS-negative attitudes; thus training programs should include these populations in the ongoing clinical work.

Therapists treating HIV-involved gay men must assess when and how to involve family members, and how to decide which family to involve: family of origin, and/or family of choice. The latter may include a lover as well as close friends who support the couple and function as an extended family. When both types of families exist, as in the example of Neal described earlier, tensions can arise between the two systems, especially with regard to which is the person's primary intimate group and who makes caretaking decisions.

Many gay men have been cut off from their families of origin. Sometimes the cutoff reflects the gay man's own internalized homophobia projected onto family members. Sometimes, the family's homophobia is virulent and viewed realistically. In any case, an HIV/AIDS situation often provokes a kind of second "coming out" or an initial coming out if not done earlier.

Early treatment reflection should focus on the advisability of repairing cutoffs. For example, therapists trained in classical Bowenian family therapy—which proposes that all cutoffs are unhealthy—must become more flexible in this assessment. Whereas healing a cutoff between a gay man with HIV/AIDS and his family of origin sometimes can have extremely beneficial consequences, reconnecting a gay man already weakened by the physical and social stresses of HIV/AIDS with a family system that rigidly rejects his identity may have extremely adverse effects on his physical and emotional health (Walker, 1991).

If a gay man has an enduring, committed relationship with a lover, the therapist can validate the legitimacy of the couple by treating the couple as essentially a marital pair with respect to structural hierarchy and boundary making. In other words, the therapist should assume that the couple is the primary decision-making and responsibility system with respect to HIV/AIDS. This is particularly important in working with families of origin that have not previously validated the couple's relationship. The therapist's own recognition of the couple's relationship must precede helping the family with its recognition of the couple. If therapists cannot honor and value an intimate relationship between two men, they simply are not ready to do this clinical work. Often, working with the couple to validate and create a more cohesive, intimate relationship goes beyond laying a foundation for other therapeutic work; it becomes the essence of the therapy (Tunnell, 1994a). Because gay men may initially view straight therapists with suspicion, the development of rapport based on mutual respect and trust must be consolidated before substantive issues can be addressed.

The later therapeutic work not only involves helping the couple address the practical, day-to-day issues of coping with illness, but also helping the couple negotiate the inevitable changes in roles associated with HIV/AIDS. Role changes in one partner may elicit anxiety, anger, and depression related to dependency and loss of control. Although these issues also arise for heterosexual couples, gay men may be even more ambivalent about depending on another for care since this may elicit anxiety or shame about being too feminine or dependent (Tunnell, 1994b), a sensitivity that may have originated in early childhood interactions with fathers, brothers, and peers.

More attention must be focused at all levels of training, beginning with undergraduate psychology courses on sexual diversity and developmental issues for gay and lesbian individuals and couples. Family systems therapists need to pay particular heed, as indicated by the existence of only one book on systemic couples therapy with same-sex partners (Carl, 1990). Family institutes need to incorporate more training that focuses on gay and lesbian families and on relationships between gay men and their families of origin. Chapter 4 of this volume has discussed some of the issues that clinicians might address in working with gay and lesbian families.

Diverse treatment modalities are necessary to address the special needs of male couples with HIV/AIDS. Couples therapy must be modified in specific ways in working with same-sex couples, taking into account the diverse ways gay men define and structure coupled relationships (Tunnell, in press). Special attention must be paid to the needs of serodiscordant couples (Remien, 1994), in which one partner is HIV positive and the other is HIV negative, as well as couples in which both men are HIV negative, often having witnessed numerous illnesses and deaths in their community (Forstein, 1994). Further development is needed of family therapy models that integrate both the family of origin and the family of choice. Finally, multiple couples group therapy is a beneficial treatment modality that is now implemented at Gay Men's Health Crisis in New York City (Livingston, 1994). A particularly innovative model for multiple couples group therapy, adapted by Greenan (1994) from Gonzalez, Steinglass, and Reiss (1987), divides HIV/AIDS patients and their carepartners into subgroups for part of each 90-minute session. Forming concentric circles, the subgroup occupying the inner circle discusses its unique issues, then the outer circle reflects on what they heard.

AIDS as an Inner-City Multigenerational Disease

AIDS/HIV has affected all ethnic and demographic groups. Inner-city African American and Hispanic groups have, however, been disproportionately affected. In 1990, the AIDS mortality rate per 100,000 population was 29.3 for African American, 22.2 for Hispanic, and 8.7 for non-Hispanic Caucasian individuals (CDC, 1993). More recent statistics reveal that 24% of the children with AIDS in the United States are Latino and 54% are African American, yet these groups respectively account for 11% and 14% of the nation's children (CDC, 1994). Prevalence of HIV infection among black women was found to be 3 to 35 times greater than among white women in nine key states (Wasser et al., 1993). Those committed to working with AIDS/HIV in the inner city, therefore, must broaden their knowledge of societal and cultural factors that may play a role in the prevention and treatment of HIV illnesses. For example, Dalton (1989) has written clearly and eloquently of the interface of the racist history of our society and the responses to AIDS in the black community. The "healthy cultural suspicion"

(Boyd-Franklin, 1989; Grier & Cobbs, 1968) that many African Americans feel toward the medical profession is also evident in the denial of the impact of the AIDS epidemic in African American communities. Researchers have found that many African Americans consider HIV/AIDS to be a "white gay man's disease" (Bouknight & Bouknight, 1988; Boyd-Franklin, Steiner, & Boland, 1995; Brown et al., 1992; Dalton, 1989; Flaskerud & Rush, 1989; Mays & Cochran, 1988; Mitchell, 1990; Peterson & Marin, 1988), which results in denial among this population that injection drug use, needle sharing, prostitution, and heterosexual sex can also be risk factors (Brown et al., 1992; DiClemente, Boyer, & Morale, 1988; Mays & Cochran, 1987; Selik, Castro, & Papparoanou, 1988; Fullilove, Fullilove, Bowser, & Gross, 1990). Mandatory reporting of HIV testing would deter African Americans and Latinos from being tested (Fordyce, Sambula, & Stonebruner, 1989).

At present, few graduate programs in psychology include general courses on ethnicity, sexual diversity, or urban psychology, nor are these topics much addressed at the internship stage or in the early years of developing a professional identity and theoretical orientation. In this volume, Chapter 10 considers some of the special challenges an urban environment provides the family.

Within inner-city black and Hispanic communities, HIV and AIDS are often multigenerational family diseases demanding family systems conceptualizations in the development of effective responses (Boyd-Franklin, Steiner, & Boland, 1995). HIV and AIDS, unlike most chronic illnesses, impact several generations. Mourning the loss of children, partners, and parents takes place while the demands of raising infected and noninfected children continue. Survivors experience denial, rage, acceptance, loss, fear of further contagion and illness, and profound and ongoing sadness and grief.

Parenting often becomes interrupted, dysfunctional, or obstructed completely whether children are themselves infected or whether an adult family member carries the virus or is sick with AIDS. Infected and noninfected children of infected mothers will need to be cared for by others from the immediate kin or nonblood kin system.

For generations, a strength of African American families has been the practice by extended blood and nonblood family members (e.g., friends, neighbors, godparents, fellow parishioners) to adopt informally or "take in" children in times of trouble. Mental health professionals must be open to these and other culture-specific resources that, without such openness, might be ignored or, at worst, pathologized.

Besides family therapy, which can be an effective resource for such families to reorganize themselves in positive ways, mental health professionals can provide support and therapy groups for caretakers. Most caretakers will be women—many of them grandmothers—already overburdened by dealing with the oppression and crises that go with poverty, racism, and the other plague of the inner cities—drug abuse. These caretakers may resist asking for or receiving support, believing that a "pillar of strength" must always stand firm.

New ways of joining with and meeting the needs of these caretakers must be developed.

Therapists working with inner-city families must also accept and respect the reservoir of rage and suspicion that exists for many inner-city people as a result of generations of poverty, racism, and demoralization. Only further study and acquaintance with the lifestyles and mores of the inner city and the two cultures most represented there, Latino and African American, will yield appropriate interventions that empower black and Latino families and further liberate their resources (Barbarin, 1993; Valdez & Vargas, 1994).

Fears of casual transmission tend to be higher in the inner city. Issues of disclosure, stigma, isolation, shame, fear of rejection or attachment, and rage are heightened by secrecy. Although issues of secrecy are common to all AIDS/HIV families, they may have additional significance for many African American families. The experience of facing racism for generations has resulted in many families adopting strict privacy rules regarding family-related matters. This emphasis on privacy often translates into considerable wariness ("healthy cultural paranoia") on the part of family members who come into contact with social welfare and health professionals (Dalton, 1989).

Issues of secrecy may also translate into difficulties finding an appropriate caretaker for a child orphaned by AIDS. Therapists working with a multigenerational genogram that includes all the extended family including nonblood kin, will be better equipped to assist in the family's reorganization.

Secrecy and stigma may further obstruct families in the inner city from reaching out to potential support systems such as schools and churches. Therapists must be ready to help families deal with issues of secrecy and stigma so that they are able to connect with supportive groups. Families need help in differentiating between constructive disclosure and disclosure that could put members at risk for discrimination.

Mental health providers should also make themselves available for talks and workshops at schools and churches in the inner city to reduce stigma and discrimination. Churches need to be recognized as a source of spiritual succor for many inner city residents, especially those that may end up in caretaking roles. Therapists need to support the connection with church as a way to expand the family system and gather additional resources.

Children and Adolescents

Because of the disproportionate incidence of AIDS/HIV in the inner city, clinicians and other professionals who come into contact with inner city children presenting with behavioral or emotional problems should develop informal screening methods for assessing the likelihood that a child's psychiatric symptoms are related to the appearance of HIV/AIDS in a family system. Such symptoms may develop because the stigma/secrecy constellation prevents the family from applying its usual approaches for dealing with crises. The child knows something terrible has happened but lives in confusion and isolation regarding the event. Symptoms may also develop simply because the demands of HIV/AIDS on caretakers have resulted in neglect of a particular child.

Pediatric HIV and AIDS are largely diseases of the inner city, affecting predominantly impoverished African American and Latino families (Macklin, 1989). Whether the children are themselves infected or they are dealing with an infected family member, they have a great need to express and clarify their thoughts and feelings regarding the family situation or their own illness. Support and therapy groups that employ a variety of techniques, including storytelling, artistic expression, play, enactment, and just plain talking may provide the appropriate context and methods for a child to do this (Gomez et al., 1995; Boyd-Franklin, Steiner, & Boland, 1995). Consider the following case:

> Brian is an 8-year-old African-American boy who was referred for family therapy by his school because of disruptive activities, including fighting. His family consisted of his mother, his grandmother, and his 2-year-old sister. Brian indicated in the first session that his fights arose from other kids saying "bad things" about his mother. He looked embarrassed and refused to elaborate.
>
> The mother and grandmother appeared for the next session without Brian and told the therapist that Brian was teased by other children at school because his mother had AIDS. Brian had been perinatally infected and diagnosed at birth, although he had never been told of this, despite his being treated at a pediatric AIDS program. When the therapist explored this, the grandmother stated that his family feared the he would "blurt out" this secret in the community and that the entire family would suffer from the stigma. The therapist shared with the mother and the grandmother that it was likely that Brian already "knew" the secret on some level and was acting out because he was not able to talk about his feelings.
>
> The therapist had a number of sessions with the grandmother and the mother discussing the concerns of these caretakers in talking to Brian directly about his and his mother's disease. In a few months, they were ready to talk to Brian about his medical condition. They were surprised to discover that he suspected the truth. He was frightened and angry and felt that he could not talk to his mother and grandmother directly about this. The session was a very emotional one with all three crying, comforting, and supporting each other. Brian's relief and that of his caretakers was obvious as they left the session.

This case is very typical of the attempts by families to protect children and the family's privacy from the stigma attached to AIDS. Because of the fear associated with the illness, it is not unusual for families to deny the extent of a child's knowledge. Unfortunately, the burden of this secrecy creates additional stress for the child and family. Timing is extremely important in the therapeutic process, and it is important for clinicians to respect the family's wishes and work with them until they are ready to discuss HIV/AIDS with the child.

More research is necessary on the physical, emotional, and neurological development of children with HIV disease. Many of these children also face social and environmental handicaps or may be developmentally delayed as a result of congenital drug intoxication or addiction. As medical treatments for HIV disease improve longevity and health, these discriminations become more important.

Since symptoms may not appear for ten or more years, it is impossible to know how many adolescents in the United States are currently infected with HIV, although recent studies indicate an alarming rate of increase (Conviser, 1993). The National Pediatric HIV Resource Center recently pilot-tested prevention and service delivery programs for adolescents in seven locales around the country, taking into account the special needs and developmental factors affecting young people coping with the threat or reality of HIV (Conviser, 1993; National Pediatric HIV Resource Center, 1994).

Intravenous Drug Users

Because sharing contaminated needles has become the dominant mode of transmission for inner city adults, mental health practitioners working with AIDS/HIV in the inner city need to learn more about the psychology, family dynamics, and treatment of drug abuse (Batki et al., 1988; Faltz & Rinaldi, 1988; Patton, 1990; Stanton & Todd, 1982). Drug abuse is often a multigenerational family disease in the inner city (Boyd-Franklin, Steiner, & Boland, 1995). Therefore, therapists working with drug-related AIDS/HIV will also encounter the residue of anger, guilt, rescue fantasies, and shame that families with one or more drug-using members may have faced for years. As illustrated in the chapter's initial case example, the rage associated with knowing a loved one has been infected by a drug-using partner can be enormous, may lead to family splinterings, and must be addressed, especially if the partners have children together.

Although drug use may be the dominant cause of AIDS infection in the inner city, homosexual transmission and sexual transmission to women from infected drug-using male partners are also significant modes. Therefore, it is important for mental health professionals to study and teach about issues of gender and sexual diversity among urban ethnic groups (Boyd-Franklin, 1989; Medina, 1988). For example, the incidence of homosexuality in both black and Hispanic populations is far greater than generally acknowledged in these communities (Peterson & Marin, 1988). Moreover, the levels of shame and stigma associated with homosexual behavior are generally considered to be greater in these communities (Morales, 1990; National Task Force on AIDS Prevention, 1990).

Therapists need to recognize and increase their understanding of cultural forces, such as the Hispanic machismo ideal, which contribute to negative attitudes, secrecy, and risk behavior (New York State AIDS Institute, 1991).

Women

More study and teaching of the lives of urban women in these communities is also necessary (Boyd-Franklin, Steiner, & Boland, 1995; Eric et al., 1989; Mays & Cochran, 1988; Worth & Rodriguez, 1987). Although AIDS is currently the eighth leading cause of death among women aged 25 to 44 nationally, in New Jersey and New York, states with huge inner city populations, AIDS is the leading cause of death for women in this age group (CDC, 1991). Why is it that the levels of HIV infection and AIDS are growing fastest among inner city women? What role is played by the Hispanic ideals of machismo and marianismo (the ideal Latin woman) in the transmission of HIV and its aftermath? What beliefs about gender obstruct or promote safer sex practices and compassionate treatment in the African-American community? Most importantly, what values and beliefs about women, the poor, and persons of color, obstruct or promote a compassionate commitment on the part of the middle- and upper-class majority in this country? Research on women with HIV/AIDS has been minimal. More study is needed to improve prevention and treatment interventions for the growing number of women with HIV illness.

THERAPIST FACTOR

Therapists need to examine their own individual and family attitudes, myths, and history regarding illness, sexuality, and death to be able to work most effectively with HIV/AIDS families. Vestiges of homophobia, ethnic stereotyping, and "addictophobia" need to be explored and addressed either through education, supervision, or the therapist's own psychotherapy if the work is to be effective and not counterproductive. The lack of such examination may limit the effectiveness of psychological services through the therapist's attempts to reduce personal discomfort or avoid working with certain populations. In the worst-case scenario, it could be harmful to patients through the communication of the therapist's own fears and biases.

Mental health professionals need to develop training programs to assist their peers in this endeavor. Research into effective methods for exploring and understanding countertransference in therapy with AIDS/HIV families is also needed.

Support and therapy groups for therapists working with AIDS/HIV families are essential. In the face of the intense emotional responses and profound mysteries that the therapist working with AIDS/HIV must confront, therapists must know their own limits and seek ongoing support and comfort, as well as a forum for clarifying the personal meanings of their experiences. Indeed, any therapist working with AIDS/HIV in isolation is a prime candidate for burnout.

In addition to support and therapy groups for therapists, hot lines should be established for therapists who need more immediate feedback and/or support. Gay Men's Health Crisis in New York City already has such a hot line for its workers and volunteers.

Working with HIV/AIDS, like working with other societal plagues (homelessness, racism, poverty), can be heartbreaking. Indeed, any mental health practitioner working in these areas whose heart has not been broken must be so cut off as to be ineffective, at best. Clinicians, therefore, need to find ways to honor and deal with their own very human reactions of hopelessness and pain. Sometimes a recalibration of expectations is in order. For example, as therapists, we are clearly not in a position to offer a guarantee of longevity to our clients. We can offer significant and even profound assistance, however, in other forms, such as pain management, psychotherapeutic exploration of the meaning of these life events, as well as movement toward a more functional and loving family system.

Because working with AIDS always involves issues of life and death, it becomes essential for therapists to explore their own spiritual beliefs and avail themselves of their own spiritual resources (Rosenthal, 1990, 1992). Denial of the spiritual dimension of work with AIDS/HIV can lead to a loss of connection with the therapist's most important resource in this work—love and compassion.

POLITICAL ADVOCACY

Finally, as front-line mental health professionals in the struggle against HIV/AIDS, family practitioners can advocate for the families they work with by taking responsible political action. Individual or group lobbying of lawmakers for more drug programs, education, and job programs, and HIV/AIDS programs is one way. Working with communities to develop community-based programs sensitive to the mores and special needs of each community is another. Walker (1991) has written of the importance of developing ecosystemic models of service delivery for communities with a high incidence of HIV/AIDS. Ecosystemic models seek a harmonious blending of individual, family, and environmental factors. Walker cites Gay Men's Health Crisis and Montefiore Women's Center in New York City as examples of effective ecosystemic delivery systems.

Family practitioners can present testimony to government bodies, speak to community groups, publish clinical and research articles, develop grants for innovative programs, provide input to lawmakers' staffs, generate publicity through news articles or television appearances, and work with activist groups. In short, any activity that exposes the social disease of racism, poverty, and homophobia, and promotes an expanding commitment to healing families of the ravages of these plagues as well as the medical plague of HIV/AIDS is part of the job of mental health professionals and others interested in alleviating the suffering of these families.

REFERENCES

Anderson, H., & Goolishian, H. A. (1990). Beyond cybernetics. *Family Process, 29,* 157–163.

Barbarin, O. (Ed.). (1993). Emotional development of African American children. *The Journal of Black Psychology, 13*(4).

Bateson, M. D., & Goldsby, R. (1988). *Thinking AIDS: The social response to the biological threat.* Reading, MA: Addison-Wesley.

Batki, S. L., Sorenson, J. L., Faltz, B., & Madover, S. (1988). Psychiatric aspects of treatment of IV drug abusers with AIDS. *Hospital and Community Psychiatry, 39*(4), 439–441.

Belgrave, F. Z., & Randolph, S. M. (Eds.). (1993). Psychosocial aspects of AIDS prevention among African Americans. *The Journal of Black Psychology, 19*(2).

Bellemare, D. (1988). AIDS: The challenge to pastoral care [Special issue]. *Journal of Palliative Care, 4*(4), 58–60.

Bouknight, R. R., & Bouknight, L. G. (1988). Acquired immunodeficiency syndrome in the black community: Focusing on education and the black male. *New York State Journal of Medicine, 88,* 232–235.

Boyd-Franklin, N. (1989). *Black families in therapy: A multisystems approach.* New York: Guilford.

Boyd-Franklin, N., Steiner, G. L., & Boland, M. (Eds.). (1995). *Children, families and HIV/AIDS: Psychosocial and psychotherapeutic issues.* New York: Guilford.

Brachio de Carpio, A., Carpio-Cedrado, F. F., & Anderson, L. (1990). Hispanic families learning and teaching about AIDS: A participatory approach at the community level. *Hispanic Journal of Behavioral Sciences, 12*(2), 165–176.

Breunlin, D. C., Schwartz, R. C., & Mac Kune-Karrer, B. (1992). *Metaframeworks: Transcending the models of family therapy.* San Francisco: Jossey-Bass.

Brown, G., Mitchell, J., & Williams, S. (1992). The African-American community. In M. Stuber (Ed.), *Children and AIDS* (pp. 21–31). Washington, DC: American Psychiatric Press.

Carl, D. (1990). *Counseling same-sex couples.* New York: Norton.

Centers for Disease Control. (1990). Estimates of HIV prevalence and projected AIDS cases. *Morbidity and Mortality Weekly Report, 39,* 110–112, 117–119.

Centers for Disease Control. (1991). HIV/AIDS Surveillance: AIDS cases reported through January 1991. Atlanta, GA.

Centers for Disease Control and Prevention. (1993, February). HIV/AIDS Surveillance (Year-end edition). Atlanta, GA.

Centers for Disease Control and Prevention. (1994, November). HIV/AIDS Surveillance Report (Mid-year edition). Atlanta, GA.

Centers for Disease Control and Prevention. (1995, January). HIV/AIDS Surveillance Report (Year-end edition). Atlanta, GA.

Cohen, P. T., Sande, M. A., & Volberding, P. A. (Eds.). (1990). *The AIDS knowledge base.* Waltham, MA: The Medical Publishing Group.

Conviser, R. (1993). *Case studies of adolescent-focused HIV prevention and service delivery programs.* Newark, NJ: National Pediatric HIV Resource Center.

Dalton, H. L. (1989). AIDS in blackface. *Daedalus, 118*(3), 205–227.

DiClemente, R. J., Boyer, C. B., & Morales, E. S. (1988). Minorities and AIDS: Knowledge, attitudes and misconceptions among black and latino adolescents. *American Journal of Public Health, 78,* 55–57.

Eric, K., Drucker, E., Worth, D., Chabon, B., Pivnick, A., & Cochrane, K. (1989). *The Woman's Center: A model peer support program for high risk IV drug and crack using women in the Bronx.* Paper presented at the Fifth International AIDS Conference, Montreal, Canada.

Faltz, B., & Rinaldi, J. (1988). *AIDS and substance abuse.* San Francisco: University of California AIDS Health Project.

Flaskerud, J. H., & Rush, C. E. (1989). AIDS and traditional health beliefs and practices of Black women. *Nursing Research, 38*(4), 210–215.

Forstein, M. (1986). Psychodynamic psychotherapy with gay male couples. In T. S. Stein & C. J. Cohen (Eds.), *Contemporary perspectives on psychotherapy with lesbians and gay men.* New York: Plenum.

Forstein, M. (1994). Psychotherapy with gay male couples: Loving in the time of AIDS. In S. A. Cadwell, R. A. Burnham, Jr., & M. Forstein (Eds.), *Therapists on the front line: Psychotherapy with gay men in the age of AIDS.* Washington, DC: American Psychiatric Press.

Frierson, R. L., Lippmann, S. B., & Johnson, J. (1987). AIDS: Psychological stresses on the family. *Psychosomatics, 28*(2), 65–68.

Fullilove, R. E., Fullilove, M. T., Bowser, B. P., & Gross, S. A. (1990). Risk of sexually transmitted disease among black adolescent crack users in Oakland and San Francisco, California. *Journal of the American Medical Association, 263,* 851–855.

Gomez, K., Haiken, H., & Lewis, S. (1995). HIV children's support groups. In N. Boyd-Franklin, G. L. Steiner, & M. Boland (Eds.), *Children, families and AIDS/HIV: Psychosocial and psychotherapeutic issues.* New York: Guilford.

Gonzales, S., Steinglass, P., & Reiss, D. (1987). *Family-centered interventions for people with chronic disabilities.* Washington, DC: Department of Psychiatry and Behavioral Sciences, George Washington University Medical Center.

Green, S. K., & Bobele, M. (1994). Family therapists' response to AIDS: An examination of attitudes, knowledge, and contact. *Journal of Marital and Family Therapy, 20,* 349–367.

Greenan, D. E. (1994). *Family-centered groups: A clinical study of the design and implementation of multiple family structured groups for gay men with human immunodeficiency virus.* Unpublished doctoral dissertation, Teachers College, Columbia University, New York, NY.

Grief, G. L., & Porembski, E. (1988). AIDS and significant others: Indications from preliminary exploration of needs. *Health and Social Work, 13,* 259–265.

Grier, W., & Cobbs, P. (1968). *Black rage.* New York: Basic Books.

Hoffman, L. (1990). Constructing realities: An art of lenses. *Family Process, 29,* 1–12.

Isay, R. A. (1989). *Being homosexual.* New York: Avon Books.

Kelly, J., & Sykes, P. (1989). Helping the helpers: A support group for family members of persons with AIDS. *Social Work, 34,* 239–242.

Kreibick, T. (1995). Therapeutic intervention: Caregiver groups. In N. Boyd-Franklin, G. L. Steiner, & M. Boland (Eds.), *Children, families, and AIDS/HIV: Psychosocial and psychotherapeutic issues.* New York: Guilford.

Leiblum, S. R., & Rosen, R. C. (Eds.). (1989). Principles and practice of sex therapy: Update for the 1990s (2nd ed.). New York: Guilford.

Livingston, D. (1994). Group counseling for gay couples coping with AIDS. In W. Odets & M. Shernoff (Eds.), *The second decade of AIDS: A mental health handbook.* New York: Hatherleigh.

Macklin, E. (Ed.). (1989). *AIDS and families.* New York: Haworth.

Mays, V. M., & Cochran, S. D. (1988). Issues in the perception of AIDS risk and risk reduction activities by black and Hispanic/Latino women. *American Psychologist, 43*(11), 949–957.

McWhirter, D., & Mattison, A. (1984). *The male couple.* New York: Prentice-Hall.

Medina, C. (1988). Latino culture and sex education. *SIECUS Report, XV*(3), 1–4.

Mitchell, A. (1990, November). AIDS: We are not immune. *Emerge,* 30–44.

Morales, E. (1990). HIV infection and Hispanic gay and bisexual men. *Hispanic Journal of Behavioral Sciences, 12*(2), 212–222.

National Pediatric HIV Resource Center. (1994). Proceedings Document from the National Workshop on HIV and Adolescents, March 17, 1993. Newark, NJ: National Pediatric HIV Resource Center.

National Task Force on AIDS Prevention. (1990). *National HIV research study of Black men: A study of AIDS knowledge, attitudes and risk behaviors for HIV infection among Black males who have sex with other men* (pp. 237–294).

New York State AIDS Institute. (1991). *Cultural factors among Hispanics: Perception and prevention of HIV infection.* Albany, NY: New York State AIDS Institute.

Patton, C. (1990). *Inventing AIDS.* New York: Routledge & Kegan Paul.

Pearlin, L. I., Semple, S., & Turner, H. (1988). Stress of AIDS caregiving: A preliminary overview of the issues. *Death Studies, 12,* 501–547.

Peterson, J. L., & Marin, G. (1988). Issues on prevention of AIDS among black and Hispanic men [Special issue]. *American Psychologist, 43*(11), 871–877.

Rampton, D. (1989). Quoted in L. Segal, Lessons from the past: Feminism, sexual politics and the challenge of AIDS. In S. Watney (Ed.), *Taking liberties* (pp. 133–146). London: Serpents Tail.

Remien, R. (1994). *Sexuality and intimacy among serodiscordant male couples.* Paper presented at the American Psychological Association, Los Angeles, CA.

Rosenthal, J. M. (1990, September–October). The Meditative Therapist. *The Family Therapy Networker.*

Rosenthal, J. M. (1992). The Bodhi-Therapist. *Journal of Couple Therapy, 3*(1), 27–50.

Selik, R. M., Castro, K. G., & Papparoanou, M. (1988). Racial/ethnic differences in the risk of AIDS in the United States. *American Journal of Public Health, 78,* 1539–1545.

Sontag, S. (1989). *AIDS and its metaphors.* New York: Farrar Straus & Giroux.

Stanton, M. D., & Todd, T. (1982). *The family therapy of drug abuse and addiction.* New York: Guilford.

Steinglass, P. (1978). Conceptualization of marriage from a systems theory perspective. In T. J. Paolino & B. S. McCready (Eds.), *Marriage and marital therapy: Psychoanalytic, behavioral and systems theory* (pp. 298–365). New York: Brunner-Mazel.

Temoshok, L., & Baum, A. (Eds.). (1990). Psychosocial perspectives on AIDS: Etiology, prevention and treatment. Hillsdale, NJ: Lawrence Erlbaum.

Tunnell, G. (1994a). *Gay male couples and HIV/AIDS: A model for treatment.* Workshop presented at the American Association for Marriage and Family Therapy, Chicago, IL.

Tunnell, G. (1994b). Special issues in group psychotherapy for gay men with AIDS. In S. A. Cadwell, R. A. Burnham, Jr., & M. Forstein (Eds.), *Therapists on the front line: Psychotherapy with gay men in the age of AIDS*. Washington, DC: American Psychiatric Press.

Tunnell, G. (in press). Couples therapy with gay men: The task of "joining." In M. de Nicholi, M. Andolfi, & C. Angelo (Eds.), *Feelings and systems*. Milan, Italy: Cortina.

Valdez, D. M., & Varga, L. A. (Eds.). (1994). Treatment issues with Hispanic children. *Hispanic Journal of Behavioral Sciences, 16*(1).

Walker, G. (1991). *In the midst of winter*. New York: Norton.

Wasser, et al. (1993). Urban-non-urban distribution of HIV infection in childbearing women in the United States. *Journal of Acquired Immune Deficiencies, 6,* 1035–1042.

Worth, D., & Rodriguez, R. (1987, January/February). Latino women and AIDS. *SIECUS Report,* 5–7.

Zich, J., & Temoshok, L. (1987). Perceptions of social support in men with AIDS and ARC: Relationships with distress and hardiness [Special issue]. *Journal of Applied Social Psychology, 17*(3), 193–215.

CHAPTER 14

When Addictions Affect the Family

RONALD D. WYNNE, BARBARA S. McCRADY, CHRISTOPHER W. KAHLER,
HOWARD A. LIDDLE, RUTH BAUGHER PALMER, LAWRENCE K. HORBERG,
and STEPHEN E. SCHLESINGER

In the past decade, American society increasingly has become concerned about alcohol and drug abuse. The U.S. government launched the "war on drugs," augmented federal efforts to decrease the supply of drugs entering the country, and increased legal sanctions against those selling drugs. Concern about drugs has affected the private sector, and drug testing in the workplace has become a lucrative industry. Attempts to control the negative effects of alcohol and drug consumption have also increased, with more severe penalties for driving while intoxicated, expansion of employee assistance programs (EAPs) and student assistance programs (counseling programs, similar to EAPs, to help troubled students), and creation of citizen-led groups such as Mothers Against Drunk Driving (MADD). Federal funding for and interest in prevention programs has increased as well, with particular emphasis on programs for adolescents.

Governmental and industry attention to the impact of drug and alcohol abuse on family functioning has been minimal, however. By contrast, the clinical community is giving increasing attention to the families of drug and alcohol users. A variety of treatment and prevention approaches have been advanced that focus on families, and there has been increasing research on the family's role in addiction and the impact of addiction on the family.

This chapter will discuss the impact of alcohol and drug abuse on family functioning, describe models for conceptualizing and treating the problems these families experience, and suggest directions family clinicians might take to improve research and practice in this field.

DEFINING ADDICTIVE BEHAVIORS

A variety of behaviors—alcohol and drug use, gambling, over-and undereating, sexual behavior, exercise—may be called addictive behaviors. In this chapter, we will focus on psychoactive substance use disorders, resulting from excessive use of a variety of psychoactive substances—alcohol, opiates, barbiturates, cocaine, tranquilizers, hallucinogens, marijuana, amphetamines, inhalants, and nicotine.

At the individual level, two major diagnoses can be established: psychoactive substance *abuse* or substance *dependence.* Criteria for diagnosis are virtually identical across substances, although certain criteria may not apply to all substances. To be diagnosed as *dependent* on a psychoactive substance, an individual must meet at least three of seven criteria concerning behavior in the past year that relate to inability to abstain or loss of control, physical tolerance, withdrawal, interference of the substance with daily functioning, or continuing to use the substance despite negative physical or psychological consequences (American Psychiatric Association [APA], 1994). *Dependence* is defined as mild, moderate, or severe, depending on the number of criteria met. *Psychoactive substance abuse* (of a particular substance) is diagnosed only if a person has never been diagnosed as dependent on that substance, and if the person meets any one of four criteria: use resulting in failure to fulfill social roles; use in a manner that creates the potential for harm (such as drinking and driving); use that leads to repeated legal problems; or use that continues despite known negative social or interpersonal consequences.

The *Diagnostic and Statistical Manual of Mental Disorders* (DSM-IV; APA, 1994) diagnostic schema is individual-specific and does not take into consideration the effects of family functioning or of other family members. Further, the literature uses varied terminology for "abusers" and "dependents" such as users, substance abusers, alcoholics, persons with alcohol/drug problems, addicts, or drinkers. This variety merely reflects the existing imprecision in the diagnostic domain.

RESEARCH ON THE IMPACT OF SUBSTANCE ABUSE ON FAMILIES

Statistical and Demographic Data

Prevalence

Psychoactive substance abuse affects a vast number of Americans both directly and indirectly. It is estimated that in 1988, 15.3 million people in the United States met criteria for alcohol abuse, alcohol dependence, or both, as determined from the precursor diagnostic manual to the DSM-IV (National Institute on Alcohol Abuse and Alcoholism [NIAAA], 1993). Prevalence rates of alcoholism are significantly higher for males than for females, with estimated lifetime prevalence rates of 23.8 percent for males and 4.6 percent for females and 1-year prevalence rates of 11.9 and 2.2 percent respectively. Prevalence *may* be increasing in the overall population and faster among females than males (NIAAA, 1993).

The United States has the highest rate of adolescent drug abuse among the world's industrialized nations (Falco, 1988), and substance abuse is increasing in the early adolescent population (Johnston, O'Malley, & Bachman, 1989).

The major national surveys likely underestimate the prevalence of problems among adolescents because of their reliance on data from students or youth over the age of 12 residing in a household. They do *not* include chronic absentees; high school dropouts; or transient, runaway, or homeless youth—all populations at extreme risk for drug abuse problems (Dryfoos, 1990). Severity of drug use among urban minority youth may be especially underestimated because until recently this population has been largely overlooked in prevalence and intervention studies. This is especially unfortunate since there is evidence that inner-city, minority adolescents have limited access to early-intervention programs and are likely to participate in mandated rather than voluntary treatment, which often takes on a punitive rather than a supportive connotation (Thompson & Simmons-Cooper, 1988).

Family Consequences

It is also clear that the effects of alcoholism and other drug abuse reach beyond the individual users, to their families. It has been estimated that 23% of Americans have a first-degree blood relative who is alcoholic (Harford, 1992). Further, the vast majority of substance abusers live in family settings—with parents, siblings, or spouses. It is estimated that fewer than 5% of alcoholics live by themselves (Steinglass, Bennett, Wolin, & Reiss, 1987).

Because alcoholism is most prevalent from ages 18 to 44, many individuals are actively alcoholic at the time in their lives when they would typically be married and raising children. Further, although alcoholics are no less likely than nonalcoholics to get married,their divorce rate is about four times higher than that of the total population (Paolino, McCrady, & Diamond, 1978).

Violence and Abuse

Many studies show a very strong association between substance use and violence both inside and outside the home. No causal relationship between substance abuse and violence has been established. It may be that substance abuse and violent behavior co-occur because they stem from a common underlying psychological mechanism, or there may be a direct causal link. To date, limited conceptual models and problems with research designs, methodologies, and the samples used have limited the power of research to explain the observed correlations (Leonard & Jacob, 1988; Martin, 1992; Sher, 1991).

Martin's (1992) literature review reports that alcohol may be involved in 33% to 50% of all homicides, 25% to 50% of serious assaults, 25% to 50% of wife beatings, and more than 25% of all rapes. Estimates of alcoholism in the husbands of abused wives range from 35% to 93% (Leonard & Jacob, 1988). Alcohol use is related to partner aggression even in couples about to be married (Arias & O'Leary, 1988).

Rates of parental alcoholism in families with reported child abuse have ranged from 0% to 92% (Sher, 1991). Estimates of the incidence of incest and alcoholism also vary, with two reviews of the literature reporting alcohol problems in 20% to 75% of incestuous fathers (Hurley, 1991; Miller, 1990). Although the exact nature of the relationship between alcoholism, incest, and child abuse is not yet known, a history of physical and sexual abuse is a risk factor for future illicit drug use, adult alcoholism, juvenile delinquency, and adult criminality (Miller, 1990).

Impact on Physical and Psychological Health

Health Care Costs

Heavy alcohol and other drug use have significant medical consequences for both the individual and for family functioning. Not only are alcoholics susceptible to a wide range of traumas and diseases, but their families also utilize health care services at higher rates than the population as a whole (Langenbucher, McCrady, Brick, & Esterly, 1994). In a 4-year comprehensive study of the employees of a large corporation, dependents of addicts consumed $8,400 more in medical services than expected, while dependents of mental health patients consumed $11,000 more than expected (McDonnell Douglas Corporation & Alexander Consulting Group, 1989).

Alcohol use during pregnancy can have serious health consequences for the fetus and has been the only factor associated with Fetal Alcohol Syndrome which is now "the leading known environmental cause of mental retardation in the Western World" (NIAAA, 1993, p. 923).

Impact on Spouses or Partners

Spouses of alcoholics are more likely to experience psychological or physical problems than spouses of nonalcoholics (Moos, Finney, & Gamble, 1982). Depression, anxiety, and psychophysiological symptoms are common, and are likely indicators of the stress under which these spouses live (Coleman, 1987). The decreased functioning of the drinking or drug-using family member may place increased role responsibilities on other family members, often leading to role overload for the nonalcoholic partner, who assumes increased responsibility for finances, household management, child rearing, and the emotional life of the family.The relationship between alcoholism and spouse functioning is not at all straightforward, however. Jacob and Leonard (1988) described two types of alcoholics whose drinking patterns have very different impacts on family functioning. Spouses of steady drinkers who drink primarily in their homes, report greater relationship satisfaction when their partners are drinking than when sober, and observational studies suggest that these couples' communication is more effective when the alcoholic is drinking than when sober. In contrast, spouses of episodic drinkers who drink primarily outside their homes, report greater relationship distress, and communication in such couples becomes less effective when the alcoholic is drinking.

Impact on Children and Adolescents

Children growing up with an alcoholic parent experience a variety of psychological, behavioral and school problems (Moos & Billings, 1982), and are at increased risk for developing drinking problems themselves (Cloninger, Bohman, & Sigvardsson, 1981).

The psychological and developmental sequelae for young people who are themselves abusers are particularly tragic. Drugs retard social and emotional growth by preventing normal problem-solving experiences and their concomitant skill development. These youngsters "emerge from adolescence without having experienced it, without having addressed its tasks, without being able to carry into adulthood the legacy of conflicts resolved, obstacles overcome, fears conquered, social skills mastered, values defined, and relationships established" (Milman, Bennett, & Hanson, 1983, p. 53). Consequences of this disrupted development include impaired interpersonal relationships and school failure, the aftermath of which is carried into adulthood. Adolescent drug users bypass the typical maturational sequence of school, work, and family formation, and make the transition prematurely into adult roles of jobs and family without the necessary skills for success in such tasks.

THEORETICAL MODELS OF ADDICTIONS AND FAMILY FUNCTIONING

Behavioral/Coping Models

Behavioral models draw on the literatures of stress, coping, and problem behavior; of social learning; of functional analysis; and of family interactional models to provide a comprehensive conceptualization of the relationships between substance use and family functioning (Schlesinger, 1988).

Stress and coping models suggest that families of substance abusers are living in a chronically stressful environment, characterized by unpredictability, emotional lability, lack of economic and emotional resources, and a high frequency of negative life events. Family members attempt to cope with this stressful behavior as best they can, but they may use a variety of ineffective coping strategies, such as avoidance or emotional withdrawal when other coping strategies are ineffective. Research on wives of alcoholics has suggested that they show significant levels of emotional distress when their partner is drinking, and that this emotional distress decreases and is comparable to that of women married to men without alcohol problems if the husband recovers from his drinking problem (Moos, Finney, & Gamble, 1982). Thus, behavioral models assume that partners and families of substance abusers are in a stressful environment and typically lack the skills needed to cope effectively with that environment.

Social learning models view substance abuse as socially learned and purposeful behavior (Rhodes & Jason, 1988). There are external antecedents that have a lawful relationship to substance use, through repeated pairings with positive or negative reinforcement, or through the anticipation of reinforcement. These antecedents may be individual, familial, or related to other interpersonal systems (e.g., friends, co-workers). The model assumes that thinking and emotional states mediate the relationship between external antecedents and drug-using behavior, and that expectancies about the reinforcing value of substances play an important role in determining subsequent drug use behavior. The model also assumes that substance use is maintained by its consequences, and that these consequences may be at a physiological, psychological, or interpersonal level.

Family Antecedents

Alcohol or drug use may be integral to the lives of some families; alcohol and other drugs may be available in the home, and the addicted person may be exposed to a variety of cues for use when other family members are drinking or using drugs. Where alcohol or drugs are not central to the family, family members may engage in a variety of attempts to influence the user, such as nagging him or her to stop, or attempting to control the availability of alcohol or drugs through control of finances or the liquor supply. Resentment or anger at these aversive control strategies may become cues for the person to continue the substance abuse. Families with alcohol or drug problems also, typically, have communication and problem-solving deficits. Consequently, marital, sexual, financial, and child-rearing problems develop and intensify over time (Coleman, 1987). Such problems may also serve as cues for further substance abuse as the user attempts to cope by avoiding these difficult situations or changing negative feelings associated with them.

Family Consequences

Families respond to drug use in a variety of ways. These responses are sometimes called "enabling." Enabling is the degree to which family members support or reinforce addictive behavior and/or the extent to which they fail to encourage or reinforce healthy patterns that are incompatible with addictive behavior. Family actions support addictive behavior to the extent that they buffer its negative consequences, provide positive consequences for such behavior, or alter the addict's environment to make the behavior possible. Family "support" can be in the form of material assistance, effort, companionship, or confirmation and approval of the addict. Enabling often continues despite family members' awareness that the behavior may be counterproductive.

Families high in enabling tend to provide material support that makes addictive behavior possible, to spend time with addicted family members when they are engaging in the addictive behavior, to expend effort to help reduce the painful consequences of such behavior, and/or to hide disapproval of the behavior and its effects. They are slow to respond warmly and positively when the addict is committed to recovery and appears to be doing well. These family members may fail to acknowledge beneficial changes and withhold support for healthy behavior (i.e., confirmation). Family members may also hold grudges and fail to work out their differences after recovery is well underway, withholding companionship.

Families low in enabling tend to withhold material support that makes addictive behavior possible, avoid spending time with family members who engage in addictive behavior, refuse to expend effort to help reduce the painful consequences of addictive behavior, show disapproval of such behavior and its effects, and are quick to respond warmly and positively when the addict is committed to recovery and appears to be doing well. These families are likely to encourage healthy patterns when—during times the addict is doing "well" and committed to making progress—they respond warmly, supportively, and help each other achieve their goals.

Families may also respond negatively to substance use by withdrawing attention or expressing negative comments about the addictive behavior. These negative responses usually do not result in a decrease in drinking. Instead, they are likely to have two undesired effects. First, the user may avoid interactions with the family or try to hide the use. In some families, hiding leads to a pattern of interactions characterized by avoidance of negative interactions and lying by the user, and hypervigilance on the part of the spouse or other family member. Second, negative consequences from family members often serve as cues to further use, thus maintaining a complex circular interaction between the use and family interactions. When family members refuse to pitch in and participate in the recovering addict's life, they withhold effort and material assistance that helps support progress.

With adolescent substance abusers, additional behavioral principles have been implicated. Family modeling of drug use is key, with parental use consistently shown to influence children's decisions regarding drug use (e.g., Huba & Bentler, 1980). Also important are perceived parental attitudes toward drug use. Adolescents who perceive their parents as having permissive views about drug abuse are more likely to use drugs than those who perceive their parents as holding nonpermissive views (McDermott, 1984).

Family management strategies have also been linked to adolescent substance abuse (Glynn & Haenlein, 1988). Specifically, parents appear to shape prosocial attitudes and behavior (and thus deter substance use) when they make clear behavioral expectations (such as demands for maturity and consistent monitoring of behavior) and implement consequences in a nonpunitive way (Baumrind, 1991). Conversely, discipline and supervision at either extreme (harsh, autocratic, intrusive or permissive, neglectful) have been linked with adolescent drug use. Patterson, Reid, and Dishion (1992) describe a typical scenario:

> A parent who is continually defeated in face-to-face discipline confrontations with a child will begin to feel there is no way to control the child's behavior. Eventually, the parent will stop monitoring what the child is doing. When the child's behavior is no longer being monitored by parents and teachers, the stage is set for learning about clandestine acts such as stealing, lying, truancy, experimenting with drugs, and spending time with antisocial peers. (p. 29)

Family Systems Models

Family systems models (e.g., Steinglass, Bennett, Wolin, & Reiss, 1987) also stress the reciprocal interactions between substance use and family functioning.

Family systems perspectives have incorporated many core concepts of family systems theory into models of the alcoholic or drug-abusing family system. Steinglass et al. (1987) posit that all families obey the general laws of all systems, including organization, homeostasis, circular causality of events, and feedback. Alcoholism or drug abuse is an organizing principle for some families, and the presence or absence of the drug is the most important variable defining interactional behavior. Steinglass et al.'s (1987) research on the functioning of alcoholic families has found that they have characteristically different patterns of interaction, depending on whether the alcoholic is abstinent, drinking, or in an unstable state of transition from drinking to abstinence or vice versa. Drinking families and unstable, transitional families tend to have the most rigid patterns of behavior, whereas stable, abstinent families have the most flexible patterns of interaction. In earlier work, Davis and his colleagues suggested that alcohol provides "adaptive" consequences to the family, allowing for the expression of certain roles or affects not otherwise expressed within the family (Davis, Berenson, Steinglass, & Davis, 1974).

Other family systems researchers have focused on the intergenerational transmission of alcoholism (e.g., Wolin, Bennett, & Noonan, 1979). Wolin et al. have studied the degree to which alcoholism disrupts the family's rituals—the predictable, repetitive events that define the life of the family (e.g., celebration of holidays, vacations). Studies of family rituals suggest that alcoholism is least likely to be transmitted across generations in families that are able to maintain their rituals intact, and most likely to be transmitted in families for whom rituals are most disrupted.

Thus, family systems models focus on the role that alcohol or drug use plays in the overall functioning of the family. These models are most concerned with questions such as:

- What role does the substance play in maintaining the homeostasis of the family?
- To what degree has the family's functioning been modified by the presence of substance abuse in the family?
- What adaptive consequences does the family obtain from the substance use?
- What roles do family members enact in this family?
- How rigid are the boundaries between generations in this family?
- How rigid are the boundaries between the family and other social systems?
- How is the rigidity of these boundaries related to the substance use?

HOW FAMILY CLINICIANS ARE DEALING WITH ADDICTIONS

The quality and extent of research on alcohol and drug treatment and prevention approaches is varied. In general, behavioral approaches have been subjected to more stringent experimental tests than have family systems approaches or programs following the "disease model" (e.g., with a strong 12-step orientation). A fairly robust alcohol treatment literature supports several conclusions: (a) that treatment is generally more effective than no treatment; (b) that spouse and family involvement is associated with improved treatment outcomes; (c) that behavioral self-control and social skills training are effective interventions; and (d) that for certain clients, brief interventions are effective (Institute of Medicine, 1990a). Studies of treatment for adolescent drug abuse are few, but some encouraging results have been found (Liddle & Dakof, in press). Most promising are those studies that have tested theory-driven models for the prevention and treatment of adolescent substance abuse.

Both general addictions treatment (Spear & Mason, 1991) and alcoholism treatment in particular (Luckey, 1987) have been associated with substantial long-term decreases in health-care utilization for all members of the alcoholic family. As an example, the McDonnell Douglas study described previously illustrates the tremendous cost savings that result from insisting on family participation in substance abuse treatment. Overall health care cost reductions for chemically dependent employees amounted to an average of $7,370 over the course of the study, while average reductions for their families amounted to $4,400. Cost reductions for employees with mental health problems amounted to an average of $2,400, while reductions for their family members averaged $6,800 (McDonnell Douglas Corporation & Alexander Consulting Group, 1988).

In this section, we examine different treatment/prevention efforts including some promising new attempts to integrate behavioral-coping and family systems models. We also discuss "disease model" programs such as Al-Anon that target family factors.

Behavioral/Coping Models

Behavioral models include interventions at multiple levels—with the individual, the spouse, the marital or intimate relationship, the larger family, and other social systems in which the substance abuser is involved (see McCrady & Epstein, in press, for a more thorough accounting of this model). Implicit in the model is the need for a detailed assessment to determine the primary factors contributing to the maintenance of the substance use; the skills and deficits of the individual, the couple, and the family; and the sources of motivation to change (potential reinforcers that could maintain changes in drug use behavior). In this domain, interventions are targeted not only at the individual drug abuser but also the ecological variables that influence substance abuse.

Individual Level Interventions

Here, behavioral treatment focuses on the client's motivation to change. The behavior therapist may help the client assess reinforcers for substance use, reinforcers for decreased use or abstinence, and negative consequences of use and abstinence. Assessment of the relative strength of incentives for continuing to use and for changing using behavior provides an incentive framework for the rest of the therapy. A number of other strategies are also employed to enhance motivation to change. Teaching coping skills to deal with substance-related situations is a second important individual intervention. Skills may include self-management planning, stimulus control, drink refusal, or self-monitoring of drinking and/or drug-using impulses. Teaching behavioral and cognitive coping skills, individually tailored to situations that are the most common antecedents to use, is a third type of individually focused intervention, and includes assertiveness, cognitive restructuring, relaxation, lifestyle balance, and recreational activities.

In the specific domain of adolescent substance abuse treatment, several skills-based strategies have been tested that seek to enhance the social coping skills of youth thus offsetting the pressures to use drugs and providing alternative ways to establish effective interpersonal relationships (Botvin, Baker, Dusenbury, Tortu, & Botvin, 1990). Generic social and coping skills are targeted as well as domain-specific skills, knowledge and attitudes, and expectations about drugs. These models have demonstrated significant reductions in the use of one or more substances (Rhodes & Jason, 1988).

Family Interventions

A second set of interventions revolves around the coping behaviors of the partner. Behavioral models suggest that the family needs to learn a variety of coping skills to deal with drug use and abstinence. An individualized assessment of family behaviors that may either cue substance use or maintain it is essential. Spouse coping skills might include new ways to discuss using and using situations, new responses to the partner's using and substance-related behavior, or individual skills to enhance his or her own individual functioning.

Behavioral models also focus on the interactions within the family, around both the substance and other issues. In the alcoholism-treatment field, alcohol-focused couples' interventions introduce alcohol-related topics as a vehicle to discuss communication and problem-solving skills. How the couple could manage in a situation where alcohol is present, whether or not they will keep alcohol in the house, how the partner could assist the drinker in dealing with impulses to drink, or what the couple will tell family and friends about the alcoholic's treatment are all relevant issues that the couple must face in dealing with the drinking. By exploring these subjects together, the couple learns basic communication skills. Additionally, the model suggests many alcoholic couples need to learn general communication and problem-solving skills that will decrease marital conflicts that may cue substance use and increase the rate of positive exchanges. When appropriate, the treatment also incorporates general reciprocity enhancement interventions to increase the overall reward value of the relationship.

Research on behavioral couples approaches to alcoholism treatment has reported fairly consistent results. Spouse-involved treatment is associated with lower rates of treatment dropouts and better treatment compliance than individual-only treatment. Focusing on communication and problem solving appears to improve relationship satisfaction and stability, and to be associated with a pattern of improved coping with alcohol over time (McCrady, 1989; McCrady, Stout, Noel, Abrams, & Nelson, 1991). Behavioral marital therapy and a commitment to abstinence have been found to reduce the incidence of violence between alcoholic husbands and their wives. Adding relapse prevention techniques to the treatment has further beneficial effects (O'Farrell, Choquette, Cutter, Brown, & McCourt, 1993).

Social System Interventions

A third set of interventions focuses on other social systems in which the drug user and/or their partners are currently or potentially involved. Clients are helped to identify interpersonal situations in which they are likely to drink or use heavily, and are also helped to identify potential social situations and people who would be supportive of abstinence or decreased drinking or drug use. Social skills such as drink refusal or general assertiveness may be taught. Additionally, some clients are encouraged to become involved with Alcoholics Anonymous, Narcotics Anonymous, or other 12-step programs. Among other possible benefits, these 12-step programs provide a strong social support network for abstinence, provide opportunities to meet nonusers whose own struggles can serve as role models, and provide a set of time-structuring activities that are incompatible with drinking and other substance abuse.

Finally, the model includes techniques to enhance generalization to the natural environment and the maintenance of new behaviors. Homework assignments, teaching clients how to anticipate high-risk situations, and planned follow-up treatment sessions are examples of such techniques.

Family Systems Models

Family systems models shift the focus of treatment from the individual within the family to the functioning of the family as a whole. Clinicians differ in the degree to which they focus on the presenting problem (alcohol or drug abuse) or the underlying dynamics of the family system.

Although some family therapists focus almost exclusively on systemic issues, others (e.g., Zweben & Pearlman, 1983) suggest that such an approach frustrates and confuses the family, and may lead to premature termination of the treatment. They emphasize that the initial task of the therapy is to help a couple or family deal with the drinking from a collaborative and interactional, rather than individual perspective. In their model, every treatment session begins with a review of the drinking, includes a restatement of the rationale for spouse-involved treatment, and makes explicit attempts to link the drinking with the couple's interactional functioning.

Systemic therapy varies depending on the theoretical orientation of the therapist. Treatment may focus on improving communication, improving complementarity in family roles, or removing the alcoholic from the role of "identified patient." The most ambitious family therapy treatment project for alcoholism to date (Steinglass et al., 1987) provided joint hospital treatment to alcoholics and their partners, opportunities to consume alcohol and learn more about the role that alcohol played in their relationships, and feedback about interactional behavior when drinking and sober.

Other research evaluating the effectiveness of family systems approaches to alcoholism treatment is limited primarily to descriptive studies. One well-controlled study (Zweben, Pearlman, & Li, 1988) found no differences in outcome between one session of advice and an eight-session marital systems treatment program.

Adolescent family models have focused primarily on treatment. However, it is odd that families have seldom been included in prevention efforts, given the influence families have on adolescent behavior, including substance abuse. Moreover, Bry (1988) found that when families are included in prevention programs, risk factors can be reduced, family management practices can be improved, and early signs of substance abuse problems can be reversed. In fact, some researchers conclude that when it is combined with other prevention targets, family involvement is the most successful means of drug abuse prevention (Dishion, Reid, & Patterson, 1988).

As the research linking family processes and adolescent substance abuse grows, intervention studies have been initiated that target family factors in treatment. Structural and strategic family therapy techniques have been among the most frequent interventions with adolescent substance abusers and their families (Szapocznik, Kurtines, Foote, & Perez-Vidal, 1983; Szapocznik et al., 1988). Szapocznik et al. (1983) compared conjoint structural-strategic family therapy (CFT) with one-person family therapy (OPFT) in treating adolescent substance abuse. Results indicated that both treatments were highly effective and demonstrated that it is possible to change family interactions even when the whole family is not present. Thus, this model proves promising in addressing the extensive problem of getting families to come to treatment.

Involving family members in the task of resolving their problems may not be east, however, even though the evidence may be compelling that it is appropriate and helpful. Questions have been raised about the efficacy of involving the family in treatment, though recent reviews have been supportive of family involvement (see, e.g., Institute of Medicine, 1990b, pp. 83–84). The active ingredients of effective family treatment remain to be established.

Integrative Models: Family Systems Combined with Behavioral Interventions

One program of research (Dishion, Reid, & Patterson, 1988) has implemented social learning principles within a family treatment approach that specifically targets parent management practices. They have articulated four empirically derived targets for effective family intervention: (a) parent(s) monitoring practices, (b) adolescent's peer associates, (c) parent(s) modeling of drug use, and

(d) adolescent's level of skills and antisocial behavior . Two approaches to intervening on these variables that represent the major outpatient intervention modalities in the field of adolescent drug use are parent training and peer training intervention. Parent training is based on social learning principles of child management. Based on 20 years of treating families with antisocial children, researchers at the Oregon Social Learning Center have found promising results of parent management techniques with a variety of antisocial child behaviors, including substance abuse. Peer training interventions are skill-based models, often provided as prevention programs in school settings. Dishion et al. hypothesize a more powerful treatment may be a *package* that combines family management training with a skills-based approach. Combination models of treatment have been developed and tested with success (Liddle, 1994).

In a small study, Bry, Conboy, and Bisgay (1986) applied findings from adult literature on substance abuse treatment to the behavioral treatment of adolescent drug abusers and their families. Three months of targeted family problem-solving training decreased drug use and school failure by the end of a 15-month follow-up.

Other integrative models have also demonstrated effectiveness with adolescent drug abusers and their families. Lewis, Piercy, Sprenkle, and Trepper (1990) compared the Purdue Brief Family Therapy model (PBFT) with family drug education and found that family therapy produced significant pre-post decreases in drug use whereas drug education did not. PBFT integrates present-centered, problem-focused skills from structural, strategic, functional, and behavioral family therapies. Liddle et al. (1992) found similar results in a comparison of three treatments for adolescent substance abuse: Multidimensional Family Therapy (MDFT), Peer Group Therapy, and Multi-Family Therapy. Although all three treatments were at least somewhat effective in reducing adolescent drug abuse, MDFT provided the greatest decrease from pretreatment to posttreatment. Moreover, dropout rates in MDFT were significantly lower than the rates in the other two conditions. This finding is especially significant because of growing recognition in the drug abuse field that attrition should be considered one of the more important outcome variables in intervention studies, given the intractable nature of substance abuse and the difficulty of retaining subjects in treatment.

Similar retention results were found in Friedman's (1989) comparison of family therapy to parent education for treatment of adolescent substance abuse. Although there was no significant difference between the two groups in degree of improvement on outcome measures, the family therapy condition enjoyed a much higher participation rate. In 93% of the family therapy cases, one or both parents remained in treatment, whereas only 67% of the parent education cases retained one or more parent. Again because of the retention problem, the ability of family therapy models to engage and retain clients should be understood as one of the most promising findings for adolescent substance abuse treatment.

The Friedman (1989) investigation also demonstrates how empirically derived family therapy models can effectively treat related adolescent problems.

In this study, the family therapy condition utilized the functional family therapy method of Alexander and Barton (1983), which has proven to be effective with delinquents. Thus, family therapy models targeting delinquency, an established correlate of adolescent drug abuse, may also offer promise with drug-abusing youth.

All the family-based models target family factors that have been linked to the etiology of substance abuse. A 20-year literature review of treatment research (Kazdin, Bass, Ayers, & Rodgers, 1990) showed that family therapy was evaluated in only 4.1% of all the investigations, so it is not surprising that there are relatively few studies of family therapy for adolescent substance abuse. Reviews of these intervention studies confirm the potential for family-based models, particularly those that are comprehensive in conceptualization and treatment delivery (Liddle & Dakof, in press).

Schlesinger and Horberg's "Taking Charge" Model

This integrative model (Schlesinger & Horberg, 1988) borrows elements from systems theory as well as from cognitive-behavioral and psychodynamic approaches to family functioning, and it assembles these elements into a stepwise model intended to help family members and therapists pursue an organized journey through the developmental tasks of recovery. It was conceived to help addicts and their families repair damage, create more satisfying lives, and prevent long-lasting deleterious effects (Cooper, 1988).

The tasks of recovery are presented sequentially to facilitate the assessment of differences among families and among members of the same family. Once the assessment is complete, the family's attention is directed to the next logical tasks. This model differs sharply from those approaches that view the family as an instrument to coerce the addict into recovery (e.g., Johnson, 1986), from those that ignore the addiction, from those that ignore the family's needs, and from those that require the entire family to participate. Family members participate as they are ready to work on the problem, and others are invited to participate as they become interested. The aim is to reach a state in which family members feel hopeful about, in charge of, and competent to handle their lives.

Schlesinger and Horberg (1988) present a series of exercises to help family members assess their progress, to guide them through these tasks, to prompt actions, and to focus attention on issues that promote health.

Families begin treatment at varying points. Some have not yet identified the links between family problems and addictive behaviors; others seek help after having accomplished many of the tasks of recovery. Within each family, individual members differ from one another. Assessing the extent to which tasks have already been accomplished is extremely valuable in guiding treatment and bolstering hope and self-efficacy.

Many families decide that they will take action on their problems—including coming for professional help—at a point at which they are depleted emotionally and physically, and enmeshed psychologically. Schlesinger and Horberg's model emphasizes helping family members refocus their attention on their own lives, apart from the addict, to fortify themselves and begin the process of psychological separation. Family members cannot confront problems associated with addiction either in an exhausted state or in an enmeshed state. In a series of "strengthening the family" tasks, family members learn to take better care of themselves, live fuller lives and develop the supportive relationships they will need to face the addiction once again. Once they have begun to strengthen themselves, family members are better prepared for "confronting the addiction." Here, family members focus on what generally is termed enabling. The aim is to help family members confront the addiction itself by engaging in a stepwise process of withdrawing from destructive experiences related to addiction and avoiding inadvertent support for addiction. Setting limits is a crucial part of the process but is not a method of controlling the addict. Limits are set both to protect the family and to communicate the family's healthy resolve. When family members have withdrawn from the poisonous experiences so often associated with chaotic behavior, they are ready to focus their attention on what the authors term "flourishing as a family." The aim here is to replace a "survivor" mentality with a "flourishing" mentality. Family members are helped to learn to let go of the lingering traumatic effects of living with an addict, navigate some common pitfalls in recovery, build healthy communication patterns, and move on to resume normal family development.

Although the clinical usefulness of these ideas seems to have been borne out with their implementation in a variety of settings, data do not yet exist to verify their validity and reliability. But this model suggests a program of research aimed at testing the tenets of the model and its utility.

Self-Help, "Disease Model" Approaches

In addition to the formal treatment models presented in the preceding sections, clinicians should be aware of the variety of self-help resources available to family members. Most of these programs are grounded in the disease conception of alcohol or drug problems, and have extended this conception to the functioning of family members.

Al-Anon

The best known of the self-help groups is Al-Anon, a program available to families and friends of alcoholics. Al-Anon meetings, like AA, are anonymous, open to anyone, and require no membership fee. Al-Anon teaches that alcoholism is a disease, and provides a 12-step recovery program for its members. Included in the program is recognition of the family's powerlessness over alcohol, reliance on a Higher Power, a searching self-evaluation, and commitment to help other family members. Meetings offer practical advice on how to cope with alcohol-related situations and emphasize detachment from the alcohol and learning to take care of personal needs.

ACOA and Other Codependency Programs

In the 1980s, there was increasing popular attention to the experiences of family members of alcoholics. Clinicians introduced the terms "codependency" and "adult children of alcoholics," and self-help and clinician-led groups proliferated to provide services to so-called codependents and ACOAs. These programs have provided a positive service in recognizing and acknowledging the real pain that families experience. Unfortunately, however, they have introduced pathological terminology and labeling of family members that goes far beyond what has been supported to date in the empirical literature.

Labeling a spouse "codependent" or a person who grew up on an alcoholic family an "adult child" can be stigmatizing and can reify problems in living into pathological syndromes. Several attempts have been made to make codependency into a formal DSM-type psychiatric diagnosis, with suggestions that it be considered one of the Axis II personality disorders. Providing a diagnosis implies that a unique constellation of symptoms characterizes many family members; calling it a personality disorder implies that this constellation of symptoms evolved early in life, is relatively enduring, and is little influenced by situational contexts.

Most definitions of codependency are also problematic as they are overinclusive and imprecise, including so many symptoms (e.g., Beattie, 1987, provides more than 200 symptoms of codependency) that virtually anyone could be considered to be codependent. The data on the functioning of spouses of alcoholics directly contradicts codependency constructs. Several research studies have found a direct relationship between the positive psychological functioning of the spouse and the cessation of drinking by the alcoholic (e.g., Moos, Finney, & Gamble, 1982). Were codependency a personality disorder in the classical sense, it should not disappear with improved circumstances.

A final problem with the codependency and ACOA movements are that both make negative some characteristics that could be construed, at least in some contexts, as very positive. Being able to cope and be successful in spite of adversity is a cornerstone of American culture and tradition, but the ACOA who is successful is told that he or she is just acting out the family "hero" role that is preordained by the structure of the addictive family and should examine that success carefully. The spouse of an alcoholic who is able to put his or her own needs second in order to maintain the household and care for the children is told that such a stance is not personally healthy. Although excessive self-sacrifice may have negative psychological ramifications, such a stance may sometimes be the behavior that allows a family to survive. The recent book on the resiliency of "survivors of dysfunctional families" by Wolin and Wolin (1993) underscores this argument.

INDIVIDUAL DIFFERENCES: GENDER, ETHNIC, AND CULTURAL FACTORS

Throughout this chapter, families with alcohol and drug abuse have been described without regard to their cultural and ethnic differences. In studying and treating substance abusers and their families, it is important to recognize that there may be systematic differences in the expression of substance abuse and its effect on the family according to the ethnicity or race of the family and the sex of the abuser(s) involved. Such differences are not well understood. Babor and Mendelson (1986) note that although there has been an underlying assumption in alcohol research that cultural factors impact drinking behavior and may or may not be conducive to alcoholism, relatively little "attention has been devoted to the study of differences in the symptoms of institutionalized alcoholics belonging to different drinking subcultures" (p. 47). Cultural factors may influence the etiology of substance problems, the manifestation of particular symptoms, and the response to treatment of a patient. Research on ethnic minority populations has rarely isolated particular factors that promote or prevent substance problems (Lex, 1987) and has often used biased sampling procedures, failed to recognize heterogeneity within minority groups, and been flawed by inconsistencies in the definitions of constructs used across studies, all of which could have the potential consequence of reifying ethnic stereotypes (Collins, 1992). Substance abuse in women also has been understudied (Nathan & Skinstad, 1987). However, this problem is being corrected, perhaps because more women are seeking treatment or because researchers are making an effort to include women in treatment outcome research.

Some notable age-related differences between ethnic groups have been found. As they age, heavy drinking decreases among whites but increases among blacks (Russell, Cooper, & Frone, 1990). However, although older blacks (over 64) have lifetime alcoholism prevalence rates almost twice that of their white counterparts, they are less than half as likely to have experienced symptoms of alcohol dependence in the past month (Helzer, Burnam, & McEvoy, 1991). Black youths drink less than white and Hispanic youths but have more alcohol-related problems per ounce of alcohol consumed.

Native Americans appear to have substantially higher rates of alcoholism and heavy drinking than other groups in the United States, although drinking varies greatly from tribe to tribe (Lex, 1987).

Differences in drinking patterns across subcultures are difficult to interpret but may have to do with attitudes about drinking that are perpetuated within an individual's family. For instance, Vaillant (1986) has noted that the Irish, who tend to forbid alcohol use by minors, drink in pubs, and drink high-proof whiskey, have much higher rates of alcoholism than Italians, who tend to teach children moderate alcohol use and to reduce the acute effects of drinking by using low-proof alcohol and by consuming alcohol with food. However,

Welte and Barnes (1987) report that across ethnicity and sex, "the greater the proportion of overall drinkers, the greater the proportion of heavy drinkers among those young people who drink" (p. 332), suggesting that those groups more tolerant of drinking in minors show a higher incidence of heavy drinking.

Notable gender-related differences have also been found. Men have been found to drink more and to manifest more alcoholism than women in almost all cultures studied (Helzer & Canino, 1992). However, this difference is more pronounced in Hispanic and Asian cultures than in Western and Anglo-Saxon cultures (Welte & Barnes, 1987).

The amount of drinking done by women in a given subculture could affect how a family reacts to alcoholism in a female family member and either heighten or lessen the stigma associated with being alcoholic. For instance, alcoholic black women, who appear to drink more often with heavy-drinking friends than do white alcoholic women, also appear to have their drinking criticized by their husbands less often than their white counterparts (Lex, 1987).

Age and gender factors interact. Although adult males (in U.S. culture) are more likely than adult females to use alcohol or drugs (e.g., marijuana, cocaine, hallucinogens), this is not necessarily the case for youths between the ages of 12 and 17. For youth, there are no significant gender differences in many aspects of the use of cocaine or hallucinogens (NIDA, 1991). Yet none of the adolescent treatment evaluation studies reviewed by Liddle and Dakof (in press) has addressed gender issues. And this seems the case with most other treatment programs as well, regardless of age of the target group.

The expression of alcoholic symptoms across cultures and countries is remarkably similar (Heltzer & Canino, 1992), and alcoholics may appear more similar as they manifest more severe symptoms (Vaillant, 1987). However, some notable findings reveal a complex interaction of ethnicity and alcoholism. Alcoholism appears to be particularly detrimental to the health of African Americans. Studies indicate they have more alcohol-related medical problems such as cirrhosis, alcoholic hallucinosis, and delirium tremens than whites (Lex, 1987). Alcoholic African-American women appear to have worse treatment outcomes and higher mortality rates than alcoholic white women even when factors such as education levels are equal. Hispanics seem particularly affected by liver cirrhosis and legal problems due to drinking. However, Hispanic drinking practices vary greatly according to country of origin. Native American alcoholics have been found to have the greatest amount of unemployment, the least education, and the greatest disruption of social roles. They also have particularly high rates of readmission to treatment and poor treatment outcomes. Being sensitive to particular problems within subgroups of the population may allow for more effective treatment planning and more targeted research.

Not only are there important effects of ethnicity on the consequences of alcoholism, but there are also effects of ethnicity on family function, influence, and attitudes toward drinking. Differences have been found between cultures in the importance of peer versus parental influence (Babor, 1992) and between

African-American, white, and Asian-American families in family management practices, involvement in family activities, sibling deviance, parental attitudes toward children's drinking, and family structure (Catalano et al., 1992). These authors (p. 216) conclude, "There may well be cultural differences in family processes leading to early variety of substance initiation." Cultural differences also exist in the conceptualization of alcoholism (Babor, 1992) that could influence how families react to and interpret alcohol problems in family members. Studies in other countries reveal variations in how families respond to alcoholism and what concerns they express about the consequences of alcohol use. For example, 76% of alcoholics in Puerto Rico reported that their families had objected to their drinking (Canino, Burnam, & Caetano, 1992), whereas only 36% of alcoholics in West Germany reported familial objections (Wittchen & Bronisch, 1992). Why such discrepancies exist has not been researched and will certainly be multidetermined.

One successful attempt to design a culturally specific treatment model must be noted here. Szapocznik et al. (1983, 1988), whose program was described earlier in this chapter, have utilized knowledge of Hispanic populations, then implemented that knowledge in the form of specific therapy interventions. Their problem-specific and culturally sensitive model of treatment has demonstrated excellent results by enhancing treatment engagement and outcome.

FUTURE DIRECTIONS IN THE ADDICTIONS FOR FAMILY CLINICIANS

Implications for the Training of Family Clinicians

Effective preparation for clinicians interested in working with families must go beyond traditional training in "family systems" per se to encompass such areas as coping models, specific skills training, community interventions, and cultural competencies. There needs to be more training (and research also) in the role of gender, ethnic factors, and cultural factors in treatment and prevention. And clinicians need to learn more about the "culture" of addictions programming, including the politics of the alcohol and drug abuse field.

Research

Issues of diversity in alcoholism and families are complex and will require sophisticated research procedures to address adequately. However, not addressing issues of sex and ethnicity, as well as factors such as sexual orientation, socioeconomic status (SES), and age, may hinder development of clinical models and research on substance abuse and the family because potential confounding variables and interactions may skew findings from studies that use diverse samples of subjects. It cannot be stressed too strongly that, in regard to treating substance abuse from a family perspective, not all families subscribe to the same set of values and beliefs as that of the therapist and other families.

Research efforts to develop family-based diagnostic schemes must also be increased; continuing to force diagnostic formulations to reflect only individual considerations will hamper both research and practice.

Given the focus of much of the addictions treatment field today, clinicians should be increasing their efforts to conduct rigorous clinical research on the family-related impact of ACOA programs, Al-Anon, and other "disease model" approaches. They should also be working to integrate more data-based interventions into these settings. There is also a need for research on the efficacy of so-called family interventions (Johnson, 1986), which are being conducted by many practitioners.

Intervention Settings

There should (and are likely to) be intensified efforts to spread family-based treatment and prevention approaches into settings with a high concentration of substance abusers who are motivated or at least under pressure to change their behavior: drinking driver programs, domestic relations courts, shelters for abused women, and the like. Efforts will also intensify to disseminate knowledge about family factors in substance abuse into primary care settings, so that family physicians will become an even greater resource than at present.

Modes of Intervention

The addiction interventions to be employed by family clinicians are likely to become more comprehensive in scope, targeting not only substance abuse directly, but the concomitant problem behaviors and their suspected etiological roots:

> This implies interventions that, in addition to specific, behavior-relevant information, attitudes, and skills, would orient toward the lifestyle organization of the separate risk behaviors, and therefore, toward alternative lifestyle choice. The general emphasis of such programs would be on health-promoting lifestyles that are relatively incompatible with the syndrome of risk behavior. (Jessor, 1984, p. 87)

Effective addiction interventions will increasingly draw on the literature of related fields. Liddle, Sersa, Schmidt and Ettinger (in press), for example, argue that the developmental literature can be mined for intervention guidelines. The literature on adolescent development tells us that detachment from parents makes teens vulnerable to negative peer influences. Intervening with families to strengthen the parent-adolescent bond should be expected to lessen this vulnerability. In addition to helping families cultivate developmentally appropriate attachment, there should be a complementary focus on developing appropriate parental influence (Liddle, 1994), in particular discipline, monitoring, and reinforcement strategies (Dishion et al., 1988). Families with high levels of warmth, democratic control, and psychological autonomy are most likely to produce teenagers who are competent and resistant to pressures to use drugs (Baumrind, 1991).

Integrative models that systematically combine interventions from various theoretical models are likely to be emphasized (Dishion et al., 1988). There is general agreement in treatment and intervention research that the most effective programs are (a) derived from an understanding of the causes and risk factors leading to the problem; (b) draw on theories and models of human behavior that direct the program's focus; (c) utilize intervention methods or techniques known to change behavior; and (d) monitor intervention implementation rigorously (Kazdin, 1993).

REFERENCES

Alexander, J., & Barton, C. (1983). *Functional family therapy training manual.* Salt Lake City, UT: Western States Family Institute.

American Psychiatric Association. (1994). *Diagnostic and statistical manual of mental disorders* (4th ed.). Washington, DC: Author.

Arias, I., & O'Leary, K. D. (1988). Cognitive-behavioral treatment of physical aggression in marriage. In N. Epstein, S. E. Schlesinger, & W. Dryden (Eds.), *Cognitive-behavioral therapy with families* (pp. 118–150). New York: Brunner/Mazel.

Babor, T. F. (1992). Cross-cultural research on alcohol: A quoi bon? In J. E. Helzer & G. J. Canino (Eds.), *Alcoholism in North America, Europe, and Asia* (pp. 33–52). New York: Oxford University Press.

Babor, T. F., & Mendelson, J. H. (1986). Ethnic/religious differences in manifestation and treatment of alcoholism. In T. F. Babor (Ed.), *Annals of the New York Academy of Sciences: Vol. 472. Alcohol and culture: Comparative perspectives from Europe and America* (pp. 46–59). New York: New York Academy of Sciences.

Baumrind, D. (1991). The influence of parenting style on adolescent competence and substance abuse. *Journal of Early Adolescence, 11,* 56–95.

Beattie, M. (1987). *Codependent no more.* Minneapolis, MN: Hazelden.

Botvin, G. J., Baker, E., Dusenbury, L., Tortu, S., & Botvin, E. M. (1990). Preventing adolescent drug abuse through a multimodal cognitive-behavioral approach: Results of a 3-year study. *Journal of Consulting and Clinical Psychology, 58,* 437–446.

Bry, B. H. (1988). Family-based approaches to reducing adolescent substance use: Theories, techniques, and findings. In E. R. Rahdert & J. Grabowski (Eds.), *Adolescent drug abuse: Analyses of treatment research* (pp. 39–68). NIDA Research Monograph 77, DHHS Pub. No. (ADM)88-1523. Rockville, MD: National Institute on Drug Abuse.

Bry, B. H., Conboy, C., & Bisgay, K. (1986). Decreasing adolescent drug use and school failure: Long-term effects of targeted family problem-solving training. *Child and Family Behavior Therapy, 8,* 43–59.

Canino, G. J., Burnam, A., & Caetano, R. (1992). The prevalence of alcohol abuse and/or dependence in two Hispanic communities. In J. E. Helzer & G. J. Canino

(Eds.), *Alcoholism in North America, Europe, and Asia* (pp. 131–155). New York: Oxford University Press.

Catalano, R. F., Morrison, D. M., Wells, E. A., Gillmore, M. R., Iritani, B., & Hawkins, J. D. (1992). Ethnic differences in family factors related to early drug initiation. *Journal of Studies on Alcohol, 53,* 208–217.

Cloninger, C. R., Bohman, M., & Sigvardsson, S. (1981). Inheritance of alcohol abuse. *Archives of General Psychiatry, 38,* 861–868.

Coleman, E. (1987). Marital and relationship problems among chemically dependent and codependent relationships [Special issue]. *Journal of Chemical Dependency Treatment, 1*(1), 39–59.

Collins, R. L. (1992). Methodological issues in conducting substance abuse research on ethnic minority populations. *Drugs and Society, 6,* 59–77.

Cooper, M. (1988). Review of taking charge: How families can climb out of the chaos of addiction and flourish. *Employee Assistance Quarterly, 4*(1), 97–102.

Davis, D. I., Berenson, D., Steinglass, P., & Davis, S. (1974). The adaptive consequences of drinking. *Psychiatry, 37,* 209–215.

Dishion, T. J., Reid, J. B., & Patterson, G. R. (1988). Empirical guidelines for a family intervention for adolescent drug abuse. In R. H. Coombs (Ed.), *The family context of adolescent drug use* (pp. 189–224). New York: Haworth.

Dryfoos, J. G. (1990). *Adolescents at risk: Prevalence and prevention.* New York: Oxford University Press.

Falco, J. (1988). *Preventing abuse of drugs, alcohol, and tobacco by adolescents.* Working paper for Carnegie Council on Adolescent Development. Washington, DC: Carnegie Council on Adolescent Development.

Friedman, A. S. (1989). Family therapy vs. parent groups: Effects on adolescent drug abusers. *The American Journal of Family Therapy, 17,* 335–347.

Glynn, T. J., & Haenlein, M. (1988). Family theory and research on adolescent drug use: A review. In R. H. Coombs (Ed.), *The family context of adolescent drug use* (pp. 39–56). New York: Haworth.

Harford, T. C. (1992). Family history of alcoholism in the United States: Prevalence and demographic considerations. *British Journal of Addictions, 87,* 931–935.

Helzer, J. E., & Canino, G. J. (1992). Comparative analysis of alcoholism in ten cultural regions. In J. E. Helzer & G. J. Canino (Eds.), *Alcoholism in North America, Europe, and Asia* (pp. 289–308). New York: Oxford University Press.

Helzer, J. E., Burnam, A., & McEvoy, L. T. (1991). Alcohol abuse and dependence. In L. N. Robbins & D. A. Regiers (Eds.), *Alcoholism in North America, Europe, and Asia* (pp. 289–308). New York: Oxford University Press.

Huba, G. J., & Bentler, P. M. (1980). The role of peer and adult models for drug taking at different stages in adolescence. *Journal of Youth and Adolescence, 9,* 449–465.

Hurley, D. L. (1991). Women, alcohol and incest: An analytic review. *Journal of Studies on Alcohol, 52,* 253–268.

Institute of Medicine. (1990a). *Broadening the base of treatment for alcohol problems.* Washington, DC: National Academy Press.

Institute of Medicine. (1990b). *Treating drug problems: A study of the evolution, effectiveness, and financing of public and private drug treatment systems.* Report by the Institute of Medicine Committee for the Substance Abuse Coverage Study, Division of Health Care Services. Washington, DC: National Academy Press.

Jacob, T., & Leonard, K. E. (1988). Alcoholic-spouse interaction as a function of alcoholism subtype and alcohol consumption interaction. *Journal of Abnormal Psychology, 97,* 231–237.

Jessor, R. (1984). Adolescent development and behavioral health. In J. D. Matarazzo, S. M. Weiss, J. A. Herd, & N. E. Miller (Eds.), *Behavioral health: A handbook of health enhancement and disease prevention* (pp. 69–90). New York: Wiley.

Johnson, V. E. (1986). *Intervention: How to help someone who doesn't want help.* Minneapolis, MN: Johnson Institute Books.

Johnston, L. D., O'Malley, P. M., & Bachman, J. G. (1989). *Drug use, drinking, and smoking: National survey results from high school, college, and young adults populations 1975–1988.* National Institute on Drug Abuse. Washington, DC: U.S. Government Printing Office.

Kazdin, A. E. (1993). Psychotherapy for children and adolescents: Current progress and future research direction. *American Psychologist, 48,* 644–457.

Kazdin, A. E., Bass, D., Ayers, W. A., & Rodgers, A. (1990). Empirical and clinical focus of child and adolescent psychotherapy research. *Journal of Consulting and Clinical Psychology, 58,* 729–740.

Langenbucher, J. W., McCrady, B. S., Brick, J., & Esterly, R. E. (1994). *Socioeconomic evaluations of addictions treatment.* Washington, DC: The White House.

Leonard, K. E., & Jacob, T. (1988). Alcohol, alcoholism, and family violence. In V. B. Van Hasselt, R. L. Morrison, A. S. Bellack, & M. Hersen (Eds.), *Handbook of family violence* (pp. 383–406). New York: Plenum.

Lewis, R. A., Piercy, F. P., Sprenkle, D. H., & Trepper, T. (1990). Family-based interventions for helping drug-abusing adolescents. *Journal of Adolescent Research, 5,* 82–95.

Lex, B. W. (1987). Review of alcohol problems in ethnic minority groups. *Journal of Consulting and Clinical Psychology, 55,* 293–300.

Liddle, H. A. (1994). The anatomy of emotions in family therapy with adolescents. *Journal of Adolescent Research, 9,* 120–157.

Liddle, H. A., & Dakof, G. A. (in press). Family-based treatment for adolescent drug use: State of the science. In E. Rahdert et al. (Eds.), *Adolescent drug abuse: Assessment and treatment.* Rockville, MD: National Institute on Drug Abuse Research Monograph.

Liddle, H. A., Sersa, F., Schmidt, S., & Ettinger, D. (in press). Adolescent development research: Guidelines for clinicians. *Journal of Marital and Family Therapy.*

Liddle, H. A., Dakof, G. A., Parker, K., Diamond, G., Garcia, R., Barrett, K., & Hurwitz, S. (1992, August). Effectiveness of family therapy versus multi-family therapy and group therapy: Results of the Adolescents and Families Project—A randomized clinical trial. Paper presented at the annual meeting of the American Psychological Association, Washington, DC.

Luckey, J. W. (1987). Justifying alcohol treatment on the basis of cost savings: The offset literature. *Alcohol Health and Research World, 12,* 8–15.

McCrady, B. S. (1989). The outcomes of family-involved alcoholism treatment. In M. Galanter (Ed.), *Recent developments in alcoholism, Vol. 7*, (pp. 165–182). New York: Plenum.

McCrady, B. S., & Epstein, E. E. (in press). Marital therapy in the treatment of alcohol problems. In N. Jacobson & A. Gurman (Eds.), *Clinical handbook of marital therapy* (2nd ed.). New York: Guilford Press.

McCrady, B. S., Stout, R., Noel, N., Abrams, D., & Nelson, H. F. (1991). Effectiveness of three types of spouse-involved behavioral alcoholism treatment. *British Journal of Addiction, 86,* 1415–1424.

McDermott, D. (1984). The relationship of parental drug use and parents' attitude concerning adolescent drug use to adolescent drug use. *Adolescence, 19,* 89–97.

McDonnell Douglas Corporation, & Alexander Consulting Group. (1989). *Employee assistance program financial offset study: 1985–1988.* Bridgeton, MO: McDonnell Douglas Corporation.

Martin, S. E. (1992). The epidemiology of alcohol-related interpersonal violence. *Alcohol Health and Research World, 16,* 230–237.

Miller, B. A. (1990). The interrelationships between alcohol and drugs and family violence. In M. De Las Rosa, E. Y. Lambert, & B. Gropper (Eds.), *National Institute on Drug Abuse Research Monograph Series 103: Drugs and violence: Causes, correlates, and consequences* (DDHS Publication No. ADM 90-1721, pp. 177–207). Washington, DC: U.S. Government Printing Office.

Milman, D. H., Bennett, A. A., & Hanson, M. (1983). Psychological effects of alcohol in children and adolescents. *Alcohol, Health and Research World, 7,* 50–53.

Moos, R. H., & Billings, A. (1982). Children of alcoholics during the recovery process: Alcoholic and matched control families. *Addictive Behaviors, 7,* 155–163.

Moos, R. H., Finney, J. W., & Gamble, W. (1982). The process of recovery from alcoholism. II. Comparing spouses of alcoholic patients and matched community controls. *Journal of Studies on Alcohol, 43,* 888–909.

Nathan, P. E., & Skinstad, A. H. (1987). Outcomes of treatment for alcohol problems: Current methods, problems, and results. *Journal of Consulting and Clinical Psychology, 55,* 332–340.

National Institute on Alcohol Abuse and Alcoholism. (1993). *Eighth special report to the U.S. Congress on alcohol and health* [Preprint copy] (DHHS Publication No. ADM 281-91-0003). Washington, DC: EEI.

National Institute on Drug Abuse (1991). *National household survey on drug abuse: Main findings 1990.* Rockville, MD: NIDA.

O'Farrell, T. J., Choquette, K. A., Cutter, H. S. G., Brown, F. A., & McCourt, W. F. (1993). Behavioral marital therapy with and without additional couples relapse prevention sessions for alcoholics and their wives. *Journal of Studies on Alcohol, 54,* 652–666.

Paolino, T. J., McCrady, B. S., & Diamond, S. (1978). Statistics on alcoholic marriages: An overview. *The International Journal of Addictions, 13,* 1285–1293.

Patterson, G. R., Reid, J. B., & Dishion, T. J. (1992). *Antisocial boys.* Eugene, OR: Castalia.

Rhodes, J. E., & Jason, L. A. (1988). *Preventing substance abuse among children and adolescents.* New York: Pergamon.

Russell, M., Cooper, M. L., & Frone, M. R. (1990). The influence of sociodemographic characteristics on familial alcohol problems: Data from a community sample. *Alcoholism: Clinical and Experimental Research, 14,* 221–226.

Schlesinger, S. E. (1988). Cognitive-behavioral approaches to family treatment of addictions. In N. Epstein, S. E. Schlesinger, & W. Dryden (Eds.). *Cognitive-behavioral therapy with families* (pp. 254–291). New York: Brunner/Mazel.

Schlesinger, S. E., & Horberg, L. K. (1988). *Taking Charge: How families can climb out of the chaos of addiction . . . and flourish.* New York: Fireside Books/Simon and Schuster.

Sher, K. J. (1991). *Children of alcoholics: A critical appraisal of theory and research.* Chicago: University of Chicago Press.

Spear, S. F., & Mason, M. (1991). Impact of chemical dependency on family health status. *International Journal of the Addictions, 26,* 179–187.

Steinglass, P., Bennett, L. A., Wolin, S. J., & Reiss, D. (1987). *The alcoholic family.* New York: Basic Books.

Szapocznik, J., Kurtines, W. M., Foote, F., & Perez-Vidal, A. (1983). Conjoint versus one person family therapy: Some evidence for the effectiveness of conducting family therapy through one person. *Journal of Consulting and Clinical Psychology, 51,* 889–899.

Szapocznik, J., Perez-Vidal, A., Brickman, A., Foote, F., Santisteban, D., Hervis, O., & Kurtines, W. (1988). Engaging adolescent drug abusers and their families into treatment: A strategic structural systems approach. *Journal of Consulting and Clinical Psychology, 56,* 552–557.

Thompson, T., & Simmons-Cooper, C. (1988). Chemical dependency treatment and Black adolescents. *Journal of Drug Issues, 18,* 21–31.

Vaillant, G. (1986). Cultural factors in the etiology of alcoholism: A prospective study. In T. F. Babor (Ed.), *Annals of the New York Academy of Sciences: Vol. 472. Alcohol and culture: Comparative perspectives from Europe and America* (pp. 142–148). New York: New York Academy of Sciences.

Welte, J. W., & Barnes, G. M. (1987). Alcohol use among adolescent minority groups. *Journal of Studies on Alcohol, 48,* 329–336.

Wittchen, H. U., & Bronisch, T. (1992). Alcohol use, abuse, and dependency in West Germany: Lifetime and six-month prevalence in the Munich follow-up study. In J. E. Helzer & G. J. Canino (Eds.), *Alcoholism in North America, Europe, and Asia* (pp. 150–181). New York: Oxford University Press.

Wolin, S., Bennett, L., & Noonan, D. L. (1979). Family rituals and the recurrence of alcoholism over generations. *American Journal of Psychiatry, 136,* 589–593.

Wolin, S. J., & Wolin, S. (1993). *The resilient self: How survivors of troubled families rise above adversity.* New York: Villard Books.

Zweben, A., & Pearlman, S. (1983). Evaluating the effectiveness of conjoint treatment of alcohol-complicated marriages: Clinical and methodological issues. *Journal of Marital and Family Therapy, 9,* 61–72.

Zweben, A., Pearlman, S., & Li, S. (1988). A comparison of brief advice and conjoint therapy in the treatment of alcohol abuse: The results of the Marital Systems study. *British Journal of Addiction, 83,* 899–916.

PART FIVE

Reviewing the Role of the Clinician

CHAPTER 15

Expanding Practices and Roles of Family Clinicians

LUCIANO L'ABATE and MARK ODELL

This chapter argues that in addition to psychotherapy, there are many ways of helping families that can increase the effectiveness and financial rewards of family clinicians. As the preceding chapters of this book have suggested, the clinician is likely to treat many kinds of families. Most families in need of treatment are unlikely to receive the help they need unless mental health practitioners in general and family clinicians in particular expand their traditional roles.

For the past 80 or so years, therapeutic treatment for nonphysical problems has consisted primarily of a face-to-face dialogue between a client, or more recently clients (as in a family), and a helping professional. Most clinicians today are still trained in this medium, often called "talk therapy," and it is the usual method through which the lay population seeks help. Although the efficacy of this type of treatment has received encouraging empirical support (Bergin & Garfield, 1994; Gurman & Kniskern, 1991; Gurman, Kniskern, & Pinsof, 1986; Smith, Glass, & Miller, 1980), this approach for solving the many psychosocial problems faced by most families has several limitations, such as expense in terms of time and effectiveness, high attrition rates, negative outcomes in a percentage of clients seeking help (Mays & Franks, 1985), and unrealistic, if not impossible, expectations in terms of preventive approaches for families in need of help (Goodyear, 1990). Chief among these limitations is the less than adequate access that the general population has to professional services. This problem stems from geographic or motivational reasons, costs, and/or lack of awareness, to name a few. Similarly, mastery of the majority (English) language can no longer be assumed. Thus, potential clients who are minorities or immigrants may be unable to utilize services because of a language barrier. Those minorities who speak English well enough to converse may still be subject to culturally naive professionals and consequently face another barrier (Odell, Shelling, Young, Hewitt, & L'Abate, 1994). It is time to

---

We are grateful to Dr. Harway for her dedicated and careful editing of our chapter.

expand the two models of service delivery in mental health (e.g., medication and psychotherapy) to include existing alternatives.

Family therapy started as a cost-effective treatment based on seeing members of a family together rather than individually. This approach, however, is no longer sufficient to deal with the many ills that are besetting American families, as previous chapters attest and as critical articles have suggested (e.g., Shields, Wynne, McDaniel, & Gawinski, 1994). There are not enough trained family clinicians to deal with such exorbitant numbers, nor are these clinicians trained to deal with the multifarious problems of these many families. As was true years ago when the so-called paraprofessional revolution started, this is still a personnel problem (Arnhoff, Rubinstein, & Speisman, 1969). Hence, we need to consider possible solutions that would make clinicians better able to cope with the overwhelming realities of increasing their effectiveness in a changing cultural and social climate.

Demands for accountability increasingly mandated by managed care will put more and more restraints on clinicians. Clinicians are going to be more often questioned about the cost-effectiveness of their practices and about the outcome of their interventions (Giles, 1993; Goodman, Brown, & Deitz, 1992; Wagner, 1992). L'Abate (in press, b) has argued that clinicians must change, in order to practice and survive in a changing practice marketplace. Clinicians must expand their practices and roles, as they want to expand the choices available to their clients.

Christensen and Jacobson (1994) have raised questions about the importance of the relationship in psychotherapy. They have challenged the psychotherapeutic community about the importance of degrees and credentials. The usefulness of hierarchical organizations in the delivery of mental health services to families will be described later in this chapter.

The overall focus of this chapter is to encourage family clinicians to expand traditional practices and roles to include (a) the other two, heretofore underutilized media of communication—the nonverbal and the written; (b) psychoeducational, social skills training approaches; (c) new developments in interactive technologies such as, personal computers, virtual reality, and television; and (d) other professional helpers at different levels of expertise and specialization, such as paraprofessionals versed in multicultural skills and in specifically structured, preventive, psychoeducational social skills training programs. When these expansions take place, family clinicians who assume leadership roles in this field will be able to make a significant dent in the vast number of families in need of help. Through these expansions, they might be able to reach families who heretofore have been unreceptive to helpful interventions and may increase their incomes as well.

Before expanding in practices and roles, however, the family clinician must be able to help families reinstitute controls that have been lost or that never existed. To help families learn how to control themselves better, it will be necessary to consider the importance of controls in family life. Hence, each family therapist needs to have a clear idea of what it means to teach families to achieve greater, or better, more effective controls.

THE IMPORTANCE OF ESTABLISHING CONTROLS

Issues of control supersede theoretical or therapeutic predilections. Control is the major issue that needs to be faced by all clinicians, no matter their experience or orientation.

Without the establishment of controls, therefore, it will become extremely difficult to help families cope with nonnormative events. But how is control to be achieved? The literature on this matter is limited to behavioral approaches that stress the importance of reinforcements *after* the response is completed. By stressing the end point of an interaction, this approach denies the importance of beginning an interaction. For instance, in real life, control is established at home through the habitual following of routines, such as getting out of bed, having breakfast, brushing one's teeth, and washing. At work, control is established by the employer who expects employees to arrive at a certain, *preordained* time, to follow a sequential schedule of tasks or responsibilities, finally leaving work at a *preordained* time. Hence, control is exercised from the beginning to the end of an interaction. By requiring families to meet at preestablished times (e.g., once a week at 8:00 P.M.; twice a week at 7:00 P.M.) to perform tasks assigned by the clinician (verbally or in writing), families in therapy eventually learn to regulate themselves to come together in less reactive fashions than they have done heretofore. Furthermore, they learn to come together to conduct family business in a responsible fashion that eventually will pay back in their assuming responsibility for their lives (L'Abate, 1986). Many references cited later in this chapter contain a variety of possible nomothetic tasks that clinicians can assign to families. Creative clinicians will be able to assign idiographic tasks that meet the ad hoc needs of many families. Family appointments are legitimated through an informed consent form signed at the outset of therapy.

Levy and Shelton (1990, pp. 150–159), after reviewing the type of tasks that can be required of clients, made the following recommendations to enhance homework compliance (modified by the writers of this chapter):

1. Ensure that tasks contain specific detail about the desired behavior—the best way to fulfill this recommendation is to give written instructions, as explained later in this chapter.
2. Give direct skill training in the office when necessary, including nonverbal exercises.
3. Reward compliance.
4. Begin with homework that is likely to be successfully accomplished.
5. Use a system that will remind clients of the assignment, such as having all family members write down the time of appointment in their calendars to remind each other.
6. Have clients make a public commitment to comply (e.g., L'Abate (1986) requires a written contract with informed consent from the very beginning of therapy about a parallel home appointment time for each therapy session).

7. Explain to clients the value of using homework assignments for treating their problems and attempt to convince them of their importance.
8. Practice cognitive (as well as nonverbal) rehearsal strategies in the therapist's office before assignment to the home.
9. Try to anticipate and reduce the negative effects of compliance. When problems of compliance arise, they should be discussed immediately.
10. Monitor compliance with as many sources as possible—a problem that decreases when a whole family is involved.

EXPANSION FROM TRADITIONAL PRACTICES

As the 21st century dawns, one goal for family clinicians is to make themselves more accessible to a wider range of clients without decreasing their effectiveness or jeopardizing their personal and professional integrity. Such an enlargement would not only widen the horizons of their practices, but their pocketbooks as well. Technologies are already in place to achieve this goal.

The Two Forgotten Media

The addition and expansion of oral therapy to include the two other media of communication—the nonverbal and the written—is inevitable. Traditionally, psychotherapeutic interventions have been based solely on the oral medium. Even though there have been many advances in the other two media, these advances have not been incorporated in the everyday repertoire of most psychotherapists. Almost no reference is made to either medium in two widely known references in the field. For instance, Bergin and Garfield (1994) devote 6 pages out of 830 of text, while Gurman and Kniskern (1991) devote 2 out of 697 pages of text to nonverbal behavior, without any reference as to the importance of nonverbal behavior in family life or therapy. Yet, nonverbal behavior is a basic dimension of family life and communication. No citations are made in either reference or in their previous editions to the written medium. Advances in these two other media will be reviewed and suggestions will be made on how they could be integrated into traditional psychotherapeutic practices.

The Nonverbal Medium

Therapists trained in expressive, Gestalt, and other experiential modalities may be more familiar with nonverbal approaches to treatment than the majority of clinicians (Burgoon, 1994; Kepner,1993; Middleman, 1968; Patterson, 1984; Steere, 1982; Waxer, 1978). Nonverbal messages, given through body exercises, may increase the chance of establishing the trust through more than one channel of communication (e.g., verbal, nonverbal, and written). Nonverbal exercises may allow family members to acquire a sense of mastery *through their bodies* over their immediate environment. Many disturbed families have lost this sense of mastery in their attempts to survive, losing also a sense of their worth and of their bodies. Clinicians of all persuasions need to become more familiar with the use of rituals, sculpting, and strictly behavioral (nonverbal) interventions to help families cope with nonnormative events in their lives. The underlying assumption for the use of nonverbal techniques is that this medium is developmentally and sequentially basic to the growth of the other two media (Table 15.1). Hence, it needs to be fostered through a variety of techniques. These techniques, when introduced to groups of individuals, couples, or families, will have a major impact. They can be delivered by specially trained paraprofessionals or volunteers under supervision of and with support from the family clinician (L'Abate, in press, b).

L'Abate (1994a, in press, b) developed a rationale for the use of nonverbal techniques in psychotherapy because of (a) the developmental primacy of nonverbal behavior before oral development—people learn both nonverbal and oral media automatically, before they learn to write (which is not learned automatically; see Table 15.1); and (b) the structural importance of isomorphic

TABLE 15.1   Developmental Comparisons among Media of Communication

Nonverbal	Oral*	Written*
Earliest to be learned	Learned earlier in life at home	Learned later in life in school
Easiest form of information	Easier than written language	Harder than spoken language
Effortless	Takes less effort	Takes more effort
Extremely informative on few cues	More productive per unit of time	Less productive per unit of time
Learned automatically	Learned automatically	Has to be taught
Spontaneous	Spontaneous	Deliberate
Dependent on immediate social context and difficult to fake	Dependent on immediate social context, but can be faked or subject to deception or delay	More autonomous of context; hence, subject to greater control than two earlier media
Restricted and limited to few channels of expression (face, body)	More ideas per unit of time	More ideas per number of words
No permanent record (unless videotaped)	No permanent record (unless tape recorded)	Permanent record but subject to destruction
Relatively simple	Less syntactically complex	More syntactically complex
Fairly concrete	Less abstract	More abstract
Immediate	Less time needed for planning and encoding	More time needed for planning and encoding

* Adapted from Weintraub (1981) and L'Abate (1994a). Published with permission.

relationships between the clinician's office and the world outside that office, where all three media are necessary (Table 15.2). Limiting clinical interventions to the oral medium may limit the kind of families and family problems that can be helped. Not all families use words to interact and not all family interactions are oral. There is a great deal of nonverbal communication that needs to be captured in the therapist's office to make it isomorphic with the outside world; this kind of communication can be used for therapeutic ends. For instance, sculpting has a long history of clinical applications that generate a great many feelings in families if applied at the beginning of therapy. In fact, these feelings may be so intense that sometimes it is wiser to wait until the therapist feels trusted by the family before applying this technique (L'Abate, in press, a; L'Abate, Hanson, & Ganahl, 1986).

The potential benefits of developing diverse nonverbal treatment methods are numerous. Families would be able to manage many of their symptoms more independently and would thus spend less time in the therapy room. Costs per

TABLE 15.2   Classification of Intervention Media and Links between Settings Inside and Outside the Therapist's Office

Channels of Intervention: Media	Settings	
	Inside Therapist's Office	Outside Therapist' Office
Oral[a]	Establishment of rapport	
	Evaluation	Self-dialogue
	Direction of treatment	Friends
	Confrontation of issues	Relatives and family
	Motivation for change	of origin
	Generalization to outside	Dialogue with partner
	Emotional support	Talk with children and coworkers
Nonverbal	Awareness Exercises	Sports and Exercise
	Nonverbal Communication	Nutrition-Diet
	Body Movements	Vitamins
		Meditation

	Structure	Goal	Content	*Level of Abstraction*	*Specificity*
Writing*	Open Focused Guided Programmed	Cathartic/ prescriptive	Traumatic/ trivial	High/low	High/low

* Adapted from L'Abate (1994a, in press, a, b).

[a] Most of the oral functions can also take place without face-to-face contact between therapists and clients. For instance, they can take place long distance, through the written modality computer or telephone, depending on the client and the situation.

family might thus be lessened, but by the same token, more families per unit of the professional's time might be reached. Hence, the more effective clinicians will have a greater chance of enlarging their clinical practices and their incomes. In addition, families would be empowered to develop their own creative resources to solve their own problems and would be less dependent on professionals in the future. More frequent use of nonverbal techniques could help correct one of the most widely held myths of psychotherapy—that words influence and even change behavior. This conclusion may be valid in functional families, where what is said by family members is held respectfully as being important. However, words do not influence pathological behavior, which, by definition, is out of the control of verbal influence.

Hence, if families are to change their behaviors, clinicians are going to have to change theirs. Moreover, therapists have an important role in mediating healthy functioning. Convincing families, for instance, about the importance of diet and exercise (Seraganian, 1993) will only be accomplished when clinicians themselves demonstrate directly the importance of the body and of body messages, as practiced in the clinician's office. As shown in Table 15.2, there are many links between what can happen in the clinician's office and what happens outside that office. For instance, in a married couple of former drug addicts who expressed difficulty in becoming intimate, the "Hurt Sharing" exercise, described by L'Abate (1986, in press, b), which forces couples to close their eyes, hold hands, and concentrate on their inner hurts in order to share them, produced an immediate coming together of their bodies, even though neither spouse was able to cry as expected. If the therapist can make the nonverbal sharing of crying take place inside his or her office, this occurrence may facilitate its taking place in the home.

How can clinicians help families generalize from their offices to homes, to work, and to leisure? Nonverbal behavior among family members must be practiced in the therapist's office and reinforced by homework assignments. This approach requires that clinicians adopt prescriptions for homework assignments. Such homework assignments should include all three media of communication and establish scheduled routines that will help families achieve a greater feeling of control over their lives, as mentioned earlier (L'Abate, 1994a, in press, b). Table 15.2 summarizes how each medium of communication and intervention, applied in the therapist's office, may generalize outside it. For instance, if the client opens up and actually enjoys talking with a therapist who will affirm and validate his or her feelings and perceptions, this new experience may allow the same client to open up to a partner, relatives, and friends. By the same token, if in addition to the oral medium, the therapist were to include awareness exercises as well as body movements in the client's emotional repertoire, this new experience might allow the client to take up a new sport activity, start a diet regime, and learn to meditate rather than act out impulsively. If in addition to these two media, the therapist were to require written homework assignments, in a structure, focus, content, level of abstraction, and degree of specificity that is convenient and relevant to the client's needs, a complete and comprehensive package of interventions would be available. A recent breakthrough is the nonverbal medium accounts of the new technology known as virtual reality (Rothbaum, Hodges, Kooper, Opdyke, Williford, & North, 1995).

Besides the previously described nonverbal behaviors, a great deal of communication should take place in writing, especially when the spoken word is too tinged by emotionality and loss of control.

The Written Medium

Written adjuncts to treatment are commonly used by a wide range of therapists. Clinicians from many theoretical traditions have assigned clients to journal writing, letter writing, or drawing pictures. The value of written assignments has been underscored by numerous authors. Consequently, some readers may find it surprising that we would suggest that written approaches to treatment are underutilized. However, writing, like nonverbal techniques, has not yet joined the mainstream of psychotherapeutic practice. Hence, clinicians who plan to use either nonverbal or written media need to require a written consent from clients to protect themselves from any possible liability (L'Abate, 1986, 1990, 1992, 1994a, 1994b, in press, b).

Family clinicians need to incorporate writing more systematically into their therapeutic practices. Writing programs can and should be developed for a great many problems that typically bring clients into the clinicians' offices. The development of a recipe book of writing programs to treat a range of problems would greatly reduce costs and increase efficiency for individual clinicians. As shown in Table 15.2, writing can be classified according to five (sometimes overlapping) categories or dimensions: (a) structure, (b) goal, (c) content, (d) level of abstraction, and (e) specificity. Interventions based *in part* on writing, would not replace the rapport building and healing aspects of the therapeutic relationship nor would they be appropriate for every family. By the same token, some families prefer writing to the verbal dialogue with a therapist.

As an adjunct to what is said in the therapy office, many problems could be dealt with adequately outside through the written medium (L'Abate, 1986, 1990, 1992, in press, a). For instance, a couple characterized and polarized by issues of addiction in one partner and codependency issues in the other partner, in addition to seeing the therapist on a face-to-face basis, profited by the addicted partner working on an impulsivity program (L'Abate, 1992) while the codependent partner worked on a codependency program (L'Abate, submitted for publication).

Programmed writing materials, or workbooks, make it easier for some clients to get the help they need. For instance, written, weekly homework assignments can be exchanged between clients and therapists via mail, as in the case of imprisoned felons. During the therapist's vacation, clients can continue to work on assigned lessons.

Other advantages relate to the inexpensive reproduction of programmed materials and their direct application to personal computers. With minor editing, these materials could be tailored to individual situations in far less time than it would take to develop entirely new programs. Visits to the therapist would be less frequent, with no loss of the time available for work on the presenting problems because families would complete the written homework assignments on their own time. Writing programs would also help identify families who do not wish to follow through with treatment or who are otherwise not motivated to change. Furthermore, by making all three kinds of communication available, we may be able to discover which media each family finds more comfortable and productive. By using the verbal medium exclusively, we would miss this opportunity.

Psychoeducational and Social Skills Training Approaches

Arguably, no other mental health intervention holds as much promise to do the most good for the most people as preventive psychoeducational and social skills training approaches (L'Abate, 1987b, 1990; McFarlane, 1991). Parenting training programs are an example of such interventions. Similar preventive efforts addressing psychological/ sociological/ family issues would minimize the number of families requiring therapeutic intervention or remedial services. More energy from the helping profession needs to be directed toward this end. Traditionally, psychotherapists have not been trained in the administration of these programs, nor have they interacted with specialists in psychoeducational skill training approaches. These shortcomings have limited cross-fertilization of ideas and the contribution of this speciality to the overall welfare of families. In actual practice, specialized trainers in psychoeducational skills training programs would be always under the supervision of the therapist. These programs would allow professionals to extend their clinical practice to couples and families who would not label themselves as being in need of clinical services, but who would want to learn more about becoming more effective individuals, partners, or parents. Many of the first author's former students—trained in structured social skills training programs such as couple and family enrichment (L'Abate, 1990; L'Abate & Weinstein, 1987; L'Abate & Young, 1987), as well as in psychotherapy—report a synergistic effect of both approaches in their clinical practices. Furthermore, these professionals report that they are able to serve a much larger clientele than it would be possible if they used just one of the two approaches.

Psychoeducational programs could yield significant benefits for many reasons (Accordino & Guerney, 1993; McFarlane, 1991; Snyder & Guerney, 1993; Sprafkin, Gershaw, & Goldstein, 1993). Premarital programs would prepare young people for marriage, thereby decreasing later marital problems. Remarriage programs containing much of the same material could be directed toward those preparing to marry again. Parenting programs, already in widespread use, could become more widely available once clinicians incorporate them in their practices. As the demographic characteristics of our society shift toward an aging population, programs for caregivers of both children and parents are needed to help these caregivers cope with the multiplicity of demands put on them (Arcus, Schvaneveldt, & Moss, 1993; L'Abate, 1990).

Psychoeducational programs may also be useful for other members of a client's family . For example, as a supplement to family therapy, the family of an alcoholic would benefit from psychoeducational approaches about alcohol and its aftermath. Psychoeducational training for adult children of alcoholics would increase their awareness of relationship patterns common to individuals who have experienced similar problems.

A number of social skills training modules would be effective components in the prevention of psychopathology, as demonstrated by the work of Anderson, Reiss, and Hogarty (1986). Teaching young men how to express anger in a manageable and appropriate way seems a far better strategy than trying to help already violent men "relearn" styles of relating. Anger coping programs would be of particular value in working with immigrants from cultures that still sanction violence in the home.

Therapists would need to differentiate between psychoeducational programs directed toward *social support* and *empowerment* as found in groups whose members share similar problems (e.g., Alcoholic Anonymous) and programs directed toward *enablement,* for groups learning new skills, such as problem-solving, assertiveness, intimacy, and negotiation. Noncredentialed but specifically trained paraprofessionals could work with therapists to reach populations that would not otherwise seek help. The main advantages of these programs lie in their ready content identification (e.g., "parenting"), their structured format with an exact number of sessions known beforehand, and their relatively low cost because of the group format (L'Abate, 1990).

Expansions to New Computer and Interactive Technologies

Since the mid-1980s, technological advancements have been made that will have a tremendous positive impact on psychotherapeutic endeavors. These advancements include incorporating the videocassette recorder (VCR) and the personal computer with a modem into therapeutic practice.

Videotape Recordings

The ready utility of the TV and VCR as a teaching tool has not been lost on U.S. educators, therapists, parents, and policy makers. However, the use of video-tapes in psychotherapeutic and preventive activities can be expanded. The VCR is an excellent method of teaching appropriate expressions of emotion, conflict resolution styles, parenting strategies, activities aimed at combating depression, anger management techniques, budgeting, and a host of other topics.

Videotapes can be created over a wide band of situations, ranging from a narrowly defined issue, such as anger expression, to broad issues that address a whole domain of life, as in learning how to love and to negotiate. Videotapes can be tailored to meet the unique needs and limitations of any population or group (e.g., abusive families could be shown how to discipline children properly without the use of violence). The creation of a taped program, however, requires clear thinking, planning, and input from a variety of experts. It will not work as an impulsive, clever idea produced on the spur of the moment. For instance, the first author is in the process of converting, for interactive applications, 50 structured enrichment programs for couples and families, developed with his students over a period of 20 years (L'Abate & Weinstein, 1987; L'Abate & Young, 1987).

In addition to the impersonality of tapes, another benefit is that clients can view and review useful videos as many times as they choose. Tapes can be viewed at home, possibly reducing the number of required therapy sessions, and the previous experience of a relevant tape can add focus to sessions. Therapeutic gains also could be engendered at a pace that is more appropriate for clients. With more control from clients, cooperation and motivation would increase.

Personal Computers and Modems

Along a similar line, the increasing ubiquity of personal computers and modems makes it possible for clients to experience a whole new range of therapeutic and preventive programs. In fact, the first author has argued that computers can serve as the third avenue of service delivery after medication and psychotherapy. In addition to personal computers at home, in the future it will be possible to have computers available in public and university libraries. By the same token, why should clinicians not offer the same service for a fee to their clients? There are many clients, in the first author's practice, who respond to written homework assignments through their computers. In addition to the convenience and utility of being an "at-home" approach to service delivery with all its concomitant benefits, clients have the opportunity to make use of many writing programs. It is necessary, of course, that these programs be written and debugged prior to their consumption via electronic mail. Such a matter seems to us, though, to be a rather small problem relative to the value of this approach. Clients in isolated geographic areas, for example, would be able to receive a range of therapeutic services as easily as those living in urban areas. Furthermore, the opportunity to work on specific issues is made available for clients in the same way as any other homework assignments. Rather than bouncing from one clinician to another, a client could be referred to an electronic library of preprogrammed lessons as well as a reference list of clinics and private practitioners with whom to work, if it is so desired (L'Abate, 1986, 1990, 1992, in press, a, submitted for publication). The preventive, relatively inexpensive, mass-oriented aspects of this approach are only now beginning to be appreciated.

Expanding to Supporting and Assisting Personnel

Increasing the modalities of treatment would require a broadening of support personnel. Everyone from computer programmers to photographic consultants would be needed to make these expansions work. In addition, building a system of professional associates to do some of the hands-on work of the clinician is proposed as a way to meet the needs of the increasing numbers of families who need help.

Some practitioners may take offense or feel threatened at the implication that they give up some of their hard-earned "turf." Christensen and Jacobson (1994) present a provocative argument asserting that empirical evidence proclaiming the superiority of the experienced professional over trained paraprofessionals in psychotherapy has not been found. They go on to suggest that professional therapists may be put to better use by doing less actual service delivery and more program development, implementation, and supervision. Mental health practitioners may follow the lead of industrial, medical, and commercial organizations structured along hierarchical lines. Hierarchical structuring produces positive results for employees because whoever is more experienced profits by the work of less experienced personnel. The latter are ultimately responsible for most service delivery. Using paraprofessionals who are less broadly educated but trained in a specific service delivery modality would allow the credentialed professional to spend more time with more critical and difficult families, later on delegating many of them to assistants, after taking care of the crisis phase (Kochalka, Buzas, L'Abate, McHenry, & Gibson, 1987).

This perspective appears to be the direction of the future for degreed clinicians. The question of how to accomplish this shift in professional responsibility remains open. A hierarchical arrangement of service providers working as an organized and multidisciplinary team may be the most efficient and expedient solution (L'Abate, 1965a, 1965b, 1990, 1994a). At the top of this hierarchy would be the degreed clinician at the doctorate level, who develops programs, trains assisting personnel, and supervises the implementation of services. This individual has the final responsibility for the case and holds the highest credentials. Groups of degreed professionals may want to band together to increase the breadth of expertise available to clients in any one location or practice setting. A family clinician could arrange for consultation from other specialties in different disciplines to provide input on a regular basis to specific programs or cases.

Below the doctorate, there would be an associate, with an MA degree plus years of psychotherapy experience. Diversifying associates in terms of their primary areas of expertise would be an effective way to provide help to clients. For example, a case in which marital issues predominate may be assigned to an associate with training and interest in working with couples, whereas an associate who specializes in mood disorders may be more appropriate for the depressed individual. This associate would have the majority of direct, face-to-face therapy contact hours with clients and would be under the doctoral professional's direct supervision. Videotaping therapy sessions would be the standard operating procedure allowing direct access to the content and process of therapy for treatment planning.

Under the associate would be a tier of paraprofessionals, with a bachelor degree or equivalent, who could act as assistants (Arnhoff, Rubinstein, &

Speisman, 1969; Ellsworth, 1968; Grosser, Henry, & Kelly, 1969; Guerney, 1969). They would be trained (and supervised) in areas such as the administration and scoring of standard psychological tests (but not the interpretation or reporting), skills training for specific psychoeducational interventions, and the administration of written homework assignments. Depending on the institutional or organizational structure of the setting and the expertise of team members, assistants could be under the supervision of the doctorate or of an associate. For example, a client may need to take a battery of psychological tests to rule out psychosis. The administration of these tests would be the domain of the assistant, who would pass on the protocols and results to the doctorate for interpretation and report writing (L'Abate, 1965a, 1965b, 1994b). The treatment team would convene to develop appropriate therapeutic strategies on a case-by-case basis. When the first author was the director of the Georgia State University Family Study Center, the following system was used: First-year graduate students would learn how to evaluate families (L'Abate, 1983a, 1994b). In the second year, they would learn how to administer structured enrichment programs under the supervision of third- or fourth-year graduate students (Jessee & L'Abate, 1981; L'Abate & Weinstein, 1987; L'Abate & Young, 1987). The latter were responsible for therapeutic interventions and, together with the director, planned how therapeutic interventions would be combined with enrichment programs (L'Abate, et al., 1983).

The treatment team approach would lend itself well to the development of a fairly standard set of operating procedures. Standard procedures for evaluation and assessment, for intervention and therapy, for crisis and emergency situations, and for prevention could all be developed. These written protocols would be tied to empirical research delineating effective methods for handling particular problems and issues. Protocols would reduce mismatches between client and clinician, while increasing the likelihood for implementation of effective interventive strategies. They would have the same function as blueprints in the construction of skyscrapers (L'Abate, 1992, submitted for publication).

This differentiation of skills for family clinicians is no different from other spheres of work. Skyscrapers are not built by architects and engineers, but by a hierarchical organization of personnel necessary for cost-efficiency and productivity; workers' skills and abilities are complementary, proceeding simultaneously along parallel tracks. The first step in this differentiation of skills lies in distinguishing professional from technical skills. For instance, the administration and the scoring of a standard psychological test require the ability to read the instructions in a manual as well as a certain amount of personal sensitivity to subtle or not too subtle emotional nuances in people. Interpretation of test results and report writing, on the other hand, require a knowledge of statistics, personality adjustment and psychopathology, and other professional skills that are learned at the doctorate level. The same kind of distinction could follow an increasingly complex sequence, going upward from clerical to technical, from technical to semiprofessional, and from semiprofessional to professional.

Under this proposal, therefore, technical-level personnel would administer standard operating procedures in evaluation and structured intervention approaches, with crisis intervention and psychotherapy being the responsibility of semiprofessional and professional personnel. To implement this proposal, however, changes would need to occur at the level of clinical training programs.

IMPLICATIONS FOR TRAINING

No changes can take place in any profession unless changes occur in training programs at the graduate as well as at the postgraduate level. Fox (1994), in a criticism of current educational practices for the training of professional psychologists (equally applicable to other mental health professions), argued:

> At a time when the public is increasingly aware that the major health problems of modern society stem from habits, lifestyles, and behaviors that increase the risk of a variety of costly illness or decrease the coping ability of people and their support groups [we would substitute the term "family" for the term "support groups"], professional . . . . specialists [have been] trained to work with the mentally ill rather than [as] experts broadly knowledgeable about the amelioration and change of problematic behaviors. (p. 204)

Proposed here is a fairly radical shift in thinking about mental health services. A number of implications for mental health professionals about expanding into other modalities of treatment affect not only training and supervision but also to licensing and costs for services.

Training at the Graduate Level

First, because of the increasing breadth of theoretical and clinical information it is likely that professionals will need to become specialized in one area of expertise (L'Abate, 1987a). One doctoral person could be an authority on eating disorders, another on substance abuse, and another on trauma survivors. It may be necessary in the future to become even more narrowly specialized as our understanding of the etiology and treatment of psychological disorders becomes clearer.

Second, whereas professionals would prefer the basics (e.g., theories of personality and psychopathology from both individualistic and family perspectives) specialized interests would be identified early and in-depth training could be undertaken. Training of semiprofessional and technical assistants also would need to reflect this specialization (Shapiro & Wiggings, 1994). Training generalists would no longer be valued—the field is becoming too complex to allow generalists. The fact that students would be choosing a position in a structured and recognized hierarchy from the outset must be appreciated by both trainees and those who train them. Because some would find working under direct supervision difficult, these concerns must be addressed as early in training as possible.

Perhaps the most controversial implication of this proposal revolves around the requirement that certain long-held postulates among particular mental health disciplines would need to be reexamined. Turf wars would have to be addressed directly as the helping community becomes more interconnected even while maintaining disciplinary distinctions. Systems thinkers would need to consider the importance of the individual's pathology even while individualistic theorists would need to take into account the contextual parameters that affect their client. A more holistic approach to treating human problems would result, presumably with a much more effective system of interventions and a better set of outcomes (L'Abate, 1994a). The general population is more likely to accept these suggestions than are those in the mental health professions. Having operated under this model for many years, we can testify to its effectiveness for clients as well as professionals although we are aware that it will take more than our testimony to accomplish change.

Additional courses would introduce students to the various media described briefly in this chapter—psychoeducational social skills training programs, and computer and VCR interactions. At the clinical internship level, specialization would begin. Students would be trained in a sequence from generalists to specialists (Kochalka & L'Abate, 1983; L'Abate, 1983a, 1983b, 1985, 1987a). This position is supported by Fox (1994), who suggested:

> Clearly, the field has evolved to the point that we very much need to have educational programs that are generic, that include some contributions from other relevant professions and disciplines, and that are oriented toward training practitioners for broad-gauged interventions in changing or improving the effectiveness of human behavior (p. 202). . . . If we wish to ensure, rather than hope, that students are not trained for obsolescence, then we must see to it that they have a *broad working knowledge of the entire spectrum of professional practice, theory, and the research basis that undergirds it* [italics added] (p. 203). . . . Because the science of psychology is concerned with the total range of human behavior, the compass of our profession should be very broad indeed (pp. 204–205). . . . Specialization in mental health should be left—to a larger extent than is true at the present—to postdoctoral experiences. (p. 205)

Training at the Postgraduate Level

The major implication of the foregoing proposal lies in postgraduate training being much more extensive in a specific specialty than it has been the case in the past. For instance, Fox recommends that clinical services would include (a) preventive care, primary, secondary, and tertiary linked to diagnostic and evaluative instruments; (b) short-term, brief- and crisis interventions; (c) rehabilitation for people with long-term effects of physical injuries (that would include also nonverbal and written media); (d) long-term care of chronic conditions, which in our view would include structured, psychoeducational social skills training programs. All these specializations will have to take place at a postgraduate level, either through formal postdoctoral training, or through continuing education workshops and conferences.

At this level, training would be tailored toward working with professional associates and assistants. A great deal of this training would be on the job, if and when such a training is required by an institution. In private practice, family clinicians will be able to experience new practices and roles once it is understood that such professional differentiation will enlarge practices and increase income.

Training in Multicultural Helping Skills

Our increasingly multicultural society requires that practically all clinical training programs include such a multicultural component in their curricula (Odell, Shelling, Young, Hewitt, & L'Abate, 1994). Especially in mental health clinics and psychiatric hospitals in large metropolitan areas, it will be necessary to have specialists on staff who will be able to speak the language of many families. We know of a police department in Doraville, Georgia, a suburb of Atlanta, that keeps on call a list of interpreters in 200 languages, just to keep ahead of problems that are increasingly cropping up in this multicultural suburb. Perhaps, some clinicians will be able to bypass such training by specializing in working strictly with English-speaking Anglo-American families. The number of these clinicians, however, will become smaller and smaller with the increasing multicultural mosaic of our society.

CONCLUSION

Family clinicians face a great challenge as the 20th century closes. This chapter has suggested a number of ways to enlarge current mental health practices and roles to reach a much larger number of families than in the past. Such an expansion will be possible through acquisition of new therapeutic skills in the use of nonverbal and written media as well as personal computers and television. The addition of psychoeducational social skills programs to the existing therapeutic repertoire would also mean an enlargement of traditional roles to include noncredentialed paraprofessional specialists who would develop a hierarchy of helpers differing in skills and interests. Just as bare hands cannot build skyscrapers, isolated clinicians cannot help families as efficiently as a hierarchy of professionals and paraprofessionals working together for the common good of families.

REFERENCES

Accordino, M. P., & Guerney, B. G., Jr. (1993). Effects of the relationship enhancement program on community rehabilitation staff and clients. *Psychosocial Rehabilitation Journal, 17,* 109–144.

Anderson, C. M., Reiss, D. J., & Hogarty, G. E. (1986). *Schizophrenia and the family: A practitioner's guide to psychoeducation and management.* New York: Guilford.

Arcus, M. E., Schvaneveldt, H. D., & Moss, J. J. (1993). *Handbook of family life education* (Vol. 1 & 2). Newbury Park, CA: Sage.

Arnhoff, F. N., Rubinstein, E. A., & Speisman, J. C. (Eds.). (1969). *Manpower for mental health.* Chicago, IL: Aldine.

Bergin, A. E., & Garfield, S. L. (1994). *Handbook of psychotherapy and behavior change.* New York: Wiley.

Burgoon, J. K. (1994). Nonverbal signals. In M. L. Knapp & G. R. Miller (Eds.), *Handbook of interpersonal communication* (pp. 229–285). Thousand Oaks, CA: Sage.

Christensen, A., & Jacobson, N. S. (1994). Who (or what) can do psychotherapy: The status and challenge of nonprofessional therapies. *Psychological Science, 5,* 8–14.

Ellsworth, R. B. (1968). *Nonprofessionals in psychiatric rehabilitation: The psychiatric aide and the schizophrenic patient.* New York: Appleton-Century-Crofts.

Fox, R. E. (1994). Training professional psychologists for the twenty-first century. *American Psychologist, 49,* 200–206.

Giles, T. R. (1993). *Managed mental health care: A guide for practitioners, employers, and hospital administrators.* Boston, MA: Allyn and Bacon.

Goodman, M., Brown, J., & Deitz, P. (1992). *Managing managed health care: A mental health practitioner's survival guide.* Washington, DC: American Psychiatric Press.

Goodyear, I. M. (1990). *Life experiences, development and child psychopathology.* New York: Wiley.

Grosser, C., Henry, W. E., & Kelly, J. G. (Eds.). (1969). *Nonprofessionals in the human services.* San Francisco, CA: Jossey-Bass.

Guerney, B. G., Jr. (Ed.). (1969). *Psychotherapeutic agents: New roles for nonprofessionals, parents, and teachers.* New York: Holt, Rinehart and Winston.

Gurman, A. S., & Kniskern, D. P. (1991). (Eds.). *Handbook of family therapy* (Vol. 2). New York: Brunner/Mazel.

Gurman, A. S., Kniskern, D. P., & Pinsof, W. M. (1986). Research in the process and outcome of marital and family therapy. In S. L. Garfield & A. E. Bergin (Eds.), *Handbook of psychotherapy and behavior change* (pp. 565–624). New York: Wiley.

Jessee, E., & L'Abate, L. (1981). Enrichment role-playing as a step in the training of family therapists. *Journal of Marriage and Family Therapy, 7,* 507–514.

Kepner, J. I. (1993). *Body process: Working with the body in psychotherapy.* San Francisco, CA: Jossey-Bass.

Kochalka, J., & L'Abate, L. (1983). Structure and gradualness in the clinical training of family psychologists. In L. L'Abate (Ed.), *Family psychology: Theory, therapy, and training* (pp. 287–299). Washington, DC: University Press of America.

Kochalka, J., Buzas, H., L'Abate, L., McHenry, S., & Gibson, E. (1987). Structured enrichment: Training and implementation with paraprofessionals. In L. L'Abate (Ed.), *Family psychology II: Theory, therapy, enrichment, and training* (pp. 279–287). Lanham, MD: University Press of America.

L'Abate, L. (1965a). *The laboratory method in clinical child psychology.* Unpublished manuscript.

L'Abate, L. (1965b). *The laboratory method in clinical psychology.* Unpublished manuscript.

L'Abate, L. (1983a). The laboratory evaluation of families. In L. L'Abate (Ed.), *Family psychology: Theory, therapy, and training* (pp. 159–168). Washington, DC: University Press of America.

L'Abate, L. (1983b). Training in family psychology. In L. L'Abate (Ed.), *Family psychology: Theory, therapy, and training* (pp. 277–285). Washington, DC: University Press of America.

L'Abate, L. (1985). A training program for family psychology: Evaluation, prevention and therapy. *American Journal of Family Therapy, 13,* 7–16.

L'Abate, L. (1986). *Systematic family therapy.* New York: Brunner/Mazel.

L'Abate, L. (1987a). In favor of specializations within clinical psychology. In L. L'Abate (Ed.), *Family psychology II: Theory, therapy, enrichment, and training* (pp. 239–246). Lanham, MD: University Press of America.

L'Abate, L. (1987b). Recent developments in psychoeducational skills programs for families: A review of reviews. In L. L'Abate (Ed.), *Family psychology II: Theory, therapy, enrichment, and training* (pp. 195–203). Lanham, MD: University Press of America.

L'Abate, L. (1990). *Building family competence: Primary and secondary prevention strategies.* Newbury Park, CA: Sage.

L'Abate, L. (1992). *Programmed writing: A self-administered approach for interventions with individuals, couples, and families.* Pacific Grove, CA: Brooks Cole.

L'Abate, L. (1994a). *A theory of personality development.* New York: Wiley.

L'Abate, L. (1994b). *Family evaluation: A psychological approach.* Thousand Oaks, CA: Sage.

L'Abate, L. (in press, a). Writing in individual, couple, and family interventions: Prevention and therapy. *Directions in Marriage & Family Therapy, 2.*

L'Abate, L. (in press, b). Nonverbal techniques in marriage and family therapy. *Directions in Marriage & Family Therapy, 4.*

L'Abate, L. (in press, c). The paradox of change: Better them than us! In R. S. Sauber (Ed.), *Managed mental health care: Clinical applications for practitioners.* New York: Brunner/Mazel.

L'Abate, L. (submitted for publication). *Writing and computer-assisted training.*

L'Abate, L., Hanson, J. C., & Ganahl, G. (1986). *Methods of family therapy.* Englewood Cliffs, NJ: Prentice-Hall.

L'Abate, L., & Weinstein, S. E. (1987). *Structured enrichment programs for couples and families.* New York: Brunner/Mazel.

L'Abate, L., Wildman, R. W., II, O'Callaghan, J. B., Simon, S. J., Allison, M., Kahn, G., & Rainwater, N. (1983). The laboratory evaluation and enrichment of couples: Applications and some preliminary results. In L. L'Abate (Ed.), *Family psychology: Theory, therapy, and training* (pp. 169–175). Washington, DC: University Press of America.

L'Abate, L., & Young, L. (1987). *Casebook of structured enrichment programs for couples and families.* New York: Brunner/Mazel.

Levy, R. L., & Shelton, J. L. (1990). Tasks in brief therapy. In R. A. Wells & V. J. Giannetti (Eds.), *Handbook of the brief psychotherapies* (pp. 145–163). New York: Plenum.

McFarlane, W. R. (1991). Family psychoeducational treatment. In A. S. Gurman & D. P. Kniskern (Eds.), *Handbook of family therapy* (Vol. 2, pp. 363–395). New York: Brunner/Mazel.

Mays, D. T., & Franks, C. M. (1985). *Negative outcome in psychotherapy and what to do about it.* New York: Springer.

Middleman, R. R. (1968). *The nonverbal method in working with groups.* New York: Association Press.

Odell, M., Shelling, G., Young, K., Hewitt, D., & L'Abate, L. (1994). The skills of the marriage and family therapist in straddling multicultural issues. *American Journal of Family Therapy, 21,* 145–154.

Patterson, M. L. (1984). Nonverbal intimacy and exchange [Special issue]. *Journal of Nonverbal Behavior, 8,* 233–293.

Rothbaum, B. O., Hodges, L. F., Kooper, R., Opdyke, D., Williford, J. S., & North, M. (1995). Effectiveness of computer-generated (virtual reality) graded exposure in the treatment of acrophobia. *American Journal of Psychiatry, 152,* 626–628.

Seraganian, P. (Ed.). (1993). *Exercise psychology: The influence of physical exercise on psychological processes.* New York: Wiley.

Shapiro, A. E., & Wiggins, J. G. (1994). A PsyD degree for every practitioner: Truth in lending. *American Psychologist, 49,* 207–210.

Shields, C. G., Wynne, L. C., McDaniel, S. H., & Gawinski, B. A. (1994). The marginalization of family therapy: A historical and continuing problem. *Journal of Marital and Family Therapy, 20,* 117–138.

Smith, M. L., Glass, G. V., & Miller, T. I. (1980). *The benefits of psychotherapy.* Baltimore, MD: Johns Hopkins University Press.

Snyder, M., & Guerney, B. G., Jr. (1993). Brief couple/family therapy: The relationship enhancement approach. In R. A. Wells & V. J. Giannetti (Eds.), *Casebook of the brief psychotherapies* (pp. 221–234). New York: Plenum.

Sprafkin, R. P., Gershaw. N. J., & Goldstein, A. P. (1993). *Social skills for mental health: A structured learning approach.* Boston, MA: Allyn and Bacon.

Steere, D. A. (1982). *Bodily expressions in psychotherapy.* New York: Brunner/Mazel.

Wagner, N. (1992). *The clinician's guide to managed mental health care.* New York: Havorth.

Waxer, P. H. (1978). *Nonverbal aspects of psychotherapy.* New York: Praeger.

Weintraub, M. D. (1981). *Verbal behavior: Adaptations in psychopathology.* New York: Springer.

CHAPTER 16

Capitalizing on Family Resiliency

MICHELE HARWAY

In this volume, a number of experts on families have discussed the special needs and strengths of a variety of family constellations, of families challenged by life cycle stresses and confronted by unusual events. In many of the preceding chapters, the focus has been on the resilience of families and of the individuals within them. In this chapter, we summarize findings from the preceding chapters, propose a resiliency or competency model for working with these families, and suggest special training needs of family clinicians. We conclude with a discussion of some special issues that family clinicians should consider.

WHAT IS NORMATIVE?

We have argued that traditional conceptions of what is normative in families are no longer applicable. A majority of families represent nontraditional constellations where factors such as biological ties between parents and children differ from the traditional notion, where parental marital status varies, where sexual orientation of parents may vary, and where gender roles and/or employment status of the parents may diverge from traditional expectations. Theories about individual development and the family life cycle that have provided guidance to generations of mental health professionals and that have shaped the expectations of Americans no longer provide a good fit for the life tragectory of many families. We need expanded definitions of what is normative in families and new training paradigms for family clinicians.

THE IMPACT OF CULTURE

This book underscores the importance of culture in our understanding of what is normative in families. Culture plays a key role in defining what is normal and acceptable in families. The impact of culture is broad and the families we treat will not remain unaffected by their cultural substrate. Culture affects the very definition of who is included in the family, family norms, what forms of adaption are required to meet those norms, what is considered normal and what is considered atypical, and what accounts for the effectiveness of various family interventions.

AGING AND FAMILIES

Population demographics are changing, not only in terms of family constellation, but also in terms of life expectancies. As people live longer, the effects of aging on families will make themselves known in new ways. The family's ability to adjust to the changes brought about by aging is related to how well the family has negotiated issues of autonomy, connectedness, and innovation at other times in the life cycle. Family clinicians are uniquely suited for intervention with the aged and their families and for the promotion of psychological and spiritual meaning.

VARIETIES OF FAMILY CONSTELLATIONS

Single-parent families and stepfamilies have special needs and special strengths. By focusing on the competence of these families, clinicians can help them achieve their therapeutic goals. Acknowledging the stressful transitions experienced by these families, over and above the stresses of the family life cycle, as well as helping heal the hurts from failed relationships is a key task of the mental health professional. Understanding the dynamics of single-parent families and stepfamilies is an important responsibility of professionals working with families. Clinicians also have a responsibility to broaden the definition of family, including issues of membership in the family (e.g., is the mother of the stepfather a third grandmother?).

Gay and lesbian families present particular challenges. They present some of the same dynamics in many cases as stepfamilies or adoptive families, but at the same time, these families have generally come into being in a political climate that considers their very existence as pathological. As a result, the special challenges of these families include existing in a society that, for the most part, does not acknowledge their existence and when it does acknowledge their existence attempts to end it by removing the children from their parents. Special issues of family genesis and family composition are key therapeutic concerns. Issues of custody and other interactions with the legal system are not uncommon. The precariousness of the role of the nonbiological parent needs to be considered, as does the impact on the child of being in this nontraditional family constellation with varying issues and concerns at different developmental stages.

Another family constellation that differs from expectation is that of adoptive families. Although these families appear to be no different from the traditional two-parent family, in fact they do differ in one important dimension: In most cases, adoptive families comprise persons not related to each other by biology.

Nonetheless, there are variations even within adoptive families based on the age of the child at adoption, varieties of ethnic and/or racial backgrounds between parents and children or between siblings, and extent of ongoing contact with the biological parents. Family clinicians working with issues of adoption may find themselves working with the adoptee; parents, the biological parents, or the adopted and their needs and problems will differ as a consequence. The life cycle stage of the family also impacts the material being examined in clinical sessions. It is also important to understand that in addition, adoptive families face the same strengths and challenges as other family constellations.

In addition to considering nontraditional family constellations, this volume examines how families handle unusual events and the role that family clinicians can play in helping families navigate through difficult periods.

MENTAL ILLNESS AND THE FAMILY

When a family member suffers from a chronic mental illness, the entire family is impacted. Family clinicians have an opportunity to intervene in a way that will be helpful to the family and will allow them to demonstrate areas of competency rather than pathologizing them. Among interventions clinicians can offer the families of the chronically mentally ill are those that will allow them to achieve greater control over the events in their life including the mental illness of their loved one. Both clinical and nonclinical services can be offered. Nonclinical services may include educational, skills-oriented, or supportive interventions. The focus of those services should be to educate family members about mental illness and the mental health delivery system; to train them in communication, conflict resolution, problem solving, assertiveness, behavioral management, and stress management; to allow them to grieve and to share and mobilize resources, to identify the impact of the mental illness on the family and its individual members and to teach them to utilize formal and informal support systems.

TRAUMA AND ABUSE

With families of trauma survivors, much of the work concerns acknowledging the impact that trauma has on the entire family. Grief work follows. Another important goal is to help the clients identify the strengths of the family that have allowed them to cope well with the traumatic situation. Social skills training and assigning of new meaning to the traumatic event while attempting to correct cognitive distortions are also important. Multiple interventions in trauma families are necessary, focusing on limit setting, clarification of roles and rules, creation of a routine in the home or reestablishment of a routine, education about posttraumatic stress disorder (PTSD), education about communication skills, and conflict resolution skills, and the use of appropriate touch.

For most trauma survivors, home and the family represent a safe haven from the traumatogen. For those who experience domestic violence, home is where they are most at risk from violence perpetrated by a loved one. Whether the abuse is perpetrated by one spouse on the other, by a parent on a child, or by a family member on an elder, the very fact that the trauma is caused by a family member intensifies the impact. With these families, it is important to acknowledge that behaviors which may be seen as pathological by some clinicians are evidence of the attempt of these persons to reorganize their worlds in meaningful ways—they are survival behaviors. As Root (1992) indicates, "Disorganized and unusual behavior following horrible experiences are normal responses to traumatic events" (p. 237).

THE URBAN ENVIRONMENT

Living in an urban environment presents special challenges to families, ranging from basic survival issues to dealing with their complex physical and social environments. Families in cities have been forced to confront the following major problem areas: poverty, juvenile delinquency, violence, gun use, and gangs. The chronic exposure of residents to violence makes them increasingly vulnerable to psychological and emotional sequelae. Moreover, cities have historically attracted immigrants seeking to integrate into the mainstream and special populations and marginalized groups such as runaways and the homeless who need special services. The families that come into therapy tend to be seen as multiproblem families because they experience crises and emergencies as well as the long-term consequences of poverty and inadequate resources. The successful family therapist will be one with skills in community advocacy, who is knowledgeable about the social context within which these families exist including the cultural substrate, and who is able to maintain a resiliency focus in his or her work.

CHILDHOOD DISABILITY

A different kind of stressor is encountered by families with handicapped or disabled youngsters. These families are coping with having to care for a child with special needs such as specialized medical care, special child care, and unusual educational needs. In addition, some family members may experience considerable emotional distress, especially in reaction to the social service delivery system or the family system itself. The impact on the family varies depending on whether the disability existed at birth or developed at a later stage as a result of disease, accident, or other trauma; and having a disabled child affects the family differently at different stages of the family life cycle. Mental health practitioners may intervene effectively as part of an interdisciplinary team along with medical personnel and educators. Among the goals of their intervention would be to empower parents and enhance their competence, to help the parents recognize the needs and strengths of the child, to assist other family members to make lifestyle adjustments to accommodate the needs of the handicapped child, and to facilitate the pursuit of adjunctive services for the family.

CHRONIC ILLNESS AND THE FAMILY

When a family member has a chronic illness, the entire family system is affected. The reorganization of the family is sometimes healthy, sometimes dysfunctional, but always stressful and requiring some form of support. Family clinicians can provide help to the families through education, support, and therapeutic intervention. The biopsychosocial model encourages multiple levels of explanation and allows an examination of the illness, its psychological sequelae and the systemic issues of the family. Clinicians should be prepared to deal with setbacks in the therapy, especially when dealing with illnesses of a progressive or episodic nature. The impact of the illness on the family social context, including ethnicity, gender, religion, sexuality, and alternative family structure, must be considered.

A progressive form of illness with special societal and familial impact is represented by the AIDS epidemic. A diagnosis of HIV/AIDS leads to complex reorganizational challenges for families with the disruption of the afflicted member's ability to play the usual role of parent, domestic partner, or breadwinner. Family members are at risk for emotional difficulties or behavioral dysfunctions, with direct caregivers particularly vulnerable. Children are at particular risk for emotional problems and have parenting and child-care needs that must be met despite their parents' illness.

Not all persons with AIDS have the same needs, however. Working with gay men with AIDS requires special sensitivity toward gay relationships and an assessment of when and how to involve the family of origin and the family of choice. AIDS in the inner city presents cultural issues that must be addressed. And, intravenous drug users with AIDS present the special challenge to clinicians of working with addictive disorders while confronting the disruptions brought by an HIV diagnosis. Practitioners working with AIDS/HIV-afflicted clients have a particular responsibility to take an advocacy position for the development of more programs to service this population.

ALCOHOL AND DRUG ABUSE

For some time now, alcohol and drug abuse interventions within the clinical community have incorporated a focus on families and their functioning. The development of such interventions results from an understanding that the effects of substance abuse reach beyond the individual users to their families. It is also clear that spouses and children of alcoholics, for example, are likely to experience a variety of psychological problems. Moreover, substance abuse has health care implications. Interventions have included behavior/coping models (focusing on the individual, the spouse, the domestic partners, and the larger family), family systems models (focusing on family functioning), and integrative models combining both behavioral and systemic approaches. In addition, the self-help approaches provide support for the addict and for family members. Clinicians preparing to work with substance abusers, in addition to training in a variety of intervention approaches, must be aware of the impact of gender, ethnic, and cultural factors on individual differences. More attention needs to be paid to concomitant problem behaviors and their suspected etiological roots.

NEW APPROACHES TO WORKING WITH FAMILIES

When family therapy started, it was considered a cost-effective way of seeing several members of one family at one time. This approach is no longer sufficient to deal with the many challenges that face American families, as attested by most of the chapters in this volume. Moreover, the number of families that clinicians can affect is limited when face-to-face counseling is the only approach being considered. And many families shy away from psychotherapy because of cost or popular misperceptions of what therapy is all about. Many more families can be impacted when the definition of the role of the family clinician is broadened. Several authors in this volume have proposed expansion of the traditional role of the family clinician. Suggestions and recommendations have included an expanded utilization of nonverbal and written modes of communication, increased involvement in psychoeducational and social skills training approaches, more frequent utilization of interactive technology such as personal computers and the development of practices utilizing professional associates and paraprofessional assistants with specialized knowledge of structured preventive, psychoeducational skills training programs. In an era of limited resources, clinicians have a responsibility to consider a variety of ways to help families.

A RESILIENCY MODEL FOR WORKING WITH FAMILIES

There is no doubt that families are a great deal more resilient than we give them credit for being. Considering the wide varieties of family types, the stressors that most families must confront, and those that are more out of the ordinary, it is surprising that more families are not experiencing problems. Graduate training programs, however, are largely unaware of the extraordinary resources of most families and most mental health training emphasizes pathology over resiliency. As Barnard (1994) acknowledges:

My family therapy background had enhanced my sensitivity to monitoring an obsessive proclivity for "deficit detecting" to the exclusion of acknowledging strengths and resources . . . we are encouraged to perceive everyone we come into contact with as having some disorder, or if not in clear evidence, as having some sophisticated way of disguising their various deficits. (p.136)

Why this focus on pathology over resources? For one, the theories of human behavior and psychopathology learned by all mental health professionals emphasize dysfunction. These theories and the clinical paradigms which accompany them lead to a focus on those dimensions of family functioning in need of modification rather than the acknowledgment of the family's stabilizing and supportive behaviors. Second, especially when working with third-party payers, professionals use the *Diagnostic and Statistical Manual of Mental Disorders* (DSM-IV; American Psychiatric Association, 1994) to establish a diagnosis on which a treatment plan is based. Because individual diagnoses and not relational ones are encompassed by the DSM-IV, the use of this assessment method encourages the application of individual diagnoses of pathology to each member of the family. When treatment plans are developed from this basis of pathology, then family treatment proceeds by focusing on the family's pathology. This focus, in turn, encourages looking for areas of weakness in families and ignoring the areas of strengths that all families possess.

A third perspective is that much of the literature read by mental health practitioners focuses on those individuals who develop symptoms rather than those who function well. For example, Barnard (1994) points out that much of the literature on adult children of alcoholics documents expected dysfunctional behaviors of individuals who have grown up with an alcoholic parent but fails to account for the nonpathological behavior of the great majority of such children (85% according to Wolin, 1991). Instead, Barnard encourages us to look toward the resiliency literature which attempts to understand factors that help explain why an individual who might otherwise be vulnerable to pathology would instead emerge from stressful situations unscathed. Similarly, we could learn much about resiliency in families by looking at the special strengths and assets developed by families with a chronically mentally ill member or blended families or some of the other families described in this volume.

Marsh (1992) suggests that a paradigm shift in working with these families is necessary. Such a paradigm shift would emphasize competence rather than pathology. Rather than taking a disease-based medical model in looking at families, clinicians would assess families from the perspective of health and development, identifying the special strengths the family has developed in coping with this experience. Accordingly, families are viewed as competent rather than pathological or dysfunctional, and the emphasis is on the family and the individual members' strengths, resources, and areas of wellness rather than their weaknesses, liabilities, and illnesses. Assessment is based on the family's competencies and deficits rather than on clinical typologies (as described by DSM-IV or any other diagnostic approach). Professionals working with these families and adopting this model serve as enabling agents, and the families they work with become collaborators. Such a model is ecological and educational. Focusing on the family's competency would involve some of the following interventions:

- In Chapter 1, we met a family headed by Elise, a single mother. One intervention here might be to increase the family's flexibility by reducing rigid role assignments. Elise might be encouraged to meet her need for social contact with other adults by making occasional plans with friends, at the same time allowing her daughters to cook that evening's meal.

- In Chapter 11, we met the Smythe family. Among the many interventions implemented in working with this family, the therapist encouraged alternative care arrangements for their Down syndrome daughter yielding more independence for the teenage son and respite care that would allow the parents time to enhance their own relationship. With these kinds of interventions, families are encouraged to take control over their life rather than remaining powerless victims of life's circumstances.

- We also saw in Chapter 12, Benita and Roberto struggling with Roberto's illness and his increasing dependence on his wife. Therapy, there, was designed to encourage Roberto to adopt a proactive posture in relation to his life and his illness and the limitations placed on him. One intervention involved showing him his options for contacting his neighbors when his wife had to leave the home.

- Other interventions that enhance coping effectiveness of families include developing new rituals better suited to their lifestyle. This is particularly important for families in nontraditional family constellations where traditional rituals conflict with the family's composition (e.g., blended families where the traditional Christmas celebration has to be modified to include a celebration with the custodial parent and his or her spouse and another celebration with the noncustodial parent and spouse). Another example is that of the gay family where two fathers must be acknowledged on Father's Day.

- Trauma survivors need particular assistance to reframe their experience and to change their perception of themselves from that of victims to that of survivors. The change to terminology from victim to survivor describes the change of self-perception that a trauma survivor can undergo. Along with it, it is necessary to construct new meaning for the trauma and to reconceptualize the world as a safe place once again. This reframing of the phenomenological experience of the trauma survivor serves to empower clients and encourages them to focus on the future rather than on the past.

Working from a competence model assumes that in working with these families, clinicians work to empower and enable the families rather than treat their pathology. The goal of intervention then is to enhance their coping effectiveness rather than providing psychotherapy.

IMPLICATIONS FOR TRAINING OF FAMILY CLINICIANS

New generations of mental health practitioners will need to be trained to work with the families of today and tomorrow. What this means is that clinicians must prepare both to be generalists who are knowledgeable about the types of families that will present for therapy and to be specialists who know their own therapeutic limitations and have access to the types of referrals that meet the adjunctive needs of the families described here. We recommend that specialized training in family diversity begin with new students enrolled in master's and doctorate programs and extend to licensed practitioners as part of their continuing education requirement. Clinical supervisors, too, must be sensitized to the varying needs of families and to the importance of approaching family work from a competence paradigm rather than one of pathology.

Suggested course content might include the following special topics (the list based on specific recommendations contained in the chapters of this book):

1. An understanding of what is normative in families: family demographics, family constellations, dimensions of family functioning (Harway & Wexler, Chapter 1).

2. A sensitivity to cultural diversity and its impact on family functioning Cuéllar & Glazer, Chapter 2).

3. Knowledge about the special issues of single-parent families, stepfamilies, and blended families (Seibt, Chapter 3) and adoptive families (Schwartz, Chapter 6).

4. An understanding of the genesis of gay and lesbian families, the interaction of family life cycle issues in gay and lesbian families, and the parent's individual development of a lesbian or gay identity and its impact on the family (Carlson, Chapter 4).

5. An understanding of issues of aging and how they impact on families at various stages of the life cycle (Peake, Rosenzweig, & Williamson, Chapter 5).

6. Knowledge about the needs of families of the chronically mentally ill, the disabled, and those suffering devastating diseases such as HIV. Learning interventions that acknowledge their strengths and resources and that strengthen family functioning (Marsh, Lefley, & Husted, Chapter 7; Edmister, Chapter 11; Strozier, Chapter 12; and Rosenthal, Boyd-Franklin, Steiner, & Tunnell, Chapter 13).

7. Awareness of the high-prevalence statistics of families affected by trauma, in general, and trauma caused by domestic violence in particular. Knowledge about the impact of trauma on family members and about the dynamics of domestic violence and its impact on children, spouses, and the elderly (Williams, Chapter 8; Harway, Hansen, Rossman, Geffner, & Deitch, Chapter 9).

8. Sensitivity to the issues of multi- problem families living in urban areas and the impacts of urbanicity on families (Sanchez-Hucles, Chapter 10).

9. Awareness of the impact of addictions on families and the interventions that have been most successful (Wynne, McCrady, Kahler, Liddle, Palmer, Horberg, & Schlesinger, Chapter 14).

10. Skill in incorporating nonverbal and written modes of therapy, and interactive technologies such as personal computers into traditional oral modalities of therapy, willingness to work in interdisciplinary teams (L'Abate & Odell, Chapter 15).

11. Skill in advocacy for families of the mentally ill, domestic violence survivors, the chronically ill, urban families and many of the other families discussed here.

12. Training in working collaboratively with medical personnel and educators.

Finally, therapists in training need to be taught to reconceptualize families and focus on their strengths rather than their pathologies, as suggested earlier in this chapter. Accomplishing the paradigm shift that is required may best be accomplished in a supervised internship setting.

Although the preceding list of topics is not inclusive, a family clinician who has been exposed to each of these issues will certainly be better prepared to work with the diverse families who need support and assistance.

SPECIAL ISSUES

This volume has presented another look at families. But families will not stay static. Families of tomorrow probably will not be exactly like families of today. It is hoped that focusing on the diversity of families described here has left the reader with an appreciation of variety in families and an understanding that families may continue to change and yet remain the mainstay of our culture. What this volume has left unanswered are a number of questions that originate in the chapters preceding this one. Some of these questions are:

1. How should clinicians apply the competence model to the families we have described? How do we move from pathology to competence with each family type?

2. How do we attract families who need help and yet do not come into therapy?

3. What are the different issues of working with families where the identified client is a child in contrast to an adult?

4. Do skills training or educational interventions work better than clinical interventions with some families? Will these types of interventions be covered by managed care?

5. How do we collaborate in working with primary care physicians and what special training do family clinicians need in working with these professionals?

REFERENCES

American Psychiatric Association. (1994). Diagnostic and statistical manual of mental disorders (4th edition). Washington, DC: Author.

Barnard, C. P. (1994). Resiliency: A shift in our perception. *The American Journal of Family Therapy, 22*(2).

Marsh, D. T. (1992). Working with families of people with serious mental illness. In L. VandeCreek, S. Knapp, & T. L. Jackson (Eds), *Innovations in clinical practice: A sourcebook* (Vol. 11, pp. 389–402). Sarasota, FL: Professional Resource Press.

Root, M. P. P. (1992). Reconstructing the impact of trauma on personality. In L. S. Brown & M. S. Ballou (Eds.), *Personality and psychopathology: Feminist reappraisals.* New York: Guilford.

Wolin, S. J. (1991). *The challenge model.* Presented at the 49th Annual Conference of the American Association for Marriage and Family Therapy, Dallas, TX.

About the Contributors

Nancy Boyd-Franklin, PhD, teaches family therapy and courses on ethnic and racial diversity at Rutgers University Graduate School of Applied and Professional Psychology in Piscataway, New Jersey. She is the author of numerous articles on these topics and two books, *Black Families in Therapy: A Multi-Systems Approach* (New York: Guilford Press, 1989) and *Children, Families and HIV/AIDS: Psychosocial and Psychotherapeutic Issues* (New York: Guilford Press, 1995).

Karen Carlson, MA, is a Marriage, Family, and Child Counselor in private practice in South Pasadena, California. She specializes in children's issues. She is faculty associate at the Phillips Graduate Institute (formerly California Family Study Center) in North Hollywood, California.

Israel Cuéllar, PhD, is an Assistant Professor of Psychology, Department of Psychology and Anthropology, The University of Texas-Pan American, Edinburg, Texas. He is coauthor (with Dr. Bill R. Arnold and Roberto Maldonado) of the *Acculturation Rating Scale for Mexican-Americans-II* (ARSMA-II). He has 16 years of experience in the delivery of mental health services primarily to Mexican American populations (adults, couples, families, and children) in public and private institutions, hospitals, and outpatient settings. He has written numerous scientific articles and book chapters on psychological disorders in Mexican Americans.

Irene Deitch, PhD, is a Professor of Psychology at The College of Staten Island, City University of New York where she chairs Options: College Study Program for Older Adults. A New York State licensed clinical psychologist, Dr. Deitch is also a Fellow of the American Psychological Association. Dr. Deitch is actively involved with issues of family violence, later adulthood, and intergenerational family therapy. She also serves on the New York State Legislature assembly subcommittee on the elderly.

Patricia Edmister, PhD, has been Director of Developmental Psychology and Children's Services at the Phillips Graduate Institute (formerly California Family Study Center) in North Hollywood, California, for the past six years. She specializes in working with children, adolescents, and their families. Prior to this, she was Coordinator of Early Childhood Handicapped Programs for the Montgomery County, Maryland, public school system where she administered programs for handicapped and developmentally disabled young children for 14 years. Dr. Edmister is a developmental psychologist licensed in Maryland, California, and Washington DC. She has written extensively on early childhood development and has also written monographs and book chapters focusing on due process in the field of service provision for disabled and handicapped young children and their families.

Robert Geffner, PhD, is Founder and President of the Family Violence and Sexual Assault Institute in Tyler, Texas, and a former Professor of Psychology at the University of Texas at Tyler. He is a Licensed Psychologist, a Licensed Marriage, Family and Child Counselor, and he directs a large private practice mental health clinic in Tyler. Dr. Geffner is the editor of the *Journal of Child Sexual Abuse, Aggression, Assault and Abuse,* and the *Family Violence and Sexual Assault Bulletin.* His publications include treatment manuals, book chapters, and books on spouse abuse, family violence, sexual abuse, child psychology, neuropsychology, and psychological assessment. Dr. Geffner has a Diplomate in Clinical Neuropsychology from the American Board of Professional Neuropsychology.

Mark Glazer, PhD, is a Professor of Anthropology, Department of Psychology and Anthropology and Head of the Rio Grande Folklore Archive at The University of Texas-Pan American, Edinburg, Texas. He is the author of *Flour from Another Sack,* (2nd ed.; Pan American University Press, 1994), and *A Dictionary of Mexican-American Proverbs* (Westport, CT: Greenwood Press, 1987). He is also coeditor with Paul Bohannan of *High Points in Anthropology* (2nd ed.; New York: Knopf, 1988). His current research is on emic approaches to studying acculturation in Mexican Americans.

Marsali Hansen, PhD, is a licensed psychologist and the curriculum development specialist for the Pennsylvania CASSP Training Institute. Her duties include the development of a competency-based core curriculum for children's mental health workers throughout the state of Pennsylvania. She also maintains a part-time private practice with a special focus on children and families. Dr. Hansen consults with community, state, and national organizations, and has published and presented widely on the topic of therapists' perceptions of spouse abuse.

Michele Harway, PhD, is Director of Research and Core Faculty at Phillips Graduate Institute (formerly the California Family Study Center), an accredited graduate program in marriage and family therapy in North Hollywood, California. She is also a member of the Consulting Faculty at the Fielding Institute and she maintains a small private practice as a Licensed Psychologist and a Licensed Marriage, Family and Child Counselor. Dr. Harway is the author or editor of five other books, most recently *Battering and Family Therapy: A Feminist Perspective* (Beverly Hills, CA: Sage Publications, 1993) and *Spouse Abuse: Assessing and Treating Battered Women, Batterers and Their*

Children (Sarasota, FL: Professional Resource Press, 1994) both with Marsali Hansen.

Lawrence K. Horberg, PhD, maintains a private practice in clinical psychology, with offices in Chicago and Skokie, Illinois. He is Assistant Professor of Psychiatry and Behavioral Sciences at the Northwestern University Medical School in Chicago, and he is a member of the Affiliated Professional Staff of the Medical Staff at Northwestern Memorial Hospital. He directed the outpatient department of the Northwestern Chemical Dependence Program for six years prior to beginning a full-time practice. He is coauthor of *Taking Charge: How Families Can Climb out of the Chaos of Addiction and Flourish* (New York: Simon and Schuster, 1988). His research, publications, and presentations are in the areas of addictions and the family.

June R. Husted, PhD, is retired Chief of the Day Treatment Center at the Long Beach Veterans Affairs Medical Center. She is a Clinical Assistant Professor at the UCLA/NPI Department of Psychiatry and Biobehavioral Sciences. Dr. Husted is active in the National Alliance for the Mentally Ill and serves on the Criminal Justice Advisory Committee of the California Alliance for the Mentally Ill. Reflecting her interest in forensic issues, she is involved in many educational efforts designed to prevent the criminalization of untreated mentally ill citizens.

Christopher W. Kahler is a graduate student in the Clinical Psychology PhD program at Rutgers University. He has worked as a counselor for adolescent substance abusers and is currently involved in research on cognitive factors in substance abuse relapse, Alcoholics Anonymous, and alcohol-focused behavioral marital therapy.

Luciano L'Abate is Professor Emeritus of Psychology at Georgia State University and Clinical Director of Multicultural Services at Cross Keys Counseling Center in Atlanta, Georgia. He is author or editor of 27 books, his most recent *A Theory of Personality Development* (New York: John Wiley & Sons, 1992) and *The Self in the Family: Toward a Classification of Personality, Criminal Behavior, and Psychopathology* (New York: John Wiley & Sons, in press). In 1994, Dr. L'Abate was selected as Family Psychologist of the year by the Division of Family Psychology of the American Psychological Association.

Harriet P. Lefley, PhD, is Professor of Psychiatry and Behavioral Sciences, University of Miami School of Medicine. Dr. Lefley is coauthor or coeditor of seven books, including *Families of the Mentally Ill: Coping and Adaptation* (New York: Guilford, 1987); *Families as Allies in Treatment of the Mentally Ill* (Washington, DC: American Psychiatric Press, 1990); *Helping Families Cope with Mental Illness* (Newark: Harwood Academic, 1994). A licensed psychologist and the author of over 100 publications, she has been involved in cross-cultural and community mental health research and services for 25 years and is active nationally and internationally as a workshop moderator and presenter. A National Switzer Scholar, Dr. Lefley received a Special Achievement Award from the American Psychological Associations's Division of Psychologists in Public Service in 1992 and the Stephen V. Logan Award for Outstanding Psychologist from the National Alliance for the Mentally Ill.

Howard A. Liddle, EdD, is Professor of Counseling Psychology and Director of the Center for Research on Adolescent Drug Abuse at Temple University. He is regular grant reviewer for the National Institute on Drug Abuse and has been involved as a consultant in their new Behavioral Therapies Development Initiative. Dr. Liddle is an editorial board member on six scientific journals, including *Family Process* and the *American Journal of Drug and Alcohol Abuse.* His most recent writings will appear in the forthcoming *NIDA Monograph on Adolescent Drug Abuse* ("Adolescent Drug Abuse: State of the Science," with Gayle Dakof), the *Journal of Marital and Family Therapy* ("The Effectiveness of Family Therapy for Drug Abuse: Promising but Not Definitive Evidence," with Gayle Dakof), and the *Journal of Family Psychology* ("Changes in Parenting Practices in Multidimensional Family Therapy," with Susan Schmidt and Gayle Dakof). In 1991, Dr. Liddle was the recipient of the Psychologist of the Year Award from the Division of Family Psychology of the American Psychological Association.

Diane T. Marsh, PhD, is Professor of Psychology at the University of Pittsburgh at Greensburg. Dr. Marsh is the author or editor of six books, including *Families and Mental Illness: New Directions in Professional Practice* (Westport, CT: Praeger, 1992); *New Directions in the Psychological Treatment of Serious Mental Illness* (Westport, CT: Praeger, 1994); *Anguished Voices: Personal Accounts of Siblings and Adult Children of Persons with Psychiatric Illness* (Boston: Boston University Center for Psychiatric Rehabilitation, 1994); and the forthcoming *Troubled Journey: Siblings and Children of People with Mental Illness* (Los Angeles: Tarcher/Putnam). Active nationally as a psychologist, an advocate, and a workshop presenter, she has many years of experience as a psychotherapist and consultant.

Barbara S. McCrady, PhD, University of Rhode Island, Kingston, is a professor in the Graduate School of Applied and Professional Psychology, Director of Training for the PhD clinical psychology training program, and Clinical Director of the Center of Alcohol Studies at Rutgers—The State University (Piscataway, New Jersey). McCrady is the Secretary-Treasurer elect of the Association for Advancement of Behavior Therapy, and coeditor (with W. R. Miller) of *Research on Alcoholics Anonymous: Opportunities and Alternatives* (Alcohol Research Documentation, Rutgers University, New Brunswick, NJ). She has published more than 100 peer-reviewed articles, chapters, and books on alcohol problems.

Mark Odell, PhD, is an Assistant Professor of Marriage and Family Therapy and Human Development/Family Studies at Bowling Green State University in Ohio. Dr. Odell has practiced in a wide variety of clinical settings, ranging from inpatient to intensive outpatient to private practice. He is a clinical member and approved supervisor of the American Association for Marriage and Family Therapy and is a licensed marriage and family therapist in the state of Georgia. His research interests include therapy process, clinical training, adult development, and values and ethics. He has authored papers on topics such as multicultural therapy, ethics in marriage and family therapy, and marital satisfaction. In addition to the clinical training of graduate students, research and scholarship, and undergraduate teaching, he is in private practice at the Center for Solutions in Brief Therapy in Sylvania, Ohio.

Ruth Baugher Palmer, PhD, is an adjunct faculty member at the Philadelphia Theological Seminary in Roxborough, Pennsylvania, where she teaches courses in pastoral psychology pertaining to adolescence and the family. She is also in private practice in Jenkintown, Pennsylvania, focusing on family therapy for adolescent behavior problems. Throughout her doctoral training, Dr. Palmer served as a graduate research assistant for the Center for Research on Adolescent Drug Abuse and the Center for Education in Inner Cities. Within those settings, she contributed to ongoing research projects, conducted her own research, and coauthored several publications pertaining to the treatment of various adolescent problems in the context of the family.

Thomas H. Peake, PhD, is a Clinical Diplomate of the American Board of Professional Psychology, a Charted Clinical Psychologist (British Psychological Society) as well as an approved supervisor for the American Association for Marriage and Family Therapy. He is Professor of Psychology in the clinical doctoral program at the Florida Institute of Technology (Melbourne). He is also adjunct Professor in the Department of Aging and Mental Health at the Florida Mental Health Institute (Tampa). Formerly, he held faculty and clinical training positions with Michigan State University and Eastern Virginia Medical School. His practice and publication are in the area of psychotherapy, clinical training, neuropsychology, and life-span development.

Joseph M. Rosenthal, PhD, teaches family therapy in New York City at Beth Israel Medical Center, Pace University and Lenox Hill Hospital, where he is a member of the affiliate staff of the Department of Psychiatry. He is also a faculty member of the Ackerman Institute for Family Therapy and, as a member of Ackerman's AIDS Project team, received the American Family Therapy (AFTA) Distinguished Service Award in 1992. He is the author of recent articles on spirituality and psychotherapy.

Susan G. Rosenzweig, PsyD, divides her time between private practice and the Pacific Northwest Clinical Research Center in Portland, Oregon. She received her doctorate in 1994 from the School of Psychology at Florida Institute of Technology.

B. B. Robbie Rossman, PhD, is part of the Child Clinical Faculty in the Psychology Department at the University of Denver. Her interest in family violence and abuse began about eight years ago in a study with Dr. Mindy Rosenberg to examine children's beliefs about their control over interparental conflict and violence. Since that time, additional projects have been completed regarding the well-being of children who experience abuse and/or parental violence. Dr. Rossman is particularly interested in forging an understanding of the impact of family violence on children that brings together the literatures on trauma, abuse, domestic violence, and child development. Dr. Rossman contributes to and reviews for professional journals, is on the editorial boards of the *Journal of Child Sexual Abuse* and the *Family Violence and Sexual Assault Bulletin,* will coedit the new *Journal of Emotional Abuse,* and is coeditor of an upcoming book, *Multiple Victimization of Children: Conceptual, Developmental, Research, and Treatment Issues.* She is currently serving on the Colorado Legislative Task Force on Battered Woman Syndrome.

Janis V. Sanchez-Hucles, PhD, is a clinical psychologist with a full-time appointment as associate professor in the Psychology Department of Old Dominion University in Norfolk, Virginia. She also serves as a faculty member for the Virginia Consortium for Professional Psychology and holds an adjunct appointment with the Medical College of Hampton Roads. Dr. Sanchez-Hucles has also maintained a part-time private practice and regularly does consultation and training with public and private agencies locally, regionally, and nationally. The focus of her clinical work and research includes families, children, women, diversity issues, and training.

Stephen E. Schlesinger, PhD, maintains a private practice in clinical psychology, with offices in Chicago and Oak Park, Illinois, and he is an Assistant Professor in the Department of Psychiatry and Behavioral Sciences of Northwestern University Medical School. He is coauthor of *Stop Drinking and Start Living* (Blue Ridge Summit, PA: TAB Books) and *Taking Charge: How Families Can Climb out of the Chaos of Addiction . . . and Flourish* (New York: Simon and Schuster), and coeditor of *Cognitive-Behavioral Therapy with Families* (New York: Brunner/Mazel). His research and publications are in the areas of addictions, and marital and family therapy.

Lita Linzer Schwartz, PhD, is Distinguished Professor of Educational Psychology Emerita and Professor of Women's Studies Emerita at Penn State University Ogontz Campus, and holds a Diplomate in Forensic Psychology (ABPP). She is the author of several articles on adoption and surrogate motherhood, as well as *Alternatives to Infertility* (New York: Brunner/Mazel, 1991) and has also written frequently on the impact of divorce, women's issues, ethnic studies, and gifted children.

Thomas H. Seibt, MA, is a marriage and family therapist and an AAMFT Approved Supervisor. He is the director of Post-Degree Training and Supervision at the Phillips Graduate Institute (formerly California Family Study Center) in North Hollywood, California, where he lectures on intact, divorced, and single-parent families, and stepfamilies. Since he has had the practical experience of raising three teenage stepchildren (and two biological teenagers), he has specialized in the area of stepfamilies for 20 years. He has been a regular presenter at annual AAMFT conferences. He has written articles on the subject of teenagers in stepfamilies and has appeared on various television talk shows. He has a private practice in Santa Clarita, California, and teaches marriage and family relations at the California State University in Northridge.

Gloria L. Steiner, EdD, is clinical associate professor and former Director of Child Psychology Training of the Department of Psychiatry, University of Medicine and Dentistry of New Jersey. She was a psychology consultant to the National Pediatric HIV Resource Center. She is coeditor of *Children, Families and HIV/AIDS: Psychosocial and Psychotherapeutic Issues* (New York: Guilford Press, 1995).

A. Melton Strozier, Jr., PhD, is a Licensed Psychologist and Clinical Member of the American Association for Marriage and Family Therapy. He holds degrees in psychology from Mercer (BA) and Southwestern (MA, PhD). He currently is Director of Behavioral Science for the Family Practice Residency Program at The Medical Center in Columbus, Georgia. He is also Instructor in Marriage and Family Therapy for The University College, Mercer University, and Clinical Assistant Professor in Psychiatry for the Mercer University School of Medicine, Macon, Georgia.

Gil Tunnell, PhD, is Director of the Family Studies Program in the Department of Psychiatry at Beth Israel Medical Center, New York City. He is a clinical professor of psychology at New York University, where he teaches family therapy. He is former chair of the Task Force on AIDS for the New York State Psychological Association.

Kathy Wexler, MA, teaches human growth and development at the Phillips Graduate Institute (formerly California Family Study Center) in North Hollywood, California. She is a licensed Marriage, Family and Child counselor, and an Approved Supervisor for the American Association for Marriage and Family Therapy.

Mary Beth Williams, PhD, LCSW, CTC, is a therapist in private practice in Warrenton, Virginia. She is also a school social worker in Falls Church,

Virginia. A 1990 graduate of The Fielding Institute, she specializes in the treatment of posttraumatic stress and dissociative disorders. She is the coeditor of *Handbook of Post-traumatic Therapy* (Westport, CT: Greenwood Press, 1994) and *Violence Hits Home* (New York: Springer Publishing, 1990), and has authored numerous articles and chapters on trauma.

Jeffrey M. Williamson, PhD, received his doctorate from the University of Missouri-Columbia. His clinical and research interests include developmental psychopathology, family therapy, brief psychotherapy, and neuropsychological assessment. He is currently in private practice in Merritt Island, Florida.

Ronald D. Wynne, PhD, ABPP (Family Psychology) is director of Washington Assessment & Therapy Services (WATS), a private behavioral health-care clinic with offices in Washington, DC, and Landover, Maryland. Clinic services include outpatient treatment, interventions, and relapse prevention for substance abusers and their families. His publications include *Effective Coordination of Drug Abuse Programs: A Guide to Community Action* (Bethesda, MD: NIDA, 1973) and *Cocaine: Mystique and Reality* (New York: Avon, 1980, coauthored by Joel L. Phillips). He is a past president of the Washington, DC, Psychological Association (DCPA).

Author Index

Subject Index